THE ANARCHY OF
KING STEPHEN'S REIGN

THE ANARCHY OF
KING STEPHEN'S REIGN

Edited by

EDMUND KING

CLARENDON PRESS · OXFORD
1994

Oxford University Press, Walton Street, Oxford OX2 6DP

Oxford New York
Athens Auckland Bangkok Bombay
Calcutta Cape Town Dar es Salaam Delhi
Florence Hong Kong Istanbul Karachi
Kuala Lumpur Madras Madrid Melbourne
Mexico City Nairobi Paris Singapore
Taipei Tokyo Toronto

and associated companies in
Berlin Ibadan

Oxford is a trade mark of Oxford University Press

Published in the United States
by Oxford University Press Inc., New York

© *The Several Contributors 1994*

British Library Cataloguing in Publication Data
Data available

Library of Congress Cataloging in Publication Data
The Anarchy of King Stephen's reign | edited by Edmund King.
p. cm
Includes bibliographical references.
1. Great Britain—History—Stephen, 1135–1154. 2. Anarchism—
Great Britain. I. King, Edmund.
DA198.5.A7 1994
942.02'4—dc20 94–5443
ISBN 0–19–820364–0

Set by Hope Services (Abingdon) Ltd.
Printed in Great Britain
on acid-free paper by
Bookcraft Ltd., Midsomer Norton, Bath

PREFACE

On 10 April 1892 F. W. Maitland wrote to J. H. Round: 'I am glad the worthy peer King Stephen is off your mind and look forward with great interest to learning all about him.' The reference was to Round's *Geoffrey de Mandeville*, published in the same year. Round enjoyed an extensive correspondence, but for this very important book Maitland's letter stands alone in the surviving record. And so it is to the book itself that we must look for clues as to why Round published on this subject, at this time. As to subject, the Preface explains that Geoffrey de Mandeville represented 'the most typical presentment of the feudal and anarchic spirit that stamped the age of Stephen'. Geoffrey de Mandeville was the first earl of Essex, given this dignity by Stephen in 1140, 'to hold with all the dignities and liberties and customs by which my other earls most honourably and most freely hold'. As to the author, Round was created a Deputy-Lieutenant of Essex in 1892, the year in which his volume on the county's first earl appeared. Round himself was not unconscious of his own dignity as a member of one of the landed families of the county. He would have been drawn to his subject also by his interest in the county of Boulogne. The centre of the honour of Boulogne in England was at Colchester. Its lord in the second quarter of the twelfth century was Stephen himself. Stephen's earl of Essex was a fitting subject for Round's first major book.

Geoffrey de Mandeville, as has often been commented upon, was the closest Round ever came to writing a consecutive history. It should be recognized that writing such a history was never Round's objective. To understand this, a few further points from Round's

biography are necessary. Round at Oxford had been a pupil of
William Stubbs, then the Regius Professor of History and later
Bishop of Oxford. Amongst the other pupils of Stubbs at this time
were Reginald Lane Poole, Thomas Frederick Tout, and Charles
Harding Firth. Poole, Tout, and Round himself may each be seen
as in different ways producing *Studies Supplementary to Stubbs'
Constitutional History*, to use the title of Petit-Dutaillis. This attitude of mind is most clear in the work of Round, who always
remained very much in awe of his master Stubbs. Thus the Preface
to *Geoffrey de Mandeville*:

'The reign of Stephen', in the words of our greatest living historian, 'is
one of the most important in our whole history, as exemplifying the
working of causes and principles which had no other opportunity of
exhibiting their real tendencies.' To illustrate in detail the working of
those principles to which the Bishop of Oxford thus refers, is the chief
object I have set before myself in these pages.

Round went on to say that the charters for Geoffrey de Mandeville
would form 'the very backbone of my work'. It was his hope, he
said, introducing a new metaphor, to break 'a few stones towards
the road on which future historians will travel'.

A century after Round wrote those words, a group of historians
travelled to Battle in East Sussex, looking forward with great interest to hearing a group of papers intended to provide a new study of
Stephen's important reign. It may be suggested that Round would
not have felt the venue inappropriate. He, like so many of the
Anglo-Norman aristocracy, had a strong base in more than one
county. It was in Sussex, at 15 Brunswick Terrace, Brighton, that
he was born on 22 February 1854, and he lived in the same house
for all but the period 1887–1903 (his most productive years) until
his death on 24 June 1928. At Battle, Mrs Joan Counihan kindly
arranged an exhibition relating to Round's connections with the
county. Amongst the exhibits was a copy of the death certificate,
which gives the date of death given above, a day earlier than that
found in the *Dictionary of National Biography*. Round was well
versed on the topography of the Battle of Hastings, and was always
happy to tour the battle site with interested visitors, particularly if
he had the opportunity to address them in French.

The venue of the conference was appropriate also because since
1978 there has met annually the Battle Conference on Anglo-

Norman Studies, whose proceedings (at times also bilingual) are published as *Anglo-Norman Studies*. The Battle Conference's decision to hold its 1992 meeting at Palermo in Sicily in early April left its normal venue at Pyke House, Battle, free at its normal time in mid-July. Our conference was thus able to take advantage of the excellent facilities at Pyke House, and the skill of Mr Peter Birch and his staff. It was a pleasure to welcome the Convenor of the Battle Conference, Dr Marjorie Chibnall, who gave one of the papers. The only sadness of a most happy and productive conference was the absence of Professor Ralph Davis, who had accepted an invitation to speak on Geoffrey de Mandeville. Happily we have the third edition of his *King Stephen*, which was published in 1990; but sadly he died on 12 March 1991. With the kind permission of Mrs Eleanor Davis, the contributors offer this volume to his memory.

The chapters in this volume are, with the exception of my own introduction, those delivered at the 1992 conference. I am grateful to the contributors for accepting the invitation to take part, for their promptness in delivering the papers, and their tolerance as those papers have been edited. Their acknowledgements appear in their own chapters. For comments on my own Introduction, I must thank the contributors, and additionally Mr John Prestwich. For chairing the final 'debriefing' session, all the delegates would wish to thank Professor T. N. Bisson. Whilst the conference was held at Battle, it was organized from the University of Sheffield. Within the Department of History, Mrs Barbara Hickman managed the administration with her customary efficiency. Closer still to home, I must thank my son Michael, for help in copying all the footnotes on to disk and with the indexing, and my wife Jenny. If, after all this assistance has been offered, any anarchic tendencies are detected within the volume, the responsibility is mine.

EDMUND KING

Sheffield
May 1993

CONTENTS

LIST OF PLATES

(between pages 136–137)

I. Castle Hedingham, Essex: interior of the great hall (*© RCHME, Crown copyright*)

II. Castle Rising, Norfolk: the keep seen from the gatehouse (*© RCHME, Crown copyright*)

III. New Buckenham, Norfolk: aerial view of castle and new town (*Cambridge University Collection, Crown copyright*)

IV. Burwell, Cambs.: aerial view of castle site (*Cambridge University Collection, Crown copyright*)

V. The coinage of the anarchy: substantive types (*British Numismatic Society*)

VI. The coinage of the anarchy: non-substantive types (*Ashmolean Museum, British Numismatic Society, Fitzwilliam Museum, National Museum of Wales*)

VII. The coinage of the anarchy: the empress and the baronage (*Ashmolean Museum, British Numismatic Society, National Museum of Wales*)

VIII. The coinage of the anarchy: miscellaneous coins (*Ashmolean Museum, British Numismatic Society*)

LIST OF FIGURES

LIST OF MAPS

ABBREVIATIONS

AC	*Annales Cestrienses,* ed. R. C. Christie (Rec. Soc. of Lancashire and Cheshire 14, 1886) (citations are by year)
Actes de Henri II	L. Delisle, *Receuil des Actes de Henri II, roi d'Angleterre et duc de Normandie, concernant les provinces françaises et les affaires de France,* Introduction (Paris, 1909), vols. i–iii, ed. E. Berger (Paris, 1916–27)
ANS	*Anglo-Norman Studies,* being the Proceedings of the Battle Conference on Anglo-Norman Studies
ASC	*The Anglo-Saxon Chronicle* (citations are by year)
Barrow, *Anglo-Norman Era*	G. W. S. Barrow, *The Anglo-Norman Era in Scottish History* (Oxford, 1980)
Barrow, *David I*	G. W. S. Barrow, *David I of Scotland (1124–1153): The Balance of New and Old* (Stenton Lecture for 1984; Reading, 1985)
Barrow, *Kingdom of Scots*	G. W. S. Barrow, *The Kingdom of the Scots* (London, 1973)

Blackburn, 'Coinage under Henry I'	M. Blackburn, 'Coinage and Currency under Henry I: A Review', *ANS* 13 (1991)
BMC	G. C. Brooke, *A Catalogue of English Coins in the British Museum: The Norman Kings*, 2 vols. (London, 1916)
BNJ	*British Numismatic Journal*
Boon, *Welsh Hoards*	G. C. Boon, *Welsh Hoards 1979–1981* (Cardiff, 1986)
Brut	*Brut y Tywysogyon or the Chronicle of the Princes*, ed. T. Jones; *Red Book of Hergest Version*, 2nd edn. (Cardiff, 1973); *Peniarth MS. 20 Version* (Cardiff, 1952) (citations are by year)
CDF	*Calendar of Documents Preserved in France*, i, ed. J. H. Round (London, 1899)
Chartrou, *Anjou*	J. Chartrou, *L'Anjou de 1109 à 1151: Foulque de Jerusalem et Geoffroi Plantagenet* (Paris, 1928)
Chibnall, *Matilda*	M. Chibnall, *The Empress Matilda* (London, 1991)
Chronicles	*Chronicles of the Reigns of Stephen, Henry II and Richard I*, ed. R. Howlett, 4 vols. (RS, 1884–9)
Councils and Synods	*Councils and Synods with Other Documents Relating to the English Church*, vol. i in two parts, ed. D. Whitelock, M. Brett, and C. N. L. Brooke (Oxford, 1981)
CP	*The Complete Peerage of England, Scotland, Ireland, Great Britain and the United Kingdom*, by G.E.C., rev. edn., 13 vols. in 14 (London, 1910–59)
Cronne, *Stephen*	H. A. Cronne, *The Reign of Stephen 1135–54: Anarchy in England* (London, 1970)

Crouch, *Beaumont Twins*	D. Crouch, *The Beaumont Twins: The Roots and Branches of Power in the Twelfth Century* (Cambridge, 1986)
CS	Camden Society; Royal Historical Society, London
Davies, *Wales*	R. R. Davies, *Conquest, Coexistence and Change: Wales 1063–1415* (Oxford, 1987)
Davis, *Stephen*	R. H. C. Davis, *King Stephen 1135–1154*, 3rd edn. (London, 1990)
Dialogus	*Dialogus de Scaccario*, ed. C. Johnson (NMT, 1950)
Earldom of Chester	*The Earldom of Chester and its Charters: A Tribute to Geoffrey Barraclough*, ed. A. T. Thacker (*Journal of Chester Arch. Soc.* 71 (1991))
EHR	*English Historical Review*
English Lawsuits	*English Lawsuits from William I to Richard I*, ed. R. C. Van Caenegem, 2 vols. (Selden Soc. 106–7, 1990–1)
EYC	*Early Yorkshire Charters*, i–iii ed. W. Farrer (Edinburgh, 1914–16); iv–xii, ed. C. T. Clay (Yorkshire Archaeological Soc., 1935–65)
FW	Florence of Worcester, *Chronicon ex chronicis*, ed. B. Thorpe, 2 vols. (English Historical Soc.; London, 1848–9)
GC	*Gervase of Canterbury: Historical Works*, ed. W. Stubbs, 2 vols. (RS, 1879–80)
GF, *Letters*	*The Letters and Charters of Gilbert Foliot*, ed. A. Morey and C. N. L. Brooke (Cambridge, 1967)
Gloucester Charters	*Earldom of Gloucester Charters:*

	The Charters and Scribes of the Earls and Countesses of Gloucester to A.D. 1217, ed. R. B. Patterson (Oxford, 1973)
Green, *Henry I*	J. A. Green, *The Government of England under Henry I* (Cambridge, 1986)
Green, *Sheriffs*	J. A. Green, *English Sheriffs to 1154* (PRO Handbook 24; London, 1990)
GS	*Gesta Stephani*, ed. K. R. Potter and R. H. C. Davis (OMT, 1976)
Haskins, *Norman Institutions*	C. H. Haskins, *Norman Institutions* (Cambridge, Mass., 1925)
HH	Henry of Huntingdon, *Historia Anglorum*, ed. T. Arnold (RS, 1870)
HMC	Historical Manuscripts Commission
Hollister, *Anglo-Norman World*	C. Warren Hollister, *Monarchy, Magnates and Institutions in the Anglo-Norman World* (London, 1986)
Howden	*Chronica Rogeri de Houedene*, ed. W. Stubbs, 4 vols. (RS, 1868–71)
HR	*Bulletin of the Institute of Historical Research* (until 1986); *Historical Research* (from 1987)
JS *HP*	John of Salisbury, *Memoirs of the Papal Court*, ed. M. Chibnall (NMT, 1956)
JW	*The Chronicle of John of Worcester 1118–1140*, ed. J. R. H. Weaver (Anecdota Oxoniensia 13; Oxford, 1908)
King, 'Anarchy'	E. King, 'The Anarchy of King Stephen's Reign', *TRHS* 5:34 (1984)

Lawrie, *Charters*	A. C. Lawrie, *Early Scottish Charters* (Glasgow, 1905)
Le Patourel, *Norman Empire*	J. Le Patourel, *The Norman Empire* (Oxford, 1976)
Lloyd, *Wales*	J. E. Lloyd, *A History of Wales from the Earliest Times to the Edwardian Conquest*, 2 vols., 3rd edn. (London, 1939)
Mack, 'Coinage of Stephen'	R. P. Mack, 'Stephen and the Anarchy: 1135–1154', *BNJ* 35 (1966)
Monasticon	W. Dugdale, *Monasticon Anglicanum*, ed. J. Caley, H. Ellis, and B. Bandinel, 8 vols. (London, 1817–30)
Mowbray Charters	*Charters of the Honour of Mowbray 1107–1191*, ed. D. E. Greenway (London, 1972)
NC	*Numismatic Chronicle*
NMT	Nelson Medieval Texts, London
OMT	Oxford Medieval Texts, Oxford
OV	Orderic Vitalis, *The Ecclesiastical History*, ed. M. Chibnall, 6 vols. (OMT, 1969–80)
PR	Pipe Roll (cited by regnal years)
PRS	Pipe Roll Society
Red Book	*Red Book of the Exchequer*, ed. H. Hall, 3 vols. (RS, 1897)
Religious Houses	D. Knowles and N. Hadcock, *Medieval Religious Houses: England and Wales*, 2nd edn. (London, 1971)
Renn, *Norman Castles*	D. F. Renn, *Norman Castles in Britain*, 2nd edn. (London, 1973)
RH	Richard of Hexham, *Chronicle*, in *Chronicles*, vol. iii
Round, *Geoffrey*	J. H. Round, *Geoffrey de Mandeville* (London, 1892)
RRAN	*Regesta regum Anglo-*

	Normannorum, vol. i, ed. H. W. C. Davis (Oxford, 1913), vol. ii, ed. C. Johnson and H. A. Cronne (Oxford, 1956), vols. iii and iv, ed. H. A. Cronne and R. H. C. Davis (Oxford, 1968–9)
RRS	*Regesta regum Scottorum*, vols. i and ii, ed. G. W. S. Barrow (Edinburgh, 1960–71)
RS	Rolls Series, London
RT	Robert of Torigny, *Chronicle*, in *Chronicles*, vol. iv
Saltman, *Theobald*	A. Saltman, *Theobald Archbishop of Canterbury* (London, 1956)
SD	*Symeon of Durham: Historical Works*, ed. T. Arnold, 2 vols. (RS, 1882–5)
Stenton, *First Century*	Sir Frank Stenton, *The First Century of English Feudalism 1066–1166*, 2nd edn. (Oxford, 1961)
Stubbs, *Constitutional History*	W. Stubbs, *The Constitutional History of England*, 3 vols., 6th edn. (Oxford, 1897)
TRHS	*Transactions of the Royal Historical Society*
Van Caenegem, *Royal Writs*	R. C. Van Caenegem, *Royal Writs in England from the Conquest to Glanvill* (Selden Soc. 77, 1959)
VCH	*Victoria History of the Counties of England*
Warren, *Governance*	W. L. Warren, *The Governance of Norman and Angevin England 1086–1272* (London, 1987)
WM *GP*	Wlliam of Malmesbury, *De gestis pontificum Anglorum*, ed. N. E. S. A. Hamilton (RS, 1870)
WM *GR*	William of Malmesbury, *De gestis regum Anglorum*, ed. W. Stubbs, 2 vols. (RS, 1887–9)

WM *HN*   William of Malmesbury, *Historia Novella*, ed. K. R. Potter (NMT, 1955)

WN   William of Newburgh, *Historia rerum Anglicarum*, in *Chronicles*, vols. i and ii

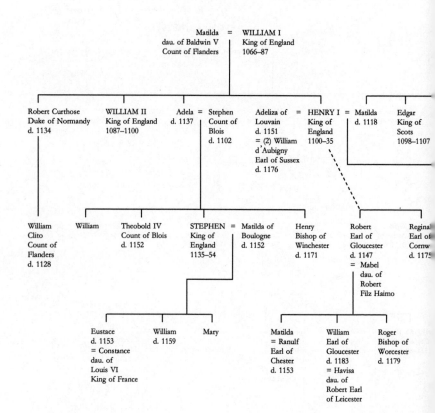

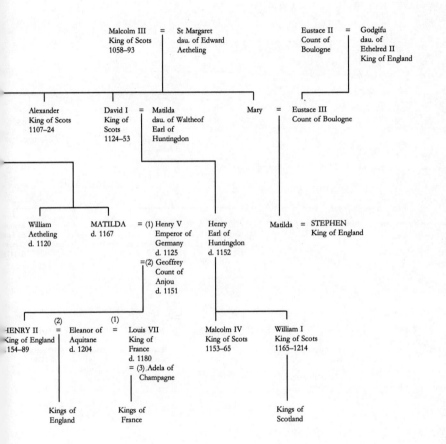

```
Malcolm III     =  St Margaret              Eustace II  =  Godgifu
King of Scots      dau. of Edward           Count of       dau. of
1058–93            Aetheling                Boulogne       Ethelred II
                                                           King of England


Alexander        David I   =  Matilda          Mary  =  Eustace III
King of Scots    King of      dau. of Waltheof          Count of Boulogne
1107–24          Scots        Earl of
                 1124–53      Huntingdon


William      MATILDA  = (1) Henry V        Henry          Matilda  =  STEPHEN
Aetheling    d. 1167      Emperor of       Earl of                    King of England
d. 1120                   Germany          Huntingdon
                          d. 1125          d. 1152
                      =(2) Geoffrey
                          Count of
                          Anjou
                          d. 1151


           (2)                (1)
HENRY II     =  Eleanor of   =  Louis VII       Malcolm IV      William I
King of England Aquitane        King of         King of Scots   King of Scots
1154–89         d. 1204         France          1153–65         1165–1214
                                d. 1180
                                = (3) Adela of
                                      Champagne


         Kings of         Kings of                         Kings of
         England          France                           Scotland
```

INTRODUCTION

Edmund King

THE classic description of what has become known as the anarchy of King Stephen's reign is that provided by the *Anglo-Saxon Chronicle*.[1] It saw a weak kingship manifested in the breakdown of public order.

When they saw that the king was a mild man and gentle and good and did not exact the full penalties of the law they inflicted every enormity. They had done him homage and sworn oaths of fealty to him, but their oaths were not kept. They were all forsworn and their oaths broken. Every great man built himself a castle and held it against the king; and they filled the whole land with these castles. They sorely burdened the unhappy people of the country with forced labour on the castles; and when the castles were built, they filled them with devils and wicked men. . . . I do not know how to, nor am I able to tell of all the atrocities nor all the cruelties that they wrought on the unhappy people of this country. It lasted throughout the nineteen years that Stephen was king, and always grew worse and worse.

The conclusion was fatalistic. 'These things we suffered nineteen long years for our sins. It was said openly that Christ and his saints were asleep.' These passages translate an original written in Old English in the abbey of Peterborough on the edges of the fenland, a community defiantly keeping alive a tradition of writing in the vernacular, through to the accession of Henry II.

There are signs that the anonymous monk of Peterborough,

---

[1] *ASC*, placed as the entry for the year 1137, but written in the 1150s. The standard modern edition of this section of the chronicle is *The Peterborough Chronicle 1070–1154*, ed. C. Clark, 2nd edn. (Oxford, 1970); translations include *The Anglo-Saxon Chronicle*, ed. D. Whitelock *et al.* (London, 1962).

writing in the mid-1150s, was here echoing a passage from another
monk, writing when no end to the disorder was in sight. This was
William of Malmesbury—in his own estimation, which later historians have accepted, England's finest historian since Bede.[2] His
work was early entitled, picking up a phrase in his Preface, the
Historia Novella, a 'history of recent events', what we would now
call contemporary history.[3] He wrote in the middle of the civil war,
when a myriad of trackless events made it almost impossible to
gain a perspective. For him, however, the most tiresome feature of
the local landscape was the castle that had been built within the
abbey precinct by the local bishop, Roger of Salisbury. When he
came to generalize, this was where he started: 'there were in
England as many lords or rather tyrants as there were lords of
castles, each claiming to protect but in fact exploiting the surrounding area.' The same ideas were developed, in the same order,
in the *Anglo-Saxon Chronicle*, strongly suggesting that this text
from Malmesbury was available at Peterborough in King Stephen's
lifetime. There are also local links between William of Malmesbury
and the monk John of Worcester. John of Worcester introduced his
generalizations immediately after Stephen's accession: 'It was not
long before, in every part of England and Normandy, the greatest
disorder prevailed. . . . It was every man for himself. They stored
their castles and towns with provisions, and guarded them with
armed men.'[4]

Of similar importance for an understanding of the reign, though
more limited in circulation at the time, is the work of a monk who
wrote in southern Normandy, Orderic Vitalis.[5] For events in
Normandy his *Ecclesiastical History* is the key source. And not just
in Normandy. Orderic had been born near Shrewsbury, and for
events in the west country of England he is an important and independent authority. Orderic and William of Malmesbury are the
two heavyweight historians of the Anglo-Norman period. It may

---

[2] WM *GR* i. 1–3; ii. 518; D. Knowles, *The Monastic Order in England*, 2nd edn.
(Cambridge, 1963), 175–6, 499–500; R. W. Southern, 'Aspects of the European
Tradition of Historical Writing, 4. The Sense of the Past', *TRHS* 5:23 (1973), 253–6.

[3] WM *HN*. The NMT edition is currently being revised by Edmund King for publication in OMT.

[4] JW 40.

[5] OV. The history of Stephen's reign up to 1141 will be found in Book XIII,
printed in vol. vi of the OMT edition.

make sense to recognize that their standing was fully appreciated by contemporaries, who on occasion would seek them out to supply the perspective offered by historical study, and to have their own views placed on record. Now, to Orderic, Stephen is the king who came too late, and did not do enough: 'The province was left without a protector and a prince.' This left the Normans prey to external enemies, and, more damaging still, to internal feuding—to which, in the absence of strong leadership, they were particularly prone. In many areas this was manifested in pillage and burning, the shattering of the peace offered by earlier rulers. 'Meanwhile,' commences a typical passage, 'the Normans were tearing each other to pieces in their native land, and many evil deeds were committed everywhere.'[6] As Haskins put it, 'its venerable author saw no hope of better days when he brought his work to its noble close in 1141'.[7]

Neither Orderic Vitalis nor William of Malmesbury lived through more than half of the 'nineteen long winters' of Stephen's reign. For the second half of the reign the coverage by chroniclers is more patchy, though still—by standards applicable elsewhere in western Europe—plentiful. Writing within the annalistic tradition was Henry, archdeacon of Huntingdon, producing a *History of the English* that in its day was even more popular than the *Gesta Regum* of William of Malmesbury. He, in a passage that parallels those cited earlier, pauses in 1140:

Where the king spent Christmas and Easter it matters not; for now all that made the court splendid, and the regalia handed down from the long line of his predecessors, had disappeared. The treasury, left well filled, was now empty; the kingdom was prey to intestine wars; slaughter, fire, and rapine spread throughout the land; cries of distress, horror and woe rose in every quarter.[8]

There follows a lengthy verse on civil war, which concludes: 'All hell's broke loose, and chaos reigns'—essentially the same image as that Christ and his saints were asleep.

In contrast to the popular and populist archdeacon of

---

[6] OV vi. 524–5; on such passages as typical of Orderic's reactions at times of weak ducal authority, see M. Chibnall, *The World of Orderic Vitalis* (Oxford, 1984), 118–19.

[7] Haskins, *Norman Institutions*, 128.

[8] HH. A new edition is in preparation by D. E. Greenway for OMT.

Huntingdon, the author of the *Gesta Stephani* has left no name and few clues as to his identity. These led R. H. C. Davis to Robert of Bath, the first bishop appointed by Stephen: 'there can be little doubt that he is the man we have been looking for.'[9] Not all have been convinced.[10] The work is *sui generis*. Unusually for the time, it is the biography of a king, and a spirited defence of that king's title to rule. But it does not attempt, any more than the other texts, to conceal the state of England during the civil war. Thus of Stephen himself towards the end of the reign:

> gathering together a large body of finely equipped knights, his son [Eustace] too with his men and some of the barons massed on the opposite flank, he set himself to lay waste that fair and delightful district, so full of good things, around Salisbury; they took and plundered everything they came upon, set fire to houses and churches, and, what was a more cruel and brutal sight, fired the crops that had been reaped and stacked all over the fields, consumed and brought to nothing everything edible that they found. They ravaged with this bestial cruelty especially round Marlborough, they showed it also very terribly round Devizes, and they had it in mind to do the same to their adversaries all over England.[11]

There are many other chroniclers whose work is drawn on in this volume of essays, but these quotations from the most influential writers should be sufficient to make clear that 'the anarchy of Stephen's reign' as a historiographical concept originates within the reign. The chronicles can be analysed to show the way in which information and ideas circulated during the reign. They also provided a means by which ideas circulated; but here their position was secondary. More important were letters and charters, varieties of correspondence more clearly distinguished by modern historians than they were at the time. The great men of the day kept up an active correspondence, most of which would later have no evidentiary value, and so would survive only if the sender kept copies.[12] The let-

---

[9] *GS*, pp. xviii–xxxviii (quotation from p. xxxviii).

[10] A. Gransden, *Historical Writing in England c.550 to c.1307* (London, 1974), 189–90; F. Barlow, *The English Church 1066–1154* (London, 1979), 21 and n. 83, 92–3.   [11] *GS* 220–1.

[12] Gilbert Foliot's letters as abbot of Gloucester and then as bishop of Hereford are the most important surviving collection: GF, *Letters*; and for commentary Morey and Brooke, *Gilbert Foliot and his Letters* (Cambridge, 1965), 8–31. Note also the important study of G. Constable, *The Letters of Peter the Venerable*, 2 vols. (Cambridge, Mass., 1967), ii. 1–44 (noting the loss of the correspondence of Ailred of Rievaulx, 5 and n. 20).

ters that we call charters survive in great numbers, and increasingly the dynamic that lies behind charters is being brought out.[13]

All these sources reveal the problems of the anarchy, and at different levels reflect historical thinking on those problems. They make it clear that during the nineteen long winters of Stephen's reign the nature of authority was discussed at every level. The main attitudes were formed by 1140, the same year in which we have the first notice of a proposal for a settlement of the civil war. The events of the year 1141 added further complications, but essentially by 1140 the Anglo-Norman political community had identified the main issues of the succession dispute and the civil war consequent upon it, had noted the problems that had arisen, and had proposals for their resolution. The delay was in persuading the protagonists that a settlement was in their best interests also.

It is a feature of Stephen's reign, and in a part a reflection of the interest in politics engendered by it, that particular episodes come to be highlighted and to be dramatized. I take as a first example the final event in the *Historia Novella*. In December 1142 the Empress Matilda found herself besieged in Oxford by troops of her rival, King Stephen. William of Malmesbury says that she escaped by a side door and walked all the way to Abingdon, from there going by horse to the castle of Wallingford, which was under the control of one of her supporters, Brian fitz Count. In the *Anglo-Saxon Chronicle*, which, as has been shown, was indebted to the *Historia Novella*, we have the additional information that she was let down from the tower by ropes. But how then did she effect her escape? The *Gesta Stephani* supplies the information that 'the ground was white with an extremely heavy fall of snow and there was a thick crust of ice on the water'. Henry of Huntingdon supplied a further refinement, that for camouflage the empress was 'wrapped in a white cloak, [and so] deceived the eyes of the besiegers, dazzled by the reflection of the snow'. It was a natural progression for the authors of *1066 and All That* to make this their symbol of anarchy, with the empress and the king chasing one another over the country clad only in their night-attire.[14]

---

[13] e.g. P. R. Hyams, 'The Charter as a Source for the Early Common Law', *Journal of Legal Hist.* 12 (1991), 173–89.

[14] WM *HN* 76–7; *ASC*, one of a composite group of entries *s.a.* 1140; *GS* 142–5; HH 276; W. C. Sellar and R. J. Yeatman, *1066 and All That* (Harmondsworth, 1960), 28 (with illustration).

Many examples could be cited of the way in which, in a similar fashion, the personalities and the politics of the reign became established in the popular mind. The different texts contribute to this at different levels. They provide information and commentary in a balance that is different in each case. In the *Historia Novella* commentary and analysis predominate, as shown by another dramatic episode in the empress's career—her expulsion from Westminster in the summer of 1141. From the author of the *Gesta Stephani* and from Gloucester abbey we are given the story that had gone the rounds, and with which all were familiar—that the empress had been driven out by the Londoners in disarray, leaving a meal half-finished. William of Malmesbury says that she left 'with a kind of military discipline'. It is tempting to say that William, because of his bias, is trying to conceal the nature of the débâcle, but this would be to misread his intentions. Here, as elsewhere, he has heard the story, and presumes his readers have done so too.[15] The phrase was meant to raise a laugh, or at very least a wry smile; if a modern historian pulls a long face, and adds this to a list of a medieval chronicler's deceits, the text is being misread. The audience must always be borne in mind.

The preface to *Historia Novella* says that it was written in response to a request from Robert of Gloucester for a historical explanation of 'those things that by a wonderful dispensation of God have befallen in England in recent times'.[16] William of Malmesbury says that to understand it is necessary to go back and set out the relevant events in a proper order. No better authority is needed for a similar treatment in the remainder of this introductory chapter. It will follow William of Malmesbury in seeing Stephen's reign as the story of a succession dispute which plunged the Anglo-Norman realm into civil war.

Henry I had two legitimate children, Matilda born in 1102 and William born in 1103; he was also survived by a long line of bastards, the senior and probably the eldest of whom was Robert, earl of Gloucester. In the first paragraphs of a text dedicated to Robert of Gloucester, William of Malmesbury introduces the key events which concerned the two legitimate children. He alludes to the death of William Aetheling in the *White Ship* off Barfleur in

<hr />

[15] *GS* 124–7; FW ii. 132; WM *HN* 56–7.   [16] WM *HN* 1.

November 1120, an episode whose importance he had stressed in the *Gesta Regum*: 'when the death of the young man became known it produced remarkable changes in politics.'[17] It led to Henry I's remarriage, to Adeliza of Louvain, a marriage that proved childless. When this became apparent, Matilda—who had been married in 1114 to the German Emperor Henry V, and had been widowed in 1125—was recalled to England. The empress was named as having the right of succession; oaths were sworn that the Anglo-Norman nobility would accept her after Henry's death; and she was married to Geoffrey of Anjou.

William of Malmesbury's text is closely focused on the succession. He provides for the most part a brisk and at times allusive commentary on it, with occasional set-piece meetings in which the main issues are brought into focus.[18] The first of these is provided by the council that met between Christmas 1126 and Epiphany 1127, in which the succession was discussed and the oaths to Matilda sworn. The dramatis personae are here introduced by means of a dispute as to who should have the honour of swearing first after David, king of Scots: Robert, earl of Gloucester, or Stephen, count of Mortain.[19] It was stated elsewhere that the oaths were administered by Roger, bishop of Salisbury.[20] They swore. But just what did they swear? William of Malmesbury makes a clear distinction between the title of the son and that of the daughter, the son as the heir and the daughter as the lawful successor.[21]

Whatever was sworn on this occasion, it was sworn to a lady recently widowed and not yet remarried. The second marriage took place in the summer of 1128. The couple lived apart for a time, and Marjorie Chibnall has shown that policy not personal antipathy lay behind their separation.[22] After they did come together, three male children were born to them: Henry in March 1133, Geoffrey (after a difficult childbirth) at Pentecost 1134, William in July 1136. The marriage had its critics, though men were well advised to choose their words with care. They allowed themselves to be reported as saying that marrying the son of a count was a bit of a come-down for an empress; that there was insufficient

---

[17] WM *GR* ii. 497; the fullest treatment of the episode is in OV vi. 294–307.
[18] There is an admirable treatment of the sources in Hollister, 'The Anglo-Norman Succession Debate of 1126', in *Anglo-Norman World*, 145–69.
[19] WM *HN* 4, not mentioned in any other source.
[20] HH 256; JW 27.   [21] WM *HN* 3–4.   [22] Chibnall, *Matilda*, 56–60.

discussion of the match; and that an Angevin marriage was inexpedient. After the marriage the oaths were resworn in 1129 and 1131; and after the birth of the first child in 1133 some additional security was asked for. Henry I, far from rejoicing in his grandchildren, as the hereditary archdeacon of Huntingdon believed,[23] found himself resisting claims made by his daughter and son-in-law on their behalf. It can be argued that this was the accident that stood in the way of a succession that was otherwise assured. It might also be argued that a perception of the insecurity of oaths sworn most solemnly lay behind a request for security in the form of castles.

Henry I died at Lyons-la-Forêt in Normandy on the night of 1 December 1135. Fifteen years after the loss of his son and heir he left behind not a secure succession but a power vacuum, which after three weeks was filled not by his daughter Matilda but by his nephew Stephen of Blois, count of Mortain. Stephen, like Matilda, was a grandchild of the Conqueror. His mother, Adela of Blois, was now the last survivor of the Conqueror's children, in retirement at the Cluniac nunnery of Marcigny, where she kept up an active correspondence with the great men of the day. Her prestige, her experience, and her network of contacts were still at the service of her sons.[24] Those sons had been generously treated by Henry I. A first indication of the fragility of Henry's plans for his daughter was the offer made by the Norman nobility to the eldest of Adela's sons, Theobald, count of Blois, that he should succeed—an offer which they would repeat in similar circumstances in 1141.[25] Discussions in Normandy, however, were overtaken by events in England, which led to the succession of another of Adela's sons, Stephen, count of Mortain and of Boulogne. Stephen had powerful bases in the Anglo-Norman world, and attracted powerful support. He made first for London, 'the capital, the queen of the whole kingdom', whose citizens, he found, claimed that, 'it was their own right and particular privilege that if their king died from any cause a successor should immediately be appointed by their own choice'; consequently, 'they appointed him king with universal approval'.[26]

[23] HH 253.
[24] A letter to her from Peter the Venerable, abbot of Cluny, is quoted by Davis, *Stephen*, 12–13 (= *Letters of Peter the Venerable*, no. 15).
[25] OV vi. 454–5, 548–9.
[26] *GS* 6–7; on the Londoners' claims, see M. McKisack, 'London and the

Next Stephen went to Winchester, the administrative capital, now the centre of the exchequer, under Roger, bishop of Salisbury, who had been at Henry I's right hand (occupying a post that would later be institutionalized as that of justiciar) throughout his long reign.[27] The bishop of Winchester was Henry of Blois, Stephen's younger brother. A Cluniac, earlier appointed and still remaining abbot of Glastonbury, he had his own agenda, in which ties of family formed only one part.[28]

It was not in doubt that of all the interest groups the Church in December 1135 would be particularly influential. While in its broadest definition, the Church at this time constituted the whole of the Christian faithful, or (a little more narrowly) the clerical order, it had a command structure in which the key role was occupied by the diocesan bishops, whose spiritual and secular obligations were fully buttressed by landed wealth.[29] It was the churchmen who by canon law claimed jurisdiction over oaths, oaths such as those sworn to Matilda. It was the churchmen who by custom crowned and anointed the new king. They had their own demands, to which Stephen had to accede before being accepted. But the churchmen would not have proceeded to the coronation on 22 December without a consciousness of the broader support within the lay community that has already been referred to. They would have been foolish to have done so. And these men were not fools.

The first presidency of F. D. Roosevelt has familiarized all subsequent political commentators with the concept of the 'First Hundred Days'.[30] The basic idea can be taken back without

Succession to the Crown in the Middle Ages', in R. W. Hunt, W. A. Pantin, and R. W. Southern (eds.), *Studies in Medieval History Presented to F. M. Powicke* (Oxford, 1948), 76–89; on their sustained support for Stephen, see J. Green, 'Financing Stephen's War', *ANS* 14 (1992), 106–14.

[27] E. J. Kealey, *Roger of Salisbury: Viceroy of England* (Berkeley, Calif., 1972); Green, *Henry I*, 38–50.

[28] The only monograph on Henry is L. Voss, *Heinrich von Blois: Bischof von Winchester (1129–71)* (Berlin, 1932); an influential short essay is found in Knowles, *Monastic Order*, 281–93; and a valuable additional perspective will be found in the edition of his charters by M. J. Franklin (*English Episcopal Acta 8: Winchester 1070–1204* (Oxford, 1993).

[29] Barlow, *English Church 1066–1154*, 29–53.

[30] A. M. Schlesinger, jun., *The Age of Roosevelt*, 2. *The Coming of the New Deal* (London, 1960), 1–22.

anachronism, for it says no more than that the first impressions created by a new regime are crucial in the establishment of its authority. Indeed, it can be argued that, for any medieval ruler, reputation and authority are so closely intertwined that they cannot be separated. What then of King Stephen? It was rather under a hundred days from Stephen's coronation just before Christmas 1135, through Henry I's burial at Reading at the Epiphany, to the Easter court of 1136.[31] The press could not have been more positive. Henry of Huntingdon stated that the king 'held his court during Easter at London, in a more splendid manner than had ever been before known, both for the number of attendants, and the magnificent display of gold, silver, jewels, costly robes and everything that was sumptuous'.[32] How had this come about?

A useful starting-point comes at the beginning of a document which the new regime took care to have widely disseminated. It is a document that has become known as Stephen's 'Charter of Liberties for the Church'. There are three surviving originals, from Exeter, Hereford, and Salisbury; copies from the metropolitan sees of Canterbury and York;[33] while the text was available to and used almost verbatim by William at Malmesbury in Wiltshire,[34] and Richard at Hexham in Northumberland.[35] The text started by spelling out Stephen's title: he had been *elected* by the clergy and people; *consecrated* by the archbishop of Canterbury; *confirmed* by the pope. The papal confirmation can have been only recently received, for it took a good hundred days, particularly in winter time, for a messenger to get to Rome, for business to be discussed,

---

[31] Easter Day in 1136 fell on 22 March, the earliest possible date under the Gregorian calendar.

[32] HH 259; cf. GS 24–9. The famous description of Arthur's crown-wearing at Caerleon was written by Geoffrey of Monmouth early in Stephen's reign (as Christopher Holdsworth kindly reminded me): *History of the Kings of Britain*, ix. 12–14; ed. L. Thorpe (Harmondsworth, 1966), 225–30; and see C. Brooke, 'Geoffrey of Monmouth as a Historian', in C. Brooke *et al.* (eds.), *Church and Government in the Middle Ages* (Cambridge, 1976), 77–91.

[33] RRAN iii, no. 271 (with facsimiles of originals in RRAN iv, plates iii, iv, and v); *Councils and Synods*, i:2, no. 137.

[34] WM HN 18–20. Malmesbury lay in the diocese of Salisbury, but William's close connection with Henry of Winchester suggests him as a more likely source.

[35] RH 148–50. The obvious source of this text was York. On the links between Hexham and York, see D. Nicholl, *Thurstan Archbishop of York (1114–1140)* (York, 1964), 46–8, 128–9; note also Gransden, *Historical Writing*, 288 n. 151.

and for the messenger to return.[36] The pope at this date was not in Rome but in Pisa. Christopher Holdsworth in his chapter explains very clearly why, in the circumstances of a schism, Stephen's case for acceptance would have seemed extremely strong.[37] At times of political uncertainty in England (as elsewhere), papal support was very important. In England and Normandy that political uncertainty lasted for most of Stephen's reign.

Stephen was the first of the kings after the Norman Conquest to be recognized as ruler both of England and Normandy. This gave him a long series of frontiers to defend, each with its own particular history and tensions. A first challenge came from the Scots, and the response to this provided the main political effort of Stephen's first hundred days. David, king of Scotland, had been the first layman to swear allegiance to the empress in 1127, and, as his troops descended on the north of England even before Henry I went to his grave, he took oaths of support from the northern magnates for his niece's cause. These oaths were potentially more insidious than the invasion itself. Stephen quickly brought a large army north to Durham, and commenced negotiations. These resulted in a carefully worked-out agreement, by which some territorial concessions were made to the Scots, including the city of Carlisle. In return, David's son Henry did homage to Stephen for his English earldom, and came south, first to York and then to the Easter court. 'In the short run the Scottish treaty was a triumph.' In the long term it did nothing to discourage the view that parts of 'northern England' were territory to which both kings had a proper claim.[38]

The ceremonial of the Easter court was designed to impress the long list of clergy and laity who attended. In attending, all had accepted Stephen's authority, the legitimacy of his title. The laymen would have done homage. An interesting narrative from Glastonbury which was written by Henry of Blois puts the matter as follows: 'King Henry my uncle having gone the way of all flesh, and my brother Stephen having succeeded in the kingdom, the aforesaid Robert [fitz Walter the Fleming] did homage and swore an oath of fealty as was the custom, together with the other

---

[36] R. L. Poole, *Studies in Chronology and History* (Oxford, 1934), 263–4.
[37] See Ch. 6.
[38] For this paragraph, see Barrow, Ch. 7; the quotation is from Davis, *Stephen*, 20.

magnates of the land.'[39] Behind each homage and oath of fealty there will in many instances have lain individual negotiation. Here lay the problem for the king. With the clergy he was dealing with a coherent group, claiming privileges in respect of their order. The privileges claimed by the magnates were, perfectly properly, a good deal more specific and more selfish.

What the king was prepared to concede is shown in grants made to Miles of Gloucester at the time of Henry I's burial. He was granted in inheritance the sheriffdom of Gloucester and the custody of the royal castle in Gloucester, as well as lands.[40] J. H. Round, always alert to the nuances of charters, thought this one 'not so much a grant from a king to a subject as a *convencio* between equal powers'.[41] It was certainly a privilege for a layman to have royal promises confirmed in writing. There cannot be much doubt that the reason for the king's generosity to Miles of Gloucester was because of his uncertainty as to the attitude of Robert of Gloucester. Robert joined the royal court at some point (quite possibly at Wallingford) on its itinerary from Westminster to Oxford, where the charter was issued, with Robert named (as earl and king's son) at the head of the lay witnesses. The earl of Gloucester did homage to the king, in a form acceptable to the royal court,[42] and was to join him in meeting the challenge offered by Baldwin de Redvers. Here was a son of one of the lords of the Cotentin linked to Henry I before he came to the throne, who prospered under his rule. Baldwin occurs in the *Gesta Stephani* as occupying Exeter castle, and as refusing to surrender it, and in another text as having been refused 'a certain honour'; the king was not uniformly generous.[43] The siege of Exeter lasted three months, and was successful, but the garrison was allowed to go free.[44] The king seems to have been present throughout, along with a considerable number of the great magnates, investing a good deal of time and authority on this one siege. What was reported, and what Robert of Gloucester would have seen, was division in the ranks.

[39] *English Lawsuits*, i, no. 292; the full text is *Adami de Domerham historia de rebus gestis Glastoniensibus*, ed. T. Hearne, 2 vols. (Oxford, 1727), ii. 303–31.

[40] *RRAN* iii, nos. 386–8.   [41] Round, *Geoffrey*, 14.

[42] *GS* 12–15; WM *HN* 17–18.

[43] There is a good discussion in Davis, *Stephen*, 22–4.

[44] The fullest treatment is in *GS* 30–47; the leniency to the garrison is strongly criticized by HH 259.

For Orderic Vitalis at least, the king would have been better occupied in coming to Normandy. He left it to others also to meet the challenge offered by the Welsh, and David Crouch suggests that Stephen may have been suspicious of Marcher authority.[45]

It was only in Lent of the following year, 1137, that Stephen crossed over to Normandy. His coffers were still full; and a whole series of truces and agreements were concluded which cash helped to lubricate. His brother Theobald can hardly have been a threat, but he was given a retainer at Evreux, where the count had recently died.[46] The king of France had supported Stephen by letters to the pope early in 1136, but now in 1137 could require homage for Normandy, which was performed by the king's son Eustace.[47] Here Stephen was dealing with people well disposed to him, and the cash they received, while welcome, will not have been the main consideration in their support. It was Stephen's wish also to bring to a head the challenge from Anjou. In 1136 Geoffrey had invaded the duchy, and he had also asked for oaths of support to his wife. As Marjorie Chibnall shows, the empress had established an advance post at Argentan, where in July of that year she had her third child. In 1137 Stephen made a truce with Anjou, but what he had wanted was a decisive battle. That chance was lost by divisions in his own camp. It is seen as having a racial element to it, with the Flemings and the Normans at loggerheads. There is seen also division in the Norman ranks, for some would never trust Robert of Gloucester, whom William of Malmesbury reports as only narrowly escaping an ambush which the king himself had prepared. The last chance went when the younger Norman nobility deserted his camp. 'When they have elected me king why do they abandon me. By the grace of God, I will never be called a king without a throne!'[48]

As Stephen reached the third year of his rule in 1138, his actions continued to be well reported, and (as with any political leader) his performance was re-evaluated with every fresh bit of news. In the opinion of Henry of Huntingdon, the king was doing well enough: 'These first two years of Stephen's reign were very propitious; in the next year, of which we shall speak, his fortunes were middling and things were beginning to fall apart; for the two years thereafter they

[45] See Ch. 8.   [46] RT 132.   [47] RH 147; OV vi. 482–3; HH 260.
[48] WM *HN* 21–2; OV vi. 484–7, and other sources cited there at 485 n. 4.

were pernicious, with everything torn to pieces.'[49] His account for
the third year balanced two things: events in the south, where the
public defection of Robert of Gloucester, rumoured in the spring,
became a reality in the summer; and, in the later summer, the battle of the Standard, in which the Scots were confronted the
moment they had crossed the Tees, and suffered a heavy defeat.[50]
Orderic Vitalis saw the defection of Robert of Gloucester as the key
to a wider rebellion: 'In England a considerable number of bishops
and castellans, on learning that the earl, who was very powerful in
both kingdoms [i.e. in England and in France], had joined the
Angevins, revealed the evil designs they had cherished in secret and
rebelled against the king.' Many resultant sieges were successful,
though crucially that of Bristol failed, energies being devoted to
easier targets.[51] Perhaps more revealing than those who rebelled
were the greater number who stayed loyal but perceived the need
for self-help. This was a year, seen from the cloister at Winchester,
one of the most stable environments in Britain, when 'there was no
man of any rank or standing in England who did not build anew
and munition his fortifications'. This passage parallels that of John
of Worcester quoted earlier in this chapter; and he went on to say,
by way of explanation, that men behaved in this way because they
were fearful of change.[52] There were good reasons for this.

   It was in 1139 that incipient rebellion, focused on the empress's
title, turned to civil war in the Anglo-Norman realm. That it
started then was not just a reflection of continuing uncertainty but
also the result of a vacuum of power which had developed amongst
the key figures who had stood behind Stephen's accession. It was
the archbishop of Canterbury who crowned the king, and who by
tradition stood first amongst his advisers. William of Corbeil, one
of the more invisible holders of this public office, died in August

---

[49] HH 260; trans. and comment by D. E. Greenway, 'Henry of Huntingdon and
the Manuscripts of his *Historia Anglorum*', *ANS* 9 (1987), 111.

[50] Ailred, *Relatio*, in RH 159–65; and noted in most of the chronicles, though not
in WM *HN*; but the relevant portion of *Gesta Stephani* has been lost. A useful collection of source material in translation is A. O. Anderson, *Scottish Annals from English
Chroniclers: A.D. 500 to 1286* (London, 1908; repr. Stamford, 1991), 185–207.

[51] On Robert of Gloucester's renunciation of fealty and Stephen's reaction thereto,
see WM *HN* 22–4; OV vi. 514–19 (at 516–17); *GS* 56–71; JW 49–50.

[52] Annals of Winchester, in *Annales monastici*, ed. H. R. Luard, 5 vols. (RS.
1864–9), ii. 51; JW 40.

1136, and the see was vacant until, following the battle of the Standard, the papal legate Alberic travelled to the British Isles to announce the end of the Schism and the Lateran Council to be held at Easter 1139. At the Christmas court of 1138–9 Theobald, abbot of Bec, was granted the archbishopric; and from this court he travelled with a number of his suffragans to Rome.[53] When at the Council the empress took the opportunity to challenge Stephen's title, the Anglo-Norman church put up a united front, and her case went by default.[54]

At the same time Thurstan of York came to the end of his career. York never had the resources or the prestige to fight a battle for the primacy on equal terms, but its archbishop was a leader of northern society in a way that no other diocesan bishop could emulate. In this perspective, Thurstan's involvement in the battle of the Standard represents the apotheosis of an unrivalled political and spiritual leadership. As he sickened unto death, that leadership was lost and would not be replaced. John of Hexham saw his death in February 1140 as leading to 'the insolence and roving licence of unrestrained disputes, shameless contempt of the clergy, irreverence of the laity towards ecclesiastical laws and persons; the unity of the kingdom was destroyed because each man's will was his law'.[55] The battle of the Standard had been followed in 1139 by the second treaty of Durham, concluded between the Scottish and English kings, which the legate Alberic helped to mediate. Most significantly, it conceded the earldom of Northumberland to Henry, son of the king of Scots. From this date until the end of Stephen's reign the Scots had untramelled authority over both Cumbria and Northumberland (except for the bishopric lands of Durham).[56] Even further south, Stephen's effective control was by no means clear. He was never able to nominate a successor to Thurstan whose title would remain unchallenged.[57]

[53] *Councils and Synods*, i:2, no. 139; Saltman, *Theobald*, 12–15.

[54] JS *HP* 83–5; for the date, see *Letters of Peter the Venerable*, ii. 252–6; for letters issued at the time of the Council, see E. King, 'King Stephen and the Anglo-Norman Aristocracy', *History*, 59 (1974), 183 n. 19.

[55] SD ii. 305; Nicholl, *Thurstan*, 213–38; P. Dalton, 'William Earl of York and Royal Authority in Yorkshire in the Reign of Stephen', *Haskins Soc. Journal*, 2 (1990), 155–65.

[56] RH 177–8; P. Dalton, *Conquest, Anarchy and Lordship: Yorkshire 1066–1154* (Cambridge, forthcoming), ch. 5; Barrow, below, Ch. 7.

[57] D. Knowles, 'The Case of St William of York', in *The Historian and Character*

More suddenly, in the south of England, the career of another great statesman came to a dramatic end. This was Roger of Salisbury. The great churchmen had been amongst the most active of the builders of the previous decade. Roger of Salisbury was proverbially wealthy, and much of that wealth was converted into buildings, which, in William of Malmesbury's view, his successors would strive in vain simply to keep in good repair.[58] In the summer of 1139 Roger and his two nephews, Alexander of Lincoln and Nigel of Ely, were arrested at court at Oxford and required to surrender their castles as security for their good behaviour. 'The arrest of the bishops' was well reported—so well reported that the significance of the episode is difficult to place in focus.[59] For many it would have been relished as a scandal in high places, a story that had everything. Roger of Salisbury was a married bishop. Matilda of Ramsbury, 'the wife of whom no one spoke',[60] was now given a walk-on role not in a tragedy but in a farce.[61] This was at Devizes, where she and Nigel of Ely, who had remained outside the royal court at the time of the arrests, fortified the castle against the king until compelled to submit. This behaviour will have gone some way to support the charge that the loyalty of Nigel, at least, was suspect; for a time he was driven from his see, and thereafter was never trusted.[62]

The immediate damage consequent on the arrest of the bishops was contained. Henry of Winchester summoned a legatine council at which the legality of the king's behaviour, in requiring the surrender of the castles as a surety against the bishops' good faith, was called in question. The king had good lawyers, and, on the narrow ground on which he chose to fight, he seems to have gained a points decision. The boxing metaphor is not chosen idly here. William of Malmesbury commented that he had witnessed no

and Other Essays (Cambridge, 1963), 76–97. In similar fashion, the election to Durham after the death of Geoffrey Rufus in May 1141 was disputed: A. Young, William Cumin: Border Politics and the Bishopric of Durham 1141–1144 (Borthwick Paper, 54; York, 1978).

[58] WM GR ii. 483–4; WM HN 37–9.

[59] There is a good discussion in Kealey, Roger of Salisbury, 173–89.

[60] R. W. Southern, 'King Henry I', in Medieval Humanism and Other Studies (Oxford, 1970), 231.

[61] As the story was embroidered at St Evroult: OV vi. 532–5.

[62] E. O. Blake, 'The Historia Eliensis as a Source for Twelfth-Century History', Bull. of John Rylands Library, 41 (1958–9), 318–26.

scholastic disputation but a fight for men's life-blood. The king was asked by the churchmen 'not to suffer a divorce to be made between the *regnum* and the *sacerdotium*'.[63] The significance of the arrest could not have been better put. The close alliance between Church and State up to this point had been lost. Innocent II from Rome late in 1140 sent a letter to Alexander of Lincoln calling for the restitution of one of the confiscated castles, that of Newark.

The magnates who should protect churchmen and their goods, and defend them against the incursions of wicked men, led on by their sins have become transformed into tyrants, and disturb churchmen with unprecedented exactions and oppressions.[64]

By this time, Roger of Salisbury was dead. In Roger, the king lost another, in the eyes of many the key, link with the good government of Henry I. His memory had been for Stephen the source of some strength. He had, if anything, strengthened his power, occasionally issuing writs in the king's name.[65] Had he not been disgraced, he would have presided over the exchequer board at Michaelmas 1139. On the following day the empress landed.

The landing was something of a gamble, for Robert of Gloucester's bases in the west country were closely invested, and could only be reached through hostile territory. In search of a safe haven, the empress had applied to her stepmother, Adeliza, the widow of Henry I, who held Arundel as part of her dower lands. She was admitted to the castle, which was forthwith surrounded by Stephen's troops. In the meantime, Robert of Gloucester went on to Bristol to mobilize support. After discussion, the empress was allowed to proceed to the west country, and given an escort of Henry of Winchester (through whose diocese the first, and for her the most difficult, part of the journey lay) and Waleran of Meulan.[66] She was to settle first at Bristol, which thereupon ceased to be an isolated outpost of defiance and became the centre of a territory which withdrew its allegiance from the anointed king. All at the time perceived as a key event in this transformation the defection of Miles of Gloucester, who, as has been seen, had been

---

[63] WM *HN* 34.   [64] *Registrum antiquissimum*, 1, no. 283.
[65] *RRAN* iii, nos. 313, 397; *Registrum antiquissimum*, 7, no. 2050. White suggests that such writs emanated from the Exchequer: below, Ch. 4.
[66] The chief sources here are WM *HN* 34–5; *GS* 86–91; JW 55–6; HH 266; OV vi. 534–5.

well treated by Stephen against such an eventuality. He now, as the
empress declared in one of her later charters, 'came to me at
Bristol, and received me as lady, and as she who was considered the
rightful heir to the kingdom of England; and thence he brought
me to Gloucester, and there did me liege homage against all other
men'.[67] Gloucester was strategically a very important centre, the
key to communications with south Wales and the Marches. It was
also a historic centre of royal authority, one of three cities where
(within living memory) the kings of England had been accustomed
to wear their crown at the great religious festivals.[68] Here at Bristol
and at Gloucester the English had the first sight of the lordship of
their new lady. Not all were impressed. According to the monks of
Gloucester, she 'received homage from all, and dispensed the laws
of the kingdom of England according to her pleasure . . . but on
those who refused to submit to her, and preferred to remain faithful to the king, torments worthy of the age of Decius or Nero were
inflicted, and death in many cases ensued'.[69]

    If, at this time, some of the outlines of the empress's character
were starting to become clear, that of the king was already well
established in the popular mind. The *Anglo-Saxon Chronicle*, in a
passage already quoted, is succinct: '*When* the traitors saw that he
was a mild man, and gentle and good, and did not inflict the full
penalties of the law', *then* every kind of enormity, which we are
quite justified in calling anarchy, ensued. Other writers, widely
scattered over the Anglo-Norman realm, say the same thing.
Stephen was a good-natured man; he inflicted no punishments.
They cited different examples. Henry of Huntingdon felt the rot
started with the treatment of the Exeter garrison in 1136; for John
of Worcester it was allowing the Hereford garrison to go free in
June 1138.[70] The comments got back to him. The public-relations
men advised a tougher image, and Stephen obliged as best he
could. When the Shrewsbury garrison surrendered late in 1138,
Orderic Vitalis records nearly a hundred executions, and says that
the king's severity was 'because unruly men regarded his gentleness
with contempt'.[71] The king's good nature had lain behind his election to the kingship, but now it became a liability to him. The

---

    [67] *RRAN* iii, no. 391.
    [68] M. Biddle, 'Seasonal Festivals and Residence', *ANS* 8 (1986), 51–72.
    [69] FW ii. 118.   [70] HH 259; JW 49.
    [71] OV vi. 520–3, and the discussion of other sources at 522 n. 2.

story of the empress's treatment after her arrival at Arundel removed any doubts on this score, being reported as an object lesson in misplaced chivalry.[72] The style was the man.

At Christmas 1139 Stephen had been king for four years. He spent the festival at Salisbury, where Bishop Roger had just died.[73] If we pause now to take stock, all the ingredients of the lack of focus and the loss of royal power that we call the anarchy can be seen to be in place. There was a vacuum in the clerical leadership that marked the most obvious continuity from Henry I's reign. The anointed king was perceived as good-natured and easily led; and yet he had received the homage of all but a handful of the Anglo-Norman nobility, and now the renunciation of homage on a growing scale weakened the feudal bond in which the lay aristocracy had invested so much capital. The homage sworn to Matilda by a man like Miles of Gloucester, who was one of Stephen's sheriffs, took from the king also capital of a different kind. He and others like him would no longer make returns to the exchequer of the county farms. Stephen at Salisbury reportedly taking money from the altar that had been saved for building works is also an image of financial weakness.[74] Few could doubt that a vital point had been reached, when sporadic dissatisfaction outside and dissension within Stephen's government had turned to civil war. It was a civil war caused by a disputed succession. The war would not be settled until the succession ceased to be a matter for dispute.

There were well-established procedures for dispute-settlement in medieval Europe.[75] Every possible network was used. The links of feudal homage, on which the main emphasis of this chapter has fallen, were important here, but so also were other ties no less strong—those of family and of neighbourhood. The succession to the kingdom was a highly complicated dispute involving two

[72] GS 88–9 ('as was reported'); OV vi. 534–5 (the king was either naïve or irresponsible); HH 266 (the king was badly advised or the castle was too strong).

[73] Kealey, *Roger of Salisbury*, 205; a charter for the canons of Salisbury was dated on Christmas Day 1139: *RRAN* iii, no. 787.

[74] WM *HN* 39.

[75] P. Wormald, 'Charters, Law and the Settlement of Disputes in Anglo-Saxon England', in W. Davies and P. Fouracre (eds.), *The Settlement of Disputes in Early Medieval Europe* (Cambridge, 1986), 149–68; E. King, 'Dispute Settlement in Anglo-Norman England', *ANS* 14 (1992), 115–30; M. Chibnall, 'Anglo-French Relations in the Work of Orderic Vitalis', in J. S. Hamilton and P. J. Bradley (eds.), *Documenting the Past: Essays in Honour of G. P. Cuttino* (Woodbridge, 1989), 5–19.

families. Representatives of those two families were convened by a
member of one of them, Henry of Blois, bishop of Winchester, as
papal legate, near Bath on neutral ground. It seems to have followed skirmishing in the neighbourhood in August 1140. 'On the
Empress's side her brother Robert was sent and the rest of her
advisers; on the king's the legate and archbishop, and likewise the
queen.' First negotiations would seldom be successful, and were
not in this instance, but Henry of Winchester gained enough
encouragement from these discussions then to go to France; and,
in turn, gained enough encouragement from discussions with,
among others, Louis VII and Theobald of Blois to bring back proposals 'that would have benefited the country if there had been
anyone who could combine both words and deeds'. It is interesting, and not entirely inconclusive, to work out the terms of the discussion from William of Malmesbury at his most allusive.[76] It may
be deduced that Louis VII was involved as overlord of the whole
kingdom of France; and that it was as a family member that
Theobald of Blois was consulted. The discussions are difficult to
interpret other than that both sides were being encouraged to look
to the next generation, and to recognize that Stephen would
remain king in his own lifetime. Events in the following year,
1141, were to change those assumptions.

The year in which one well-informed chronicler speaks of discussion for peace was also, as has been seen, the one in which there
can be detected in the literature the germ of some of the main ideas
of the anarchy. The prominent position occupied by the castles,
and the arbitrary cruelty of the castlemen; the incoherence of political life, as private feuds were pursued in the name of the public
authority—these are nowhere better seen than in the work of the
monastic chroniclers who wrote in the west country at Worcester
and at Gloucester. John of Worcester starts his treatment of the
year with Stephen marching his forces to the fenland, 'a measure
which in my opinion was entirely unnecessary', and which led to
Nigel of Ely taking refuge in Bristol. The chronicler was then taken
up with events closer to home. The king and Waleran of Meulan
came to Worcester, and then marched south, wasting the estates of
Robert of Gloucester, including his 'magnificent house' in
Tewkesbury; Waleran returned home, 'proclaiming to all that he

---

[76] WM *HN* 44–5, the only evidence for these discussions.

had hardly ever either in Normandy or in England caused such a conflagration'. Attention then turned to Devizes in Wiltshire, formerly the castle of Roger of Salisbury, which came into the hands of the mercenary Robert fitz Hubert. Here was a model for the cruelty of the castlemen, double-crossing both sides; he was finally captured by John the Marshall.[77] Here John of Worcester's chronicle ends. The Gloucester monk took up the story, recorded with satisfaction the hanging of Robert like a common criminal, and then described the skirmishing near Bath. Robert of Gloucester then turned to attack Nottingham, a 'most noble city', which was consigned in its turn to the flames.[78] These are the stories as they came in, with no pattern imposed, and no theme other than universal suffering.

William of Malmesbury prefaced his account of the events of the year 1141 by saying that Robert of Gloucester was so distressed by the manifestations of civil war in England that he preferred to hazard all on the result of a single battle.[79] The battle took place at Lincoln. The flashpoint was again the control of the royal castle, here claimed by Ranulf, earl of Chester, one of the dominant figures of the anarchy. It is now suggested that some control had in fact been conceded by Stephen, but, after protest by the townsmen, the king had changed his mind, and at Christmas 1140 had commenced a siege of his own castle. Ranulf appealed for help to his father-in-law, Robert of Gloucester. A substantial army was levied to attempt to lift the siege, including Welsh infantry, here for the first time playing a significant part in an English battle. In an engagement that was fought on the west side of the city, many of Stephen's troops abandoned the field, and the king was captured. He was taken in captivity to Bristol.[80] At no time does it appear that his life was in danger; but many would have expected his tenure of the throne now to be short. Few could have expected that

[77] JW 59–63. On Waleran of Meulan and Robert of Gloucester, see the comments of D. Crouch, 'Robert, Earl of Gloucester, and the Daughter of Zelophehad', *Journal of Medieval History*, 11 (1985), 234–6. On Robert fitz Hubert, see further *GS* 104–9; WM *HN* 43–4.

[78] FW ii. 127–9.   [79] WM *HN* 47–8.

[80] The fullest treatment is provided by Henry of Huntingdon, an archdeacon of the Lincoln diocese: HH 268–75. There are good modern discussions in Davis, *Stephen*, 48–51, and P. Dalton, '. . . Ranulf II Earl of Chester in King Stephen's Reign', *ANS* 14 (1992), 39–59; see further Crouch, below, Ch. 8 (on the significance of the Welsh forces), and Coulson, below, Ch. 2 (on Lincoln castle).

so clear a victory for one side would prolong the civil war, but this is what happened.

The victorious party now opened discussions with Henry of Winchester, the papal legate, as to the terms on which the empress would be recognized as ruler of England. Those discussions are referred to in one of the empress's own charters: 'On the third Sunday of Lent he came to me and spoke with me at Wherwell, and on the following Monday the same prelate and the citizens of Winchester received me honourably within the cathedral and the city of Winchester.'[81] The price of the support of Henry of Winchester was that his existing authority within the Church be maintained. The empress became *domina Anglorum*, lady of the English; and this was added to her titles: 'Matilda the Empress, the daughter of king Henry, lady of the English.' This new title recognized her *de facto* authority within England. It allowed those who had done homage to Stephen now with a clear conscience to do homage to the empress. Events would prove whether it could be made to mean more than that. The empress still needed to be received within London. Around and within London were bases of the honour of Blois, from which Stephen's queen could still muster substantial support. The empress needed an endorsement from the papacy; and may well have delayed her arrival in London for at least an initial reaction from Innocent II, who up to this point had offered her no encouragement at all.

What more could the empress achieve? The answer, as it turned out, was very little. With the authority of her new title still untested, twice, in the summer and early autumn of 1141, she was forced to retreat, first from London and then from Winchester, the twin capitals of the monarchy which she claimed. All the while, the spotlight never left her. Her every move, almost her every gesture, was closely watched. The modern reader continues to have excellent witnesses as to what men at the time took to be common knowledge. The two great chroniclers of the day, William of Malmesbury and Orderic Vitalis, were to find in the events of this year their last great challenge; while Henry of Huntingdon, the Gloucester continuator of Florence, and the author of the *Gesta Stephani*, can be taken as additional witnesses of a lively contemporary debate. The

---

[81] *RRAN* iii, no. 343, reading *dominica tercia* for *dominica intrantis*, as in WM *HN* 50–1.

English writers stressed the importance of the empress's character. She was seen to be imperious (which might have been thought understandable), to be stubborn, to be impetuous, and to be reluctant to take advice. These faults impacted in different ways on three interest groups in particular: first, her own followers; secondly, the Londoners; and, thirdly, Henry of Winchester, the legate. The detail given differs in each case, as did the importance attached to the different groups. It was the dealings with Henry of Winchester that William of Malmesbury saw as being crucial, 'the origins of all the evils that would follow'. The focus of this disagreement was the provision to be made, while Stephen was in captivity, for his son and heir Eustace. The senior members of Eustace's family—Matilda (his mother); Henry of Winchester (his uncle); Theobald, count of Blois (also his uncle)—all urged the empress that Eustace be given the (extensive) lands that his father had controlled before he became king; but this was refused. It is important to realize—what many of the chroniclers were a little too close to events to see[82]—that the provision for Eustace was the key to the settlement of the civil war. In leaving him nothing, the empress was rejecting compromise. More people than just Eustace may have felt themselves threatened by this episode.[83]

In this perspective, the capture of Robert of Gloucester in the retreat from Winchester (early in September 1141), and his subsequent exchange for the king (two months later), made for tidiness but did not alter the balance of power. Each man went back to his power base. Each was to 'maintain his cause to the best of his advantage'.[84] The generals attempted to motivate tired troops by claiming that the enemy was on its last legs, and one push would lead to a breakthrough.[85] It was not true. And those generals had

[82] Apart from William of Malmesbury, the exception to this statement is the well-briefed monk of Gloucester, who concluded his treatment of the year 1141 when the peace negotiations broke down, not with the exchange of king and earl: FW ii. 131–6.
[83] The author of the *Gesta Stephani* takes pains to emphasize the insecurity engendered by the empress's actions: *GS* 120–1.
[84] WM *HN* 61 (this being a comment on stories, which were well known, that Stephen had tried to buy off the earl: WM *HN* 67–8; FW ii. 136).
[85] William of Malmesbury records that Stephen was seriously ill, 'so that in nearly the whole of England he was proclaimed as dead' (WM *HN*, 71). The author of the *Gesta Stephani* records that, after the retreat from Winchester, the empress (whom he always calls the countess of Anjou) was 'worn out almost to the point of utter collapse' (*GS* 138–9).

lost much of their authority. From this perspective the importance of the events of 1141 can hardly be exaggerated. King and earl had suffered the degradation of imprisonment,[86] while the empress's attempts to lead from the front had left her exposed and vulnerable. Discussions for peace had no sooner been opened than they were overtaken by the results of war. The whole idea of peace-making had suffered a set-back. Theobald of Canterbury and Henry of Winchester, 'the archbishop and the legate', suffered the natural fate of failed mediators in being derided by both sides. In councils of 1141 the laymen had been told first to support the empress, and then to change their allegiance back again to Stephen. Amongst those who continued to support the empress feelings ran high, as a fragment of correspondence between Brian fitz Count and Henry of Winchester makes very clear. The layman gave necessity as the reason for seizing goods bound for Winchester fair; reproached the bishop for his inconsistency; and claimed that it was the clergy not the laymen who were responsible for the breakdown of order.[87] 'I am sorry for the poor and their plight, when the church provides scarcely any refuge for them, for they will die if peace be longer delayed.'[87]

The most important strategic result of the battle of Lincoln was that Stephen lost control of Normandy. It did not happen immediately, but (not for the first time since the Conquest) between 1144 and 1154 Normandy and England were under different rule. Marjorie Chibnall's chapter shows the stages by which this came about.[88] It is emphasized that Matilda in her dower lands had an important foothold in Normandy from the beginning of the reign. When, however, Geoffrey of Anjou commenced the systematic conquest of Normandy, it was he who received the homage of the Normans, and who in 1144 was invested as duke. Moreover, it was the suggestion of Haskins, in his classic work on Normandy, that Geoffrey viewed himself as ruling not for himself but as regent for his son.[89] From this perspective, it is reasonable to go forward to

---

[86] Orderic concluded his text whilst Stephen was in captivity, and this was the conclusion that he drew: 'I see the princes of this world overwhelmed by misfortunes and disastrous setbacks' (OV vi. 550–3).

[87] WM HN 63; H. W. C. Davis, 'Henry of Blois and Brian fitz Count', EHR 25 (1910), 297–303 (at 302).　　　　　　　　　　　　　　　　[88] See Ch. 3.

[89] Haskins, Norman Institutions, 130–5; SD ii. 322–3; GS 214–17, 224–7; Davis, Stephen, 104–7.

the knighting of Henry at Carlisle in 1149, and his investment as duke in his father's place and in his father's lifetime, immediately after his return to Normandy. These few sentences have taken the story of the reign forward at some speed. The justification for doing so is that these developments were at the time seen as coherent and inevitable. Neither while Normandy was being over-run by Geoffrey of Anjou, nor after it had fallen under his control as duke, did Stephen make any attempt to bring forces from England to restore his authority in Normandy.

The loss of Normandy to the Angevins was but one of the ways in which by the 1140s the range of Stephen's authority was reduced. We turn now to consider the extent and the nature of royal government within England. Mark Blackburn in his chapter offers for the first time a survey of the coinage which brings an extensive literature into the mainstream of historical debate.[90] The coins are important because they are amongst the most precise evidence we have from medieval England. An estimate of 5,000 surviving coins is here given for the reign. Each of these coins, though only the size of an adult's thumb-nail, contains precise information on the place of issue, on the moneyer, and on the authority in whose name the coin was issued. Up to this point in England that authority had been the king. It was the image of royal authority that circulated most widely. Stephen upon his accession struck a coinage at forty-five or more mints, from Newcastle and Carlisle in the north to Canterbury and Exeter in the south. It is an interesting reflection of a national economy that coins from forty mints (all but two of the then-known mints of Stephen's first type) were found in 1972 in a hoard buried at Prestwich in Lancashire some time in the early 1140s. By the early 1140s the control reflected in the wide issue of a standard coinage from centrally issued dies had disappeared. The empress and Robert of Gloucester had control of several of the mint towns of the west country within a short time of her landing in England in 1139, and from these coins were issued in her own name after 1141. In the north of England the issuing of coins by David of Scotland, from mints and by moneyers who had previously struck for Stephen, is a clear sign of the extension of the Scots' authority in Northumbria and Cumbria. The loss of control, however, was not confined to these two areas. The

[90] See Ch. 5.

centrally issued coinages of the 1140s cover only the south-east of
England. Outside this area, coins were issued for Stephen (amongst
others), but not from dies that were centrally issued. Mr Blackburn
suggests this may have been because the moneyers, and the royal
officials to whom they were responsible, were reluctant to pay the
fee for new dies or the *geld de moneta*, the tax payable for operating
the minting, which was how the Crown took most of its profit
from minting. Since, of course, no one pays taxes with any enthusiasm, this would mean that in these regions the sanctions behind
the centrally issued coinage (whose memory could still have been
very clear) were seen to be ineffectual. These coins thus show some
of the features of the most remarkable, and the most *anarchic*,
coins of Stephen's reign, those issued by the magnates in their own
names. For king as for aristocracy there is a truncated version of
the images of their power on the seals: on that of Patrick, earl of
Salisbury, head, helmet, and sword. At the end of the reign, after
peace had been agreed, came the return again to a genuinely
national coinage. Only in 1158 were coins issued in the name of
Henry II.

The coinage was just one element of routine administration
which continued after Stephen's accession, under the overall control of Roger of Salisbury. The exchequer served as the accounting
body, its routines reflecting the accountability of the local officers
of the Crown. This is one of the areas considered by Dr Graeme
White in his chapter. A number of clear breaks in administrative
routine have been identified. The first was the public humiliation
in 1139 of Roger of Salisbury and of Nigel of Ely, his nephew, and
a possible successor. With the authority of Stubbs to second the
opinion of Henry of Huntingdon, this has long been seen as *the*
hiatus in the reign—for Ralph Davis one of the king's crucial *mis-
takes*. It has more recently been argued that continuity in personnel, at the levels below the top, show a bigger change in 1141.[91] If
we again focus on the exchequer session that should have been held
at Michaelmas 1141, it is difficult to see many sheriffs (if any at all)

[91] HH 266 ('this prepared the way for the eventual ruin of the house of king
Stephen'); Stubbs, *Constitutional History*, i. 326 ('the most important constitutional
event that had taken place since the Conquest'); Davis, *Stephen*, 28–33 ('one of the
turning points of Stephen's reign'); E. J. Kealey, 'King Stephen: Government and
Anarchy', *Albion*, 6 (1974), 201–17; K. Yoshitake, 'The Arrest of the Bishops in 1139
and its Consequences', *Journal of Medieval Hist.* 14 (1988), 97–114.

setting off with satchels of cash. The king was in prison in Bristol. The lord of Bristol, Robert of Gloucester, was in prison in Rochester, one of the fortresses of the king. The payment of taxes is one habit that is easy to break.

It is not in question that a weakening of authority at the centre, a virtual disappearance of any effective accountability of local officers of the Crown, was accompanied by an increase in the power and the independence of local magnates. The literature here has come in particular to focus on the power of the earls—and for good reason. The reign of Stephen was marked by a positive explosion of new earldoms, granted both by Stephen and by the empress, to the point at which several counties in the 1140s had an earl appointed by each of the two sides who were struggling for authority.[92] Several questions have here been raised. Was it all along the intention that the centralization which Roger of Salisbury personified should be put in reverse as soon as this could be arranged? Paul Dalton's case study of Yorkshire argues not.[93] What was the nature of the earl's dignity, and did this change in Stephen's reign? Here there is a substantial literature. Round did indeed 'throw some fresh light' on the subject in his study of Geoffrey de Mandeville, and after him further light has been shed first by Stenton, then by Davis.[94] Davis, in a study of the reign that had grown out of an edition of the charters, was in no doubt that a different and more directive role was now, through changing circumstances, placed upon the earls: 'Earls were an essential part of government in a kingdom divided by war.'[95] The discussion is continued by Warren Hollister and by Graeme White in their chapters on (respectively) the aristocracy and the administration.[96]

As the effective power of the great magnates increased, so inevitably did their vision of their authority. One of the simplest of the charters of creation of an earldom, that for Geoffrey de Mandeville *c.*1140, provided that he was to hold 'with all dignities and liberties and customs with which the other of my earls most

---

[92] See the table in Davis, *Stephen*, 130; there is a list of county officials, including the earls, in *RRAN* iii, pp. xxiv–xxv.

[93] Warren, *Governance*, 89–95; Dalton, 'William Earl of York'.

[94] Round, *Geoffrey*, 267–77; Stenton, *First Century*, 227–34; Davis, *Stephen*, 125–41. Note also D. Crouch, *The Image of Aristocracy in Britain, 1000–1300* (London, 1992), published as the present volume was about to go to press.

[95] *RRAN* iii, p. xxvi. [96] See Ch. 1 and Ch. 4.

honourably and most freely hold'.[97] Robert of Gloucester as a matter of routine, his brother Reginald of Cornwall, and his son-in-law Ranulf of Chester on occasion, took the title *consul* and not *comes*.[98] Stephen, when trying to mollify Robert of Gloucester in Normandy in 1137, took care to emphasize his rank.[99] Several of the earls took to describing themselves as holding their authority 'by the grace of God';[100] as having acquired territory through the same favour;[101] and dated their charters from the dates of their acceptance of the comital dignity.[102] Ralph Davis pointed out that within their own counties the earls were accustomed to issuing writs modelled on those of the royal chancery, addressing the officers of the shire as their own officers.[103] In charters and on the seals that authenticated charters their leading men emphasized their official status.[104]

There are in private charters, the more telling for being so matter of fact, references to time of war, and recognition that the economic value of property was lessened because of it. Stenton printed a charter by which a church in Wiltshire granted to Lewes Priory was valued at 10*s.* in time of war and 13*s.* 4*d.* in time of peace, a 25 per cent loss of value.[105] There survive figures for 'waste', in the danegeld collected in Henry II's second year, which might seem to offer a nation-wide statistics of the damage caused by war. The argument was first put by H. W. C. Davis in 1913, and first questioned by A. L. Poole in his Oxford history volume in 1946; thereafter there has been extensive discussion, but no consensus has been reached.[106] Nor can one be suggested in this short survey. It

[97] *RRAN* iii, no. 273.

[98] *Gloucester Charters*, 22–3; *Earldom of Chester*, 155; *Sarum Charters and Documents*, ed. W. D. Macray (RS, 1891), 23–4.

[99] WM *HN* 21 (a point lost in the translation); cf. *GS* 14–15.

[100] *Earldom of Chester*, 70–1; and see further Crouch, *Aristocracy*, 13–14, 67–8.

[101] *The Cartulary of Worcester Cathedral Priory*, ed. R. R. Darlington (PRS NS 38, 1963), no. 252.

[102] Miles of Gloucester in 1141, 'iamque consulatus honorem adeptus' (Stenton, *First Century*, 233 n. 1).

[103] Davis, *Stephen*, 127–8.

[104] The seal of Geoffrey de Waterville identified him as 'the earl's steward' (*dapifero consulis*); the earl, who did not need to be identified, was Robert of Gloucester: King, 'Dispute Settlement', 115. See in general Crouch, *Aristocracy*, 292–3.

[105] Stenton, *First Century*, 246.

[106] H. W. C. Davis, 'The Anarchy of Stephen's reign', *EHR* 18 (1903), 630–41; A. L. Poole, *From Domesday Book to Magna Carta*, 2nd edn. (Oxford, 1955), 151–3;

may be helpful, however, to bear in mind that these variant interpretations are based on taxation records. These, in ways that vary
considerably between societies, record assessments of wealth and of
capacity to pay. Medieval English taxation was based on an assess-
ment of surplus over and above immediate consumption needs.
Those needs varied with status, for an individual needed to be
maintained at the level of his or her estate; yet for the tax-man
there were some obvious targets. Grain safely gathered into barns
and destined for the market; sheep whose wool could be woven
into cloth, and other livestock destined for market; these were pre-
eminently surplus. Build up your stock, came the advice of Bishop
Grosseteste to the countess of Lincoln a century later, and 'in the
end your stock will pay for your wine, your robes, your wax, and
all your wardrobe'.[107] Now the targets of the tax-man were also the
targets of those seeking to deprive an enemy of sustenance or provide provisions for the garrison of a castle in time of war. Thus an
early letter from Gilbert Foliot as abbot of Gloucester complained
to the diocesan bishop that William de Beauchamp had seized '44
measures of threshed corn, which were being carried to meet the
needs of our brothers', while more recently 'he has broken into our
houses, seized our grain, and borne it off'.[108] If the plough beasts
were driven off, and the seed-corn stolen, then (until an estate was
restocked) fertile land might indeed lie as waste. According to the
Ramsey abbey chronicle, after the depredations of Geoffrey de
Mandeville, the incoming abbot found 'on all the demesne lands of
the abbey only one and a half plough teams, and no provisions'.[109]

We turn now to consider the changes in attitudes which allowed
the country to move from war to peace, a peace embodied in a settlement late in 1153, consequent upon which Henry II would succeed Stephen less than a year later in 1154. The first point that
needed to be accepted was that Henry should indeed succeed.
William of Malmesbury throughout his text emphasizes that the
empress his mother had the right of *succession*, while her son Henry

Green, 'Financing Stephen's War', 104 and n. 99; and further literature cited by
Hollister, Ch. 1 n. 39.

[107] D. Oschinsky, *Walter of Henley and other Treatises on Estate Management and
Accounting* (Oxford, 1971), 398–9.

[108] GF, *Letters*, no. 3.

[109] *Chronicon Abbatiae Rameseiensis*, ed. W. D. Macray (RS, 1886), 333–4, one of a
number of similar texts cited in Knowles, *Monastic Order*, 268–72.

was the *lawful heir*. This by 1142 was clearly the view of the
Angevin camp, and it came to be much more widely accepted. It
was quite possible, and quite consistent, for individuals in the
1140s to believe both that Stephen was the lawful *king* and that
Henry was the lawful *heir*. We are fortunate to have here the evidence of John of Salisbury in his *Memoirs of the Papal Court*. He
shows very clearly that Theobald by the late 1140s had established
an effective primacy on the model of his predecessor Lanfranc. He
had done so by insisting on unity: 'although individual dignitaries
followed different lords, the church as a whole recognized only
one.'[110] It was in every way consistent both to say this, and to support Henry's claims to the succession. It has been remarked on
that, when Henry came to England in 1147, and again in 1149
(when he was knighted by David of Scotland at Carlisle), the
author of the *Gesta Stephani* on each occasion describes him as 'the
lawful heir to the kingdom of England'. There is no need to see
such passages as written after the peace settlement of 1153. They
reflect the best opinion of the late 1140s.[111]

So Henry should succeed. But what would he succeed to? When
the inevitability of his succession was recognized, England was a
wartorn country, in which the institution of monarchy had fallen
to a low ebb. So the nature of kingship was under discussion, at
least from the late 1140s, and its relation to magnate authority;
and here again the churchmen took a leading role. One point in
the indictment of the castlemen in the famous passage in the
Anglo-Saxon Chronicle states that, 'at regular intervals they levied a
tax known as *tenserie* [protection money] upon the villages'.[112]
Those who levied the tax, of course, did not lack justification for it.
The ideas came from the rights of castellans within the area of their
castleries, over the peasantry, and over religious houses, particularly
where they claimed rights as an advocate. The Church's defence
drew, just as the assertion of these claims, on continental precedent. Behind what seem to be bland claims—peasants forced to
work on castles; to give renders in grain—lay big issues. The laymen could appeal to custom, for in current usage 'customs' (*consuetudines*) were renders in cash and in kind. The churchmen drew on

[110] JS *HP* 47–9.
[111] Davis, *GS*, pp. xx–xxi (though he thought the phrase might have been 'a last
minute revision of the text'); cf. Davis, *Stephen*, 113–14.
[112] On the term *tenserie*, see Round, *Geoffrey*, 414–16.

their armoury of texts, improper levies were exactions, the manifestations of tyranny.[113] Where in all this was legitimacy to be found? It was found in the idea of royal sanction. Here is how the problem and the solution appear in the canons of Theobald's first legatine council in 1151. They started with the particular problems of the anarchy. New diseases called for new remedies.

We therefore provide that the church and all its possessions shall in all respects remain free of works and exactions that go under the name of *tenserie* or tallages, nor should anyone presume to trouble them hereafter in respect of these. Anyone who is tempted to go against this decree shall be subject to the suspension of divine office in his lands until he shall make appropriate satisfaction, and be subject to anathema. Only works due to be done for the king are excepted, if they have been specifically authorised by him.[114]

Here, in the thinking of the great churchmen, concerned to protect themselves against what they saw as local tyranny, is prefigured Henry's insistence, as duke and as king, that he would restore the rights of the Crown. The units here—the building-blocks, as it were, in the re-establishment of royal authority—were castles and hundreds, the centres of local administration.[115]

The castle was the dominant image of the day. At whatever level politics was discussed at the time, *a* castle (or a number of castles) or *the* castle tended to move to centre stage. At the simplest level the description of political action listed a series of sieges. Thus a passage from John of Worcester, dealing with Stephen's actions after Robert of Gloucester had renounced his homage in 1138:

The king having wasted and burned the surrounding lands and townships of the earl of Gloucester, laid siege to the castle [of Bristol]; but at length, weary of the tedious blockade, he diverted to besiege the earl's other

[113] King, 'Anarchy'; but a much wider reference to continental literature would have been both possible and helpful. Note in particular M. Bur, *La Formation du comté de Champagne v.950–v.1150* (Nancy, 1977), 358–78.

[114] *Councils and Synods*, i:2, no. 150; the mention of the council in Henry of Huntingdon was the occasion for his complaint about the novelty of appeals to Rome: HH 282.

[115] King, 'Anarchy', 139–43; on hundreds, see further Dalton, 'William Earl of York'. H. G. Richardson ('The coronation in medieval England: the evolution of the office and the oath', *Traditio*, 16 (1960), 153–6) suggested that, once peace had been agreed, Nigel of Ely became an important figure in the restoration of alienated crown property.

castles, [Castle] Cary in Dorset and Harptree in Somerset; and then, having thrown up and manned castles in front of them, he departed and marched with the whole of his army to Dudley castle, which Ralph Paynel held against him. There he set fire to the surrounding country, and took and carried off much cattle; and then went by sea, together with a large body of his soldiers, to besiege Shrewsbury castle, which William fitz Alan held against him.[116]

The castles must be seen not just as real estate, but as a focus of the ideas and aspirations both of monarch and of magnate. Thus Baldwin de Redvers at Exeter saw the control of the castle as a key to his integrity; the king equally: 'there could be no doubt that it was a royal castle.'[117] What then of cases in which it was equally no doubt that it was a private castle, as were the great majority of those built by barons and bishops on their demesne manors? What restrictions affected individual magnates in their castle policy, particularly in time of war? Charles Coulson's chapter argues that there was no agreed concept of royal 'licensing' of castles in this period, but rather a series of ideas clustered around the continental concept of 'rendability'. The council of Winchester which followed 'the arrest of the bishops' in 1139, and the agreement between the earls of Chester and Leicester late in the reign, are among the episodes reinterpreted with these ideas in mind. It is argued further in this chapter that the 'adulterine' castle was not an unlicensed castle. Here a different set of ideas was in operation. The adulterine castle was an invention of the churchmen, no less a part of the clerical peace movement than was the condemnation of taxes not authorized by the king. The passage from the *Anglo-Saxon Chronicle*, under the year 1137, describing the tyrannies of the castle-men, is seen as firmly within this tradition.[118]

In the early 1150s events were moving fast towards a final settlement of the civil war, though whether it would be an agreed settlement was still an open question. With the knighting in 1149 first of Eustace, King Stephen's elder son, and then of Henry of Anjou, the initiative had clearly moved to a new generation. Robert of Gloucester had died in 1147, and was buried at Bristol; the empress had left Devizes castle, one of the fortifications of Roger of Salisbury, and retired to Rouen, where she died in 1167; Stephen's

---

[116] JW 50. Castle Cary is in fact in Somerset.   [117] *GS* 32–3.
[118] See Ch. 2.

queen Matilda died in 1152, and was buried at the monastery she
and her husband had founded at Faversham in Kent. The impetus
to Henry's eventual success in England was provided by his going
very quickly from being a landless pretender to the English throne
to one of the greatest magnates of northern Europe.

The first stage in the establishment of Henry was his succession
to the duchy of Normandy, after he had returned empty-handed
from his third visit to England in 1149. This was in his father's lifetime. Then in 1151 Geoffrey of Anjou died, and Henry became
count of Anjou. The following year 1152 saw the divorce of Louis
VII from his wife Eleanor of Aquitaine, and her marriage with
Henry of Anjou. This marriage was both a great *coup* and a great
risk, for it destabilized western France, and a great accretion of
power brought with it a great accretion of enemies. There came
Eustace from England, recognizing that the battle for succession to
the English monarchy was now to be fought in northern France;
the younger brothers of Henry of Anjou, claiming some share of
their father's accumulated lands; the heirs to Theobald of Blois; the
king of France himself, who had lost face and was threatened with
the diminution of his lordship. Robert of Torigny, in the middle of
a detailed treatment of the manoeuvrings of these different groups,
comments simply: 'Many men thought that Duke Henry would
rapidly lose all of his possessions.'[119] If he did not, it was because
Henry was well advised; his enemies of his own generation had no
common focus for their ambition, while his overlord was a cau-
tious man, advised in his turn by men favourable to Henry. Henry
remained calm; the coalition of his enemies unravelled; and he was
left to confront them in his own time.

Within England, however, time was not on his side. Little has
been said in this introduction of the course of the civil war in
England, but there was every sign that Stephen was gaining some
ground. Reginald, earl of Cornwall, and Roger, earl of Hereford,
are each recorded as informing Henry that there was no time to
lose.[120] Early in 1153 he landed in England.[121] Twice in this year
Henry and Stephen came together as though for a decisive military
engagement; twice they broke off, finding their own supporters

[119] RT 165–6.   [120] Ibid. 164 (Cornwall); *GS* 228–31 (Hereford).
[121] For contrasting views as to the extent to which Henry's success was at this point
inevitable, see J. Leedom, 'The English Settlement of 1153', *History*, 65 (1980),
347–64; G. White, 'The End of Stephen's Reign', *History*, 75 (1990), 3–22.

reluctant to fight.[122] The first occasion was at Malmesbury, where
the castle to which William of Malmesbury had taken such objec-
tion was surrendered to Duke Henry. The second time was at
Wallingford, lone bastion of Angevin support in the Thames
Valley. We are told that immediately after this meeting, which
must have been in late July or early August, Stephen's son Eustace
left court in disgust, 'for the war in his opinion had reached no
proper conclusion'; and he died shortly thereafter. We may take his
withdrawal as the sign that Stephen had accepted the need to make
terms.[123] All knew what those terms would be with regard simply
to the succession. There remained a good deal more to discuss.

Sir James Holt's chapter, from a close study of the relevant charters and chronicle sources, makes clear how a settlement of the succession dispute became at the same time a settlement of the civil
war, a genuine peace settlement. The protagonists had to be
satisfied that they had achieved the best result they could by negotiation. Those negotiations, as has been seen, went back at least a
decade. The history behind the settlement is longer than that.
Henry, in looking for security, looked to the custody of the key castles,[124] in which it is tempting to see a comment on the arrangements that Henry I had attempted to make for his succession. As
leaders of the discussions, the clergy mention both clergy and laymen. Among the clergy, Theobald now had a clear primacy with
the granting of the legateship, but no attempt was made to remove
Henry of Winchester from discussions on which he had long been
engaged.[125] Indeed the settlement was ratified at Winchester,
Henry of Anjou sitting on Henry of Blois's episcopal throne,[126]
though, as Holt shows, the notification comes from later, at

[122] The events are clearly set out in Davis, *Stephen*, 115–18 (map at 116).
[123] An interesting sign of how far discussions had progressed is a charter of Henry
confirming and standing surety for Ranulf of Chester's grant to Lincoln, witnessed by
the archbishop of Canterbury: *RRAN* iii, no. 491.
[124] Richard de Lucy held the tower of London and Windsor castle, Roger de Bussy
Oxford, Jocelin de Bussy Lincoln, while the duke asked for extra security also in
respect of Henry of Winchester's tenure of Winchester castle and 'the fortifications' of
Southampton: *RRAN* iii, no. 272. Note the reference to 'the castles which pertain to
the crown'.
[125] The *Gesta Stephani* and John of Hexham have Henry of Winchester as the chief
mediator; Henry of Huntingdon mentions Theobald in first place and Henry as his
coadjutor: *GS* 240–1; SD ii. 331; HH 289.
[126] GC i. 156.

Westminster. Among the laymen the first two witnesses to that document were William d'Aubigny and Robert of Leicester, preceding a list of earls that then seems to divide on, party grounds, and it is tempting to see them as the leading peace-makers.[127] What they wanted as individuals can be seen in Holt's chapter, which has a full discussion of the charters for Robert of Leicester and his son. All needed to be satisfied. The complicated exchange of homages sorted some of the confusion in feudal relationships, in general terms respecting the integrity of those who had fought on each side. This was important, but more was needed. No one felt more strongly than Henry himself that he was the lawful heir, and that Stephen had been a usurper. What then of all the business which, in our phrase, had passed under the king's signature—in medieval practice, under his seal—for nearly twenty years. Holt shows the principles that were in operation, the distinction between inheritance and acquisition.

The selling of the settlement provided one last challenge for the public-relations men. What was reported in the shires was what men wanted to hear. The disinherited should be restored; and Henry of Anjou in his own person provided the model study.[128] Castles should be destroyed. And the mercenaries should be sent home. A new coinage would have symbolized in many areas the agreement that had been reached. This could be done quite quickly. There is the suggestion that the homages were expected to be sworn by the following Easter.[129] It took longer to take down the castles, and Henry is recorded as complaining that progress was

---

[127] Robert of Leicester was named as Duke Henry's most influential counsellor in *GS* 234–5.

[128] This may be seen from a study of the language of Duke Henry's charters. The terms in which he spoke in Normandy of Reginald of St Valery, 'cum autem deo juvante hereditarium jus suum in Anglia recuperaverint' (*RRAN* iii, no. 329), are the terms he used of himself once he had landed in England in 1153, 'cum autem deo volente jus meum Anglie adeptus fuero', 'si annuente deo regnum Anglie adeptus fuero', 'cum hereditatem meam dei gratia adquisitus fuero' (*RRAN* iii, nos. 81, 90, 126).

[129] Thus a general confirmation to the influential abbey of Reading speaks of a time 'ab illo Pascha in retro quod fuit proximum post compositionem inter me et Henricum ducem Normannie factam', whilst one for the Templars confirms to them lands 'de quibus saisiti erant in primo Pascha quod fuit post pacificationem et concordiam quam feci cum comite Normannorum' (*RRAN* iii, nos. 696, 866). Henry of Huntingdon said that 'all the great men of the realm did homage and promised fealty' to Henry at Oxford in mid-January: HH 289–90.

slow.[130] There was little that could be done save with the small-fry; and much scope for negotiation. Henry himself can be seen in 1153 in negotiation with the bishop of Salisbury for the control of Devizes, 'than which there was no finer castle in Europe', which had been his mother's base from 1143 to 1148, and a fortress whose fortunes closely mirror those of the civil war as a whole.[131] Henry of Huntingdon had commented on Henry I that, by comparison with what came later, all his actions seemed to be admirable. A new generation of chroniclers, building on the texts of their predecessors, and their perception of the civil war, would make the same point about Henry II. When Stephen died on 25 October 1154, Henry of Anjou was in France. He did not need to hurry back to England, not sailing from Barfleur until 7 December. He and Eleanor of Aquitaine were crowned at Westminster by Theobald on 19 December. There was an impressive array of attenders.[132] Matilda at Rouen, like Adela at Marcigny in 1135, awaited with some interest the arrival of the messengers who still held together the Anglo-Norman world.

[130] HH 290.   [131] *RRAN* iii, no. 796; HH 265.   [132] RT 182.

1

THE ARISTOCRACY

C. Warren Hollister

ON this centenary of John Horace Round's *Geoffrey de Mandeville*, it is my purpose to evaluate Round's portrait of the so-called 'turbulent baronage' of Stephen's so-called anarchy in the light of recent scholarship. Let me begin by providing, as Round did not, a bird's-eye-view or, better, a satellite picture of Stephen's upper aristocracy. Thanks to a recent satellite photo of a more scientific kind, astrophysicists have gained a much clearer comprehension of the origins of our universe by tracing its evolution back to the immediate aftermath of the Big Bang, which occurred some fifteen billion years ago. In this same venturesome spirit (but across a somewhat shorter time frame), I propose to trace the aristocracy under King Stephen back to the immediate aftermath of that Anglo–Norman Big Bang, the Norman Conquest.

Thanks to the researches of Dr David Bates and others, we know that the great Norman landholders of 1066 had evolved over the previous half century along lines parallel to those of the aristocracy elsewhere in eleventh-century France. They had become lineage-based, with the succession to the patrimony determined by primogeniture; with toponyms derived from the site of their chief castle or their county or vicecomital town (Beaumont, Evreux, Avranches, Montfort, Montgomery, Mortain); with family *leitnamen* (the Roberts and Rogers and Richards and Williams and Hughs that infest the witness lists of contemporary charters); and with family abbeys that served their founding families as necropolises, old age homes, status symbols, and powerhouses of intercessory prayer (Lyre, Troarn, Sées, Préaux, Grestain, Le Tréport,

Saint-Sauveur, and others).[1] A family's chief castle, or *sedes*, after which its eldest sons were usually named, along with its religious foundation (or foundations), had by 1066 become an integral part of the family's sense of identity, of being. How could the Beaumonts exist apart from their castle and priory of Beaumont and their abbey-necropolis at Préaux, or the counts of Evreux without the town, castle, and abbey with which they had long been associated and whose names they bore? William the Conqueror's aristocracy had thus established deep roots in Normandy before being further, often lavishly, enriched in England in the wake of the Norman Conquest.

The manorial values of the great Domesday honours, calculated by William J. Corbett in his ground-breaking study of 1926 and subsequently refined, disclose the relative wealth of the new aristocrats of post-Conquest England who profited so prodigiously from the Conqueror's redistribution of English lands among his kinsmen and friends (Table 1.1).[2] And the relative wealth of members of this same aristocracy in Conquest Normandy is disclosed by other sources, less straightforward but no less revealing: the Conqueror's Ship List, evidence of Norman aristocratic abbey foundations, the proud name-dropping of contemporary writers, and, surprisingly, data from the Norman *Infeudationes militum* of 1172, more than a century later (Table 1.2).[3] These sources show that the three greatest landholders in Domesday England—Odo, bishop of Bayeux and earl of Kent, Robert, count of Mortain and earl of Cornwall, and Roger of Montgomery, earl of Shropshire—were also, unsurprisingly, among the very greatest landholders in Conquest Normandy. But, as one moves further down the list of landholders

---

[1] Robert of Torigny, 'De immutatione ordinis monachorum', in *Chronique de Robert de Torigni*, ed. L. Delisle, 2 vols. (Rouen, 1872–3), ii. 184–206; J.-M. Besse, *Abbayes et prieurés de l'ancienne France*, 7. *Province ecclésiastique de Rouen* (Paris, 1914), *passim*; D. Bates, *Normandy before 1066* (London, 1982), 34–6, 115–16, 133–4, 218–25; M. Chibnall, *Anglo-Norman England 1066–1166* (Oxford, 1986), 162; C. W. Potts, 'Les Ducs normands et leurs nobles: La Patronage monastique avant la conquête d'Angleterre', *Études normandes*, 3 (1986), 29–37.

[2] W. J. Corbett, 'The Development of the Normandy and the Norman Conquest of England', *Cambridge Medieval History*, v (Cambridge, 1926), 505–13; Hollister, *Anglo-Norman World*, 97–9, and 'The Greater Domesday Tenants-in-Chief', in J. C. Holt (ed.), *Domesday Studies* (Woodbridge, 1987), 219–21, 242.

[3] Ibid. 221–6, 243–8; E. M. C. Van Houts, 'The Ship List of William the Conqueror', *ANS* 10 (1988), 159–83.

Table 1.1. *The upper aristocracy of Conquest England, 1066–1086*

Name	Domesday Book Value (approx.)	Disposal of Honour, 1066–1135[a]
1. Odo, bishop of Bayeux	£3,240	Forfeited by Odo, 1082, recovered 1087, forfeited again 1088
2. Roger of Montgomery	£2,080	Forfeited by son Robert, 1102
3. Robert, count of Mortain	£1,975	Forfeited by son William, 1104
4. William fitz Osbern	£1,750?[b]	Forfeited by son Roger, 1075
5. William of Warenne	£1,140	Remains in family
6. Alan of Richmond	£1,120[c]	Remains in family
7. Eustace, count of Boulogne	£915	Remains in family (to Stephen of Blois *jure uxoris*, 1125)
8. Hugh, earl of Chester	£795[d]	Remains in family (to nephew, Ranulf I, 1120–1)
9. Richard fitz Gilbert	£795	Remains in family
10. Geoffrey, bishop of Coutances	£788	Forfeited by nephew Robert, 1095
11. Geoffrey de Mandeville	£740	Part remains in family; grandson Geoffrey II recovers remainder by 1141

[a] The bulk of all the forfeited honours listed remained in the king's hands in 1135.
[b] W. J. Corbett's rough estimate: 'The Development of the Normandy and the Norman Conquest of England', *Cambridge Medieval History*, v (Cambridge, 1926), 510–11.
[c] Plus waste lands worth £118 TRE (1066).
[d] Plus waste lands worth £270 TRE (1066).

whom Corbett described as Domesday 'Class A barons', one finds significant discrepancies between Norman and English holdings. Roger, earl of Hereford, the younger of the two sons and heirs of the Conqueror's friend and kinsman William fitz Osbern, had lost his earldom in the rebellion of 1075, while the elder son, William, retained the extremely valuable Norman patrimony of Breteuil and Pacy.[4] Similarly, the Beaumonts held vast lands in Normandy but,

[4] Hollister, 'Domesday Tenants-in-Chief', 231; *CP* vi. 447–50; OV vi. 40, 44 and nn.

Table 1.2. *The upper aristocracy of Normandy, 1066–1086*

Name	Ships (knights)	Abbey founded before 1075	Knights' fees in 1172	(quotas)
1. Robert, count of Mortain	120	Grestain	Unknown	(30)
2. Odo, bishop of Bayeux	100	—	120	(20)
3. William, count of Evreux	80	Saint-Sauveur, Evreux	No report	
4. Roger of Montgomery	60	Troarn, Sées; Almenêches	111	(20)
5. William fitz Osbern	60	Lyre; Cormeilles	99	(?)
6. Roger of Beaumont	60	Saint-Pierre, Préaux; Saint-Leger, Préaux	79 or 89	(25)
7. Robert, count of Eu	60	Saint-Pierre-sur-Dives; Le Tréport	No report	
8. Hugh d'Avranches, earl of Chester	60	Saint-Sever	52 (incl. Bessin)	(10)
9. Walter I Giffard	30 (100)	(Longueville in 1093)	99 or 103	(?)
10. Hugh of Montfort	50 (60)	—	56	(?)
11. Ralph of Tosny and Conches	—	Conches	50	(?)

For the methodology and data on which this list is based, see C. Hollister, 'The Greater Domesday Tenants-in-Chief', in J. C. Holt (ed.), *Domesday Studies* (Woodbridge, 1987), 219–48 with appendices. See also T. K. Keefe, *Feudal Assessments and the Political Community under Henry II and his Sons* (Los Angeles, 1983) app. I (143–53), and C. W. Potts, 'Norman Dukes and their Nobles: Monastic Patronage before the Conquest' (Seminar paper, UC Santa Barbara, 1985), app. 2.

until long after Domesday Book, relatively few estates in England.[5] The counts of Eu, although also lords of the Rape of Hastings, cut a distinctly more imposing figure in Normandy, where they had founded two great abbeys, than in England, where they were over-shadowed by the royal abbey of Battle.[6] Similarly Walter Giffard and his heirs, although they acquired the relatively empty title of earl of Buckingham, were, more importantly, lords of Longueville in Upper Normandy, where they founded a great Cluniac priory in 1093.[7] And the powerful counts of Evreux were mere leprechauns north of the Channel.[8]

Conversely, the Clare brothers, Richard and Baldwin, were rela-tively impoverished in Normandy after their father, the ducal kins-man Count Gilbert of Brionne, had lost his lands and his life around 1040; they made their fortunes and founded their religious houses after the Conquest in their extensive English honours cen-tring on Suffolk and Devon.[9] The same was true of William of Warenne, a middling landholder of Upper Normandy with castles at Mortemer and Bellencombre, who acquired extensive lands in southern England, including the Rape of Lewes in Sussex. There, having catapulted into the ranks of the rich and famous, he founded the great Cluniac priory of St Pancras.[10] Indeed, William of Warenne had the audacity to build, next to his priory of Lewes, two great motte-and-bailey castles side by side, one for himself and one, so R. Allen Brown suggested, for his wife Gundreda. In 1088 William Rufus raised the Warennes to comital status as earls of

[5] S. N. Vaughn, *Anselm of Bec and Robert of Meulan* (Berkeley, Calif., 1987), 78–93, 101–4; Crouch, *Beaumont Twins*, 3–10; *CP* vii. 521–30; xii:2, 358–9, and app. 2–3; *VCH Northamptonshire*, i. 387; J. Green, 'William Rufus, Henry I and the Royal Demesne', *History*, 64 (1979), 345; Hollister, 'Domesday Tenants-in-Chief', 227–8, 234–5.

[6] Ibid. 221–6, 243–7; I. J. Sanders, *English Baronies 1086–1327* (Oxford, 1960), 119–20; E. Searle, *Lordship and Community: Battle Abbey and its Banlieu, 1066–1538* (Toronto, 1974), 48–55, 201–12; *CP* v. 151–6.

[7] Ibid. ii. 386–7; Besse, *Abbayes et prieurés*, 70; Hollister, 'Domesday Tenants-in-Chief', 222, 238–9, 243, 246.

[8] Ibid. 222–3, 226–8.

[9] Ibid. 220, 228, 230, 236, 242; Hollister, *Anglo-Norman World*, 180–1; *Religious Houses*, 87, 92; M. Altschul, *A Baronial Family in Medieval England: The Clares, 1217–1314* (Baltimore, 1965), *passim*; *CP* ii. 44.

[10] Hollister, 'Domesday Tenants-in-Chief', 228–9; *Anglo-Norman World*, 137–44, 181–2; L. C. Loyd, 'The Origin of the Family of Warenne', *Yorkshire Arch. Journal*, 31 (1933), 104–11; *Religious Houses*, 100; *EYC* viii. 1–12, 40–6, 54–5; W. Farrer, *Honors and Knights' Fees*, 3 vols. (London and Manchester, 1923–5), iii. 296–300.

Surrey—a promotion that brought little additional income but much prestige.[11]

The Class A magnate Geoffrey de Mandeville, grandfather of Round's anti-hero, was similarly enriched by the spoils of the Conquest; indeed, Geoffrey's pre-Conquest Norman lands were so modest as to be untraceable.[12] The disequilibrium of the post-Conquest Anglo-Norman aristocracy, like the clumpiness of the primordial cosmic gas clouds of our universe, had a determining influence on the future.

In Normandy aristocratic estates were relatively stable across the entirety of the Anglo-Norman era, from the Norman Conquest to the reign of Henry II (Tables 1.2 and 1.3). There, the great Conquest honours remained virtually unaltered, although some changed hands. The county of Mortain, having been forfeited by William of Mortain in 1106, passed c.1113 to Stephen of Blois, then (after a prolonged interruption resulting from the Angevin conquest) to his son William IV of Warenne, and, on William's death in 1159, it reverted to the king–duke. The honour of Montfort-sur-Risle, after the rebellion and incarceration of Hugh de Montfort in 1123–4, passed to the neighbouring Beaumont count of Meulan—partner in Hugh's rebellion and beneficiary of his misfortune. And William fitz Osbern's honour of Breteuil, on the forfeiture of his illegitimate grandson Eustace in 1119, passed, through a marriage arranged by Henry I, to the Beaumont earl of Leicester. The one new Norman honour of vast extent that emerged in the first half of the twelfth century, that of the hereditary chamberlains of Tancarville, resulted from marriages by Tancarvilles to two very wealthy heiresses across two successive generations. The Tancarvilles devoted part of their resulting fortune to the building of the only new family abbey of the era, Saint-Georges de Bocherville, whose splendid church in the late Norman Romanesque style, artfully refurbished (and flanked by a splendid Gothic chapter-house), stands today in much of its former glory. But, apart from these changes, the Norman upper aristocracy of the mid- and later-twelfth century consisted of the descendants of notable Conquest families: Beaumont, Evreux, Eu, Giffard, Avranches, Tosny, and Montgomery.[13]

---

[11] *CP* xii:1, 491–6.

[12] Hollister, 'Domesday Tenants-in-Chief', 229–30; *CP* v. 113 n. (c).

[13] Hollister, 'Domesday Tenants-in-Chief', 225–6; *CP*, ix. 243; *RRAN* iii, no. 272; Crouch, *Beaumont Twins*, 13–14; RT 227, 251; T. K. Keefe, *Feudal Assessments and the Political Community under Henry II and his Sons* (Los Angeles, 1983), 141–53.

Table 1.3. *The upper aristocracy of Normandy, 1135–1137*

Name	Knights' fees in 1072	(quotas)	1066 Holder (ships)
1. King Stephen, count of Mortain	Unknown	(30)	Robert, count of Mortain (120)
2. Richard III, bishop of Bayeux	120	(20)	Odo, bishop of Bayeux (100)
3. Amaury of Montfort, count of Evreux	No report	(?)	William, count of Evreux (80)
4. William Talvas	111	(20)	Roger of Montgomery (60)
5. Robert, earl of Leicester	99	(?)	William fitz Osbern (60)
6. Waleran, count of Meulan	79 or 89	(25)	Roger of Beaumont[a] (60)
7. Henry, count of Eu	No report	(?)	Robert, count of Eu (60)
8. Ranulf II, earl of Chester	52	(10)	Hugh d'Avranches and Ranulf of Bayeux (60)
9. Walter II Giffard, earl of Buckingham	99 or 103	(?)	Walter I Giffard (30 ships, 100 knights)
10. Rabel of Tancarville	95	(10)	none[b]
11. Roger II of Tosny	50	(?)	Ralph I of Tosny (—)

For the methodology and data of this table, see Table 1.2, note.

[a] In 1136 Waleran accepted custody of the lands and minor heir of his brother-in-law, Hugh of Montfort, who had been a royal prisoner since 1124: Crouch, *Beaumont Twins*, 29–30. William the Conqueror's Ship List credits the honour of Montfort-sur-Risle with 50 ships and 60 knights; 56 knights were enfeoffed on the honour in 1172 (Table 5.2).

[b] The Tancarville family acquired, through marriages to heiresses, the lands of Eudes Stigand, founder of the priory of Sainte-Barbe-en-Auge (J.-M. Besse, *Abbayes et prieurés de l'ancienne France*, 7. *Province ecclésiastique de Rouen* (Paris, 1914), 204–5) and those originally possessed by Goscelin, vicomte of Rouen, who, with his wife Emmelina, had founded the abbeys of La Trinité-du-Mont, Rouen, and Saint-Amand, Rouen (both before 1040): see Hollister, 'Domesday Tenants-in-Chief', 246, n. 4; Potts, 'Norman Dukes', app. 2; *CP* x, app. F, 40.

In England, on the other hand, the aristocracy changed considerably during the half century between the Domesday survey and Stephen's accession in 1135. English landholders of Norman ancestry were becoming increasingly English or Anglo-Norman. Many of them continued to hold lands on both sides of the Channel, but some, whose English holdings equalled or overshadowed their Norman holdings (if any), began to assume English toponyms (Clare, Leicester, Warwick, Clinton, Gloucester), and began founding or refounding English religious houses (St Werberg's Chester, Shrewsbury, Colchester, Whitby, Montacute, Furness, the aforementioned priory of Lewes, and the many cut-rate twelfth-century Augustinian foundations, such as Bodmin, Bridlington, Guiseborough, Kenilworth, Kirkham, Launceston, Leeds, Little Dunmow, Merton, Missenden, and Osney).[14]

Meanwhile, the positions of the great families raised up in England by William the Conqueror after 1066 proved to be highly unstable over the next fifty years. One reason is that the major post-Conquest families in England would at first have been perceived not as rooted in their estates but as squatting on them, and therefore much easier to dislodge than the landholders of Normandy. Another source of instability was the division of Anglo-Norman aristocratic allegiances between the kings of England and Robert Curthose, duke of Normandy, until Henry I reunited the two lands by his victory over Duke Robert at Tinchebray in 1106.[15] By then all three Conquest super-magnates, Bishop Odo and the *comites* of Shropshire and Mortain, had opted for the luckless Curthose and had consequently forfeited their English lands. Odo, whose final exile from England occurred in 1088, died on the First Crusade and was entombed in Palermo Cathedral. The Montgomerys, while deprived of Shropshire and Arundel in 1102, remained important lords in Normandy and along its frontiers long thereafter, under the family names of Bellême and Talvas, and eventually became counts of Alençon.[16] William, the hot-headed

[14] C. A. Newman, *The Anglo-Norman Nobility in the Reign of Henry I* (Philadelphia, 1988), 38–9, (more generally) 68–90; *Religious Houses*, 62–3, 76, 80, 100, and 137–80 *passim*; J. C. Dickinson, *The Origin of the Austin Canons and their Introduction into England* (London, 1950), 109 and *passim*.

[15] C. W. David, *Robert Curthose: Duke of Normandy* (Cambridge, Mass., 1920); Le Patourel, *Norman Empire*, 181–7; Hollister, *Anglo-Norman World*, 77–95, 247–49.

[16] Ibid. 188; D. Bates, 'The Character and Career of Odo, Bishop of Bayeux', *Speculum*,

young son and heir of Robert, count of Mortain, joined Curthose's faction in 1104 and thereby forfeited his English lands; in 1106 he was among the many nobles whom Henry I captured at Tinchebray (William's own castle), and he subsequently spent three interesting decades as a prisoner in the Tower of London before entering the monastic community at nearby Bermondsey Abbey a few years after King Henry's death. One source alleges that William was blinded during his imprisonment; another reports, perhaps less reliably, that in 1118 he was released from the Tower, or at least furloughed, in consequence of an unspecified but doubtless very impressive miracle wrought by the True Cross, which, by good fortune, had been rediscovered just the previous year near the Thames.[17]

For some years after 1106 great men and families in England continued to tumble—Montfort of Haughley, Malet, Abetôt, Lacy—and new ones to ascend—Beaumont, Bigod, Gloucester, Clinton, Brian fitz Count, and Roger of Salisbury, with his ecclesiastical friends and relations. But these unsettled conditions eventually came to an end. Forfeitures of English lands under Henry I virtually ceased after 1114, and by the mid-1120s a stable aristocracy of new and old families had emerged.[18] These families, like those of Normandy and elsewhere in France, tended more and more to identify with the castles and towns after which they named themselves, and with their family religious houses. In short, the English aristocracy was transformed during the middle years of Henry I's reign (Table 1.4). Having established firm roots in their lands, the great families became increasingly difficult for a king to

50 (1975), 1–20; J. F. A. Mason, 'Roger of Montgomery and his Sons', *TRHS* 5:13 (1963), 1–28; *CP* xi. 689–97.

[17] HH 255; Annals of Bermondsey, in *Annales monastici*, ed. H. R. Luard, 5 vols. (RS, 1864–9), iii. 432, 436; M. Brett, 'The Annals of Bermondsey, Southwark and Merton', in D. Abulafia *et al.* (eds.), *Church and City 1000–1500: Essays in Honour of Christopher Brooke* (Cambridge, 1992), 286–99. The Bermondsey Annals, although very late, may well preserve a house tradition with regard to William of Mortain. They report his entry into the Bermondsey religious community *s.a.* 1140. Even if he had indeed been released in 1118, he was safely under lock and key again by 1130: *PR 31 Henry I*, 143.

[18] Sanders, *English Baronies*, 6, 46–7, 61, 75, 93, 120, 138; *CP* vii. 523–7, 683–6; D. Crouch, 'Geoffrey de Clinton and Roger, Earl of Warwick', *HR* 55 (1982), 113–24; E. J. Kealey, *Roger of Salisbury: Viceroy of England* (Berkeley, Calif.: 1972); Vaughn, *Anselm of Bec and Robert of Meulan*, 313–17; Green, *Henry I*, 38–50, 247–8, 263–4, 273–4; Hollister, *Anglo-Norman World*, 154, 178–80, 186–7, 215–16, 243–4; R. DeAragon, 'The Growth of Secure Inheritance in Anglo-Norman England', *Journal of Medieval Hist.* 8 (1982), 381–91.

Table 1.4. *The upper aristocracy of England in 1135*

Name[a]	1130 danegeld exemption (rank order)	Knights' fees in the time of Henry II
1. Roger, bishop of Salisbury	£150 (1)	n.a.[b]
2. Stephen of Blois	£135 (2)	301 (honours of Boulogne, Eye, & Lancaster)
3. Robert, earl of Gloucester	£125 (3)	275
4. Robert II, earl of Leicester	£29 (7)	157
5. *William II of Warenne, earl of Surrey*	£104 (4)	140
6. *Stephen of Richmond*	n.a.	176
7. *Ranulf II, earl of Chester*	n.a.	118 + Cheshire
8. *Hugh Bigod*	£20 (8)	161
9. *Richard II of Clare*	n.a.	150
10. *Roger, earl of Warwick*	n.a.	104
11. Brian fitz Count	£72 (5)	100
12. Geoffrey de Mandeville	n.a.	110 (including the three lost manors, recovered in 1141)
13. Geoffrey of Clinton	£59 (6)	n.a.

For the methodology on which this list is based, see Hollister, *Anglo-Norman World*, 177–9 and nn. 22, 24. For further statistics, see ibid. 71 n. 2, and Keefe, *Feudal Assessments*, app. II (154–88). The evidence is too exiguous for the above rank order to be regarded as anything but approximate.

dislodge. To confiscate their English ancestral estates would by now rob them of their very identity and would scandalize other aristocrats. Indeed, even during the disorders of Stephen's reign, the configuration of estates of the upper aristocracy remained surprisingly resilient to disruption, more so, for example, than during the period 1075–1114.

Henry I's aristocracy of the 1120s, like that of his father in the 1070s, was dominated by three men of surpassing wealth, but they were all new men. One of them was King Henry's natural son Robert, who in the early 1120s became the first earl of Gloucester. Another was Henry's nephew, Stephen of Blois, and the third was Henry's chief administrator, Roger, bishop of Salisbury.[19] These three, each with a new configuration of estates, filled the emptied shoes of the earlier triumvirate of William I's kinsmen: Odo of Bayeux, Robert of Mortain, and Roger of Montgomery. Almost comparable in wealth in Henry I's England was Robert of Beaumont, count of Meulan in the French Vexin and lord of extensive estates in and around the Risle Valley in Normandy, who, as King Henry's principal adviser, acquired vast lands in England from the forfeited honours of Grandmesnil and Mortain and from the *terra regis*.[20] When Count Robert died in 1118, he left a comital title to each of his two eldest sons. He bequeathed his county of Meulan along with the Beaumont ancestral lands in Normandy and a modest estate in Dorset to his son Waleran, and left his earldom of Leicester to Waleran's twin brother Robert (younger by only minutes). In the early 1120s the young Robert, earl of Leicester, established himself as a great lord in Normandy by acquiring, as we have seen, the lordship of Breteuil *jure uxoris*. When, early in Stephen's reign, Waleran of Meulan received the earldom of Worcester and the promise of marriage to Stephen's infant daughter, both twins had become formidably powerful on both sides of the Channel and were positioned to play crucial roles in the politics of the subsequent generation.[21]

The other leading magnate families of England in 1135 included several Class A Conquest survivors (Warenne, Clare, Richmond, and Chester), along with the Beaumont earl of Warwick (who missed Domesday Book by only a couple of years),

[19] Hollister, *Anglo-Norman World*, 186–7.
[20] Vaughn, *Anselm of Bec and Robert of Meulan*, 238, 313–17.
[21] Crouch, *Beaumont Twins*.

the more recently enriched Bigods and Redvers, Brian fitz Count, and, among those of slightly less wealth, two Clare cadet lines with *caputs* at Netherwent and Little Dunmow.[22] Of these families, only the earls of Chester were also among the most powerful magnates in Normandy. Their forebears had founded Benedictine abbeys on both sides of the Channel, Saint-Sever in the Avranchin and St Werburgh's, Chester. When the young Earl Richard of Chester, vicomte of Avranches, died without direct heirs in 1120 in the wreck of the *White Ship*, Henry I permitted Richard's English earldom and Norman vicomté to pass to his first cousin Ranulf, vicomte of Bayeaux, who was already lord of Cumberland and a great landholder in Lincolnshire by virtue of his marriage to the thrice-married and genealogically mysterious Countess Lucy. In exchange for granting him Chester, Avranches, and the comital title, Henry required, not unreasonably, that Ranulf return Cumberland and many of his Lincolnshire holdings to the Crown. Ranulf, who stood to profit handsomely in the exchange, agreed without any recorded grumbling.[23] But other members of his family were less accommodating. Ranulf's stepson, William of Roumare, rebelled for a time in the hope of uniting the lost Lincolnshire estates of his mother Lucy with his considerable patrimonial honour in Normandy. And Ranulf's son and heir, Earl Ranulf II, coveted Cumberland and other estates that his father had traded in for the earldom of Chester.[24] Holding his peace while Henry I lived, Ranulf II began to make trouble under the looser, more lenient rule of King Stephen.

Similarly, Geoffrey II de Mandeville—Round's Geoffrey, grandson of the *nouveau riche* Conquest Geoffrey—was anxious to make good the forfeiture by his blundering father, William de Mandeville, of the family's most valuable Domesday manors (Sawbridgeworth, Great Waltham, and Saffron Walden), along with its ancestral claims to the shrievalty and justiciarship of Essex and custody of the Tower of London. The young Geoffrey joined Henry I's entourage during the final years of the reign, evidently

[22] Hollister, *Anglo-Norman World*, 179–88.

[23] Ibid. 182–4; *CP* ii. 164–7.

[24] J. E. A. Jolliffe (*The Constitutional History of Medieval England*, 4th edn. (London, 1961), 172) discusses the vast extent of the lands to which the earls of Chester could theoretically lay claim after 1120. For a wise and measured discussion of the problem, see Chibnall, *Matilda*, 93–4.

hoping to cajole the king into restoring his family's losses.[25] Thus the upper aristocracy of England—refashioned by Henry I, entrenched by the passage of time, and inherited by Stephen—included two magnates who, rightly or wrongly, were more than ordinarily covetous of lost ancestral possessions: Ranulf II of Chester and Geoffrey II de Mandeville. These two, as is well known, proved to be among the most intractable of Stephen's magnates.

Apart from Ranulf and Geoffrey, the great landholders of 1135 appear to have constituted an aristocracy that had prospered and was generally content with its lot. Its leading members had become accustomed to functioning under the canopy of a firm royal peace, enforced by a king whose policies and patronage meshed with their own interests. Graphic metaphors suggesting that the English aristocracy at Henry's death was like a pressure cooker or a bomb ready to explode are wildly off target. The aristocracy was prosperous and flourishing in 1135 and hoped to remain so. It only sought, to quote the Wizard of Oz, 'the simple things of life: wealth, power, and prestige'. And during the closing years of Henry I's reign, it enjoyed all three.

Having sketched this general picture of the wealthiest Anglo-Norman aristocrats of 1135 and their background, let me now enquire how they behaved during the civil struggles that followed. How have scholars over the past century reinterpreted Round's vision of 'the feudal and anarchic spirit that stamps the reign of Stephen'? Most have responded with a good measure of scepticism, concluding that Round's 'anarchy' is a fantasy propagated by a few doom-crying churchmen generalizing wildly from local and temporary conditions. I am among the minority, however, who continue to see the reign as 'a true and terrible anarchy' (to quote David Crouch).[26] Despite the more-or-less peaceful inclinations of the great English landholders, the ineptness of the new central authority and its drawn-out rivalry with the house of Anjou led to

[25] Hollister, *Anglo-Norman World*, 117–27; D. Crouch, 'Earl William of Gloucester and the End of the Anarchy', *EHR* 103 (1988), 69–75.

[26] Crouch, *Beaumont Twins*, 138; for classic statements minimizing the anarchy, see Stenton, *First Century*, 218–19, 245–8, and A. L. Poole, *From Domesday Book to Magna Carta*, 2nd edn. (Oxford, 1955), 151–4; see, further, the exchange of views between R. B. Patterson, E. J. Kealey, T. Callahan, and C. W. Hollister in *Albion*, 6 (1974), 189–239.

civil chaos. Although, as has been argued, parts of England were placid during much of Stephen's reign (Brother Cadfael's Shropshire, for example, apart from one unfortunate mass slaughter in 1138), the same could be said of Vietnam in the 1960s or Lebanon in the 1980s.

Let me elaborate. The Anglo-Saxon chronicler, in an oft-quoted passage, tells us in bloodcurdling detail of diabolical castle garrisons ravaging neighbourhoods and villages throughout the kingdom and torturing, robbing, and starving their inhabitants.[27] Although sometimes dismissed as an over-reaction to conditions singular to the region around the chronicler's home abbey of Peterborough, his impressions are corroborated by many other observers writing elsewhere. John of Worcester from the west, Henry of Huntingdon from deep within the diocese of Lincoln, John of Hexham from the north, the chronicler of Abingdon from the heart of old Wessex, and many others, having become accustomed to the placid years of Henry I when there was little to complain of except high taxes and bad weather, express grief and outrage at the conditions of brutality and social chaos in Stephen's England.[28] William of Malmesbury, echoing the Anglo-Saxon chronicler, speaks of castle garrisons plundering the surrounding countryside, stealing cattle and sheep, looting churches, and kidnapping and torturing peasants for their ransoms.[29] The first continuer of the *Historia Dunelmensis ecclesiae* writes of the horrible cruelties perpetrated by the men of William Cumin in the region around Durham.[30] And the author of the *Gesta Stephani* complains of men breaking faith with King Stephen and raging savagely all across England, 'wickedly committing everywhere the most grievous of criminal acts they could think of'.[31] The notion that conditions were relatively peaceful under Stephen, with occasional episodes of violence occurring only here and there, appears nowhere in the sources of the Middle Ages; it first emerges among writers of the twentieth century, who evidently find it difficult to imagine the eternal peace of the English countryside having been disrupted in long-ago times by tumult and mayhem.

---

[27] *ASC, s.a.* 1137.

[28] JW 40; HH 256, 267; SD ii. 286, 302; *Chronicon monasterii de Abingdon*, ed. J. Stevenson, 2 vols. (RS, 1858), i. 178. Also GC i. 142; *Liber Eliensis*, ed. E. O. Blake (CS 3:92, 1962), 320.

[29] WM *HN* 40–1.   [30] SD i. 152–4, 163–4.   [31] *GS* 90; cf. 152–6, 218–19.

The anarchic conditions of Stephen's England resulted not only from battles, of which there were few, and castle sieges, of which there were many, but also from the far more destructive tactics of devastating the lands and villages around an enemy castle in order to deprive the enemy of sustenance, or, conversely, sallying forth from a castle to loot and destroy defenceless farms and manors in order to resupply the garrison and starve its besiegers. The devastation of productive lands was, indeed, the most characteristic feature of medieval warfare,[32] and it was rampant in Stephen's England. Orderic Vitalis describes Nigel, bishop of Ely, going off in a rage after the downfall of his family in 1139, attacking enemy lands, and, by recklessly scorching the earth, condemning many thousands to starvation.[33] The *Gesta Stephani* alludes to the frequent raids and reckless destructiveness of the king's enemies throughout the south-west, to the depredations of Miles, earl of Hereford, in the region around Gloucester, to Stephen's policy in 1149 of burning his enemies' crops and destroying all their possessions, and to the scorched-earth raids of the castle garrisons at Trowbridge and Devizes that 'reduced the surrounding country everywhere to a lamentable desert'.[34] And the tactic of reducing an enemy castle by burning the surrounding town, although employed only very rarely under Henry I (Bayeux in 1105, Evreux in 1119), recurred with depressing regularity under Stephen.[35]

The damning evidence from these narrative sources, which I have by no means exhausted, finds strong corroboration in the record evidence. An abundance of private charters of the reign make allowances for the widespread incidence of domestic violence and destruction by setting substantially lower dues, rents, and services on grants of property until such time as the war should end, or by recompensing religious houses for losses and damages sustained during the *tempus werre*.[36] Similar testimony is found in the early pipe rolls of Henry II, where substantial portions of the king's normal revenues from shires and boroughs are reported as being unpaid owing to waste.

[32] See the illuminating discussion by J. Gillingham, 'William the Bastard at War', in C. Harper-Bill *et al.* (eds.), *Studies in Medieval History Presented to R. Allen Brown* (Woodbridge, 1989), 141–58.
[33] OV vi. 532.   [34] *GS* 82, 90, 96, 218–19.
[35] WM *HN* 59–60, 73–4; HH 282; Annals of Winchester, in *Annales monastici*, ii. 52.
[36] Stenton, *First Century*, 243–8.

The remarkably high incidence of waste in the pipe roll of 1155–6 has been much discussed and variously interpreted. Early in the century H. W. C. Davis concluded from an analysis of these waste figures that they powerfully corroborate the lamentations of Stephen's chroniclers: for example, Warwickshire, 63 per cent waste; Nottinghamshire and Derbyshire, 52 per cent waste; Leicestershire, 51 per cent waste; Berkshire, 33 per cent waste; Wiltshire, 25 per cent waste; 50 per cent waste in the towns of Cambridge, Huntingdon, and Shrewsbury, etc.[37] A literal interpretation of the meaning of 'waste' in these accounts has since been challenged, on the grounds that the term refers not to devastated lands but to uncertainties on the part of sheriffs and exchequer clerks as to title, tax liability, and danegeld exemptions on the estates in question. For, although, as we now believe, the exchequer system survived the anarchy in parts of England, it nevertheless suffered serious damage.[38] The term 'waste' thus indicates, so it is argued, not that the land failed to produce crops but that, for whatever reason, it failed to produce taxes.[39] R. H. C. Davis pointed out, however, that the Midlands shires through which Henry Plantagenet campaigned in 1153 tend to be among those with the highest percentages of waste in 1156,[40] and it is likely that Henry's progress through these shires was accompanied by significant destruction. Although our (very sketchy) contemporary accounts of Henry's 1153 campaign supply few details, the *Gesta Stephani* reports that he 'attacked the king's party everywhere with determination and spirit and severely assailed those who resisted him with fire, sword, and pillage'.[41]

A parallel has sometimes been drawn with the significant number of Domesday manors described as 'waste' in Yorkshire in 1086. Here, too, the evidence of waste in a royal record has been associated with extremely destructive military activity, in this case the Conqueror's harrying of Yorkshire in 1069, when, according to narrative sources, the royal army destroyed all the crops, herds,

---

[37] H. W. C. Davis, 'The Anarchy of Stephen's Reign', *EHR* 18 (1903), 630–41.

[38] K. Yoshitake, 'The Exchequer in the Reign of Stephen', *EHR* 103 (1988), 950–9.

[39] J. Green, 'The Last Century of Danegeld', *EHR* 96 (1981), 252; King, 'Anarchy', 133–53; G. J. White, 'Were the Midlands "Wasted" during Stephen's Reign?', *Midland History*, 10 (1985), 26–46. For a good, even-handed discussion of the question, see Newman, *Anglo-Norman Nobility*, 164–7.

[40] Davis, *Stephen*, 83.   [41] *GS* 234.

houses, chattels, and foodstuffs throughout the whole region, leaving many thousands to starve.[42] Again, recent historians have doubted the testimony of Domesday Book as evidence of massive and lasting devastation, arguing that the impact of William's harrying is unlikely to have endured for seventeen years, and that the pattern of wasted manors in Yorkshire Domesday is the product of resettlements, consolidation of manors, reallocation of resources, Danish and Scottish raids, and accounting short cuts.[43] But, regardless of how resources and settlements may have been shuffled about within aristocratic honours, the fact remains that between 1066 and 1086 the Yorkshire estates of Robert of Mortain, taken as a whole, lost 30 per cent of their value, those of Ilbert de Lacy 34 per cent, those of Robert Malet 43 per cent, those of Alan of Richmond 58 per cent, and those of Hugh, earl of Chester, virtually all their value; the entirety of Yorkshire declined in value by approximately two-thirds.[44] These declines, comparable in magnitude to the waste figures of 1156, clearly reflect devastation resulting from military campaigning. And the fact that Cheshire Domesday discloses a similar pattern of massive waste along the path of William's marauding army of 1069[45] confirms the traditional view that the wasted manors of Yorkshire in 1086 bear witness to the disaster that occurred seventeen years before. The warfare of Stephen's reign may have been less systematically destructive than William's harrying of the north, but it was also much closer in time to the document that recorded its consequences.

This literal interpretation of 1156 waste finds conclusive support in an article by Emily Amt, who demonstrates, on the basis of geography and a meticulous analysis of pipe-roll terminology, that

---

[42] OV ii. 230–2; iv. 94; WM *GR* ii. 207–8; *ASC, s.a.* 1069 (D and E); FW ii. 4; HH 205; SD ii. 188.

[43] T. A. M. Bishop, 'The Norman Settlement of Yorkshire', in R. W. Hunt, W. A. Pantin, and R. W. Southern (eds.), *Studies in Medieval History Presented to F. M. Powicke* (Oxford, 1948), 1–14; W. E. Wightman, 'The Significance of "Waste" in Yorkshire Domesday', *Northern History*, 10 (1975), 55–71.

[44] Robert of Mortain held Yorkshire lands worth £85 a year in 1086 along with waste lands that had been worth £37 in 1066. Comparable figures for Ilbert de Lacy were £158 and £82; for Robert Malet, £11 and £8; for Alan of Richmond, £86 and £117; and for Hugh of Chester, £10 and £260. See also Bishop, 'Norman Settlement of Yorkshire', 2.

[45] *VCH Cheshire*, i. 336–7; the location of most of the wasted Cheshire manors rules out attributing their destruction to Welsh raids.

the term 'waste' normally means what it seems to mean. Even allowing for a degree of self-interested bookkeeping on the part of royal officials, the evidence suggests very strongly that most of the 'waste' lands recorded in 1156 were in fact unproductive.[46] By 1162, after a massive effort at restocking manors, 'waste' had virtually disappeared from the pipe rolls, a clear indication that Christ and his saints were up and about once again.

The narrative sources, charters, and pipe-roll accounts thus provide abundant, mutually consistent evidence of systematic devastation of arable lands, burning of towns and villages, scorched-earth tactics employed on a vast scale, mass imprisonments, and plundering of crops, cattle, and goods during the virtually incessant military campaigns that afflicted England between about 1138 and 1153. If the term 'anarchy' is to have any substance at all, this was it. And because these conditions were so widely deplored by contemporaries, it is difficult to accept the notion expressed recently by some historians that in the twelfth century weak central government was a perfectly viable alternative to strong central government. Such broadmindedness should be firmly rejected in favour of the old-fashioned royalist view of Orderic Vitalis, William of Malmesbury, and all other contemporaries, no matter how whiggish their attitudes toward royal peace-keeping may seem.[47]

The degree to which the central administration faltered under Stephen can best be understood by looking briefly at English royal governance in the final decade of Henry I's reign. Sheriffs were attending to the king's interests in all the shires except the earldom of Chester—the one survivor among the Conqueror's three semi-autonomous Welsh Marcher earldoms—and the Marcher lordship of the bishop of Durham. Henry's sheriffs were carefully supervised by the twice-yearly audits of the exchequer under its masterful director, Roger, bishop of Salisbury.[48] Similarly (and this has not

[46] E. Amt, 'The Meaning of Waste in the Early Pipe Rolls of Henry II', *Economic History Review*, 2:44 (1991), 240–8.

[47] Among the historians who argue that local autonomy and kingdom-wide centralization were equally effective arrangements for the maintenance of stable societies are F. Barlow, *William Rufus* (London, 1983), 433–4, and Warren, *Governance*, 91–5.

[48] Hollister, *Anglo-Norman World*, 239–42; cf. J. Green, 'The Sheriffs of William the Conqueror', *ANS* 5 (1982), 129–45. On this point I disagree with David Crouch, in *Earldom of Chester*, 69–71, and 'Geoffrey de Clinton and Roger, Earl of Warwick', 115–16.

always been adequately understood), itinerant justices closely associated with the royal curia were hearing pleas of the Crown in
nearly every shire, constituting a kingdom-wide network of judicial
visitations. This network fades from view in Stephen's reign and,
indeed, would remain unmatched until the mid-1160s.[49] But,
under Henry I, the central government was so ubiquitous that not
even earldoms were exempt from the intense scrutiny of royal
officials. Of the eight earldoms in Henry's England, all but Chester
were supervised in or around 1130 by a small coterie of sheriffs and
justices with strong ties to the royal curia: Richard Basset, Aubrey
de Vere, Geoffrey of Clinton, Miles of Gloucester, and Payn fitz
John.[50]

It is a point of crucial importance that the surge of aristocratic
autonomy under Stephen involved not only the lavish proliferation
of earldoms—twenty-six to Henry's eight—but also the metamor-
phosis of many counties from political subdivisions administered
by sheriffs and royal justices into semi-autonomous districts governed by earls. The shift in governing style between Henry's
England in 1125–35 and Stephen's England after mid-1138 was
drastic. For, although the aforementioned concentration of
shrievalties and justiciarships in the hands of a few of Henry I's
curiales began only in 1130, sheriffs long before that date had been
responsible primarily not to a local earl, if any, but to the king and
exchequer.

To establish this vital point, which has been questioned, let me
survey briefly the affiliations of some pre-1130 sheriffs of shires
that were the seats of earldoms.[51] Buckinghamshire in the time of

[49] Hollister, *Anglo-Norman World*, 236–42.

[50] Ibid. 239–42; Green, *Sheriffs, passim*. In 1130 Richard Basset and Aubrey de Vere
were co-sheriffs of five of the seven shires on which earldoms were based: Buckinghamshire
Huntingdonshire, Northamptonshire, Leicestershire, and Surrey; Miles of Gloucester was
sheriff of Gloucestershire, and Geoffrey of Clinton was sheriff of Warwickshire. Royal justices, although more difficult to identify, can be traced in 1130 and the years immediately
preceding it to all seven of these shire-earldoms: Geoffrey of Clinton in Huntingdonshire,
Northamptonshire, Buckinghamshire, Surrey, and Warwickshire; Richard Basset in
Leicestershire, and Miles of Gloucester and Payn fitz John in Gloucestershire. These same
men served in a number of other shires as well.

[51] Green, *Sheriffs*, 15, 17, 53, 55, 63, 83. Henry I's government also dominated the
Norman counties. The frontier magnate Amaury de Montfort, who was accustomed to exercising firm control over his French castleries, complained on inheriting the countship of
Evreux in Normandy that royal bailiffs and provosts were 'running wild' in his newly
acquired county: OV vi. 330–2.

Earl Walter Giffard was one of at least six shires administered by the tireless royal sheriff Hugh of Buckland; it subsequently passed, along with several other shires, to Hugh's son, William of Buckland, before landing in the busy hands of Richard Basset and Aubrey de Vere.[52] Gilbert the Knight and his nephew Fulk, who served in turn between the early 1100s and 1129 as sheriffs of Cambridgeshire, Surrey (under Earl William II of Warenne), and Huntingdonshire (under Earl Simon and then Earl David), constituted another family of professional local officials with court connections. Gilbert enjoyed the friendship of Henry I's wife, Queen Matilda, who contributed to his foundation of Merton Priory. Gloucestershire in the time of Earl Robert had as its sheriffs two successive royal *curiales*, father and son, Walter and Miles of Gloucester—and Earl Robert was himself, of course, an even more devoted *curialis* than they.[53]

Warwickshire in the time of Earl Roger had as its sheriff the omnicompetent *curialis* and treasury chamberlain Geoffrey of Clinton. Before Geoffrey (who took over in about 1121), the sheriff of Warwickshire was a certain Hugh of Leicester, who also served for a time as sheriff of Lincolnshire and, for some twenty years before 1130, as sheriff of Leicestershire and Northamptonshire.[54] Hugh of Leicester has been identified as a client of the Beaumont earls of Leicester and Warwick, but on grounds that are so tenuous as to be unacceptable. Despite his toponym, Hugh is not known to have had any connections with the earl of Leicester before he became a sheriff; we know only that he had previously served as the steward of Matilda, daughter of Simon of Senlis, the first Norman earl of Huntingdon and Northampton. But during most of Hugh's tenure as sheriff of Northamptonshire (*c.*1106–29) the earl of Northampton and Huntingdon was David, future king of Scots, who acquired the earldoms *c.*1113 by marrying Earl Simon's widow.[55] David was of course Queen Matilda's brother

[52] OV vi. 28; Hollister, *Anglo-Norman World*, 239–41; Green, *Henry I*, 196, 201, 237.

[53] Ibid. 197–8, 256–7; Green, *Sheriffs*, 29, 42, 47, 78; *Religious Houses*, 166; Dickinson, *Austin Canons*, 117–18; *CP* vi. 640–2; xii:1, 491–6.

[54] Green, *Sheriffs*, 53, 55, 63–4, 83; Green, *Henry I*, 198.

[55] It has been suggested that Hugh of Leicester 'was linked with the house of Senlis, the close ally and kin of the Beaumont family' (Crouch, 'Geoffrey de Clinton and Roger of Warwick', 115). No such kinship tie linked the Senlis and Beaumont families at the time of Hugh of Leicester's appointment to the shrievalty of Northamptonshire under Earl Simon I of Senlis *c.* 1107, or during Hugh's service under that earl (*c.*1107–11); the link was forged

and a *curialis* of Henry I. Hugh of Leicester had previously founded a priory at Preston Capes on land formerly belonging to the Conquest family of Mortain and therefore quite possibly given to him by Henry I, who had disseised William of Mortain in 1104, shortly before the priory's founding.[56] Everything points to the conclusion that, as sheriff, Hugh of Leicester, although doubtless friendly towards the two Beaumont earls and acceptable to them, was a royal servant.

Indeed, the whole question of comital versus royal influence on Henry I's sheriffs and justices loses much of its force in the light of Henry's intimate friendships with several of the earls themselves— men such as Robert of Meulan, earl of Leicester, his brother Henry, earl of Warwick, Queen Matilda's brother David, earl of Northampton and Huntingdon, and the extravagantly favoured royal bastard, Robert, earl of Gloucester. The king would doubtless have avoided appointing local officials who were offensive to the earls; sometimes he might even have heeded the earls' suggestions of nominees to shrievalties. But royal authority over the sheriffs, even within earldoms, was strong throughout the reign of Henry I and grew stronger as the reign progressed. It is reported that, of all Henry I's sheriffs, only Gilbert the Knight, the queen's friend, could render his accounts to the exchequer cheerfully and without fear.[57]

After Stephen's accession, Henry I's system of highly centralized government persisted, but only for a time. Roger of Salisbury continued to supervise the sheriffs and to audit their accounts. And, despite recent arguments to the contrary, he did so with the full

---

many years later when Simon II of Senlis (Simon I's son) married Isabel of Beaumont, daughter of Robert II, earl of Leicester: *CP* vi. 643. This marriage occurred long after Simon I's earldoms passed to David *c.*1113, at which time the future groom was still a very young child (he remained a ward of his stepfather David until 1124) and the bride was as yet unborn; her father was about 9 years old at the time.

[56] *CP* vi. 640–2; ix. 663; Green, *Henry I*, 198; *The Cartulary of Daventry Priory*, ed. M. J. Franklin (Northamptonshire Rec. Soc. 35, 1988), pp. xvii–xxiii, nos. 609, 666, 860. Our less than satisfactory evidence indicates that Hugh of Leicester first established a very small Cluniac community at Preston Capes *c.* 1106–7, and shortly afterwards, with the support of his lord Earl Simon I, moved it to a more suitable site at Daventry; and that Daventry Priory received further support from Earl David: ibid., p. xxvi, nos. 1–2; *RRS* i, no. 146.

[57] Green, *Henry I*, 198; *Sheriffs*, 12.

support of the new king.[58] If, as has been argued, Stephen planned from the beginning to rid himself of Roger of Salisbury, it is hard to understand why Roger and his two episcopal kinsmen, Alexander of Lincoln and Nigel of Ely, enjoyed the royal favour for three and a half years after Henry I's death and why King Stephen appointed Roger's kinsman Adelelm as royal treasurer and Roger's natural son, Roger le Poer, as chancellor.[59]

But, with the unresolved Angevin claim to the throne, the business of the royal administration could not go on as before. Stephen's regime, in the opening months of his reign, comprised at least four potentially antagonistic factions: (1) the king and the immediate royal family, including his younger brother Henry, bishop of Winchester, and his courageous, knightly wife, Queen Matilda; (2) Roger of Salisbury and his kinsmen and supporters, who, at least at first, were hostile to the Angevin claim and worked in close collaboration with the king and his family; (3) the Beaumonts and their kin by blood or marriage (Philip of Harcourt, the Warennes, the Clares, Simon II of Senlis, and others), who also supported Stephen against the Empress Matilda almost from the beginning, and (4) the group that had backed the empress at the court of Henry I in 1126–7 and would back her again at the opportune time: Robert, earl of Gloucester, Brian fitz Count, and David, king of Scots, soon to be joined in the empress's camp by Robert of Gloucester's vassal, sheriff, and now fellow earl, Miles of Gloucester, earl of Hereford.[60] I have suggested elsewhere that Brian, Earl Robert, and King David constituted, at Henry I's court of autumn 1126, an identifiable faction supporting the empress's succession, and that Roger of Salisbury (and presumably his kins-

---

[58] On this point I differ from Green (*Henry I*, 45–7), stating that Bishop Roger 'was not employed as viceroy after 1126'; cf. WM *HN* 25–6, 37–8; OV vi. 530 (writing of Roger of Salisbury after Henry I's death): 'toti Angliae omni uita Henrici regis prefuerat'. See further Blackburn, 'Coinage under Henry I', 75–6. I differ too from Warren (*Governance*, 93), declaring that the fall of Roger of Salisbury in 1139 'must . . . be seen as a move intended from the beginning and delayed only until it could be conveniently contrived'. This view seems inconsistent with the evidence not only of Stephen's lavish patronage to Bishop Roger's family 1135–6 (see below, n. 59), but also of Roger's unmitigated support of Stephen's dash for the throne: Hollister, *Anglo-Norman World*, 164–6; see also J. Bradbury, 'The Early Years of the Reign of Stephen', in D. Williams (ed.), *England in the Twelfth Century* (Woodbridge, 1990), 23–5.

[59] *RRAN* iii, pp. ix, xxi; Davis, *Stephen*, 28–9.

[60] Ibid. 18–19, 39–41; Hollister, *Anglo-Norman World*, 164–7.

men) opposed the plan.[61] Again, Robert of Gloucester and Brian
fitz Count represented the interests of Henry I and his daughter,
the empress, in the delicate marriage negotiations with Anjou in
1127, negotiations from which Roger of Salisbury was evidently
excluded.[62] Eight years later, during the tense weeks and months
following Henry I's death in December 1135, members of the first
two groups coalesced. Henry of Winchester, with Roger of
Salisbury and his episcopal nephews, rushed to Stephen's support:
his coronation on 22 December was attended, so William of
Malmesbury reports, by 'three bishops (the archbishop and those of
Winchester and Salisbury), no abbots, and very few nobles',[63] and
Malmesbury's testimony is corroborated by the attestations of King
Stephen's earliest charters.[64]

The issue separating these factions was not strong versus weak
royal government but, rather, who should rule? The lack of an
immediate Angevin military bid for the throne, which left potential Angevin supporters with no place to hide, prompted most of
the English aristocracy to close ranks behind Stephen by Easter
1136. But thereafter, in the absence of decisive royal leadership and
with the growing threat of a landing in England by the empress,
the four factions tended to split apart. The Beaumonts joined the
bishops in rallying behind Stephen, whereas Brian fitz Count,
Robert of Gloucester, and others opposed him or, at best, gave him
only tepid and temporary support.[65] Until about 1138 Stephen
endeavoured to perpetuate the regime of Henry I, but his lavish
outpouring of royal treasure on such urgent challenges as rebellion
in the south-west and attacks from the Scots emptied his coffers.[66]

---

[61] Ibid. 145–69.   [62] WM *HN* 5; *ASC*, s.a. 1127.

[63] WM *HN* 15–16.

[64] *RRAN* iii, nos. 45, 99, 187, 204, 255, 270, 341, 355, 373a, 382, 386–7, 465, 500,
591, 678, 716–17, 832, 904–7, 919, 942, 979; Hollister, *Anglo-Norman World*, 166.

[65] The causes and circumstances of Robert of Gloucester's entry into the Angevin faction
have been much debated: R. B. Patterson, 'William of Malmesbury's Robert of Gloucester:
A Re-Evaluation of the *Historia Novella*', *American Hist. Rev.* 70 (1965), 983–97; J. W.
Leedom, 'William of Malmesbury and Robert of Gloucester Reconsidered', *Albion*, 6
(1974), 251–65; D. Crouch, 'Robert, Earl of Gloucester and the Daughter of Zelophehad',
Journal of Medieval History, 11 (1985), 227–43; Bradbury, 'Early Years', 17. In this long-
standing controversy I opt for Leedom, as emended by Crouch. For a succinct recent evalua-
tion of Brian fitz Count's motives and character, see Chibnall, *Matilda*, 84–5.

[66] J. O. Prestwich, 'War and Finance in the Anglo-Norman State', *TRHS* 5:4 (1954),
37–42.

The resulting tensions and, after mid-1138, warfare between the curial factions strained the system of centralized government to the breaking-point.

Stephen's proliferation of earldoms was a product of these tensions. He instigated the policy in the latter part of 1138 and it reached full throttle around 1140.[67] It did not represent, as was recently proposed, a conscious rejection on Stephen's part of the long-evolving Anglo-Norman trend towards centralization and bureaucracy.[68] Stephen's political philosophy, if any, played no part in this development. Rather, it was an accommodation to a swiftly disintegrating political situation in which an epidemic of baronial rebellions was, to quote the *Gesta Stephani*, dragging Stephen 'hither and thither all over England. It was like the fabled hydra of Hercules; when one head was cut off two more grew in its place.'[69] The crumbling of Stephen's authority in 1138 caused him virtually to abandon Normandy, with dire consequences, and Wales, with consequences almost equally dire. It also impelled him to subdivide much of England into quasi-autonomous earldoms—a policy of radical decentralization in which, unlike the arrangements of Henry I, the earl superseded the sheriff and royal justice as the primary agent of shire government.[70] This was not always the case; Stephen's earldoms were not peas in a pod. Some earls were frequently named in the address clauses of Stephen's charters pertaining to their earldoms, others less often or not at all. But by and large earls replaced sheriffs as castellans of formerly royal castles; they became dispensers of formerly royal justice; and in many instances they received great tracts of formerly royal demesne lands. In four shires, earls served as their own sheriffs. Some earls even minted their own coins.[71] As William of Malmesbury explained it, Stephen won a pretence of peace from the magnates 'by the gift of great honours or castles. Finally he also established many as earls who had not been earls before, with endowments of landed estates and revenues that had belonged directly to the king.'[72] In brief, decentralization meant a drastic reduction not only of royal power but of royal property and royal wealth as well.

---

[67] Davis, *Stephen*, app. I, 'Earls and Earldoms', 125–41; see also the table in *RRAN* iii, pp. xxiv–xxv.

[68] Warren, *Governance*, 91–4.   [69] *GS* 68.   [70] Davis, *Stephen*, 125–8.

[71] Cronne, *Stephen*, 236–44; Warren, *Governance*, 96–8; *RRAN* iii, p. xxix.

[72] WM *HN* 23.

The multiplication and transformation of earldoms was probably undertaken at the urging of Stephen's leading nobles—in particular, the Beaumonts and Ranulf, earl of Chester, whose families and kinsmen (comprising some of England's foremost magnates under Henry I) received most of the new earldoms.[73] The downfall in June 1139 of Roger of Salisbury and his nephews, with their comprehensive network of sheriffs and justices, was another facet of this same radically decentralizing trend and seems also to have been instigated by the Beaumonts.[74] Although the exchequer managed to survive these new conditions, it was nevertheless deeply undermined.[75] Roger's fall and immediately subsequent death left Henry I's remaining two super-magnates to confront one another directly: Robert, earl of Gloucester, who fought on behalf of his half-sister and the house of Anjou, and King Stephen, a younger son of the house of Blois, who had joined his own immense aristocratic holdings in England with the far greater *terra regis* (and whose treasury was momentarily replenished by Bishop Roger's confiscated wealth).

Stephen decentralized his realm not out of choice but in order to win badly needed support and military assistance from his aristocracy. The new policy failed because the allegiance of Stephen's magnates was by no means firm, being governed by their territorial ambitions and their instinct for survival. In a kingdom disputed between evenly matched antagonists who could not reach an accommodation, the nobles were anxious to come down on the winning side, or at least to hedge their bets and lie low. Most of them, like Anglo-Norman magnates in the past, shunned decisive military encounters. As at Rochester in 1088, Alton in 1101, and Shrewsbury in 1102, the magnates in Stephen's army at Lincoln in 1141 chose not to risk their lives, estates, or freedom on the uncertain outcome of a fight to the finish.[76] They might well have pondered the lessons of 1106 and 1124, when barons of the defeated armies at Tinchebray and Bourgthéroulde suffered long years of

---

[73] Bedford, Cambridge, Hereford, Hertford, Lincoln, Worcester.

[74] Crouch, *Beaumont Twins*, 43–4 with references.

[75] Yoshitake, 'Exchequer', 950–9; Cronne, *Stephen*, 222–4; Chibnall, *Matilda*, 122–3; Davis, *Stephen*, 84.

[76] C. W. Hollister, *The Military Organization of Norman England* (Oxford, 1965), 120, 122, 223–4, 226–8 with references. For another example of baronial reluctance to engage in battle, see *GS* 236–8 (1153, Wallingford).

captivity—men such as the aforementioned young William of Mortain, now a wretched old man shuffling around the cloister at Bermondsey after a generation of captivity, and the once-powerful Norman baron Hugh of Montfort-sur-Risle, still languishing in prison after his capture in 1124. Robert of Bellême had survived the defeat at Tinchebray by fleeing the battlefield, and Stephen's magnates did likewise at Lincoln.[77] Stephen's own capture and imprisonment, resulting in part from his magnates' defection, taught him most convincingly to be wary of them in the future and to cease enriching them with earldoms. Indeed, the raising of new earls was a policy that Stephen pursued for only sixteen or seventeen months of his reign.[78] But, in the years following his release from captivity, despite his reliance on non-magnates such as William Martel, Richard de Lucy, and the Flemish mercenary captain William of Ypres, he lacked the strength and support to re-establish the centralized kingship of his opening years.[79] The new earldoms endured until the accession of Henry II, whose policy of restoring the tenurial conditions of 1135 was aimed not only at the resolution of baronial land disputes but also at the recovery of royal estates that Stephen had alienated *en masse*. In the opening years of his reign, Henry took firm action to recover the large chunks of *terra regis* that had slipped into private hands under Stephen's faltering regime.[80]

The urgency of Stephen's fight for survival in England, beginning in 1138, and his subsequent capture at Lincoln in 1141, left Normandy largely unattended and therefore highly vulnerable. Twice the Norman landholders had appealed to Theobald, count of Blois, to come to their rescue and take charge of their defence against the Angevins and other potential enemies, and twice he had declined.[81] After Stephen's one unsuccessful foray into the duchy in 1137, he left it virtually ungoverned. Of the men whom he appointed on his departure as Norman 'justiciars' (of whom only two are named), Roger of Saint-Sauveur, *vicomte* of the Cotentin,

---

[77] OV vi. 84, 90, 94–8, 350, 356, 540–2; HH 235–6, 245, 273–4; Crouch, *Beaumont Twins*, 22, 29–30, 49–50. Robert of Bellême fled to safety in 1106 only to be taken captive in 1112: OV vi. 178, 256. On the high risks of pitched battles, see Gillingham, 'William the Bastard at War', 146–8.

[78] See the table of county officials in *RRAN* iii, pp. xxiv–xxv; Davis, *Stephen*, 125–41.

[79] Davis, *Stephen*, 65–7.   [80] W. L. Warren, *Henry II* (London, 1973), 262–4.

[81] OV vi. 454, 548; RT 128–9.

died in battle shortly afterwards, and William of Roumare, Lucy's son, vanishes from Norman sources after 1138; by 1141 he had defected to the Angevins in England.[82] Count Geoffrey's conquest of Normandy during the early 1140s, and his assumption of the ducal title in 1144,[83] tended to draw to the Angevin cause barons with very large Norman holdings—for example, Waleran of Meulan and Walter Giffard.[84] It left in Stephen's camp others with relatively modest Norman holdings—for example, William III of Warenne and the Clares.[85] Robert, earl of Leicester, who possessed great wealth on both sides of the Channel, stuck with Stephen until nearly the end and lost his Norman lordship of Breteuil as a result, whereas Waleran of Meulan, Earl Robert's twin, managed, with Robert's help, to retain his earldom of Worcester despite his defection to the Angevin cause.[86] Since the Angevins remained strong in the west of England, Waleran ran little risk of losing the earldom when he joined them.

But allegiances were sometimes determined less by geopolitics than by such non-strategic factors as the quality of a baron's personal relationship with Stephen. This was true of Geoffrey de Mandeville, whose Norman holdings were minimal but whose relations with the king after 1141 were marred by deep mutual hostility that culminated in Geoffrey's rebellion and death.[87] Mutual hostility also marred Stephen's relations with Ranulf, earl of Chester, whose loyalties were further complicated by his conflict with King David—a staunch supporter of the empress—over Lancashire and Cumberland. Ranulf's Norman and English lands were both considerable, but he ended on the Angevin side because of personal difficulties with Stephen and his men, and in 1149 he

---

[82] OV vi. 494, 538–42; Haskins, *Norman Institutions*, 91, 127; L. Delisle, *Histoire du château et des sires de Saint-Sauveur-le-Vicomte* (Valognes, 1867), 27–31, 59–65.

[83] Discussed in two as yet unpublished papers by R. Helmerichs: 'Geoffrey le Bel, *Dux Normannorum*', and 'The "Norman Conquest" of Geoffrey de Bel' (Univ. of California, Santa Barbara, 1992).

[84] Crouch, *Beaumont Twins*, 51–2; Davis, *Stephen*, 129.   [85] Ibid. 131, 133.

[86] Crouch, *Beaumont Twins*, 50–2, 55, 87. In 1153 Henry, duke of Normandy, re-granted Breteuil to Earl Robert, along with the associated honour of Pacy, which had been held jointly with Breteuil by Eustace of Breteuil, the last of William fitz Osbern's heirs. Eustace had forfeited Breteuil in 1119 in consequence of having rebelled against Henry I. Duke Henry also granted Earl Robert the stewardship of England and Normandy: *RRAN* iii, nos. 438–9.

[87] Davis, *Stephen*, 78–81, 157–60.

settled with David: all of Lancashire to Ranulf; Carlisle and Cumberland to David.[88]

At this point, and in conclusion, I must challenge Round's inter-pretation of Stephen's aristocracy on a matter of fundamental significance. Having agreed with Round that the reign was indeed anarchic, I must also insist that the civil strife was not the deliber-ate product of an incorrigibly turbulent, land-grabbing aristocracy infected, as Round imagined, by a 'feudal and anarchic spirit'.[89] Indeed, the risks and uncertainties of anarchy ran counter to the inclinations of most magnates, who were, as Edmund King has cogently argued, accustomed to survive and flourish in conditions of peace under a strong monarchy that, in Stephen's time, no longer existed.[90]

Above all, the magnates were interested in enjoying the full income from their lands. Many and perhaps all of them were keep-ing close track of their profits and losses. William of Warenne, while suffering temporary banishment in Normandy in 1101, was painfully and acutely aware that his forfeited earldom of Surrey 'had produced an annual revenue of a thousand pounds of silver for him'.[91] Such awareness of annual income on the part of the baronage can only have been intensified by the growth of the royal exchequer, with its associated writs of exemption for specific amounts of danegeld, *murdrum*, and *auxilium civitatis*. By no later than 1118 the earl of Leicester had developed an exchequer of his own, and another baronial exchequer emerged in the course of the century at Bristol under the earls of Gloucester. By mid-century the earls of Chester were employing similar accounting machin-ery.[92] Henry I had such respect for the numeracy of Robert, earl of Gloucester, and Brian fitz Count, lord of Wallingford, that he com-missioned them to conduct an audit of the royal treasury.[93] Having enjoyed a generation of uninterrupted peace, patronage, and abun-

---

[88] Davis, *Stephen*, 78–81, 157–60 ; J. Green, in *Earldom of Chester*, 97–108.

[89] Round, *Geoffrey*, p. v.

[90] E. King, 'King Stephen and the Anglo-Norman Aristocracy', *History*, 59 (1974), 62.

[91] OV vi. 12; the figure approximates the total value of William's Domesday honour: £1140 (Table 1.1).

[92] Crouch, *Beaumont Twins*, 163–6, and in *Earldom of Chester*, 82; Stenton, *First Century*, 70; *Gloucester Charters*, no. 188; Vaughn, *Anselm of Bec and Robert of Meulan*, 355–6.

[93] *PR 31 Henry I*, 129–31.

dant profits under Henry I, the aristocracy can only have been cha-
grined at the widespread scorched-earth warfare of Stephen's
reign.[94] Brian fitz Count, literate, numerate, and vastly enriched by
Henry I, complained that the destruction of all his tillable land in
the course of the civil war had constrained him to 'take things from
other people in order to sustain my life and the lives of my men'.[95]
Such lamentations by great lay landholders were very seldom committed to writing, but the same story is told in the abundance of
baronial charters that provide recompense for the impoverishment
brought about by the anarchy.[96] And on a much larger scale, we
can well imagine the mortification of the earls of Warwick,
Leicester, and Derby at the wasting of over half their home shires.
Certainly, the onset of weak kingship might encourage a magnate
to raid his neighbour's lands, especially if he had an old family
claim to them or if his neighbour was on the wrong side of the succession dispute. But, as the pillaging dragged on year after year, the
terrible costs of military destructiveness, shared by all participants,
were not only hellish for ordinary folk but deeply subversive to the
interests of the upper aristocracy as well.

The magnates of Stephen's England engaged in civil war and yet
they sought peace. Many were driven to arms by family ambitions
that had been buried in deep storage during the peaceful years of
Henry I but now emerged as realizable goals in the confusion and
instability of a society with its monarchy in dispute. Consequently,
in the absence of an authoritative royal referee, they fought to fulfil
old family claims or to defend lands that they already possessed
against others who claimed them. In R. H. C. Davis's cogent
words, 'There were too many claimants for too few baronies.'[97]
Similar free-for-all conditions had occurred, for similar reasons, in
the intervals immediately following the deaths of William I and
William II.[98] But under Stephen there seemed no end to the turmoil.

In time, however, the violence in Stephen's England was miti-
gated by compromise agreements, such as those negotiated by the

[94] Stenton, First Century, 245.
[95] H. W. C. Davis, 'Henry of Winchester and Brian fitz Count', EHR 25 (1910),
297–303.
[96] Stenton, First Century, 246.   [97] Davis, Stephen, 39.
[98] OV iv. 100–4, 112–14, 124–6; v. 292, 300–4; WM GR ii. 378–9; HH 213–14;
Barlow, William Rufus, 429.

earls of Chester and Leicester 'in the fields between Leicester and Mountsorrel', by the earls of Gloucester and Hereford, Derby and Chester, and by other great men—'the magnates' peace', as it has been called.[99] And when most barons concluded that Henry of Anjou was the best hope for the healing of hostilities, the war ended.[100] Far from striving to prosper by playing one side against the other, as Round supposed, the magnates longed for the security of a strong monarchy, and in Henry II they found it.

[99] Stenton, *English Feudalism*, 250–6, 286–8; Davis, *Stephen*, 108–11; Crouch, *Beaumont Twins*, 82–5; E. King, 'Mountsorrel and its Region in King Stephen's Reign', *Huntington Library Quarterly*, 44 (1980), 1–10.

[100] See especially J. W. Leedom, 'The English Settlement of 1153', *History*, 65 (1980), 347–64; also H. G. Richardson and G. O. Sayles, *The Governance of Mediaeval England* (Edinburgh, 1963), 251–64; Davis, *Stephen*, 115–18.

2

THE CASTLES OF
THE ANARCHY

Charles Coulson

THE study of castles in the reign and wars of King Stephen has been bedevilled by a tendency to treat all fortifications of the period as a single category. The shortcomings of such an approach become apparent if castles are considered instead with a threefold structural classification in mind. First, there were the castles which were regularly founded, mostly soon after the Conquest, and which were active residentially and administratively; some may have been defensively refurbished, as Sir Frank Stenton suggests; these form the vast majority. Secondly, there were the castles which in the ordinary course of any nineteen years of twelfth-century tenurial and economic development would have been created or modernized by the largely autonomous mechanisms of growth and seignorial ambition. Thirdly, there were the notorious castles built in direct furtherance of usurpation; these, because new, must be grouped with the siegeworks and campaign works which were intentionally ephemeral.[1]

These categories serve to highlight the central question of the role of the castle in the anarchy. Even when instruments of violence

For reading this chapter in draft and for bibliographical help, I am grateful to Richard Eales. The assistance of Derek Renn with the archaeology and illustrations has been invaluable, and I have greatly benefited from affirmative discussion with Marjorie Chibnall, my former teacher, on rendability in Normandy; Tom Bisson, on castle-customs in early Catalonia; Lewis Warren, on royal 'castle-policy'; and for the opportunity to read chapter 8 of David Crouch, *The Image of Aristocracy*, in advance of publication. To the courteous persistence of the editor Edmund King, particular acknowledgement is due.

[1] Royal castles and warfare are beyond the scope of this discussion. The basics are well adumbrated by Stenton, *First Century*, 193–5, 200–5, 223–7, 235–56.

(and its most noticed and durable symptom), castles were the result, not the cause, of local disturbances. Castle-building, as one of the consequences of the suspension of the juridical protection of property rights, might also measure the extent of disturbance. This line of enquiry, however, would require combining the narrative and other sources with the most exhaustive archaeological survey, and is not possible in this chapter. Here no more can be done than apply our categories in the investigation of what was seen to be the most crucial abnormality of Stephen's reign: that large numbers of new or revived castles allegedly came into existence without royal licence. The 'adulterine castles' are so prominent, both in the chronicles and in modern accounts, that they figure in Norman Pounds's recent and admirable survey as the root of all the evils of the reign.[2]

If castle-building was really licensed prior to 1135, so that applicants who were refused permission did not build; and if licensing was resumed after 1154 and could be shown to have become again a means of 'control', whereby only 'strategically useful' castles in loyal hands came into being, or were kept in a 'militarily effective' condition; then the intervening period would reveal a breakdown of royal power in this respect also.[3] 'Adulterine castles' notoriously afflicted the anarchy. But they are also reported of other disturbances: during Duke William's minority until c.1047; then, after his death in 1087, they are reported most emphatically until Robert Curthose departed on Crusade in 1096, a period punctuated by his and William Rufus's declaration of the Conqueror's laws in 1091; and we hear of adulterine castles again, from Robert's return late in 1100 until the subjugation of the duchy after Tinchebrai in 1106. In England, Henry I's opportunistic seizure of the throne, and the ensuing insecurity which ended only with William Clito's death in 1128, still caused no such troubles—but compare the complaints of churchmen at his and his partisans' activities in the Cotentin. He did move decisively in 1102 to break the English power of Robert of Bellême, but only Bridgnorth (not Tickhill or Arundel) was a new castle, and even that cannot be

[2] N. J. G. Pounds, *The Medieval Castle in England and Wales* (Cambridge 1990), 26–33.

[3] Royal 'castle-policy' is treated in my *Castles and Crenellating . . . 1200–1578* (in progress); the historiography in 'Freedom to Crenellate by Licence: An Historiographical Revision', *Nottingham Medieval Studies* (forthcoming).

regarded as built in defiance of royal law. Only on Henry I's death did 'adulterine castles' apparently reappear, both in England and (up to c.1137) in Normandy.[4] The supposed general outbreak in England should ideally be distinguished from local incidents during phases of hostilities, but the evidence is wanting. Sufficiently close archaeological dating of the few excavated sites is impossible. Documentary corroboration is rare. Inferences, ostensibly from topography or structural type, tend to reflect historical doctrine. Stenton is ambivalent. While not doubting that 'innumerable castles' arose during Stephen's reign, he is also sure that the large numbers of earthwork castles were 'the natural results of the feudal organization of Anglo-Norman society'. This, and his opinion that careful and lengthy construction was foreign to wartime creations (few of which featured significantly in the conflict), is deservedly respected.

Investigation must start with the Angevin accusation in 1153–4 that Stephen was so lacking in kingly qualities that he allowed a variously guessed but large number of castles to appear. Robert of Torigny, in his account of the peace settlement, says the total of new *castella* to be 'overthrown' exceeded 1,115, a figure of mesmerizing precision. Among later chroniclers, William of Newburgh wrote of 'those new castles which in the days of Henry I had in no way existed', which Henry II's heroic advent caused 'to melt away like wax before the flame' (as lodgements of brigands naturally would when order was restored). Gervase of Canterbury ascribed to Henry II an order that anonymous 'very nasty little fortlets' should disappear throughout England. William of Newburgh, with alluring royalism, tells us that 'a few of the new castles which were conveniently located' were retained to be held by 'peaceful men for the strengthening of the kingdom'. This last passage contains a useful hint that a castle's novelty was not decisive, and that discretion and partisanship were exercised. Nothing solid on numbers exists, nor is to be expected.[5] A fossilized trace of the idea that the Conqueror and his sons jealously restricted castle-building, so that a great

[4] Examples of complaints at new castles or castle-works, rarely 'adulterine' but habitually since assumed to be 'unlicensed', are: *William of Jumièges*, ed. J. Marx (Paris, 1914), 115–16, 123; *William of Poitiers*, ed. R. Foreville (Paris 1952), 14–20; Haskins, *Norman Institutions*, 38, 64, 86, 289; *GS* 104–5.

[5] WN i. 94, 102; GC i. 160; RT 177, 183. Not all the manuscripts of RT have the figure 1,115; one has 126 new castles.

many of the thousand or more castles structurally attributable to before 1189 must have been anarchic, is occasionally still encountered, despite Stenton. Robert of Torigny has thus escaped the routine scepticism applied to medieval military statistics. Estimates of numbers have been revised by Richard Eales, proposing a post-Conquest proliferation followed by a slow decline, possibly stemmed temporarily or even mildly reversed under Stephen, then resumed more steeply as obsolescence, physical decay, tenurial change, and the cost of rebuilding in masonry contracted the social range of castle-ownership. First Stephanic mentions of castles listed by John Beeler total ninety. David King counted 110 but considered only twenty-seven of all kinds stated to be new.[6]

As Stenton emphasizes, *firmare* frequently meant refortification, indeed often only munitioning, like *infortiare*. Structures tend constantly to be over-stressed and manning neglected. After all, an 'incastellated' church and a 'house held as a castle' were just buildings filled with armed men. What to moderns is *the* castle to contemporaries was only *a* castle. It was a structure with features of fortification, both utilitarian and symbolic, ranging from a kit of prefabricated timber *bretasching* to equip an earthwork, via a bewildering variety of buildings, up to a major honorial *caput* or a walled town like the ancient hill-fort of Old Sarum. All these were 'castles', though not consistently so described, as many terms were in literary vogue. Most regrettably no medieval equivalent existed of the Victorian engineer's distinction between 'permanent fortification' and 'fieldwork', which weaker forces always relied on. Thus the empress and her partisans met their 1141 crisis and the king's release: 'she built castles over the country wherever she might to best advantage; some to hold back the king's men more effectively, others for the defence of her own people', which caused 'grievous oppression to the people, a general devastation of the realm, and the seeds of discord on every hand'. Forts are mentioned at Woodstock, at Radcot near Oxford among the Thames

---

[6] R. Eales, 'Royal Power and Castles in Norman England', in C. Harper-Bill and R. Harvey (eds.), *Ideals and practice of Medieval Knighthood*, 3 (Woodbridge, 1990), 55–63, and *passim*: J. Beeler, *Warfare in England 1066–1189* (New York, 1966), 397–422, 430–4 (with references); D. J. C. King, *Castellarium Anglicanum* (New York, 1983), pp. xxxi–xxxii. Renn (*Norman Castles*, gazetteer) notes about forty possible Stephanic foundations, including about fifteen siegeworks. A possible siege-castle has now been found by Exeter (1136?): *Fortress* 18 (1993), p. i.

marshes, and also within Cirencester. In this last reference ecclesiastical castro-phobia reinforces the chronicler's political sympathies, this castle being 'next the holy church of the religious like another Dagon before the ark of the Lord'. The *Gesta Stephani* held the empress responsible for much castle-building by her supporters, and blamed Robert of Gloucester especially for imposing the labours of castleworks.[7] Cirencester was later razed by Stephen; and he also took down the famous castle built upon and in the old stone tower of Bampton church, near Oxford, and another in 1149 at Wheldrake near York by the citizens' procurement.[8] Stephen, perhaps more than Henry II, was the great destroyer of illicit fortlets.[9]

The siege- and campaign-castles were seemingly the least obnoxious of fortifications, being ephemeral army fieldworks not entailing long-term arrogated lordly rights, nor prises of food and money. But siege-castles are elusive. Wallingford had a cluster, among them probably Crowmarsh Giffard and Brightwell; but judging a site by its slight construction or incomplete state or by its location, without documents to refine archaeological possibilities, is hazardous. Earl Robert's recorded castle nearby, identified with Faringdon, built in 1144 and destroyed by Stephen the next year, shows how suggestion can become false certainty in citation. Castles of all kinds were strong only when stocked and heavily manned—insubstantial wartime works especially so. Although depredations by the 'castle-men' are prominent in clerical condemnation, they were but one of the numerous disasters of war. Conditions requiring self-defence and an environment of seignorial competition, both distantly akin to the scramble of the Conquest decade, explain Thomas of Cuckney's slight earthwork thrown up around his estate church, which Stenton notes, and doubtless many others also.[10]

[7] *GS* 138–9 (comment in Stenton, *First Century*, 203), 150–1 (comment in Davis, *Stephen*, 73–4; and cf. 15–16, 105, 115–17, 119). Works, not castellation *per se*, were the grievance.

[8] *GS* 140–1; SD ii. 323–4.

[9] S. Painter (*Feudalism and Liberty* (Baltimore, 1961), 127) notes a minimum of twenty-one demolitions under Henry II.

[10] King, *Castellarium Anglicanum*, *sub* Berkshire; Davis, *Stephen*, 88–90; J. Kenyon, *Medieval Fortifications* (Leicester, 1990), 10, 24, 38, 141 (with excavation report references). Renn (*Norman Castles*, 189) shows the discrepancy between the archaeology at Faringdon and the sources.

The contemporary indictment of Stephen for permitting new castle-building is a specious and propagandist circular argument, rubbing in his failure to defeat the Angevins and to establish his dynasty; but the accusation that he allowed *unlicensed* castles is a modern invention. Certainly, irregular fortlets were a traditional proof of governmental incapacity and even illegitimacy, alleged as late as the Dunstable meeting of January 1154, when it was alleged that Stephen had disarmed those of his supporters with undue partiality. (Henry of Huntingdon's comment implies that few such castles remained at this date, and fewer still for Henry II to disarm.) There is no foundation for the modern charge that he allowed to lapse the royal prerogative to license castles (and hypothetically to stop unlicensed ones).[11] The historiography is complex. The prerogative is asserted as a peculiar royal right by the compiler *c.*1115 of the *Leges Henrici Primi*,[12] but it has a much longer continental pedigree. Scholars have read it into clause four of the *Consuetudines et justicie* (1091),[13] even though the whole declaration was an interim peace-keeping measure, which exempted from interference (baronial as well as ducal) just the sort of *munitiunculum* castigated in 1153–4. The *Consuetudines*, moreover, forbade absolutely brigand occupation (*fortitudo*) of natural lairs (*et in rupe vel in insula*) typical of outbreaks of lawlessness. (The Isle of Ely from Hereward's time until after the 1320s is a barometer of the state of the peace.) In 1091 there is no mention of that constant clerical grievance—the armed conversion of churches—nor in the chronicles for 1153–4, although cases recorded had been quite numerous.[14] The emphasis given to 'unlicensed' castles would be unbalanced even were they what Orderic Vitalis in another context twice, but modern writers constantly, call 'adulterine'. Whereas the *Consuetudines* say nothing about licens-

---

[11] R. A. Brown, 'A List of Castles 1154 to 1216', *EHR* 74 (1959), 250 (and *passim* 249–80); and *English Castles* (London, 1976), 82, 215.

[12] *Leges Henrici Primi*, ed. L. J. Downer (Oxford, 1972), 108, 116.

[13] Haskins, *Norman Institutions*, 277–84.

[14] e.g. Bampton, Bridlington, Cirencester, Coventry, Hereford, Lincoln, Malmesbury, Ramsey, Reading, Wallingford, Wherwell, Wilton, and perhaps Haile and Selby: Renn, *Norman Castles*, 49, 100, 117, 144, 160, 161–2, 199, 205, 226–7, 272, 289, 291, 307–8, 338, 344, 347. Roger of Salisbury intruded Malmesbury castle into the Abbey precinct, but in 1118: ibid. 239.

ing, clause four is quite clear on rendability—the duke's right to take over castles for his own use when he needed them.[15]

It is instructive to read some of the *conventiones* of Stephen's reign with French custom in mind. In the most famous of them the earls of Chester and Leicester not only agreed to refrain from fortifying castles on the sensitive marches of Leicestershire, but mutually undertook to ensure that no one else did. Neither the removal of the possibility of enforceable royal arbitration nor pervasive anarchy determined the castle-clauses of this celebrated treaty.[16] Bilaterally agreed zones where no new fortification (or refortification) was to be undertaken by the principals or their men; tolerance for contentious castles (here Whitwick), or arrangements to disarm castles (here Ravenstone); and careful provisions for the munitioning or the further strengthening of intrusive or crucial fortresses: these are all familiar elements of French practice. Similar arrangements on a larger scale occur in the successive Anglo-French treaties of 1194, 1195–6, and 1200, covering the borders of Normandy and the provinces to the south.

Other aspects of the Chester–Leicester agreement become clearer when read in the light of French custom. Chester, in granting, or accepting, Leicester possession of Mountsorrel castle, with its appurtenant *burgus* or *villa*, affirmed his continuing lordship in the conventional fashion by reserving refuge-rights there for himself and his retinue. The purpose is 'to make war on whomsoever he wished' (*ad guerreandum quencunque voluerit*), and the entitlement *ut de feudo meo*; so Leicester, despite the scrupulous respect for mutual interest which dominates the pact, could have no con-

[15] On jurability, whereby security was given that the fortress would not be injurious to the lord of the fief (here, Ravenstone may be reprieved by Chester but must not be hostile to Leicester in any eventuality), see C. L. H. Coulson, 'Fortress-Policy in Capetian Tradition and Angevin Practice', *ANS* 6 (1983), 13–38; 'Rendability and Castellation in Medieval France', *Château-Gaillard*, 6 (Caen, 1972), 59–67; 'Castellation in the County of Champagne', *Château-Gaillard*, 9–10 (Caen, 1982), 347–64. These customs have particularly early record in Catalonia and in Provence: D. Herlihy (ed.), *The History of Feudalism* (London, 1970), 99–102, 228–9 (1058 *bis*, 1115, mistranslated); C. Brunel, *Les Plus Anciennes Chartes en langue provençale* (Paris, 1926), nos. 2 (*c*.1034), 8, 10 (*c*.1103), etc. Coulson, 'The French Matrix of the Castle-Provisions of the Chester–Leicester Pact', *ANS* 18 (forthcoming).

[16] For the texts, see Stenton, *First Century*, 250–6. See further Davis, *Stephen*, 108–10, 162–3; King, 'Mountsorrel and its Region in King Stephen's Reign', *Huntington Library Quarterly*, 44 (1980), 1–10; Renn, *Norman Castles*, 53 map F.

trol over, or compensation for, Chester's use of the castle. The
lord's right was paramount, and conventionally it was expressed as
though in contemplation of war. Refuge was a component of basic
rendability, which might extend, not only to putting in troops on
demand by messenger, but to requiring the vassal to vacate his castle first to symbolize complete takeover of control. The occasions,
if not the lord's mere will, were war and the lord's necessity. Both
are present here. Chester, for warring against whomsoever he
wished, had right of entry in company to the *burgus* and castle-
baileys of Mountsorrel, but *si necesse fuerit comiti Rannulfo* he must
personally be admitted *in dominico castro*—presumably Leicester's
own *donjon* or whatever inner ward existed on this heavily damaged hill-top site. This restricted the lord's right, but is an early feature in circumstances of strict reciprocity. If Chester entered
unaccompanied, Leicester was bound by feudal etiquette (*portabit
ei fidem*), subject as throughout to the king's liege lordship. Both
parties relied on established castle-customs to define a long-term
relationship. Stenton's 'uneasy state of half-suspended hostilities'
between the earls, and the 'new feudal order' he believes had 'arisen
in reaction from the anarchy of previous years', were probably less
uneasy, novel, or impermanent in intention than he supposes.

Stephen regarded his obligations under rendability much less
scrupulously than did the two earls in the preceding agreement. In
council at Winchester in 1139 rendability was raised as a means of
trying the subordination of the bishops. Archbishop Hugh of
Rouen voiced the commonplace, according to William of
Malmesbury, that 'as it is a time of suspicion all the chief men, in
accordance with the custom of other peoples, ought to put all the
keys of their fortifications (*munitionum*; i.e. give symbolic entry) at
the disposal of the king who has to strive for the peace of all'.
Demanding castles in pledge was standard form, and was acceptable if 'reasonable', but it was not reasonable to make this demand
with the intention of depriving their owners. Temporary use only
was the superior's right. Arresting Roger of Salisbury (with
Sherborne castle, Malmesbury, and Devizes), Alexander of Lincoln
(with Newark, Sleaford, and Banbury all of his own building), and
later Nigel of Ely, gained Stephen their castles but serious repercus-
sions as well. Taking Geoffrey de Mandeville in 1143 at the St
Albans court gained at least Pleshey and Saffron Walden, but
Henry of Huntingdon thought it dishonourably done. At

Northampton in 1146 Stephen once more broke the rules, extorting Lincoln castle from Ranulf of Chester.[17]

By Henry II's standards, Stephen did well; nor did he fall short of Anglo-Norman practice regarding new castles. Even by the exemplary test of the *Leges Henrici Primi* he must be exonerated. They reserved to the king, in a spirit of Carolingian nostalgia, judgement of *castellatio sine licentia*, but in another clause it is *castellatio trium scannorum*, which meant that, even theoretically, earthworks nearly three times the size of those exempted from interference in 1091 were excluded from the king's ban, along with all works of masonry. The *scabulum* of the *Consuetudines* is undoubtedly the *scannum* of the *Leges Henrici Primi*.[18] Three casts of earth or relays of earth-moving, even stages of scaffolding, would cover all but the greatest castles. Suggestions by Liebermann and Ella Armitage, recently endorsed by L. J. Downer, that the phrase meant triple embankments would make exemption virtually total. Wartime forts were not of this order, whether fieldworks or the competitive entrenchments of minor lordlings, defending their positions or exploiting the weakness of royal and magnatial authority to enhance them.

The 'adulterine' castle must be looked for elsewhere. As a polemical term it may have been invented by Abbot Suger of Saint-Denis or by Orderic himself, writing about Normandy after 1087. In his exhaustive trawl of the French chronicles, Robert Aubenas found it used solely by Orderic and by Suger (varied by *castrum sceleratum*) in denouncing the new castles of Robert of Bellême and other great Norman lords. Orderic used also *adulterina municipia* and Aubenas notes the peculiarly English fashion, citing Stubbs's *Constitutional History*, to which much is due. It was an integral part of a long castrophobic ecclesiastical *genre* exemplified *c*.1025 by Fulbert of Chartres's invective against Count Theobald for failing to stop the vicomte of Châteaudun building two castles as scourges, 'one from the east the other from the west', to strike down upon the cathedral city. For incastellated churches, conversion into *spelunce latronum* (after Matt. 21: 13) was the stock phrase.[19] Peace of God

---

[17] Davis, *Stephen*, 29–30, 32–3, 78–9, 92–3; WM *HN* 32–3. With Devizes (1140) and Berkeley (1145) for special causes the method failed (Davis, *Stephen*, 42, 90–1).

[18] As noted by Pounds, *Medieval Castle*, 305 n. 17. E. Armitage (*Early Norman Castles of the British Isles* (London 1912), 378 n. 1) has caused some confusion.

[19] e.g. M. Chibnall, 'Orderic Vitalis on Castles', in C. Harper-Bill, C. Holdsworth,

provisions, monastic castle-free *banlieues*, and conciliar anathemas all have a common parentage. The concern in Stephen's reign with castleworks builds on these ideas. 'Undue works of castles' were forbidden in 1148 at the Council of Reims. Ecclesiastics had blamed William I for 'oppressing poor men' in this way, and the *Gesta* arraigned the empress but particularly Robert of Gloucester for it. Levying *tenserie*, to sustain chiefly the old and recognized castles, was another grievance, as was forcible provisioning from church lands particularly, even when the king did it.[20] In 1153–4 two traditions merged. The pusillanimity of the house of Blois, exemplified by Stephen's father at Antioch, blended with the fashion for branding rulers, like Robert Curthose, as incompetent (and even illegitimate) for allowing intrusive castles. The combination has condemned Stephen to posterity.

The term *adulterinus* is dear to the British. Hamilton Thompson translated it as 'counterfeit' or 'spurious', which sprang from the notion that 'adulterine castles' were misbegotten, not the genuine article. The 1217 reissue of Magna Carta, itself a pacification document, has the only authoritative definition. Its final provision (47) explains that *castella adulterina*, to be razed in principle, were 'those castles which were constructed or rebuilt from the beginning of the war waged between the Lord King John our father and his barons of England'.[21] The rule was most exactly, if selectively, applied. There is still nothing about licensing, but the feeling was that the castle was an attribute of established lordship, not one intruded by upstarts while the rule of law was suspended. Possessions 'invaded' and new castles built in 1154 concerned Robert of Torigny equally, although neither figures in the official text of the Winchester accord. The notorious 'tyrannies of the castle-men' were not this sort of usurpation, but partly the exacting of the old Anglo-Saxon *burhbot* services, to a degree unknown since the Conquest era.

and J. L. Nelson (eds.), *Studies Presented to R. Allen Brown* (Woodbridge, 1989), 52 (cf. 56 on 'spiritual castles'); R. Aubenas, 'Les Châteaux-forts des Xe et XIe siècles', *Revue historique de droit français et étranger*, 4:17 (1938), 548–86 (at 567 n. 4); H. d'Arbois de Jubainville, *Histoire . . . de Champagne*, 1 (Paris 1859), 275–8.

[20] The passage from Robert of Torigny is translated in Davis, *Stephen*, 119; *ASC*, *s.a.* 1137; William of Newburgh couples castles and tyranny (WN i. 69–70). D. C. Douglas, *William the Conqueror* (London, 1964), 373; Count Henry in the Cotentin (1087–1100) likewise, in person and by proxy: Haskins, *Norman Institutions*, 63.

[21] W. Stubbs, *Select Charters*, 9th edn. (Oxford, 1913), 344; cf. A. H. Thompson, *Military Architecture in England* (Oxford, 1912), 56 n. 3, 89 n. 1.

Despite this evidence, there is frequent reference to the Norman kings' supposed 'control of private castles'.[22] Richard Eales has emphasized the impact of the multitude of castles rapidly established after 1066, endowing their lords with customary rights and precedent, upon existing law. Only a small proportion of the 'castles of the Conquest', in J. H. Round's phrase,[23] could have been ordained. The demands of the Norman settlement, producing a range of marcher-type franchises, would have entrenched and extended seignorial liberties. Any consultation would have been chiefly by the great, who by continental precedent already had the right. The implanting of the great majority of lesser castles, along with claim-staking disputes, would fall to the magnates' courts. Eynsford castle in Kent, an early and lowly stone castle, doubtless came into being in this way under the archbishops' aegis. The vassal's castle enhanced his lord's position, whether formally rendable or not. Little encouragement was needed by William I for his tenants to build castles. Their self-interest sufficed.[24] William fitz Osbern's and Odo of Bayeux's authority to found castles was in the common spirit of the enterprise. Aubenas argued cogently that castles were built by delegation of official authority. He firmly refuted views expressed by Flach, Luchaire, Calmette, and many others (deriving ultimately from the work and fraternity of Eudes de Mézeray, 1610–83) that France 'bristled with feudal castles', so that any 'adventurer' could become count or baron in no time by building one. Jean Yver concurred, but had the ducal honour much at heart, finding no place in Normandy for the *châtellenie indepéndente* despite the great franchises, nor for the *avoué* whom ecclesiastics so disliked. Both scholars championed the legitimacy of the new feudal order. What they and Marcel Garaud have demonstrated for tenth- and early eleventh-century France is highly relevant for the anarchy. Unfortunately it is the *anarchie féodale* school which has been drawn upon, which in France is never far from the

---

[22] Painter asserted that 'the charters which were granted to Geoffrey de Mandeville . . . prove conclusively that a specific license from the crown was required for castle-building' (*Feudalism and Liberty*, 141), despite his candour about some of the difficulties, not least the lack of evidence.

[23] *Archaeologia*, 58 (1902), 313–40.

[24] Pounds (*Medieval Castle*, 30, 305 nn. 23, 24) cites FW ii. 34. His quotation from William of Poitiers refers only to putting 'energetic custodians into castles' (ii. 35).

surface. Garaud went so far as to put back the view that 'plus d'un millier de châteaux forts . . . hérissaient . . . le sol de la France' into the remote Gallo-Roman period.[25]

By the end of the eleventh century perhaps as many as a thousand castles had fixed the feudal map of England. New castles, not refortifications, affected holders of vested rights. The supply was ample for normal purposes, but earth and timber castles perished quickly from rot, wind, and erosion. Frequent repairs and alterations are the pattern shown by the meticulously excavated castle of Old Montgomery at Hen Domen. Ditches had to be re-cut, timber revetments and palisading replaced. Most vulnerable were the wooden towers shown by the Bayeux Tapestry crowning the mottes of Bayeux, Dinan, Dol, Rennes, and Hastings, the type verified by excavation. Only the large foundation-posts found at Abinger and at South Mimms (see Fig. 2.1), speculatively attributed to the anarchy, would be difficult to reinstate.[26] Whether mere sentry-box

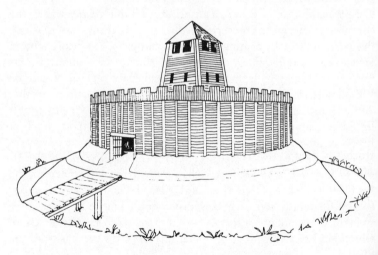

FIG. 2.1. South Mimms, keep and motte

[25] J. Yver, 'Les Châteaux-forts en Normandie jusqu'au milieu du XIIe siècle', *Bulletin de la société des antiquaires de Normandie*, 53 (1955–6), 28–115; 'Autour de l'absence d'avouerie en Normandie', ibid. 57 (1963–4), 189–283; M. Garaud, 'La Construction des châteaux et les destinées de la *Vicaria* et du *Vicarius* carolingiens en Poitou', *Revue historique de droit*, 4:31 (1953), 54–78 (at 58).
[26] Kenyon, *Medieval Fortifications*, 10, 13–17, 22, 35–7, 83–5, 98–101, etc. R. Higham and P. Barker (*Timber Castles* (1992)), now surveys the issues.

look-outs on stilts, or structures as grand as Lambert of Ardres's famous multi-chambered tower, such castles were almost as easily rebuilt as destroyed. Wooden structures of earth-fast posts, established for the fifteen or so years until the first major repair, were automatically and lawfully rebuilt (compare mills, weirs, deer-leaps, barns—all seignorial furniture, variously lucrative and prestigious). Painter justly commented, 'if it were to be even reasonably effective, royal regulation of castle-building could not be confined to controlling the creation of new strongholds on sites never before used'; but *idée fixe* then compelled him to assert that castles became dangerous only after the Settlement and Scandinavian threat were past, when 'the king could . . . begin to enforce his right to control new construction'.[27]

That licensing implemented some politico-strategic Norman castle-plan is as imaginative as supposing that the omission of castle-builders to seek this, like other privileges, contributed to the disorders of the anarchy. Even oral pacts as important as is implied would have been solemnly made and attested, surviving significantly in the record. The few documents, while not properly licences and due to extraneous motives, do offer some illumination. An agreement between Henry I and William de Corbeil, archbishop of Canterbury, dated 1127, allowed him and his successors to build a *turris* or *munitio* within the royal castle of Rochester. The archbishops enjoyed little security as custodians and had to have the new keep in full proprietorship for the expense to be justified. In 1088 Rufus had bargained with Bishop Gundulf of Rochester to wall the bailey in stone after Odo's revolt. It cost him £60 in discharge of a debt of £100. Henry's deal was sharper, since his great-grandson not only resumed the custody but got the great donjon-palace as well for no more than a brush with the Church. William of Corbeil may have hoped to strengthen his hold on the custody, as well as on his vassal the bishop, whose cathedral the great tower overawes. King Henry's terse *et concedo ut in eodem castello municionem vel turrim quam voluerint sibi faciant et in perpetuum habeant et custodiant* is outweighed by provisions for the complications of castle-guard which did not involve the tower.[28]

[27] Painter, *Feudalism and Liberty*, 141.
[28] *RRAN* ii, p. clxxxviii, nos. 1475, 1606; R. W. Southern, 'The Place of Henry I in English History', *Proc. of British Academy*, 48 (1962), 161 n. 2.

The impression that the fortifying was a subsidiary issue is stronger still in the series of privileges gained by Bishop Alexander of Lincoln to endow his fine new castle of Newark on Trent in the early 1130s. To dignify this strongly walled, palatial, and very conspicuous masonry fortress, he was allowed to divert the king's highway (otherwise *stretbreche* by the *Leges*); to erect a bank or causeway to dam up his fishponds; to build a bridge 'at the castle', subject to not diminishing the king's revenues in Lincoln nearby or at Nottingham upstream; to hold a fair 'at the castle'; and to do a third of his knight service by castle-guard at Newark. This last concession Stephen confirmed early in his reign, allowing the bishop to transfer there his Dover service also.[29] The only routine assistance Alexander lacked, which, being on the Trent, he probably did not need, was with the getting and transporting of materials. It is not surprising that lay nobles envied the superior castles of Roger of Salisbury and his clan.[30] Henry I's chamberlain, Geoffrey de Clinton at Kenilworth, had less help over his new castle with its large moats or fishponds and adjacent monastery; but this castle or Brandon could hardly have come into existence without tacit royal support, not least because of its close encroachment upon Warwick. The king's licence might legalize various novelties (markets, tolls, mills, parks, chantries) if circumstances permitted. It might even overbear objectors; but, while a form of law operated, existing rights called for circumspect evasion.

The bishop of Lincoln, builder also of Sleaford and Banbury castles, insured his gains from loss of favour and from the challenge at law to which royal charter gave little immunity, but can have expected no dispute over building castles upon his own soil and lordship. The same insouciance must be inferred in Roger of Salisbury's attitude to his new or rebuilt castles at Devizes and Sherborne; and in Henry of Winchester's to his at Downton, Farnham, Merdon, Taunton, Bishop's Waltham, and Wolvesey. When in 1155 he secretly sent his treasure out of England and discreetly followed it, and the new king in revenge for his mother's

---

[29] *RRAN* ii, nos. 1660, 1661, 1770, 1791; iii, no. 465.
[30] WM *HN* 25–6; Newark was 'a magnificent castle of very ornate construction' (HH 266). See Renn, *Norman Castles*, 100, 111, 163–4, 173, 187–8, 242, 308–10, 312–13, 319, 349, for plans and succinct descriptions of Banbury, Bishop's Waltham, Devizes, Downton, Farnham, Merdon, Sherborne, Sleaford, Taunton, Wolvesey (on which also M. W. Thompson in *Fortress*, 12 (1992), 18–22).

and his own humiliations razed his castles, including probably the magnificent enmotted stone tower revealed by excavation at Farnham (see Fig. 2.2), the rationalization that they were all 'adulterine' would have astounded him. It is equally inapt of ancient Mandeville Pleshey or Saffron Walden, dismantled in 1158. Bishop Nigel may have had doubts about his masonry rebuild at Ely, probably of the small and old motte near the cathedral, but if so they were due to the hostility of the monks and of Saint Etheldreda, to whose intervention the monks credited its disappearance following capture by Stephen and in 1143 by Geoffrey de Mandeville.[31] This so-called *munitio firmissima* can have been one of the least deserving of the grandiloquent language habitually used of castles by chroniclers, in eulogy and in anathema alike.

The stone castles of this first twelfth-century 'great rebuilding' are much undervalued, and impossible to list with confidence, but were an aesthetic and technical leap forward, whether represented by William of Corbeil's *egregia turris* at Rochester; by the moated enclosure castle at Kenilworth; by Robert of Gloucester's great tower-keep rediscovered at Bristol, where Stephen was held prisoner; or by the de Veres' beautiful ashlar tower-palace at Castle Hedingham, with its lofty and well-lit galleried hall, thrown into one stately apartment by carrying the cross-wall on a wide arch (see Pl. I). Closets, chambers, latrines, and fireplaces are lavishly provided, but, as with towers as late as Orford (1165–73) and Dover (1180–90). Hedingham contains no archery loops or even dual-purpose windows. That Geoffrey de Mandeville in 1141 may have had to be content with the extemporized fort at South Mimms near St Albans, and with other less distinguished earthworks, shows his straits. The vertically planked-up motte, with its central stone-footed timber tower with tunnel access to the basement, possibly built by him, was perhaps as powerful a symbol of the lordship he sought to gain as time and resources allowed. Masonry construction was phased over several years, with slow-setting lime-mortar wall masses. It was costly and required free movement of skilled craftsmen and materials, both scarce in many regions.

About this time, in Norfolk, the late eleventh-century great mansion within the large embanked motte or upper ward at Castle

---

[31] Brown ('Castles 1154 to 1216', 250 n. 1, 251 n. 2) had doubts; Southern, 'Place of Henry I', 137–40, 162; King, *Castellarium Anglicanum, sub.* Cambridgeshire, Lincolnshire, Oxfordshire, Warwickshire, etc.; Kenyon, *Medieval Fortifications*, 41–3.

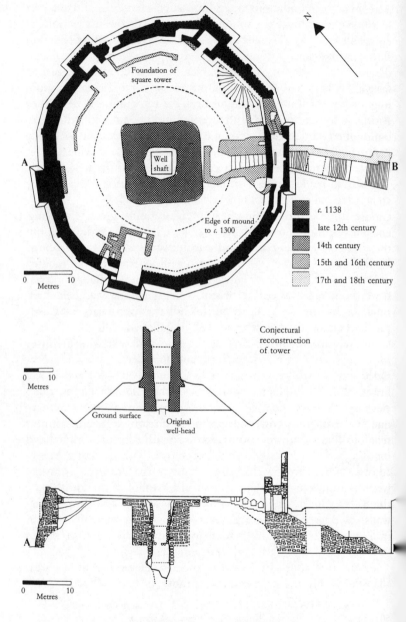

Foundation of
square tower

N

Well
shaft

A   B

Edge of mound
to c. 1300

0   10
Metres

c. 1138

late 12th century

14th century

15th and 16th century

17th and 18th century

Conjectural
reconstruction
of tower

0   10
Metres

Ground surface   Original
                        well-head

A

0   10
Metres

FIG. 2.2. Farnham, keep and motte

Acre may have been converted into a tall rectangular tower by sacrificing about half the original area and thickening and heightening the rest (see Figs. 2.3 and 2.4).[32] Even major adaptation was slow and expensive, and aesthetics not military determinism deserve respect here as elsewhere. What a great lay magnate with a taste as ambitious as that of Bishop Roger at his opulent Sherborne might seek is shown by William d'Aubigny's 'hall-keep' at Castle Rising. Roofs recessed behind upper walls are standard (the forebuilding summit is later). The block is squat in proportion, with many large windows and excellent ashlar with enriched detail, especially to the processional stairway to the first-floor *piano nobile*. The wall-arcading is like that once at Norwich and, while moderately fire-proof, the *ambiance* is of quasi-regal state. It was good enough for Isabella of France after 1330. Although the massive encircling ramparts were probably heightened at some early period, the so-called 'keep' is worlds away from any anarchic scenario (see Pl. II).

By 1146 the earl of Arundel had moved his other East Anglian seat from the large sub-rectangular moated castle at Old Buckenham, seemingly up to date but soon to be demolished, to the new castle at a more frequented site two miles away.[33] An ambitious town-plantation scheme figured also at new Sleaford, at improved Devizes (1135–9), at Mountsorrel (by 1148), and effectively also at Newark-on-Trent and at Rising. Maurice Beresford's list of new towns shows no slackening of impetus, Stephen having eleven to thirteen compared with Henry I's thirteen to twenty-one.[34] A castle on its own was much less disruptive. The many new religious houses and towns entailed more adjustment of rights and tenures. New Buckenham was enhanced by a neat grid-plan *burgus*, adjoining the carefully laid-out, almost circular, moated ringwork with a vast levelled interior about seventy yards across, containing the base of a cylindrical tower about seventy feet in diameter with walls about ten feet thick and a crosswall (see Pl. III). No lack of money, time, or care is apparent. The crude flint workmanship

[32] Kenyon, *Medieval Fortifications*, 28, 49–51; guidebook by J. G. Coad (English Heritage, 1984).

[33] *Monasticon*, vi. 419; *Religious Houses*, 138, 150.

[34] M. Beresford, *New Towns of the Middle Ages* (London, 1967), 462–3, 466–7, 504, 637–8. Land for New Buckenham itself was acquired from the bishop of Norwich on the Thetford to Norwich road.

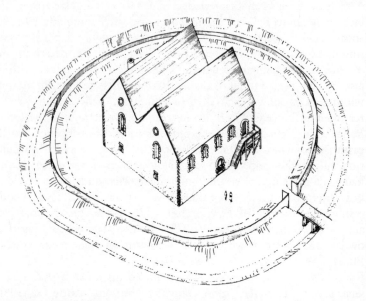

FIG. 2.3. Reconstruction of Castle Acre in the late eleventh century

FIG. 2.4. Reconstruction of Castle Acre during Stephen's reign

with sparing use of ashlar revealed by loss of the rendering is due to lack of good local stone, which may also explain the cylindrical shape. The habitual militarism about reduced vulnerability to mining and battery may certainly be disregarded.

Normal lordly castle-building, on excavated sites, is represented also by Brandon and Ascot Doilly, both smaller rectangular towers within earthwork enclosures, tentatively dated to the second quarter of the century.[35] Ascot, in the contentious Oxfordshire–Berkshire region, is one of several 'keeps' built up with mounded earth to the ground storey forming an enmotted tower. Its destruction has inevitably been attributed to Henry II. Brandon's 'keep' had a plinthed base ornamented by a decorative string course. New but 'early' castles tend doctrinally to be dated to Stephen's reign, but the probability is that aristocratic construction continued almost normally, and that the reign possessed a certain style of its own. When new or rebuilt castles occur in royal donations, as New Buckenham does and Gainsborough in favour of William de Roumare, analysis should precede the inferring of any licence.[36] That major rebuilding was known to the county community and thence to the king, and that confirmation of the privileges of the *caput* might be sought then, would be entirely natural.

To all this, the fieldworks of campaigns and sieges, essential to warfare, stand in some contrast. Positive identifications are few, but possibles, mostly slight ringworks or almost imperceptible mottes and enclosures, have been excavated at Bentley and Powderham (Hampshire), possibly attributable to Henry of Blois's siege of his own castle of *Lidelea*. Others considered by D. F. Renn include two near Arundel, Castle Cary, Corfe, Coventry, Cricklade, Harptree, Hereford, Lincoln (two), Ludlow, Oxford, and the Wallingford group. Seignorial and 'unofficial' works by emergent individuals, aspiring to permanency, may be represented by Peter of Goxhill's *capitalis curia* and by Cuckney. Therfield may be one, being of hasty construction and incomplete. Deddington, also excavated,

---

[35] Kenyon, *Medieval Fortifications*, 40–1, 43. No correlation with hostilities can be seen. Other suggested Stephanic foundations and additions are Aldingourne, Bedford, Benington, Bungay, Carisbrooke, Carlisle, Castle Cary, Christchurch, Guildford, Mileham: (Renn, *Norman Castles*, 46–8 and gazetteer). David of Scots' Carlisle is elusive.

[36] *RRAN* iii, no. 494 (cf. Round, *Geoffrey*, 159–60); also Bishopton, '1143' after John of Hexham: Renn, *Norman Castles*, 51, 111.

was an embanked Saxon residence, later perhaps a castle of Odo of Bayeux and possibly refortified in stone by Stephen's Oxfordshire captain William de Chesney.[37] Individualism, stimulated by the relaxing of social constraints, unaccustomed—as the chroniclers in 1153–4 suggest—but scarcely unlawful, must have affected castle-building; but exactly how remains uncertain.

Geoffrey de Mandeville's charters are firmer ground. Since magnates were entitled to fortify in their own land and honour, his insecurity in Essex as earl, obliging him to make accessories of each *de facto* ruler in turn, explains his 'licences', as does their context. His titular position was confirmed by the empress 'about midsummer' 1141, with hereditary custody of the White Tower and of 'Ravenger's little castle' ('with the castle nearby' in her second charter).[38] These he might munition (*infortiare*) for her. When the citizens had expelled the Angevins from the city and from Westminster, this provision had to be more emphatic; so, by the empress's late-July charter, Geoffrey might hold the Tower, *ad firmandum et efforciandum ad voluntatem suam.* The empress also promised to make no separate accord with the Londoners, 'seeing that they are his mortal enemies' (surely Geoffrey's own words). If he has to defend the Tower, she, in effect, accepts the consequences. The latent royal licensing prerogative is not invoked. She recognizes his gains, including 'his castles which he has', which 'shall stay and remain to him', with the normally superfluous 'to be munitioned at his discretion'. Saffron Walden was one such castle, with its early motte and bailey, now almost obliterated, and its large but roughly built square flint-rubble 'keep' upon and within the motte. Geoffrey can hardly have had facilities or time to build it. He had also the ancient castle of Pleshey, with its baileys and *burgus.* Any other castles he claimed, or fieldworks thrown up for his contest with Blois partisans based in East Anglia, and perhaps his 'castle on the river Lea' mentioned in late-July, might be covered; but the eloquent irregularity of it all contrasts starkly with the correct but perfunctory licence to transplant his market from Newport 'into his castle of Walden'. He too desired the enhancement of his capital complex of donjon, baileys, and *burgus* with the

---

[37] Kenyon, *Medieval Fortifications*, 10, 24, 31–3, 58–9; Renn, *Norman Castles*, 162–3.
[38] *RRAN* iii, nos. 274, 275; Davis, *Stephen*, 55–6, 57–8, 77–82, 157–60.

profits and public quality of a market. The worsened military position after the Londoners' revolt and the Angevins' flight to Oxford required Geoffrey to be confirmed in his father's and grandfather's tenures in the full panoply of established lordship, *in terris et turribus, in castellis et bailliis*. The empress undertook to make the bishop and cathedral clergy of London yield to Geoffrey the irksomely positioned castle of Stortford; and, if they refused, she would seize it and 'make it collapse and entirely fall'. The first licence to fortify two new castles follows; one retrospective, the other at a site not yet chosen by Geoffrey but still *in terra sua*, which he took as previously granted.[39] The diagnostic 'stay and remain' and 'for him to munition at his will' are reiterated, providing some colour of legality to endue his gains with permanency, while sanctioning violence with some show of propriety.

Whereas hints of hostilities in the Chester–Leicester pact, so greatly illuminated by Edmund King, are standard formulae of feudal antiquity, Geoffrey's *stet et remaneat* and the munitioning clauses are one with that disingenuous deal to eliminate Bishop's Stortford castle. A straightforward warrant to take and hold in fief, as in earlier thirteenth-century Ireland, was doubtless too blatant. Stephen could not endorse it, but based his charter closely on his rival's, her *turris Lundonie cum castello quod subtus est* becoming his *cum castello quod ei subest*; and her 'licence' being reworded as *preterea firmiter ei concessi ut possit firmare quoddam castellum ubicumque voluerit in terra sua, et quod stare possit*. Ratifying usurpation required both emphasis and caution. The castle *super Luiam* was left out, and Geoffrey's opportunities generally had shrunk. Neither he, in 1143, nor others could resist arrest and extortion of their castles by Stephen's crafty breaches of the

---

[39] The *sicut ei per aliam cartam meam concessi* are nominally the empress's words. Foundations 'tentatively identified as a defensive tower and stair-turret and dated to the mid-twelfth century', discovered at Pleshey, and remains of the keep and market emplacement at Saffron Walden, may relate: F. Williams, *British Arch. Reports*, 42 (Oxford 1977); S. R. Bassett, *Council for British Archaeology Research Report*, 45 (London 1982). 'Ravenger's little castle' is elusive: R. A. Brown, H. M. Colvin, A. J. Taylor, *The History of the King's Works*, ii (London, 1963), 707 n. 3; G. Parnell, *Trans. London and Middlesex Arch. Soc.* 36 (1985), 14, 23–5; and ibid. 33 (1982), 120. The 'castle on the Lea' could be Hertford, or one of two possible sites near Bow Bridge, or in Luton. His association with South Mimms is purely conjectural: Round, *Geoffrey*, 336–7 n. 7; J. Dyer *et al.*, *The Story of Luton* (Luton, 1964), 54–7, 63–4; J. P. C. Kent, *Bull. of Barnet and District Local Hist. Soc.* 15 (1968).

conventions of hospitality, which may have aborted castle-based revolts but generated fatal mistrust. A man of Geoffrey's stamp was forced into savage frustration. The moated sub-rectangular platform at Burwell where he was killed, built on the margin of the Fens near Cambridge, probably one of the fieldworks Stephen erected to house the troops checking his piratical operations, affords but weak witness of his name (see Pl. IV). The Peterborough chronicler's lurid passage, probably the most influential specimen of the castrophobic writing of the time, is Geoffrey's most eloquent memorial.[40]

Earl Ranulf's charter for Lincoln castle, probably of 1146 just before his own arrest, also gives no support to any practice of Anglo-Norman royal licensing of fortification. It is a specious guarantee of possession of the castle, city, and constableship, akin to the licence for the city-castle of Rochester in 1127. Both show the possessory aspects of 'fortifying' and hinge on tenure in fief of a *turris* within a royal castle held in 'perpetual' custody. It appears Ranulf obtained it to revive his claim by his late mother, Countess Lucy, to the castellanship, using the feudal leverage of his Norman lands lost in the Angevin conquest; and, since Stephen cherished Lincoln, to secure the eventual reversion of the castle and lands of Tickhill. Stephen's concessions were of expediency, as Ranulf surely knew. No resultant construction is likely, nor is any now visible or known from excavation. The charter, surviving only in a summary of 1325, provides for Ranulf, pending receipt of Tickhill, to munition (*firmare*: basically 'to establish'), and have *dominium*, over and above his custody, of one of the two tower-crowned mottes (*unam de turribus suis*). This motte, for its symbolism and other reasons, was probably the *motte-maîtresse* of c.1068, now distractingly known as the Lucy Tower. Stephen's loyal city, which he lost his liberty in February 1141 trying to regain, Ranulf was to hand over, with the *turris*, in return for his lands in Normandy 'with all his castles'.[41]

Stiff local competition came from Bishop Alexander's aggrandis-

[40] Quoted Davis, *Stephen*, 80. Burwell and other comparable local sites have been investigated: T. C. Lethbridge, *Proc. Cambridge Antiquarian Soc.* 36 (1936) 121–33; A. E. Brown, C. C. Taylor, ibid. 67, 97–9 and ibid. 68, 62–5. I have to thank Derek Renn for references in this and the preceding note.

[41] *RRAN* iii, no. 178; Davis, *Stephen*, 46–50, 88–94, 161–5; Renn, *Norman Castles*, 226–7.

ement of the complex of cathedral, palace, and precinct close by. In 1133 the bishop had annexed the city's East Gate and tower by royal licence. Further expansion was authorized in 1155–8, mainly by taking land from the city and breaching its ancient walls to extrude the intended eastern arm.[42] The castle must already have suffered some eclipse. Ranulf had seized it by a trick in 1140, which Stephen initially condoned and then tried to reverse. Although he had recognized Ranulf's title to 'the constableship of the castle of Lincoln and of Lincolnshire by hereditary right', the security of having, in full right as heir, *turris sua quam mater sua firmauit* was a natural demand. Although the Lucy Tower has since the eighteenth century at least been the 'shell-keep' upon the principal motte, and the name existed in 1225, excavation of the substructure of the smaller south-eastern mound has shown that this is the addition. Beneath the early nineteenth-century observatory, a rectangular masonry core infilled with mortared boulders was discovered, around which the earth had been heaped, making a foundation of the type at Farnham and Ascot Doilly. Upon it, finer twelfth-century and later masonry indicated a fashionable enmotted stone tower, which the excavator attributed to Ranulf, in the belief that the charter was permission to build a new tower.[43] Lucy might have had the base erected before she died *c.*1136, and perhaps a timber superstructure. Her son could have added to it, but work by either is unlikely on the Conqueror's motte, where the munitioning of temporary ownership is Ranulf's likely 'fortification'. At Rochester the archbishops after William of Corbeil long kept their 'great tower' and their custody, but Ranulf by his arrest shortly afterwards lost both his mother's tower and all his rights in Lincoln castle.

One pseudo-licence, for Berkeley in 1153, remains for discussion. As a castle-pact the Berkeley charter is significant, even though it does not incorporate any licence to fortify, despite the *Regesta* headline and index.[44] Duke Henry did not actually 'grant the Manor of Bitton and £100 of land in Berkeley with permission

---

[42] *RRAN* ii, no. 1784; *Calendar of the Charter Rolls* 4 (1912), 106–12; C. L. H. Coulson, 'Hierarchism in Conventual Crenellation', *Medieval Archaeology*, 26 (1982), 69–100 (at 75).

[43] N. Reynolds, 'Investigations in the Observatory Tower, Lincoln Castle', *Medieval Archaeology* 19 (1975), 201–5.

[44] *RRAN* iii, no. 309.

to build a castle there', but rather promised 'to fortify a castle at Berkeley to Robert fitz Harding's requirements'.[45] Henry had just landed at Wareham and bought the adherence at Bristol of the *parvenu* heir-by-marriage to this small but crucial motte-and-bailey castle on the road to Gloucester. The structural improvements show how much he valued both, and suggest that Robert was quite demanding. Some of the early Berkeley documents have been tampered with, but this one rings true,[46] being a guarantee by the leading Angevins of active support in return for Robert's homage. Had the conflict with King Stephen lasted longer, further similar pacts might have arranged a series of defensive outposts to Bristol and the empress's redoubt of the south-west. As it is, the good quality plinthed revetment encasing the scarped motte, embellished with three semi-cylindrical turrets and, not much later, by a forebuilding and ramped ceremonial stairway approximating to the increasingly fashionable 'tower-keep', testify to fitz Harding's adroit opportunism. Henry II, whom the 'feudal-anarchy' school has praised for striving with conscientious altruism against all 'private castles', may have anticipated his reign by building one himself.

Fieldworks once abandoned quickly perished, leaving faint traces, unlike the concrete, brick, and metal debris of modern war. Little can have been left for Henry II to clear up. His destructions recorded as paid for differed entirely in target and in motive. Henry of Winchester's castles were slighted, and those of his nephew William of Boulogne were seized. Punishment was the common denominator.[47] Castle-polemic has scored a famous victory for the churchmen over the 'castle-men'. Clerical self-interest and royalism have since triumphed. Expectations of licences to fortify after 1154 are in reality still less fulfilled than during the anarchy or before it, for Henry II issued none which can be substantiated; nor did Richard I. They begin with one by John (*c.*1194) as count of Mortain, for the walling of the house of a partisan at Haddon. His series of licences as king, aborted in 1204, begins with Wheldrake near York (1199), perhaps the Stephanic

---

[45] As noted by Renn, *Norman Castles*, 107–8, and King, *Castellarium Anglicanum, sub* Gloucestershire.

[46] On the authenticity of these charters, see further Ch. 9 n. 58.

[47] Brown, 'Castles 1154 to 1216', 250–3; Pounds, *Medieval Castle*, 31; William of Newburgh's *complanare* (above, n. 3) is as exaggerated as the rest.

castle.[48] The citizens seem to have outbid the grantee, Richard Malebisse. The grant is not enrolled and Howden says it was promptly revoked, a significantly solitary reference.

That organized warfare and consequential disorder in parts of England, not castles, were the problem of the anarchy hardly requires demonstration. Keeping castles on a war-footing, whether in defence or aggressively, so that the normal skeleton estate staff was enlarged to the extent of 'garrisoning', and the lord with his 'riding household' based himself there, was exceptional and expensive. Analysis of all references to castles in the sources might offer some hint as to how commonly this was done in contested and lawless zones. Established castles—being, at diverse levels of noble society, *inter alia* country mansions, estate offices, farmsteads, hunting lodges (with park and warren), court-houses, and gaols, with widely varying emergency capacities for defence if adequately stocked and manned—had 'permanent' status, unlike purely military fieldworks. Regular castle-building by episcopal and lay magnates continued little affected, producing noble capital-seats, no more overtly 'military' but as ostentatiously palatial and 'fortified' as before and since. Bishop Alexander's Banbury has gone, but traces of his rectangular, towered and moated Sleaford remain, logically laid out, as is Bishop Roger's Sherborne, with its central rectangular keep and small mural turrets to the curtain wall. Bishop Henry may have added a large keep to Taunton, and his Farnham must have been an impressive sight. His palatial castle of Wolvesey boasted a square dwelling tower ('keep') and excellent sanitary arrangements (see Fig. 2.5). Systematic survey and some bold redating would greatly strengthen the 'normal' contingent and extend its social range, provided 'anarchic' expectations are neutralized. But categories of 'warlike' and 'normal' castle-building (already problematic) will remain archaeologically unsubstantiated, even were generous excavation funding available. Very many lesser gentry-seats, some at least still administratively and residentially active and needing only to be refortified, manned, and stocked, will be among the 'normal' castles. These, the vast majority, products of the Norman settlement, differ radically from the crisis-only fortifications, mostly fieldworks serving the passing needs of a campaign. They also differ significantly from any new

---

[48] Brown ('Castles 1154 to 1216', 251 n. 10) claims a licence 1160–1180 for Pleshey; also 279 n. 8; *Historical MS Commission, Rutland MSS*, iv. 24; Howden, iv. 117.

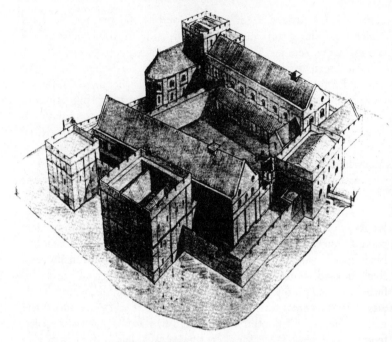

Fig. 2.5. Wolvesey Palace, Winchester

castles, permanently intrusive in intention, which the 1153–4 comments have been taken to imply. Archaeologically the two are virtually inseparable, nor can either usually be distinguished from sub-manorial farmsteads, especially if short lived. All of these diverse forms might be 'castles', as we have seen.

It has been the argument of this chapter that, with due allowance for necessary conjecture, the better-recorded fieldwork castles matter chiefly for the military history of the anarchy, of which they were the most durable symptom. The new and 'unprecedented' castles, which the traditional view has determinedly emphasized—whether brigand lairs, which could only slightly increase the predatory potential of lawless men, or, maybe, the aspiring lordship seats of 'feudal lawlessness', carved out of the confusion by genuine acts of usurpation—should both, more objectively, be regarded as the inevitable reaction of an acquisitive noble society to the state-sponsored turmoil and governmental abdication which was the anarchy of King Stephen's reign.

3

NORMANDY

Marjorie Chibnall

IN Round's massive book on Geoffrey de Mandeville, some 450 pages long, less than a dozen are concerned, even peripherally, with Normandy. Round's interest, if interest it can be called, was exclusively in Geoffrey of Anjou's claim to be in any sense the heir of his father-in-law, Henry I. His position is summed up at the outset: was the succession vested in the Empress Matilda, 'in accordance with our modern notions', or in her husband, 'in accordance with feudal ones', or in her son, 'as in the event it was'?[1] He considered that Geoffrey renounced any claim he might have had to England when in 1142 he declined to come to the support of his wife and sent his son instead, and to Normandy when he invested his son with the duchy after unsuccessfully calling on Stephen to 'give up his ill-gotten duchy' in 1148.[2] These are undeniably questions of importance. But on the fighting in Normandy, on the work of both the empress and Geoffrey in establishing a base from where they might launch an attack on England, on the effect that the Norman and French interests of the Anglo-Norman baronage had on their loyalties during the years of struggle, he is almost entirely silent. The fact that Geoffrey completed the conquest of Normandy and took the title of duke in 1144 is mentioned only in passing, in relation to the possible dating of young Henry's charters as 'son of the duke of Normandy'.[3] The key fortress of Argentan, where Matilda first secured a foothold just after her father's death, is never mentioned; the castles of Caen and Rouen are discussed

I am particularly grateful to Professor Edmund King for his helpful suggestions and comments.

[1] Round, *Geoffrey*, 33.   [2] Ibid. 259.   [3] Ibid. 418.

only in relation to the terminology used to describe castles.[4] And there is nothing on the wealthy citizens of Rouen, whose loans helped to finance the Angevin cause. On these subjects a hundred years of research call for a drastic revision of the reign of Stephen.

Even the question that seemed to Round to be worth asking needs to be rephrased. It is anachronistic to speak of the succession at this date 'being vested in' anybody. We may, however, ask who was—or who was thought to be—the rightful heir of Normandy when Henry I died? The king himself never made his intentions entirely clear. Like his Norman predecessors, he had a distinct preference for maintaining the integrity of the Anglo-Norman realm; like them, he too was hampered by circumstances. However great the power of the duke of Normandy, the duchy was a part of the realm of the French king, and the duke owed allegiance to him.[5] Since Louis VI had supported the claims of Robert Curthose, Henry's own position in the early part of his reign was insecure. After Louis had been beaten to his knees at Brémule, he was obliged to accept the homage of Henry's son, William Atheling, in 1120;[6] but the uneasy friendship broke down when William was drowned a few months later, and Louis soon began to give open support to Curthose's son, William Clito. Henry himself never did homage, even in the Marches; nevertheless he continued to call himself duke of Normandy.[7] In 1128 Clito died in battle just a few weeks after the marriage of the Empress Matilda to Geoffrey of Anjou; but Henry was apparently content to leave the question of homage in abeyance. At that date it was unprecedented for a woman to do homage to the French king;[8] but Geoffrey could

---

[4] Round, *Geoffrey*, 331, 333–6.

[5] For an account of the relations between the dukes of Normandy and the kings of France, see Hollister, *Anglo-Norman World*, 15–57; J.-F. Lemarignier, *Recherches sur l'hommage en marche et les frontières féodales* (Lille, 1945), 73–96.

[6] Hollister, *Anglo-Norman World*, 39–40.

[7] Although Henry added the ducal title only exceptionally in his early charters, the legend on the equestrian side of the seal he used from *c.*1120 was *Henricus Dei gratia dux Normannorum*: P. Chaplais, 'The Seals and Original Charters of Henry I', *EHR* 75 (1960), 260–75 (at 265).

[8] Later, in exceptional circumstances, a woman might sometimes perform homage. In July 1199 Eleanor of Aquitaine did homage formally to Philip Augustus for Aquitaine; a few days later she granted her domains to her son John and received his homage for them: J. C. Holt, 'Aliénor d'Aquitaine, Jean sans Terre et la succession de 1199', *Cahiers de civilisation médiévale*, 29 (1986), 95–100 (at 96–7); *Œuvres de Rigord et de Guillaume le Breton*, ed. H. F. Delaborde (Paris, 1882–5), i. 146. This, however,

have acted on her behalf in anticipation of ultimately holding the duchy *iure uxoris*. Henry never attempted to seek this solution.[9] Perhaps he hoped that a son of the marriage would be old enough to act before his own death; though, since young Henry was not born until 1133, when Henry himself was 65, this suggests a blinkered approach to the inescapable fact of his own mortality. And, because no understanding on the question of the succession was reached with the French king, it was only to be expected that Louis would, whenever he had the power, be ready to foment trouble in Normandy to his own advantage, and to press his claims to receive homage from the man he chose to recognize as duke.

The Angevin marriage alliance also caused complications in relations with other French magnates. 'Strangely enough,' wrote William of Malmesbury of Henry I, 'that great man . . . always regarded the power of the Angevins with suspicion. For this reason he married his daughter to the son of Fulk', count of Anjou.[10] In so doing, he also married her (though William did not add this) to the traditional rival of the man who had been one of his staunchest allies in France, Theobald, count of Blois, the son of his sister Adela.[11] The ambitions of the counts of Blois in the Touraine had been thwarted by the counts of Anjou, and Theobald had an interest in recovering full authority in the region.[12] He can hardly have viewed the prospective union of Normandy and Anjou with equanimity, and he was under no obligation to Geoffrey and Matilda, for he had taken no oath to recognize Matilda's right of succession, as had King Henry's vassals, both before and after her marriage. To this must be added Henry's failure either to clarify the status of his son-in-law (to whom no oaths had been taken), or to allow his daughter to occupy the frontier castles of her dowry during his lifetime. Geoffrey clearly fretted in his anomalous position, and it

was a formal act of homage over sixty years later, necessary to secure her son's succession to the duchy she held by hereditary right under a new king.

[9] Chibnall, *Matilda*, 55–7.   [10] WM *HN* 2–3.

[11] J. Gillingham (*The Angevin Empire* (London, 1984), 6–7) has pointed out that in the eleventh and early twelfth centuries the traditional rivals of the counts of Anjou had been, not the dukes of Normandy, but the counts of Blois and Champagne.

[12] The Touraine had been held by the counts of Anjou since its capture by Geoffrey Martel in 1044; see Olivier Guillot, *Le Comte d'Anjou et son entourage au xie siècle*, 2 vols. (Paris 1972), i. 282–3 and n. 5; L. Halphen, *Le Comté d'Anjou au xie siècle* (Paris 1906), 48–9.

contributed both to a quarrel that nearly broke the marriage in its early days, and to a fatal dispute with his father-in-law in 1135.[13]

Robert of Torigny's account of the breach, though compressed and not entirely clear, shows that both fealty and the holding of some border castles were involved.[14] Argentan was the most important of the castles assigned to Matilda's dowry; Henry busied himself with fortifying it, but kept it in his own hand. A cause of the quarrel, Torigny alleged, was that the king would not agree to do fealty to his daughter and her husband for all the castles of Normandy and England when they asked for it. This cannot be true as it stands; but perhaps Geoffrey demanded that he and his wife might be put in possession of the castles of her dowry, and that Henry's Norman vassals should swear fealty to Geoffrey. The result of the quarrel was that hostilities broke out on the southern frontier of Normandy, with which Geoffrey and his wife were occupied when Henry died at Lyons-la-Forêt on 1 December 1135. Stephen, at Boulogne, was much better placed to make a dash for Winchester and seize the Crown.[15]

Normandy played a part in the decision of the Anglo-Norman magnates to accept Stephen's *coup*. They had never been more than lukewarm about the Angevin marriage, and, though they had sworn to accept Matilda and her heirs, they had taken no oath to Geoffrey.[16] No narrative source suggests that they ever contemplated inviting him to receive their homage for their Norman lands; indeed their thoughts turned, it seems, towards Stephen's elder brother, Theobald of Blois. Then, when news of Stephen's coronation reached them, they resolved to accept him as duke of Normandy, in order to keep their Anglo-Norman inheritances intact.[17] There was at first very little resistance to Stephen in Normandy itself. Rabel of Tancarville, King Henry's chief chamberlain in Normandy, for a time held Lillebonne and his other castles—an isolated pocket of resistance for a year and a half.[18]

---

[13] Chibnall, *Matilda*, 57–62.   [14] RT 128.

[15] See Hollister, *Anglo-Norman World*, 145–69 (at 162–3).

[16] For accounts of the oaths taken to Matilda, see JW 22–3; SD ii. 281; WM *HN* 3–5, 15–16; Hollister, *Anglo-Norman World*, 154–6.

[17] OV vi. 454–5; RT 128–9. Orderic put the meeting at Neubourg, Torigny at Lisieux.

[18] OV vi. 482–5; RT 132. Rabel appears to have made his peace with Stephen and been reinstated as chamberlain in 1137; Stephen's charter to Sainte-Barbe-en-Auge was

And within a year Baldwin de Redvers, the only magnate of the first rank in England never to do homage even conditionally to Stephen, was driven out of his English estates and forced to retreat to his lands in the Cotentin, where he became a centre of disaffection for other dispossessed or discontented lords.[19]

The only strong point seized by the Angevins and never lost was Argentan. Matilda, on learning of her father's death, moved at once to take possession of her dowry. She was welcomed at Argentan by the castellan, Wigan the Marshall, as his liege lady, and with the support of her husband she kept one firm foothold on Norman soil.[20] Henry may have been niggardly in providing a territorial base for her in England,[21] but at least he had fortified Argentan so massively that it never fell. It was a necessary gateway from which the Angevins could enter Normandy in a series of invasions that at first failed to make lasting gains, but steadily eroded resistance. Other castles on the frontier of Normandy and in Maine were secured at the same time: Exmes, Domfront, Ambrières, Gorron, and Châtillon-sur-Colmont. Sées was temporarily occupied by Geoffrey and then lost. But Juhel de Mayenne, who was granted the castles in Maine on condition that he would help Geoffrey to secure the inheritance of his wife and her sons, gave loyal and steady support.[22] And Argentan stood out as a point of stability inside a turbulent frontier region.[23] The disputed inheritance, indeed, was only one element in the feuds and rivalries of the frontier lords.[24] Some of them had interests also in France; some had

granted *requisitione Rabelli de Tancarvilla camerarii mei: RRAN* iii, no. 749; see OV vi. 484 n. 1.

[19] Davis, *Stephen*, 22–4; OV vi. 510.   [20] Chibnall, *Matilda*, 66–7.

[21] In this he followed the example of his father; none of William I's sons received any substantial lands in the lifetime of the old king, and, though Robert Curthose had been invested with Maine and recognized as count of Normandy, one of his grievances was his lack of adequate resources. See C. W. David, *Robert Curthose: Duke of Normandy* (Cambridge, Mass., 1920), 18–19; F. Barlow, *William Rufus* (London, 1983), 34–5, 49.

[22] OV vi. 454–5; RT 128.

[23] Argentan indeed was well within Normandy, and provided a foothold in the duchy itself.

[24] Apart from the southern frontier, there were feuds along the border with Brittany, and Breton lords raided the region round Mont-Saint-Michel. The Vexin was a notoriously turbulent region: OV vi. 491–3; J. Green, 'Lords of the Norman Vexin', in J. Gillingham and J. C. Holt (eds.), *War and Government in the Middle Ages* (Woodbridge, 1984), 47–63.

extensive cross-Channel estates, which soon complicated their allegiance. Any lords disaffected with Count Geoffrey could join forces
with discontented vassals in Anjou, who had already given trouble
in 1129 and 1135.

The position of Theobald of Blois was complicated: as the elder
brother of Stephen, he may have resented being passed over, but as
count of Blois he wished to press his family interests. Whatever his
feelings, he was not a man to rush into action without deliberation.
About Christmas time 1135 he agreed to a truce with Geoffrey
which lasted until Pentecost.[25] His later refusal of the duchy of
Normandy when it was offered to him after Stephen's capture[26]
showed that he had no wish to become embroiled in the troubled
province. He seems deliberately to have chosen to act principally in
the interests of his own hereditary county of Blois.

Geoffrey could at least be sure of William Talvas of Bellême, to
whom he had restored some of his father's castles.[27] Initially this
may have caused the hostility of Rotrou of Perche, a traditional
rival of the Bellême for lands claimed by both families.[28] Rotrou
made his peace with Stephen in 1137.[29] The most continuing
frontier feud was that between the Tosny and the lords of Breteuil,
and in the early years of Stephen's reign the honour of Breteuil was
in ferment.[30] When Eustace of Breteuil, who had forfeited all the
honour except Pacy for his rebellion in 1119, died, his son William
of Pacy fought to recover his inheritance. Henry I, however, gave it
to Ralph of Gael, a descendant of William fitz Osbern, and gave
the hand of Amice, Ralph's sister and heir, to Robert, earl of
Leicester. He had, however, at the same time required Ralph to
grant Pont-Saint-Pierre and the lands of the Val de Pîtres, which
had come to the lords of Breteuil as dowry, to Ralph of Tosny; and

---

[25] OV vi. 454–5, 458–9.   [26] Ibid. 548–9.

[27] RT 128. Henry had confiscated all of Robert of Bellême's Norman lands in
1112, and Robert had passed the remainder of his life as a prisoner in one or other of
Henry's castles. The pipe roll of 1129–30 shows that he was then still alive (*PR 31
Henry I*, 12); it is possible that his death occurred three or four years later and that his
son William Talvas then claimed his paternal inheritance, including the castles in
Maine.

[28] OV ii, app. I; vi. 396–9.

[29] OV vi. 484–5. Orderic implies that Stephen bought Rotrou's recognition by lavish grants, including the castle of Moulins-la-Marche. Rotrou reverted to the Angevin
side after the battle of Lincoln: OV vi. 546–8.

[30] See Crouch, *Beaumont Twins*, 31–8, for an account of the frontier rivalries.

the powerful earl of Leicester wished to recover them. Ralph of Tosny made common cause with the dispossessed William of Pacy. The lesser vassals of the honour of Breteuil took advantage of the breakdown of order to fight for their own interests, as the unfortunate monks of Saint-Evroult, caught up in the midst of disorder and ravaging, learnt to their cost. Since the earl of Leicester and his twin brother, Waleran, count of Meulan, were committed to Stephen's cause, Roger of Tosny and his allies favoured the Angevins.[31]

The Beaumont twins belonged to the greatest of the cross-Channel families, and were in sharp contrast with the Tosny. The latter had carefully husbanded their Norman patrimony for some seventy years, and had used their English acquisitions to establish one branch across the Channel and provide generous endowments for their religious foundations.[32] The two branches were tending to go their separate ways. They were, therefore, unlikely to be troubled by divided loyalties if England and Normandy were in different hands. The cross-Channel links of the Beaumont family, on the other hand, had been (probably deliberately) strengthened by Henry I. Although Robert had inherited the bulk of the English estates and Waleran most of those in Normandy, Robert's marriage had brought him the honour of Breteuil, and Waleran had some lands in England even before Stephen gave him the earldom of Worcester. In Normandy he was the most powerful of all the magnates, and dominated the valley of the Seine. His position was potentially precarious, since he owed homage both to King Louis and to the duke of Normandy, and he needed to perform a very delicate balancing act. But, from 1135 until the battle of Lincoln and Geoffrey of Anjou's subsequent conquest of Normandy, the lords of all his lands were on friendly terms, and he was able to uphold Stephen's authority in the duchy.[33]

The greatest of the other magnates involved in cross-Channel loyalties were the earls of Chester and the lords of Roumare. When Richard d'Avranches, earl of Chester, was drowned in the *White*

---

[31] OV vi. 214 and n. 2, 250–1, 278–9, 330–1, 456–7.

[32] L. Musset, 'Aux origines d'une classe dirigéante: Les Tosny, grands barons normands du xe au xiiie siècle', *Francia*, 5 (1978 for 1977), 45–80. The De Courcy family similarly divided their lands between Normandy and England: Le Patourel, *Norman Empire*, 191.

[33] Crouch, *Beaumont Twins*, 29–38.

Ship in 1120, Henry I allowed Ralph of Briquessart, vicomte of Bayeux, to succeed to his cousin's lands,[34] and these passed to his son, Ranulf of Gernons. Ranulf's mother, the celebrated Countess Lucy, was also the mother (by an earlier marriage) of William of Roumare.[35] William's family's extensive patrimony lay in the Roumois, just west of Rouen; and the office of castellan of Neufmarché, which they had made almost hereditary, established them as important custodians of the Vexin frontier. William also secured some of his mother's English lands, though he had to rebel against Henry I to obtain them. As lord of the honour of Bolingbroke, he had a considerable interest in England ever before he was made earl of Lincoln by Stephen.[36] His foundation of the abbey of Revesby in England[37] suggests either a shift of interest to England or, perhaps as with the Tosny, a preference for using the acquisitions for benefactions, while husbanding the wealth of the Norman patrimony. But, notwithstanding the growing importance of William of Roumare's possessions in England, his roots in Normandy were strong: in 1137 Stephen relied on him to keep order, and he acted as justiciar for a time after the king's return to England in the autumn.[38]

Some lesser magnates were a potential source of support for the Angevins through their cross-Channel estates. Baldwin de Redvers, dispossessed in England and anxious to recover his estates, kept discontent simmering in the Cotentin until 1138. Aided by his friend Stephen of Mandeville and King Henry's bastard son Reginald of Dunstanville, he opened a kind of second front on the Channel coast.[39] The Cotentin and the Bessin were to provide a contingent of disinherited in England, who fought ferociously at Lincoln; it included Stephen's captor, William of Cahagnes.[40] Some other lords with divided interests avoided disinheritance more successfully. One was William of Moion (Mohun), lord of Dunster, who held estates balanced between Normandy and south-west England,

[34] OV vi. 308–9; *CP* iii. 166.   [35] Ibid. vii, app. J, 743–6.

[36] For William of Roumare, see F. A. Cazel, 'Norman and Wessex Charters of the Roumare Family', in P. M. Barnes and C. F. Slade (eds.), *A Medieval Miscellany for Doris Mary Stenton* (PRS NS 36, 1960), 77–88; OV vi. 322–4, 330; F. M. Stenton, *Facsimiles of Early Charters from Northamptonshire Collections* (Northants Rec. Soc. 4, 1930), 1–7; Davis, *Stephen*, 134–5.

[37] The foundation charter is printed by Stenton, *Facsimiles*, 2–4.

[38] Haskins, *Norman Institutions*, 127.

[39] *GS* 20–4, 29–30; OV vi. 511–12.   [40] HH 274; OV vi. 542–3.

where the Angevins were strong.[41] As for Hugh Bigod, his Norman
holdings were too modest in comparison with those in East Anglia
to swing his allegiance, and it is unlikely that he would have acted
very differently if he had possessed nothing in Normandy, but they
had the value of patrimonial lands.[42] His conduct might be
described not so much as sitting on the fence as keeping one hand
on it and vaulting lightly from one side to the other as his interests
dictated; like Moion, he was adroit enough to hold on to his
Norman lands while concentrating on enhancing his position in
England.

During the first phase of the conflict, Normandy was important
in providing a foothold from which further conquests could be
made, and a refuge where the disinherited might withdraw from
England and harass Stephen's supporters. That they acted as much
from self-interest as from any whole-hearted allegiance to the
Angevin cause did not reduce the value of their support for the
time being, and Count Geoffrey was astute enough to know how
to tempt them with grants that were often no more than temporary
expedients (as, indeed, Robert of Torigny recognized).[43] When
Stephen paid his only visit to the duchy in 1137, he gained some
advantage by securing the recognition of Louis VI, who received
the homage of his son Eustace, but he failed to pacify Normandy.
Indeed, some of the rivalries among his own supporters were
embittered during the campaign. Robert of Gloucester, never perhaps more than a nominal supporter biding his time, did not
return to England with the king, and in the spring of 1138 he
renounced his allegiance and joined forces with his half-sister the
empress at Argentan.[44] His presence put new heart into Count
Geoffrey's next campaign, though that too failed to make any permanent territorial gains. It also gave the Angevins new pockets of
support in Caen and Bayeux, and opened the way to their adherents in the Cotentin. Communication with England became easier,

[41] H. C. Maxwell-Lyte, *Dunster and its Lords 1066–1881* (Exeter, 1882), 1–3, 7; Le
Patourel, *Norman Empire*, 104 n. 1; *CP* ix. 18–19; *GS* 54–5, 85.
[42] *CP* ix. 580 and n. c; J. H. Round, *Family Origins and Other Studies* (London,
1930), 213; Chibnall, *Matilda*, 90; Davis, *Stephen*, 138–9.
[43] '[1154] Circa Pascha Henricus dux Normannorum transfretavit in
Normanniam, et coepit revocare paulatim et prudenter in ius proprium sua dominica,
quae pater suus, urgente necessitate primoribus Normanniae ad tempus concesserat'
(RT 179).
[44] OV vi. 484–5; RT 132; WM *HN* 23; Chibnall, *Matilda*, 73–4.

and in 1139 the Angevin counter-offensive across the Channel began.[45] With the empress in England, the conquest of Normandy was now left to her husband Geoffrey. This, in turn, was aided by Matilda's temporary triumph in England in February 1141.

Up to the last months of 1139 Waleran, count of Meulan and (by Stephen's grant) earl of Worcester, played a major part in leading the royalist campaigns in Normandy. Thereafter he was occupied, first with an embassy to Paris to make sure of the friendship of the new king, Louis VII, and then, from the spring of 1140, in England.[46] Evidently he had some responsibility for the defence of Normandy, since Robert Marmion, one of his principal tenants, replaced Richard de Lucy as castellan in Falaise. Throughout 1140 fighting in Normandy was limited and sporadic: attention had switched to England, and in the duchy the rival factions for the most part waited on events. Geoffrey returned once to the attack on Falaise, and, though he failed to take the castle, he captured Robert Marmion's castle of Fontenay-le-Marmion, just south of Caen.[47] His opportunity came with the capture of Stephen at the battle of Lincoln, which fatally weakened the resistance both of Stephen's vassals and of his allies in Normandy. Geoffrey at once renewed his attack, and Normandy began to have a new and important role in the struggle for the Crown.

During the months of Matilda's brief triumph as Lady of the English, Geoffrey established a stranglehold on Normandy that was never lost. He led his armies north and before the end of April had conquered the province as far as the Seine.[48] The Normans accepted him reluctantly; the brutality of his earlier campaigns had alienated men who had never shown much enthusiasm for an Angevin lord. Their first thought when Stephen was captured was to offer the kingdom and the duchy to Theobald of Blois; but Theobald was too prudent to become embroiled in the conflict,[49] and had his eye on the recovery of the lands in the Touraine that had been occupied by the Angevins in the eleventh century.[50] Moreover, his most serious concern was his worsening relations with the king of France, which within a year were to deteriorate

[45] Chibnall, *Matilda*, 74, 80–1.   [46] Crouch, *Beaumont Twins*, 35–8, 42–3.
[47] RT 139; OV vi. 426–7; cf. Crouch, *Beaumont Twins*, 130.
[48] OV vi. 546–51; RT 142.   [49] OV vi. 548–9.
[50] See Guillot, *Comte d'Anjou*, i. 282–3, 311–13, for the conquests of Geoffrey Martel.

into open war.[51] He renounced any claim he might have to
Normandy in favour of Geoffrey, provided Geoffrey would hand
over Tours to him and grant Stephen his freedom and former
lands. These terms were never fulfilled. Theobald remained free
to oppose Geoffrey, but for the moment he was as ready as the
greater Norman vassals for peace, and, with the assistance of
Rotrou of Perche, he negotiated a temporary truce. Robert, earl of
Leicester, crossed the Channel to secure the best possible terms for
himself and his brother Waleran,[52] and Geoffrey at once embarked
on a policy of temporary concessions to the greater vassals to
strengthen his grip on the duchy until he should be strong enough
to revoke them. So the great cross-Channel magnates were forced
to consider whether they could afford to continue supporting
Stephen and thereby lose their Norman patrimonies. This meant a
decisive shift in the balance of power between the king and the
empress.

Because his first task was to secure Normandy, Geoffrey refused
to join his wife in England. He continued mopping up operations,
and in June 1142 even persuaded Robert, earl of Gloucester, to
help in the capture of a number of castles in north-west
Normandy. His contribution to the war in England was to send
some knights and his eldest son Henry to England when Earl
Robert recrossed the Channel some three months later.[53] The fall
of Rouen in January 1144 marked his triumph in the duchy,
though Arques still held out for a time against hopeless odds. Until
Rouen fell he was not accepted as duke of Normandy by either the
king of France or the archbishop of Rouen;[54] nevertheless, from
1141 he had *de facto* authority. The greater Norman vassals made
their peace and did homage, and he was able gradually to impose
his authority on the bishops in the territory wholly under his control, notably the bishops of Lisieux and Sées.[55] He played his cards

[51] Relations between Louis VII and Theobald IV of Blois had never been cordial,
but in 1141 serious trouble began with a disputed election to the archbishopric of
Reims, when the king and the count supported different parties. The rift worsened
when Raoul of Vermandois repudiated his wife Leonora, who was Theobald's niece, to
marry the sister of the queen of France: JS *HP* 12–15. Louis's troops ravaged the lands
of Blois, and at one point the church of Vitry was burnt with about 500 people inside.
Reconciliation did not begin until 1144. See M. Pacaut, *Louis VII et son royaume*
(Paris, 1964), 42–5.

[52] OV vi. 548–9; RT 142.   [53] WM *HN* 72–4; Chibnall, *Matilda*, 116–17.
[54] Haskins, *Norman Institutions*, 128–30.   [55] See p. 109.

carefully until he had completed the conquest of the duchy and
been accepted as duke. Acceptance came first from the former vassals with most to lose. Waleran of Meulan, who submitted some
time in the summer of 1141, brought his immense power and
influence in the valley of the Seine and the Roumois; William of
Roumare and Waleran's kinsman Robert of Neubourg also made
their peace.[56] Waleran was received in Geoffrey's court and given
the hand of Agnes, sister of Count Simon of Evreux, in marriage.[57]
He was not able, however, to prevent his brother Robert's honour
of Breteuil being restored to William of Pacy.[58] His troops supported Geoffrey in 1143 and in the attack that led to the fall of
Rouen on 20 January 1144. The men and the wealth of Normandy
were not available to Stephen when, after his release in November
1141, he renewed his attack on the empress and her supporters in
England; castles changed hands there, but he was never able to
recover the territory at the heart of the Angevin resistance. Much
has been made of Stephen's attack on the bishops in 1139 as a
turning-point in his reign; it is equally or more arguable that, when
he abandoned Normandy to its fate in 1137, he fatally weakened
his position.

During the years that Geoffrey was winning the duchy and then
exercising full ducal powers, the question that interested Round
once again comes to the surface: *de facto* conquest apart, by what
right did he exercise his authority? What was the position of the
Empress Matilda and young Henry? Significantly, the names of
both Geoffrey and Henry first appear in Matilda's charters for
Geoffrey de Mandeville and Aubrey de Vere.[59] Of her three surviving writs for Normandy that possibly date before 1139, two are
addressed in her own name to officials of Argentan,[60] undoubtedly
hers by right, and the other (of more doubtful date) to the foresters
of Tinchbray.[61] By midsummer 1141 she was at the height of her
powers, but for a few months the right by which she exercised

---

[56] Crouch, *Beaumont Twins*, 51–4.   [57] Ibid. 52.

[58] Ibid. 55.   [59] *RRAN* iii, nos. 275, 634.

[60] Ibid., no. 567, Caen, AD de Calvados, A 5092, fo. 281 (discovered by monsieur
J.-M. Bouvris, and calendared with his kind permission in M. Chibnall, 'The Charters
of the Empress Matilda', in G. Garnett and J. Hudson (eds.), *Law and Government in
Medieval England and Normandy* (Cambridge, 1994), app. 1).

[61] Ibid., no. 805. The date of this writ is, however, uncertain; it might possbly be
1148, but 1138 is more likely: Chibnall, *Matilda*, 70 n. 29.

them was far from clear. When she first reached England, she spoke of herself in a charter for Miles of Gloucester as *justam heredem regni Anglie*;[62] since the charter concerned only England, the omission of any mention of Normandy is not significant. Once a substantial part of Normandy had fallen to the Angevins, the situation was different. Her first charter for de Mandeville was addressed to all her faithful men in Normandy as well as in England; in granting the justiciarship of Essex she referred to the pleas that pertain *ad coronam meam*.[63] This is the language of her father's royal chancery. In her second 'charter' (more accurately charter-treaty) to de Mandeville and her charter-treaty to Aubrey de Vere the grants included lands in Normandy, and the men were said to have entered into her husband Geoffrey's service; he is described, naturally, as count of Anjou.[64] Without here going into the question of how Matilda envisaged her authority in England, or interpreted her title of *domina Anglorum*, it seems likely that, for a time at least, she thought, in the terms of the somewhat vague oaths taken to her in her father's lifetime, of Normandy as part of her inheritance.

We should not read back into the second quarter of the twelfth century the more precise definitions of rights of inheritance that were worked out in both England and France in the course of the next century. It is at least noteworthy that after June 1141, when the empress was expelled from London and saw her hopes of ever wearing a crown beginning to fade, her son Henry begins to appear in her charters alongside his father. This change seems to have taken place in July 1141. In both the Bordesley charters he is mentioned as *heredis mei*.[65] He swore in the hand of Hugh of Ing to confirm the grants to Aubrey de Vere, made in late July 1141, as *filius filie Regis Henrici rectus heres Anglie et Normannie* and refers to the day when Earl Aubrey and his men *ad servicium domini mei Comitis Andegavie et mei adheserunt*.[66] At this date there was nothing unusual in the theoretical overlap of power between the ruler of

---

[62] *RRAN* iii, no. 391.

[63] Ibid., no. 274. The chroniclers showed a similar confusion about her status; William of Malmesbury (WM *HN* 54) said she was elected *Anglie Normannieque domina*.

[64] *RRAN* iii, nos. 275, 634. These charters and the Bordesley charters are discussed more fully in Chibnall, 'Charters of the Empress'.

[65] *RRAN* iii, nos. 115, 116. There is some doubt about the dating of these charters, but late July 1141 is the most likely date: Chibnall, 'Charters of the Empress'.

[66] *RRAN* iii, no. 635.

a duchy and his heir for some years before effective power formally changed hands. Robert Curthose had received the homage of the Norman magnates many years before his father's death, and was spoken of as count of Normandy, but his father continued to retain the title and all the powers and revenues of the duke. As in France, where the king's son might be crowned in his father's lifetime, the apparent overlap represented rather a recognition of a right to inherit than a transfer of power: an attempt to guarantee that order would not break down when the ruler died.[67]

Conditions in Normandy were complicated by the disputed succession; but it seems clear that, during the years when Geoffrey was conquering Normandy and gradually bringing his son Henry into the governance of the duchy, the Empress Matilda played no part in Norman affairs.[68] For most of the time her hands were full in England, where she remained until 1148; and she too began to involve Henry in her work. Some of her charters after 1141 had been addressed to her faithful men in Normandy, but from 1144 such an address occurs only in joint charters with her son Henry.[69] He was becoming slowly more active in Normandy. He issued several charters with his father,[70] and, when Duke Geoffrey gave a charter to the citizens of Rouen, Henry swore to observe the terms, which he later confirmed in a charter of his own.[71] Once Henry had been knighted at Carlisle by his uncle, David, king of Scots,[72] he began to be spoken of as duke, and it may well have been the knighting that marked the significant moment of change in the eyes of his father's vassals. In 1149 Arnulf, bishop of Lisieux, wrote to Robert Chesney, the new bishop of Lincoln, urging him to sup-

[67] The question is discussed by R. H. C. Davis, 'William of Jumièges, Robert Curthose and the Norman Succession', *EHR* 95 (1980), 597–606.

[68] J. Le Patourel ('Angevin Successions and the Angevin Empire', in M. Jones (ed.), *Feudal Empires, Norman and Plantagenet* (London, 1984), ch. IX, p. 14 n. 3) noted that she participated in two of Geoffrey's non-Norman acts. Her consent, with that of her three sons, was mentioned in two charters for Rouen and Mortemer: *RRAN* iii, nos. 559, 729.

[69] Ibid. nos. 43, 71 (this charter was issued in Normandy after Henry became duke, but during his father's lifetime). She issued no known joint charters with her husband.

[70] Haskins, *Norman Institutions*, 131–2; *RRAN* iii, nos. 780, 78, 79, 304; he was most usually associated with his father in privileges for the great abbeys such as Fécamp, Bec-Hellouin, and Saint-Wandrille.

[71] *RRAN* iii, no. 729.

[72] Chibnall, *Matilda*, 150. He was knighted on 22 May 1149.

port the cause of the young man whom he called *ducem nostrum cui ius successionis hereditarie regni vestre gubernacula debet.*[73] Shortly after his return to Normandy, Henry's father Geoffrey invested him with the duchy, most probably in December 1149 or January 1150,[74] though he had to wait over a year and a half for recognition by King Louis, who was absent on crusade. Whether or not Geoffrey then intended to withdraw completely from Norman affairs remains an open question.[75] We can be certain only that rights of succession at that time were more complex and fluid than Round assumed them to be.

The hard facts of pragmatic power, however, with which Round was far more familiar, meant that Normandy continued to have an important role in the succession to the whole Anglo-Norman realm after the death of Geoffrey de Mandeville, where Round's study ended. During the years from 1144, before young Henry came of age, Geoffrey of Anjou proved an able ruler of the province. He definitely made Rouen his administrative centre—a process already begun under Henry I.[76] The greater number of Geoffrey's charters for Normandy were issued at Rouen, and their language had the brevity and formality which characterized Norman writs and charters.[77] A central core of officials in his court and household acted only in Normandy; he seems to have adopted the practice he was to recommend to his son, of not transferring customs from one

---

[73] *The Letters of Arnulf of Lisieux*, ed. F. Barlow (CS 3:61, 1939), no. 4.

[74] Z. N. Brooke and C. N. L. Brooke, 'Henry II, Duke of Normandy and Aquitaine', *EHR* 61 (1946), 81–9.

[75] Le Patourel ('Angevin Successions', 13–15) raised the possibility that Geoffrey may not have given up the ducal title altogether in the last eighteen months of his life, and examined the scanty charter evidence. Geoffrey certainly helped his son in the fighting in Normandy in 1151: RT 161–2.

[76] In Henry's reign Rouen had been, with Caen, an important centre for the collection of revenue and the storing of treasure. It is probable too that the king was using the canons of the royal chapel of Saint-Cande-le-Vieux, Rouen, for the daily business of governance, in much the same way as the canons of St Martin-le-Grand in England: R. H. C. Davis, 'The College of St Martin-le-Grand and the Anarchy 1135–54', in Davis, *From Alfred the Great to Stephen* (London, 1991), 237–54. Haskins noted the exemption of the *dominica capellaria* of Saint-Cande from the diocese of Rouen, and its placing under the authority of the bishop of Lisieux, who at that time was King Henry's justiciar, John: *Norman Institutions*, 110; *Gallia christiana* (rev. edn., Paris, 1715–1865), xi. 42, 774.

[77] Haskins, *Norman Institutions*, 143–5.

province to another.[78] Geoffrey's chief innovation was the employ-
ment of *baillis* as officials under the vicomtes; they appear for the
first time in his charters, though they seem not to have had the
same importance as the *baillis* in Anjou.[79] He made some progress
too in restoring the ducal finances, and in enforcing the regular
collection of revenues. Judith Green has recently shown that,
although two or three local audits may have been carried out in the
early part of Henry I's reign, the appearance of a single exchequer
audit in Normandy cannot confidently be dated before his very last
years, if then.[80] Any exchequer court was probably too insecurely
established to survive the turmoil of the next two decades.

A series of charters for the hospital of Beaulieu de Chartres,
extending from the reign of Henry I to that of his grandson, is an
interesting barometer of financial changes during the anarchy.
Henry I granted the hospital an annual rent of ten livres in the
money of Rouen, to be paid from his treasury at Michaelmas,
when his farms and moneys were collected.[81] In 1137 Stephen
confirmed the grant in the same terms;[82] but in 1140, when
Normandy was slipping from his grasp, he ordered the payment of
the alms to be made from the mint at Rouen, not the treasury.[83]
This suggests that the regular collection of revenues had become
impossible, but that the mint was still working. When Henry
Plantagenet and his mother renewed the grant in 1150–1, the alms
were to be paid by the vicomte of Rouen out of the revenues of the
vicomté, at the Purification (2 February).[84] Their next charter, in
1154, repeated the charge on the *vicomté*, but restored the original
Michaelmas date.[85] A possible explanation of these variations is
that the financial system was in tatters when Geoffrey won the
duchy, and, although he succeeded during his years as duke in col-

---

[78] John of Marmoutier, *Historia Gaufredi ducis*, in *Chroniques des comtes d'Anjou et
des seigneurs d'Amboise*, ed. L. Halphen and R. Poupardin (Paris, 1913), 224.

[79] Haskins, *Norman Institutions*, 151–2.

[80] J. Green, 'Unity and Disunity in the Anglo-Norman State', *HR* 62 (1989),
120–3.

[81] *RRAN* ii, no. 1917; the place of payment was not named, but Haskins conjec-
tured plausibly that Rouen was intended: *Norman Institutions*, 106–7.

[82] *RRAN* iii, no. 69.   [83] Ibid. no. 70.

[84] Ibid., no. 71. Geoffrey of Anjou had previously made the vicomte of Rouen
responsible for other payments out of the ducal revenues, as a charter for the hospital
of Le Mont-aux-Malades at Rouen shows: ibid., no. 730.

[85] Ibid., no. 72.

lecting revenues from the vicomtes and prévôts, the farms and dues
were trickling in too slowly for any kind of reckoning at
Michaelmas. By 1152, however, there are signs of a revived
Michaelmas accounting at Rouen; and very likely there was also
one at Caen, which was later to become the seat of the exchequer
court.

Geoffrey's other success was with the Church. Although his handling of the two elections at Lisieux and Sées initially provoked the
wrath of both the pope and St Bernard, he succeeded in placating
both and in accepting the outward forms of election required by
canon law, while keeping intact the ducal rights claimed by his predecessor.[86] In 1147 he met Pope Eugenius III in Paris;[87] the reconciliation seems to have been complete, and it may have helped him
to secure the good offices of St Bernard as well as Suger when the
time came to negotiate the succession of his son Henry to the
duchy.[88] Such help was all the more necessary, because in 1150,
after King Louis had returned from the crusade, he invaded
Normandy to force Geoffrey to restore the castle of Montreuil in
Poitou, recently captured from Giraud de Berlai. During his campaigns Louis was joined by King Stephen's son Eustace to lay siege
to the castle of Arques.[89] The successful resistance of Geoffrey and
Henry, and Louis's own illness (which Robert of Torigny thought
providential), finally forced Louis to return to Paris, where a truce
was negotiated *sapientibus viris ac religiosis intercurrentibus,* as

---

[86] For the details of Geoffrey's relations with the Church, see H. Böhmer, *Kirche
und Staat in England und in der Normandie im xi und xii Jahrhundert* (Leipzig, 1899),
310–25; M. Chibnall, 'The Empress Matilda and Church Reform', *TRHS* 5:38
(1988); Haskins, *Norman Institutions,* 153–4.

[87] H. Gleber, *Papst Eugen III* (Jena, 1936), 71. A statement by John of Salisbury
(JS *HP* 44) has been taken to mean that Geoffrey met with persistent papal hostility.
John's comment, however, was a general one, thrown in after describing the unsuccessful embassy of Miles, bishop of Térouanne (probably in 1148, but conceivably earlier),
to charge Stephen with unjust usurpation. It combines a characteristic dig at the
avarice and cunning of the Roman curia with the statement that Geoffrey knew he had
offended the Roman church by not allowing the pope himself or any legate to enter his
lands; and it could have applied to the time before Geoffrey's reconciliation with the
pope. The reflective style of the *Historia pontificalis* shows John to have been more
concerned with explaining motive than with strict chronology. There are only three
dates in the work (ibid. 2, 52, 60), and two of them are wrong.

[88] Chibnall, *Matilda,* 153–4.

[89] For these events, see J. Boussard, *Le Comté d'Anjou sous Henri Plantagenêt et ses
fils (1151–1204)* (Paris, 1938), 69–71; Pacaut, *Louis VII,* 63; RT 160–2.

Toringy put it, no doubt with reference to Suger (until his death) and St Bernard.[90] In August 1151 Louis received Henry's homage as duke of Normandy, in Paris. Henry was obliged to accept the cession made by his father in 1144, which included Gisors and part or all of the Norman Vexin;[91] he probably intended even then to recover the lost territory as soon as possible. At least, when Geoffrey died a few weeks later, his son seemed to be firmly established as duke of Normandy.

Within a year, however, the whole structure of power in France had been transformed. A relatively small, but significant, change occurred when Count Theobald IV of Blois and Champagne died and his lands were divided between his three sons: Henry the Liberal, the eldest, received Trèves and Champagne, and Theobald V, Blois; Stephen, the youngest, was given some estates in Bourges.[92] The change of lordship meant that Henry Plantagenet should have done homage for the Touraine, as the counts of Anjou had done since the time of Geoffrey Martel; but, on the pretext that Theobald was unjustly withholding Fréteval, he refused it. He may have been encouraged by Sulpicius of Amboise, who was anxious to escape from his precarious position of owing homage to the counts of both Anjou and Blois for the castle of Chaumont, and was prepared to defy Theobald, with consequences which will be described later.[93] The major upheaval, however, resulted from the divorce of Louis VII and his wife Eleanor of Aquitaine; for within a few months, without asking the permission of the king his

[90] RT 162.

[91] There is some doubt over how much of the Vexin besides Gisors, Neaufle, and Dangu was ceded in 1144 and how much in 1151. J. Chartrou argues strongly that Geoffrey's cession in 1144 was partial, and that in 1151 he and Henry added the remainder of the Norman Vexin between the Seine, the Epte and the Andelle: Chartrou, *Anjou*, 72–3; Lemarignier, *L'Hommage en marche*, 45 and n. 53. Henry recovered the territory in 1160 as the dowry of Louis's daughter Margaret, who was betrothed to his son Henry in 1158 and declared of age in 1160: *Continuatio Becci* in RT 318; Pacaut, *Louis VII*, 63; W. L. Warren, *Henry II* (London, 1973), 71–2. Robert of Torigny alleged that Geoffrey's concessions had been a temporary expedient: he had ceded to Louis 'ad tempus, illam partem Wilcasini, que est inter Andelam et Ittam fluvium, quae ad ducem Normanniae pertinet' (RT 169). This was not the view of King Louis.

[92] RT 164.

[93] Boussard, *Comté d'Anjou*, 70–1; the position of Sulpicius is also discussed by J. Dunbabin, *France in the Making 843–1180* (Oxford, 1985), 231, 250, 334–5. See below, pp. 113–14.

suzerain, Henry Plantagenet married Eleanor and so acquired a title to her vast inheritance. Louis, outraged, at once attacked Normandy, and found support in Henry's younger brother Geoffrey, who considered, rightly or wrongly, that he had some claims to Anjou.[94] And the stability of Normandy was further threatened, since Count Waleran of Meulan, conscious of his French interests and never fully trusted by either Henry or Henry's mother the empress, was prepared to help the French in every way, short of actually taking the field against the duke of Normandy. In August 1152 he allowed Louis's armies to pass across the bridge at Meulan.[95] It was not until January 1153 that Henry felt just secure enough to cross to England and make a determined bid for the throne, after negotiating a truce with King Louis. Had he failed to make an impact in England, Waleran and the other Franco-Norman barons might definitely have thrown in their lot with the king of France. Then Normandy, which since 1141 had provided the firm base for the ultimate recovery of the whole Anglo-Norman realm by Henry Plantagenet, might have been lost.

In this final phase Henry relied greatly on his mother the empress to preserve the reality of central authority in Normandy. Permanently settled just outside Rouen, in Bec-Hellouin's priory of Le Pré, she brought her practical experience of administration and diplomacy to the task of providing a regency when Henry himself was out of Normandy.[96] Her role there was greater than it had been in her husband's lifetime; in some ways it resembled that of her formidable aunt, Adela of Blois, who had remained a power to be reckoned with in Blois and Champagne after her son, Count Theobald IV, came of age.[97] To be effective she needed the support of kinsmen and vassals, able to take the field if necessary. But, of her sons, Geoffrey was unreliable and William too young; and,

[94] Boussard, *Comté d'Anjou*, 69–70. Whether or not Geoffrey of Anjou intended his son Geoffrey to have Anjou if Henry won England, the younger Geoffrey's alliance with the French king on this occasion was two years before Henry's accession to the English throne. For a discussion of Geoffrey's intentions, see Hollister and Keefe, 'The Making of the Angevin Empire', in *Anglo-Norman World*, 265–6; Chartrou, *Anjou*, 85–6; Le Patourel, *Feudal Empires*, ch. IX; Warren, *Henry II*, 45–7; Chibnall, *Matilda*, 155 n. 65.

[95] Crouch, *Beaumont Twins*, 71, 74–5.

[96] Chibnall, *Matilda*, 158–9; L. Delisle, in *Actes de Henri II*, Introduction, 139, 169–70.

[97] See K. A. LoPrete, 'Adela of Blois and Ivo of Chartres', *ANS* 14 (1992), 131–52.

since her half-brother Reginald, earl of Cornwall, and two of the greater cross-Channel magnates (Ranulf of Chester and William of Roumare) were with young Henry in England, she was particularly sensitive to the manœuvres of Waleran of Meulan at a time when the situation in Normandy was precarious. She was accustomed to facing dangerous odds, but she had never before been so much alone. The one crumb of comfort was that there was no immediate threat on the western frontiers; Brittany, torn by a disputed succession after the death of Conan III in 1148, had troubles enough of its own.[98]

The complicated story of the foundation of the abbey of Le Valasse mirrors the uncertainties of those years in Normandy.[99] On Waleran's return from the crusade he had set about fulfilling a vow, made at a time of danger, to found a Cistercian abbey. The site he chose was at La Haye-de-Lintot, near to Lillebonne, where a part of the demesne of the counts of Evreux had been given to his wife as her dowry.[100] He bought out claims made by other religious, and approached Haimo, abbot of Bordesley in Worcestershire, for monks to form the nucleus of a new community. His motives may have been purely pious, but the proposed introduction of monks from Bordesley was at best tactless and may have had political undertones. For the empress had never conceded Waleran's right to found Bordesley out of royal demesne lands given to him by Stephen;[101] and his continued interest in the contested county of Worcester and the lands of the Seine estuary seemed to her to be a threat. She was not prepared to tolerate his establishment of a daughter-house of Bordesley in a sensitive region, and proposed instead to found a Cistercian abbey on the site herself, with monks brought from Mortemer, a Cistercian house founded by Henry I.

Difficulties of all kinds delayed the foundation of the abbey

[98] P. Galliou and M. Jones, *The Bretons* (Oxford, 1991), 193–4.

[99] For the complicated history of the foundation (or more strictly four foundations) of Le Valasse, see F. Somménil, *L'Abbaye du Valasse* (Rouen, 1868); Chibnall, *Matilda*, 183–7.

[100] La Haye-de-Lintot was one of the last fiefs acquired by the counts of Evreux in the honour of Gravenchon, and was carved out of the forest of Lillebonne: Jacques le Maho, 'L'Apparition des seigneuries châtelaines dans le Grand-Caux à l'époque ducale', *Archéologie médiévale*, 6 (1976), 5–148 (at 25–30).

[101] Chibnall, *Matilda*, 134–5; Crouch, *Beaumont Twins*, 39–40; for the situation in Worcestershire, see Davis, *Stephen*, 154–6.

until 1157.[102] Their interest here lies in their relevance to the greater struggle for power in Normandy. As long as the duchy was under threat from the king of France, Matilda would not hear of Haimo, abbot of Bordesley, being appointed abbot, and pressed the claims of Mortemer. Once Henry's position in England became more secure in the autumn of 1153, and Waleran's brother, Robert of Leicester, joined his adherents, she would have been prepared to welcome Haimo (though in fact, because the Cistercian statutes forbade an abbot to give up one abbey in order to receive another, he did not come). But the early months of the year were a time of crisis for her. There was no guarantee that the truce conceded by King Louis would last for long. Moreover, there was trouble in the Touraine. When Sulpicius of Amboise, castellan of Chaumont, refused homage to Theobald V of Blois, young Theobald launched an attack and took him prisoner with his sons. He died in captivity shortly afterwards. The exact course of events is difficult to reconstruct, since the only detailed source for this episode—the chronicle of the counts of Amboise—gives a version which is chronologically impossible.[103] It states that Henry Plantagenet led an expedition to rescue the sons of Sulpicius in August 1153, and was defeated in an engagement in which his brother Geoffrey was captured. This cannot be true, since Henry was in England at the time; if he was involved, the date must be after Easter 1154. There is another possibility, which would allow the date to be correct: that Geoffrey, not Henry, led the unsuccessful rescue expedition. We do not know precisely what the relations between the brothers may have been after their reconciliation in 1152, but Geoffrey was probably in Anjou during Henry's absence and, if he was given any responsibility, his failure in the Touraine would have provided Henry with either a justification or a pretext for not allowing him to have any further authority in Anjou after his own succession to the English throne. But, whatever the exact sequence of events, the threat from Blois certainly added to the problems of the Empress Matilda.

---

[102] For the troubled history of the foundation, see *Chronicon Valassense*, ed. F. Sommènil (Rouen, 1868), 8–9, 12–21; Chibnall, *Matilda*, 182–7, and for the part played by the abbey of Mortemer, see J. Bouvet, 'Le Récit de la fondation de Mortemer', *Collectanea Ordinis Cisterciensium reformatorum*, 22 (1960), 149–68.

[103] *Gesta Ambaziensium Dominorum*, in *Chroniques des comtes d'Anjou*, 127–31. Boussard (*Comté d'Anjou*, 70–1) gives the background to the struggle, but accepts the dating uncritically.

The disorders of the months of danger threatened the incipient foundation at Le Valasse. When the region was ravaged by a predatory neighbour, Matilda admitted that the monks of Mortemer would have to be withdrawn because she was powerless to help them.[104] Once Henry had returned, recognized as Stephen's heir, and had restored order in the Touraine, the crisis ended, and the foundation of the new house with a community of monks from Mortemer proceeded more smoothly. But during the years 1152–4, when Normandy was under threat from the king of France, the chequered history of the new house is a graphic commentary on the wider issue of the disputed succession.

Throughout the whole of Stephen's reign, Normandy was an essential element in the struggle for the succession, and it crucially influenced the course of events. The tense situation on the frontier of Normandy and Anjou when Henry I died in 1135 prevented Matilda and Geoffrey from forestalling Stephen's dash for the throne, and so gave him an initial advantage in what was to prove a bitter and protracted struggle. Nevertheless, the duchy gave them the means to mount a challenge. Until 1139 a base for the Angevins, where Stephen failed signally to establish order and gained only formal recognition from Louis VI, it became a springboard for the empress to carry her campaign to England. The conquest of the duchy by Geoffrey of Anjou, made possible by Matilda's brief triumph in England, brought an interlude of relative stability, thanks to Geoffrey's able governance and astute manipulation of his greater vassals. In Normandy young Henry learnt something of the art of government—and of manipulation. A certain number of the Norman members of his household were taken over from his father.[105] And the wealthy merchants of Rouen were able to provide some of the money needed for his later campaigns in England. The first pipe rolls of his reign show that money was being paid to the Rouen merchant, William Trentegeruns, most probably as repayment of loans made in the previous years.[106] These resources must have been particularly valuable before he succeeded, during his 1153 campaign in England, in tapping the

---

[104] *Chron. Valassense*, 14.

[105] The households of both Henry and his father are described in *RRAN* iii, pp. xxxiii–xxxix; and see Chartrou, *Anjou*, 101–11.

[106] *PR 2–4 Henry II*, 53, 60, 107, 178; and see Green, *Henry I*, 213.

wealth of the Bristol merchant, Robert fitz Harding.[107] The charters granted by both Geoffrey and Henry as dukes of Normandy to
the citizens of Rouen show the value both attached to the loyalty of
the city, and their wish to promote its prosperity.[108] One may well
ask whether, if Normandy had been lost in the years 1152–4,
Henry could ever have won England. Undeniably, he held on to
the duchy at a cost. It could be argued that too much ground had
been lost in the previous ten years for his victory to be more than
temporary. For the first time, in 1151, a duke of Normandy had
done homage in Paris to the king of France. Moreover, though
Henry was determined to restore the Norman frontier to the line
of the Epte, and succeeded in recovering the lost Vexin territory in
1160, King Louis and later his son were equally determined to
have it back one day. That, however, was for the future. In 1154,
less than a century after the conquest of England, Normandy still
remained the patrimony of the Norman kings and of a section of
the nobility that was far from negligible. Even in the face of the
increasing aggression of the French kings, the Anglo-Norman
realm was not yet ripe for dismemberment.

[107] For his career, see R. B. Patterson, 'Robert fitz Harding of Bristol', *Haskins
Society Journal*, 1 (1989), 109–22.
[108] *RRAN* iii, nos. 728–9.

4

CONTINUITY IN GOVERNMENT

Graeme White

STEPHEN'S government in England was severely criticized by those subjected to it. The Battle Abbey chronicler was one of many to complain:

Everywhere the whole liberty and prosperity of the country was thrown into confusion by malevolent men, who took advantage of the ingenuous and gentle king . . . In his time justice seldom prevailed, he who was strongest got most . . . Peace was driven out, everything lay open to plunder.[1]

Henry of Huntingdon was another:

Where the king spent Christmas and Easter is irrelevant, for now all that made the court splendid, and the regalia handed down from his predecessors of old, had disappeared. The treasury, left well filled, was now empty; there was no peace in the kingdom; everything was destroyed by slaughter, fire, and rapine.[2]

No scholar today would claim that the government collapsed as completely as these verdicts might suggest.[3] But there is room for further discussion about how far royal control was maintained under Stephen and about the extent to which the governmental

I am most grateful to several participants in the July 1992 conference at Battle for their advice and encouragement, and especially to Dr Judith Green and Professor Edmund King for helpful comment upon a draft of this paper.
[1] *Chronicle of Battle Abbey*, ed. E. Searle (Oxford, 1980), 142, 212, 238 (translation adapted).
[2] HH 267.
[3] e.g. Cronne, *Stephen*, 185–282; Warren, *Governance*, 89–103; Davis, *Stephen*, esp. 82–6.

style and administrative traditions of Henry I's reign were continued. Sketchy as the evidence is, enough survives on which to base
an argument, first, that an initial attempt to govern in the manner
of Henry I met with fair success down to 1140, and, secondly, that
recovery from less than total breakdown was already under way
before the end of the reign. Henry II's declared objective after his
accession was to restore the customs of his grandfather, but in his
early years as king he governed in many ways as Stephen would
have wished to, while also presiding over financial and judicial
reform, the pace of which quickened from 1163.

The suggestion has been made that, in the first few years of his
reign, Stephen consciously modelled himself on Henry I, and
much can be said in favour of this interpretation.[4] In his coronation charter of December 1135 Stephen deliberately posed as the
continuator of all that was best in the previous reign, confirming
the liberties and good laws which his uncle King Henry had given:
platitudinous, but a striking contrast to Henry's own coronation
charter, which had repeatedly rejected the evil ways of William
Rufus.[5] Moreover, in the details of government personnel and
practice, there was clearly an underlying concern for continuity,
expressed most obviously in the compilation of the *Constitutio
domus regis*: the fact that Stephen had this drawn up soon after
Henry I's death as a comprehensive guide to household arrangements strongly suggests a wish to maintain his predecessor's establishment.[6]

Indeed, the maintenance of the administrative traditions of
Henry I was the logical consequence of the survival in power of
Henry I's chief minister, Roger, bishop of Salisbury. Having played
a leading role in Stephen's advancement to the throne,[7] Bishop
Roger secured the treasurership and chancellorship for members of
his family, just as he had done in the 1120s for his nephew Nigel
and his protégé Geoffrey Rufus.[8] Of the people who served

---

[4] J. Bradbury, 'Early Years of the Reign of Stephen', in D. Williams (ed.), *England
in the Twelfth Century* (Woodbridge, 1990), 17–30.

[5] *RRAN* iii, no. 270; W. Stubbs, *Select Charters*, 9th edn. (Oxford, 1913), 117–19.

[6] 'Constitutio Domus Regis', in *Dialogus*, pp. xlix–lii, 129–35; cf. Green, *Henry I*,
26–7.

[7] E. J. Kealey, *Roger of Salisbury: Viceroy of England* (Berkeley, Calif., 1972), 154–9;
Hollister, *Anglo-Norman World*, 162–9.

[8] Green, *Henry I*, 160, 167, 263; Kealey, *Roger of Salisbury*, 159, 272–4.

Stephen in the period to June 1139, four of his nine known scribes, both known chamberlains, two of his six stewards, one of his two butlers, his marshal, and all four constables had previously served Henry I in these capacities.[9] Clearly there were some changes in personnel, such as the chamberlain William II Mauduit (not recognized in office) and the stewards Robert Malet, Robert fitz Richard de Clare, and Simon de Beauchamp (newly appointed).[10] But in general Stephen seems to have been content to leave the old guard in place, doing little to advance the careers of those who had served in his household before his accession: thus, Robert de Secqueville, his steward when he was count of Mortain, seems to have attested very few of his charters when he was king.[11]

In judicial administration, we cannot know how far the reforms promised by Stephen in his coronation charter—to combat sheriffs' sharp practices and to moderate financial penalties—were put into effect,[12] but royal justice itself seems to have been active in the early years of the reign and to have encompassed serious crimes, transgressions of royal rights, settlements between tenants-in-chief, and cases to which the king had been alerted, much as it had done under Henry I.[13] The claim by the prior of Holy Trinity, Aldgate, against the keeper of the Tower of London to part of the soke of the English cnihtengild, which had been brought to the notice of Henry I only to be delayed by his death, was heard before Stephen instead, in what appears to have been a council at Westminster sometime in 1136–7. The king issued a writ ordering the justice and certain burgesses of London to try the case, as a result of which the prior was vindicated through the oath of twenty-one burgesses.[14] The king was also present at a hearing in Oxford, not later than 1140, at which the burgesses acknowledged by sworn

---

[9] Scribes: Bishop's nos. X, XI, XIII, XIV; chamberlains: William de Pont de l'Arche, Aubrey I de Vere; stewards: Hugh Bigod, Humphrey de Bohun; butler: William d'Aubigny *pincerna*; marshal: John fitz Gilbert; constables: Robert de Vere, Miles of Gloucester, Robert d'Oilli, Brian fitz Count: *RRAN* ii, pp. ix–xvii; iii, pp. xiii–xxi; iv, 11; Green, *Henry I*, 226–81; T. A. M. Bishop, *Scriptores regis* (Oxford, 1960), 30.

[10] *RRAN* ii, pp. xi–xiv; iii. pp. xvii–xix; E. Mason, 'The Mauduits and their Chamberlainship of the Exchequer', *HR* 49 (1976), 3.

[11] *RRAN* ii, no. 1676; iii, nos. 234–5, 327, 550 (if variant spellings represent the same individual).

[12] *RRAN* iii, no. 270; HH 258; cf. Green, *Sheriffs*, 17.

[13] Green, *Henry I*, 102–3.   [14] *RRAN* iii, no. 506.

recognition the rights of St Frideswide's Priory in the city wall.[15] A dispute between the abbot and monks of Peterborough and the canons of Lincoln over land at Northorpe (Lincolnshire) sometime between 1136 and January 1141 was settled before him at Lincoln in favour of Peterborough.[16] And, as Henry of Huntingdon lamented, he held forest pleas at Brampton (Huntingdonshire) before the first year of his reign was over.[17]

As for justices acting on the king's behalf, the evidence is unsatisfactory: we cannot always be certain that a man addressed in a writ immediately before the sheriff, or named in a *nisi feceris* clause, was necessarily a local justice or the holder of a judicial commission. Nevertheless, from writs of 1141 at latest which imply that there was a judicial role to perform, we can compile a list to suggest royal justices at work in the early part of the reign in Essex, Herefordshire, Huntingdonshire, Kent, Lincolnshire, London, Northumberland, Rutland, Staffordshire, and Suffolk.[18] Given that the names include Miles of Gloucester and Payn fitz John, who had served the previous king as itinerant justices, and that three men— Miles of Gloucester, Adam de Beaunay, and Aubrey I de Vere— occur in more than one shire, there may be slight indications of judicial eyres. If so, they would appear, like those of Henry I, to have covered localized areas—Miles of Gloucester, for instance, near his territorial base in the Welsh borders and west Midlands; Adam de Beaunay in East Anglia.[19]

Scholars have increasingly drawn attention to the pressure brought by feudalists upon Henry I to intervene in their affairs, even where this impinged upon the jurisdiction of other court-holders. Such pressure certainly continued into the next reign. Stephen issued several prohibitions against impleading except in his

---

[15] *RRAN* iii, no. 637.   [16] Ibid., no. 656.   [17] HH 259–60.

[18] *RRAN* iii, nos. 318 (Essex: Henry of Essex, Adam de Beaunay), 382 (Herefordshire: Miles of Gloucester, Payn fitz John), 883 (Huntingdonshire: Aubrey I de Vere, William Merk or Martel), 143 (Kent: Aubrey I de Vere *et justic' mea*), 466 (Lincolnshire: *sicut eam disrationavit coram justic' mea*), 525 (London: Andrew Buccuinte), 257 (Northumberland; Eustace fitz John), 886 (Rutland: Alexander, bishop of Lincoln), cf. 885; 82, 752 (Suffolk: Aubrey I de Vere, Robert fitz Walter, Adam de Beaunay), 134 (Staffordshire: Miles of Gloucester). *RRAN* iii, pp. xxiv–xxv, would add Robert d'Oilli in Oxfordshire and Ilbert de Lacy in Yorkshire on the strength of nos. 636, 621–2, but the evidence is inconclusive.

[19] W. T. Reedy, 'The Origins of the General Eyre in the Reign of Henry I', *Speculum*, 41 (1966), 688–724; cf. Green, *Henry I*, 109.

presence or by his command, maintaining the tradition demonstrated in the 1130 pipe roll by the series of fines *ne placitet de terra
sua.*[20] He was also frequently sought out by ecclesiastical lords
embroiled in disputes over property. In the period 1135–9 royal
writs similar in intention and phraseology to many of Henry I's,
and anticipating in some respects the standardized judicial writs of
Henry II, were issued in favour of religious houses from Durham
in the north to Gloucester and Exeter in the west.[21] Many carried
the *nisi feceris* clause, which had become familiar in the previous
reign as a device to provide for a royal official to act if the addressee
did not; for instance, one writ in favour of Thorney Abbey, ordering the reseisin of property in Wing (Rutland) and naming the
bishop of Lincoln in the *nisi feceris* clause, was followed by another
to the bishop direct, although it is clear in this case that the monks'
tenure remained insecure.[22]

In the absence of pipe rolls, there are obvious limits to what can
be said about the handling of royal finances. However, Stephen's
early writs and charters assume a system for the collection, assign-
ment, and accounting of revenues in full working order. If he was
short of money by 1139, this seems to have had far more to do
with heavy expenditure than with any problems in raising
income.[23] In his first year, Stephen confirmed the gift of the previous king and queen, Henry I and Matilda, to Holy Trinity Priory,
Aldgate, of £25 *ad scalam* from the revenues of Exeter—an
allowance duly entered as £25 12s. 6d. *numero* in the pipe rolls of
1130 and 1156 onwards.[24] Royal gifts in Berkshire to the abbeys of
Cluny (the demesne manor of Letcombe, 1136) and Bec (release
of rent paid for East Hendred, 1136–9) were also acknowledged in
Henry II's pipe rolls from 1156.[25] Meanwhile in Normandy,

---

[20] *RRAN* iii, nos. 3, 10, 105, 210, 215, etc., cf. 133; *PR 31 Henry I*, 11, 14, 18, 24,
etc.; Green, *Henry I*, 81–2, 104.

[21] *RRAN* iii, nos. 257, 355, 286; Van Caenegem, *Royal Writs*, nos. 46, 87, and generally pp. 195–403, 413–64.

[22] *RRAN* iii, nos. 885–6, cf. nos. 887–8; Van Caenegem, *Royal Writs*, nos. 44a, 85.

[23] J. O. Prestwich, 'War and Finance in the Anglo-Norman State', *TRHS* 5:4
(1954), esp. 37–43.

[24] *RRAN* ii, nos. 1493, 1514 (where 'blanch' replaces *ad scalam*); iii, no. 500; *PR 31
Henry I*, 153; *PR 2–4 Henry II*, 46, 74, etc.; J. H. Round, *The Commune of London
and other Studies* (London, 1899), 85–7; K. Yoshitake, 'The Exchequer in the Reign of
Stephen', *EHR* 103 (1988), 952–3. For terminology, see *Dialogus*, pp. xxxvii–xli.

[25] *RRAN* iii, nos. 204, 74; *PR 2–4 Henry II*, 34, 80, etc.

during 1137, Stephen renewed his predecessor's gift of a hundred-mark pension to the nuns of Fontevrault, specifying that sixty marks should be taken from the farm of Lincoln and forty from the farm of Winchester, with half payable at Easter, half at Michaelmas.[26] Writs survive issued by Roger, bishop of Salisbury, at Westminster, possibly in his capacity as presiding officer at the exchequer: one commands the sheriff of Herefordshire to let the monks of Gloucester have their sixty shillings royal alms as in the time of Henry I; another instructs the sheriff and constable of Lincoln to allow the bishop twenty soli-dates of land as ordered by the king's charter and determined by two local juries.[27] As for the king's sources of income, Henry of Huntingdon says that Stephen broke his initial promise to abolish danegeld; he specifically excluded this tax from the quittances granted to Bridlington Priory sometime before June 1139.[28] Among the sheriffs responsible for gathering in the money, there was at least some continuity from the previous reign, with Ansfrid in Kent, Fulk in Cambridgeshire–Huntingdonshire–Surrey, Warin in Dorset–Somerset–Wiltshire, and William de Pont de l'Arche in Hampshire being those who, with varying degrees of probability, have been suggested as having made the transition.[29]

If we followed Stubbs, we would, of course, see this story of competent efficiency coming to a dramatic end with the arrest of the bishops in June 1139.[30] But nowadays the main reason for regarding it as an administrative watershed is that, by choosing a new seal to mark a break with the past, Stephen himself treated it as such. A good case has been made for regarding the king's capture at the battle of Lincoln in February 1141 as the real catastrophe for central government,[31] although we must recognize that the empress's invasion in September 1139 led to the south-west of England falling under an alternative administration based in Bristol and Gloucester and to the immediate defection of Stephen's stew-ard Humphrey de Bohun, constables Miles of Gloucester and Brian fitz Count, and marshal John fitz Gilbert.[32] But, in the

---

[26] *RRAN* iii, no. 327.   [27] Kealey, *Roger of Salisbury*, 259–60.

[28] HH 258; *RRAN* iii, no. 119.

[29] Green, *Sheriffs*, 13, 20 n. 49; cf. 'Financing Stephen's War', *ANS* 14 (1992), esp. 91–2.

[30] Stubbs, *Constitutional History*, i. 351–3.

[31] K. Yoshitake, 'The Arrest of the Bishops in 1139 and its Consequences', *Journal of Medieval Hist.* 14 (1988), 97–114.

[32] *RRAN* iii, pp. xviii–xxi, xxxi–xxxii.

months following June 1139, bishops and abbots continued to attend the royal court; and, although there was no replacement for the bishop of Salisbury as chief minister, nor any known successor to his presumed son Adelelm as treasurer, the chamberlains Aubrey I de Vere and William de Pont de l'Arche, and the constables Robert de Vere and Robert d'Oilli, all remained in Stephen's service.[33] The change of chancellor, with the removal of Roger le Poer, made no discernible impact upon the style of royal writs and charters; analysis of those which can be dated with any precision suggests that the chancery's output fell significantly not in 1139 but in 1141.[34] At least four of Stephen's scribes worked for him both before and after the arrest of the bishops (three writing charters bearing the 'second' seal) and, if all were at work simultaneously in the 1139–41 period, the chancery would have maintained the strength of the previous decade.[35] One new appointment may have been Baldric de Sigillo as keeper of the seal; no one can be shown to have held this office under Stephen before the end of 1140, but it had been an important post in the chancery of Henry I, especially in the last two years of the reign.[36]

Several royal charters give the impression that the business of government continued much as before, outside the Angevin southwest. A sworn recognition before the king at Oxford, at which the burgesses detailed rents within the borough due to the canons of St Frideswide's, and a grant in favour of Baldric de Sigillo from the tithe of the farm of the city of Lincoln, both suggest that burghal revenues were being handled as usual in 1139–40.[37] Also in this period, Stephen gave his annual rent of forty shillings from the mills of Huntingdon to the local priory, an allowance duly recorded in the pipe rolls from the outset of Henry II's reign.[38] Royal confirmations of property were sought from East Anglia and the Midlands, and the king issued a prohibition on impleading in favour of St Peter's Hospital, York.[39] There was as yet no generally

[33] Ibid., pp. xix–xx.
[34] Bishop, *Scriptores regis*, 12–33; *RRAN* iv, esp. 10–22; Cronne, *Stephen*, 218; Yoshitake, 'The Arrest of the Bishops', 104–5.
[35] Nos. XIV, XVIII, XIX, XX; Bishop, *Scriptores regis*, 30; *RRAN* iii, pp. xiv–xv; cf. Cronne, *Stephen*, 217, and, on numbering of seals, Davis, *Stephen*, 86 n. 34.
[36] *RRAN* iii, p. xi, nos. 478–80; Green, *Henry I*, 27.
[37] *RRAN* iii, nos. 640, 478–80.
[38] Ibid., no. 410; *Red Book*, ii. 653; *PR 2–4 Henry II*, 13, etc.
[39] *RRAN* iii, nos. 16, 261–2, 293, 991.

accepted alternative to Stephen's government: the empress's
prospects were highly uncertain and it is possible that she issued no
charters in England before the battle of Lincoln.[40]

Yet we must beware of painting too rosy a picture, for the
mounting disruption described in the chronicles, affecting parts of
the south-west, Midlands, and East Anglia during the course of
1140[41] can only have diminished the king's authority in practice.
He was obliged to order the restoration of property in Essex,
Hampshire, and Wiltshire following disseisins committed by his
own brother, Theobald of Blois.[42] Two successive writs had to be
issued in 1140 concerning the retention by Hugh and Stephen de
Scalers of property they were supposed to restore to the monks of
Ely; this suggests that the king's first writ—addressed to the disseisors—had been ignored.[43] Stephen's grant of the church of
Wolverhampton to Roger de Clinton, bishop of Coventry, sometime between June 1139 and March 1140 also seems to have been
ineffective. The canons of Wolverhampton complained to Pope
Eugenius III that the church rightfully belonged to the monks of
Worcester, but made no mention of the tenure past or present of
their diocesan bishop of Coventry: it was 'lack of funds and fear of
the laymen in whose hands we and the church are' which prevented their coming to the pope in person.[44] Inability to enforce
his will over much of the kingdom would characterize Stephen's
government for most of the 1140s and early 1150s, but these
episodes from 1139–40 suggest that, in places, he was already
losing his grip.

The issue of Stephen's control in different localities leads us to
consider his policy on the appointment of earls. The extent to
which an earldom was perceived during his reign as carrying
specific military or administrative responsibilities, as opposed to
conferring an honorific title with some financial perquisites,

[40] Yoshitake, 'The Arrest of the Bishops', 107, 111 n. 29; cf. Chibnall, *Matilda*,
90–1.

[41] Davis, *Stephen*, 41–8.   [42] *RRAN* iii, nos. 543, 790.

[43] Ibid., nos. 264–5, but cf. above, n. 22, for an earlier example of a writ apparently
being ignored.

[44] On this case, see *RRAN* iii, nos. 452–3, 962, 969; D. Styles, 'The Early History
of the King's Chapels in Staffordshire', *Birmingham Arch. Soc. Trans. and Proc.* 60
(1936), 56–95; *The Cartulary of Worcester Cathedral Priory*, ed. R. R. Darlington (PRS
NS 38, 1968), pp. xlviii–xlix, nos. 263, 266–7.

remains a matter for debate.[45] It is, however, clearly relevant to a
discussion of continuity in government, for we need to consider
how far Stephen was departing from his predecessor's practice. The
first point to stress is that, ever since the Conquest, there had been
variation in the powers and privileges attached to earldoms; indeed,
even William I seems to have changed his mind on what an earldom should involve.[46] Under Henry I, earls had frequently but
inconsistently appeared in the address clauses of royal writs and
charters, in a way which suggests that the king, while glad to
include them to add weight to his instructions, did not perceive
them as playing a defined or essential role in shire administration.
For example, c.1130 he had included the earl of Huntingdon
among the addressees of a confirmation for Huntingdon Priory but
had omitted him from a grant addressed to Huntingdonshire in
favour of Thorney Abbey.[47] There is some evidence to show earls'
entitlement to the third pennies of boroughs and of pleas of the
shires in this reign, but not enough to prove that these were automatically enjoyed by them all.[48] It is hard to disagree that, under
Henry I, as under William II, 'the title earl appears to have been
primarily a means of conferring social pre-eminence'; and an earldom was 'a recognition of local influence'—the earl was with the
bishop and the sheriff 'the most important member of the shire
court'—but 'it is difficult to detect . . . any other specific governmental function conferred by the title'.[49] As for Stephen, any general explanation of the nature and purpose of his earldoms faces the
problem that it will fit some cases better than others. We are likely
to come closer to an understanding of his intentions if we recognize differences according to time and place.

One role certainly fulfilled by some of Stephen's earls was as 'the
military . . . defenders of their counties'.[50] The *Gesta Stephani*
specifically associates the appointment of Alan of Brittany and
Hervey Brito to Cornwall and Wiltshire respectively during 1140

[45] See esp. Davis, *Stephen*, 30–1, 125–41; Warren, *Governance*, 92–5; P. Latimer,
'Grants of "Totus Comitatus" in Twelfth-Century England', *HR* 59 (1986), 137–45;
Green, 'Financing Stephen's War', 91–114.
[46] C. P. Lewis, 'The Early Earls of Norman England', *ANS* 13 (1990), 207–33.
[47] *RRAN* ii, nos. 1659, 1666; cf. (for Huntingdonshire) nos. 1064, 1438, (for
Warwickshire) nos. 1636, 1415, (for Gloucestershire) nos. 1657, 1681.
[48] Green, 'Financing Stephen's War', 92 and n. 7; P. Latimer, 'The Earls in Henry
II's reign' (Univ. of Sheffield Ph.D. thesis, 1982), 129–30, 135–7.
[49] Green, *Henry I*, 119.   [50] Davis, *Stephen*, 125.

with the need to combat the king's enemies in the region. The previous establishment of the earldoms of Richmond and Pembroke,
in areas exposed to Scots and Welsh hostility, must also have had a
defensive purpose.[51] Elsewhere, military considerations may have
been involved in the creation of the earldoms of Worcester (adjacent to Robert, earl of Gloucester's territories) and York (although
the battle of the Standard had already taken place).[52] They could,
of course, be argued as a factor in any appointment following the
empress's invasion in September 1139, including that of Geoffrey
de Mandeville in Essex, possibly a response in part to Hugh Bigod's
1140 revolt in East Anglia.[53] But military reasons lack conviction
as an explanation for some early appointments, such as that of
Gilbert de Clare to Hertford (possibly in 1138) and the ambiguous
earldom conferred upon Simon II de Senlis in 1136.[54] The transfer
of Bedford castle to Hugh le Poer has been taken to imply a
significant military role for the new earl of Bedford (created in
1137 or 1138), but custody of the castle was granted to him as part
of the Beauchamp inheritance in marriage to the heiress, not necessarily because of his comital title; Orderic Vitalis, for one, did not
make the connection.[55] The appointments of William d'Aubigny
pincerna as earl of Lincoln and William de Roumare as earl of
Cambridge, both probably in 1139 at the latest, involved the promotion of men who held no land at all in their respective shires,
and, when William de Roumare was later made earl of Lincoln, he
was still denied custody of Lincoln castle.[56] It is difficult to see a
military purpose underlying arrangements such as these.

It has also been argued that behind the new earldoms, created
even before the civil war began, there lay a deliberate 'downgrading
of the role of central government', a systematic attempt at a 'shift
of power from central to local control'.[57] It has been shown that
the sheriffs of Warwick and Worcester were controlled by their

[51] GS 102, 108; OV vi. 520; *RRAN* iii, nos. 204, 949.
[52] G. H. White, 'King Stephen's Earldoms', *TRHS* 4:13 (1930), 56–72; Crouch,
Beaumont Twins, 39; RH 165; P. Dalton, 'William Earl of York and Royal Authority
in Yorkshire in the Reign of Stephen', *Haskins Soc. Journal*, 2 (1990), 155–65.
[53] *RRAN* iii, no. 273; Davis, *Stephen*, 42, 136.   [54] Ibid. 131, 133.
[55] Ibid. 125–6, 131–2; OV vi. 510; *GS* 46–50; cf. Stenton, *First Century*, 237–8;
CP ii. 68–9; Crouch, *Beaumont Twins*, 41.
[56] Davis, *Stephen*, 134–5; Stenton, *First Century*, 233; Chibnall, *Matilda*, 93–4.
[57] Warren, *Governance*, 92, 94.

local earls not later than 1137 and 1139 respectively.[58] In 1140, by conferring the *totum comitatum* of Herefordshire, including borough, castle, and substantial lordship in the shire, upon Robert, earl of Leicester, Stephen certainly seems to have been prepared to devolve governmental responsibilities upon a favoured magnate; the grant proved ineffective, but its intention appears to have been to offer Earl Robert the resources and the incentive to carry the fight to the Angevins.[59] All this could be taken to support the view that Stephen wished an earl to be 'surrogate for the king ruling an autonomous county',[60] with real executive authority. But, if such a policy was general, it is hard to detect in Stephen's early writs and charters addressed to shire officials, which show the same inconsistency towards earls, sometimes including them in address clauses, at other times omitting them, as had been characteristic of Henry I's. Waleran of Meulan headed the address clause of a writ to the king's ministers in Worcestershire, ordering them to ensure that the bishop restore land to the monks of Worcester.[61] Among the earls inherited from the previous reign, Roger, earl of Warwick, and the officers of Warwickshire were instructed that Reading Abbey must hold Rowington as in Henry I's time;[62] but grants in Buckinghamshire and Leicestershire were addressed to the shire officials without reference to Earls Walter and Robert, while a writ ordering that Burton Abbey be reseised of land in Warwickshire of which the monks had been unjustly disseised—just the sort of case where one might expect some coercive force to have been necessary—omitted Earl Roger.[63] A writ in favour of Worcester Cathedral ordering quittance of geld on lands in Worcestershire and Warwickshire also left out both earls.[64] Address clauses are only one form of evidence, the details of their contents and formulae being of less importance to chancery and beneficiaries than the instructions the writs conveyed.

[58] D. Crouch, 'Geoffrey de Clinton and Roger Earl of Warwick', *HR* 55 (1982), 122; *Beaumont Twins*, 39–40.

[59] *RRAN* iii, no. 437; Crouch, *Beaumont Twins*, 48–9. Alternative interpretations of this grant are offered in Davis, *Stephen*, 126 and n. 1, 137, and Latimer, 'Grants of "Totus Comitatus"', esp. 140–4, but they agree on the devolution of authority in this instance.

[60] Warren, *Governance*, 94.   [61] *RRAN* iii, no. 967.

[62] Ibid., no. 688, a writ bearing Stephen's first seal.

[63] Ibid., nos. 586, 681, 135.

[64] Ibid., no. 965—although Waleran of Meulan, who might not yet have been appointed as earl, was included as a witness.

But, for what they are worth, these addresses suggest that, if earls lacked a defined or consistent function under Henry I, the same was true in the early years of Stephen. Indeed, Stephen's expectations of his earls at this time seem to have been no different from the role assigned to William Peverel of Nottingham—who never bore a comital title—when, in company with the sheriff and ministers of Nottinghamshire, he was ordered to ensure that the canons of Southwell had their woods and easements without interference.[65]

What purposes, then, lay behind Stephen's creation of earldoms? One explanation is that, between 1136 and 1139, the distribution of comital titles—titles coveted by the baronage for the immense prestige they conferred—must have seemed a relatively cheap way of consolidating support. He relied heavily on the backing of the Beaumont network, and the earldoms they received helped to reinforce their influence at local as well as central level.[66] He was indebted to those—William of Aumale and Robert de Ferrers—who had defeated the Scots at the battle of the Standard.[67] As civil war loomed, he was desperate not to antagonize others—such as William d'Aubigny *pincerna* and William de Roumare—and they in turn were anxious not to miss out on the king's largesse.[68] Where appointed, earls might sometimes be called upon to act on the king's behalf, whether as an ally or as an alternative to the sheriff: but not with any consistency. Stephen can be blamed for being far too generous and for failing to foresee the consequences of his actions; but Henry I had created at least two new earldoms, Leicester and Gloucester, had restored another, Surrey, and had allowed succession to others,[69] so in part Stephen's patronage can be seen as extensions of, not a departure from, his predecessor's policy. Like Henry I, he doubtless allowed 'third pennies' as a perquisite, at least to some of his earls, although the evidence is thin.[70] This is not the whole story, however, for even before the

---

[65] *RRAN* iii, no. 831.   [66] Crouch, *Beaumont Twins*, 39–41.

[67] RH 165; SD ii. 295; cf. OV vi. 520–2.

[68] cf. WM *HN* 23, where the widespread creation of earls is linked to fear of Robert, earl of Gloucester's, defection to the empress.

[69] Green, *Henry 1*, 118–19; *CP*, ii. 387; iii. 165–7; v. 683–5; vi. 640–2; vii. 523–6; xii:1, 495–6; xii:2, 358–61.

[70] G. H. Fowler, 'The Shire of Bedford and the Earldom of Huntingdon', in *Publications of the Bedfordshire Hist. Rec. Soc.* 9 (1925), 29, 32–3, for the third penny in Bedford borough held by Earl Simon II de Senlis; and Latimer, 'Earls of Henry II', 130–1, 137–9, for a general discussion.

empress's invasion certain earls enjoyed a real measure of autonomy or had a clear defensive role, and these administrative and military responsibilities could only increase once the civil war began—as the king himself recognized in some of the earldoms he established during the course of 1140. But several of his early creations, however short-sighted, may not have been markedly different in their original intentions from those of Henry I.

If a case can be made for continuity in government, at least to 1140, what can be said of the period after the battle of Lincoln? Writs and charters issued by the empress during the spring and summer of 1141 assumed the continued operation of the financial administration.[71] Her charters for Geoffrey de Mandeville, the first granting the shrievalty of Essex for the farm rendered at Henry I's death, the second conceding the shrievalties of London, Middlesex, Essex, and Hertfordshire for farms rendered by his grandfather, were exceedingly generous but at least expected accounts to be forthcoming.[72] Geoffrey de Mandeville was one earl able to extract extensive administrative and territorial concessions from empress and king in turn; elsewhere, it seems reasonable to suppose that most of the earls created or recognized by the empress (including men such as Miles of Gloucester and Patrick of Salisbury for whom shrievalties ran in the family) were expected both to fight and to control the administration on her behalf within their respective shires.[73] Yet she exercised considerable authority in Shropshire through a loyal sheriff William fitz Alan without ever appointing an earl,[74] never gave a comital title to her most selfless supporter Brian fitz Count,[75] and allowed Aubrey II de Vere to take his pick

[71] The barons of the exchequer were instructed to allow 5s. 5¾d. from the annual farm of Oxford as alms for the canons of Oseney; the canons of St Frideswide's, Oxford, had rent of 17s. 7¼d. remitted (later acknowledged in Henry II's pipe rolls); and grants made to the nuns of Fontevrault from the farm of London, and to the monks of Tiron from the farm of Winchester, stated that half should be deducted at Michaelmas and half at Easter: *RRAN* iii, nos. 628, 644, 328, 899; *PR 2–4 Henry II*, 36, 82, etc.

[72] *RRAN* iii, nos. 274–5 (following the dating there suggested).

[73] Davis, *Stephen*, 130, 136–9; Green, *Sheriffs*, 42, 85–6.

[74] *RRAN* iii, nos. 378, 461, 820, the abbeys concerned (Haughmond, Lilleshall, Shrewsbury) apparently preferring to seek charters from empress, not king; cf. Green, *Sheriffs*, 72, and, for a possible explanation of why no earl was appointed, Davis, *Stephen*, 140.

[75] Chibnall, *Matilda*, 84–5, 101–2.

of an earldom in any one of four shires, in none of which he held
estates.[76] If the king was flexible in his approach to the creation of
earldoms, so it seems was the empress.

As for Stephen, ten months' captivity during 1141 deprived him
of key advisers and officials who defected to the enemy. Given that
the Angevins also failed to establish firm control, earls and other
leading barons had both an opportunity and an obligation to carry
on the business of government without reference to the centre.
Authority once devolved was very difficult to recover, for as long as
the civil war persisted. Yet royal government obviously continued
in the period 1142–53, albeit on a much reduced scale. After his
release from captivity Stephen normally had only one steward,
William Martel, in attendance, although a second, Walter fitz
Robert, occurs late in the reign.[77] He was down to one constable,
Robert de Vere, succeeded on his death c.1151 by his son-in-law
Henry of Essex.[78] No royal chamberlain or treasurer is known, but
it has been plausibly suggested that William Martel and Richard de
Lucy were now given major responsibility for handling the king's
finances.[79] Only one scribe can be proved to have worked for
Stephen both before and after the battle of Lincoln and only two
other chancery hands have been identified from later in the reign;
this suggests a chancery of one, or at most two, scribes at any time,
and certainly the annual output after 1141 appears to have been
less than half that of the king's first six years.[80] All three scribes of
Stephen's later years were, however, expert practitioners and used
established chancery formulae.[81] The difference was that the government whose will they expressed now functioned over a
restricted part of the country. Stephen's own itinerary between
1141 and 1153 never took him north of Beverley and York and
only exceptionally west of a line from York through Coventry,
Winchcombe, Tetbury, and Wareham—although this in itself
proves little, since Henry I, when in England, was rarely out of the

[76] RRAN iii, nos. 634–5; Stenton, First Century, 233–4.
[77] RRAN iii, p. xviii; H. M. Cam, 'An East Anglian Shiremoot of Stephen's reign,
1148–53'; EHR 39 (1924), 568–71; Pinchbeck Register, ed. Lord F. Hervey (Brighton,
1925), ii. 297–9; English Lawsuits, i, no. 331.
[78] RRAN iii, p. xx.
[79] Green, 'Financing Stephen's War', 111–13.
[80] Bishop, Scriptores regis, 30; RRAN iii, p. xv; Cronne, Stephen, 217–18.
[81] Bishop, Scriptores regis, 13–14, pls. xxi–ii.

south and south-east either.[82] More to the point, what might be described as effective royal government was confined to the south-east and parts of the south Midlands and eastern counties.

A review of the available evidence is sufficient to demonstrate the regional nature of Stephen's control. Court cases were heard *coram rege* during the mid- to late–1140s in Kent (Battle Abbey's claims to wreck at Dengemarsh when Stephen tried to uphold Henry I's decree)[83] and Essex (St Martin's, London, versus Richard fitz Hubert over half a hide at Mashbury);[84] they also took place in 1148 at Norwich (the trial of Simon de Novers for the murder of the Jew Eleazer)[85] and at St Albans (Battle Abbey's claims to exemption from the bishop of Chichester's jurisdiction).[86] Royal justices—evidently local rather than itinerant—were addressed by name in writs of the 1140s or early 1150s to Essex (Richard de Lucy) and London (Richard de Lucy and Theodoric fitz Derman).[87] Both his stewards, William Martel and Walter fitz Robert, were assigned to a case involving the liberties of St Edmund, first heard at Norwich about 1150.[88] In 1153 the king referred a dispute between Thurstan fitz Simon and Abingdon Abbey to Henry of Oxford, sheriff of Berkshire, where the property lay.[89] Stephen's second charter for Geoffrey de Mandeville, of Christmas 1141, refers to the deduction of alienated demesne manors from shire farms when accounted for at the exchequer, but specifically in connection with Essex and Hertfordshire.[90] In so far as disputes over liability to danegeld imply its continuing collection, the evidence is confined to Surrey, Kent, and possibly Hampshire, although Stephen did succeed in levying some form of tax in Yorkshire in 1149.[91] The clearest indication of royal control

---

[82] *RRAN* iii, pp. xlii–iv (the exceptions being his sieges of Worcester in 1150–1); ii, pp. xxix–xxxi; Green, *Henry I*, 5.

[83] *Chronicle of Battle*, 142–6. Van Caenegem (*English Lawsuits*, i, no. 303) prefers the date 1139–41.   [84] *RRAN* iii, no. 550.

[85] A. Jessopp and M. R. James (eds.), *Life and Miracles of St William of Norwich by Thomas of Monmouth* (Cambridge, 1896), 92–3, 97–110; Cronne, *Stephen*, 262–4.

[86] *Chronicle of Battle*, 150–2. Cf. *English Lawsuits*, i, nos. 262, 278, for the possibility that Stephen also heard cases in Northamptonshire and Yorkshire during the 1140s.

[87] *RRAN* iii, nos. 546–7, 559, 534.   [88] See above, n. 77.

[89] *RRAN* iii, no. 13.   [90] Ibid., no. 276.

[91] Ibid., no. 934; Cronne, *Stephen*, 230; Green, 'Financing Stephen's War', 104; SD ii. 323–4.

over sheriffs in the 1140s and 1150s comes from Norfolk and Suffolk, where members of the Chesney family, tenants in Stephen's honour of Eye, had prolonged spells in office.[92] It is possible that Westminster came to replace Winchester as the centre of financial administration after 1141; if so, this would have been appropriate to a government most active in the south-east.[93]

Within these geographical limits, the king continued to intervene in the relations between lords and tenants, disseisors and disseised. In 1147–52 the justice and sheriff of Essex were ordered to hold a recognition by men of three hundreds into whether the canons of St Martin's, London, were seised of Maldon marsh between specific dates. In 1139–54 the justice and sheriff of London received a writ stating that, if Robert de Boulogne could show his father's tenure of Fleet by gift of the king, he should hold it in peace and not be impleaded unless the king so ordered. In 1152–4 the abbot of St Edmund's was instructed to let Roger de Clare have seisin of the holdings of Baldwin fitz Geoffrey and his mother, with wardship of Baldwin's son, saving lawful service due to the abbot, otherwise 'my justice of Suffolk would see that it was done'.[94] The concerns, and some of the ingredients, of Henry II's possessory assizes are apparent here. Moreover, the earliest known example of a writ providing for immediate summons to a royal court if the defaulter failed to act—akin to the later writ *praecipe*—can be found in Stephen's order of 1140–54 that Earl Warenne restore what he had taken unjustly from the monks of Reading in Catshill (Surrey) or come to plead before him; this has fairly been described as 'a decisive advance in the development of originating judicial writs'.[95] Yet under Stephen few seem to have benefited from the innovation. A royal remedy for unjust disseisin was not available outside a restricted area of the country in the middle and later years of the reign.

We are bound to acknowledge that over most of England—quite apart from the Angevin-dominated south-west—the king's control

---

[92] Green, *Sheriffs*, 13, 21 n. 54, 61–2, 77.

[93] Green, 'Financing Stephen's War', 110–11. However, if Bishop Roger's writs (see above, n. 27) are taken as having been issued from the exchequer (a debatable point), they would indicate meetings at Westminster before June 1139.

[94] *RRAN* iii, nos. 546, 536, 201.

[95] Ibid., no. 692; Van Caenegem, *Royal Writs*, no. 45; Chibnall, *Anglo-Norman England*, 178.

between 1141 and 1153 seems to have been tenuous indeed. It is hard to assess the impact of royal writs and charters to the north and Midlands in this period, many of which failed to give names to the king's ministers in the shires,[96] but collectively they continue to suggest variability in the role which the earls were expected to play. The extent of Stephen's dependence upon his earls in the 1140s seems to have rested on his perceptions of their loyalty, and possibly their efficiency, rather than on any consistent policy of delegated authority. Simon II de Senlis, earl of Huntingdon–Northampton, appeared with some frequency in the address clauses of royal writs and charters relating to his shires,[97] but this was unusual. Stephen's writs to Leicestershire, Lincolnshire, and Nottinghamshire were consistently addressed to the sheriff and other officials without reference to the earl.[98] The earls of Hertford, Warwick, and York all figured in writs addressed to their shires but none was an entirely dependable royalist—even discounting the special circumstances of 1141—and there are at least as many examples of their omission as of their inclusion.[99] All this suggests that, with the possible exception of Simon II de Senlis, Stephen had little faith in his earls to act on his behalf in their respective shires. He often seems to have been inclined to bypass them in his instructions to local officials, although the extent to which he was heeded when doing so must be in doubt: certainly, one of his grants in Warwickshire in favour of Luffield Priory had no lasting effect.[100] He saw no reason to create new earls of Bedfordshire or Worcestershire after 1141,[101] nor a new earl of Essex after 1144; we know of more royal writs addressed to Essex than to any other shire in the middle and later years of the reign, yet Stephen recognized no earl here between the fall of Geoffrey de Mandeville and the peace settlement.[102]

[96] e.g. *RRAN* iii, nos. 109 (Nottinghamshire, Yorkshire), 297 (Cambridgeshire), 889 (Huntingdonshire), with comment, p. xxvi.

[97] *RRAN* iii, nos. 611, 657, 671, 884, but cf. no. 660.

[98] e.g. ibid., nos. 682, 605–6, 737.

[99] cf. ibid., nos. 858, 219 (Hertfordshire), 689, 570, 687 (Warwickshire), 101, 124, 991–2, 109, 123, 258, 984, 987–8 (Yorkshire). On their allegiance records, see Davis, *Stephen*, 131–3; Dalton, 'William Earl of York'.

[100] *RRAN* iii, no. 570; for subsequent tenure by the Templars of Balsall, see *Monasticon*, vi:2, 834.

[101] *GS* 116; Davis, *Stephen*, 132–3; Crouch, *Beaumont Twins*, 50–3.

[102] *RRAN* iii includes over twenty writs and charters addressed to royal officials in

This is not to say, of course, that earls—and some non-comital barons—did not take substantial power for themselves. The issue of currency, the levy of taxation, the hearing of crown pleas, the attempts to control castle-building within each *potestas*, have been admirably demonstrated elsewhere.[103] The boroughs of Derby, Hereford, Huntingdon, Lincoln, Northampton, Nottingham, Stafford, Worcester, and York were all either promised to earls or came under their effective control at some stage in Stephen's reign.[104] Many of the earls installed sheriffs answerable to them. It has been pointed out that the farms of six shires were accounted for in 1155 by men who at some point in their careers were stewards of the local earls (Gloucestershire, Herefordshire, Leicestershire, Northamptonshire, Nottinghamshire–Derbyshire)[105]—testimony enough that, however far Stephen was able to go in restoring royal authority in the last months of his life, his achievement did not extend to loosening the grip these earls had established on the personnel of shire administration. Yet, where the magnates exercised a measure of autonomous government, they did their best to legitimize it by imitating that of the king. They maintained the existing framework of local government and in addressing charters to sheriffs and other officials they used the formulae of the royal chancery—even to the point of the Angevin earls Robert and William of Gloucester imposing the £10 forfeit for infringing the terms.[106] Knights still had to pay scutage, but in the west country to Robert, earl of Gloucester.[107] Monasteries still sought confirmations of property secured in lawsuits, but in Northamptonshire

---

Essex which appear to postdate Geoffrey de Mandeville's tenure of the earldom: nos. 137, 147–8, 223, 227, 230, 232, 237, 239, 239a, 307, 374, 520(?), 546–7, 549, 552, 555, 559, 733(?), 770, 877. Numerical comparisons are most unsatisfactory, but the shire with the next highest figure, datable with fair confidence to c.1143–54, is Yorkshire (above, n. 99, plus nos. 797, 923, 993).

[103] King, 'Anarchy'; cf. Stenton, *First Century*, 218–57; Cronne, *Stephen*, esp. 138–52, 178–80, 241–3; Green, 'Financing Stephen's War', esp. 102–4.

[104] Derby, Lincoln, Nottingham, Stafford: *RRAN* iii, nos. 178, 180 (cf. Davis, *Stephen*, 169). Hereford: *RRAN* iii, no. 437. Huntingdon: Fowler, 'Shire of Bedford and Earldom of Huntingdon', 28–9; Northampton: *VCH Northamptonshire*, iii. 3–4; Worcester: Crouch, *Beaumont Twins*, 30; York: Dalton, 'William Earl of York'.

[105] Green, *Sheriffs*, 13, 21 n. 52.

[106] *Gloucester Charters*, nos. 68–9; cf. e.g. *RRAN* iii, nos. 287, 476, 621.

[107] *GS* 150; cf., for Waleran of Meulan, Green, 'Financing Stephen's War', 104.

might approach Earl Simon de Senlis.[108] Lords who built castles were liable to have them demolished, but in the borders of Leicestershire at the command of the earls of Chester and Leicester.[109] It is surely no coincidence that it was Stephen's reign which saw at least one earl, Ranulf II of Chester, taking steps to improve his honorial administration, including provision of a new financial bureau.[110] At best, this fragmentation of government led, as the *Gesta Stephani* put it in reference to Angevin control in the south-west, to 'a shadow of peace but not yet peace complete'. At worst, it led to Warin of Walcote's successful career of plunder in the area around Rugby and to Osbert de Wanci's desperate efforts to insure himself, his family, and his livestock with the monks of Biddlesden Abbey.[111]

The chroniclers convey the impression of a partial recovery in royal authority from the mid-1140s. After regaining Lincoln, Stephen made a great show of wearing his crown there at Christmas 1146. He visited Yorkshire in 1149 to destroy castles, including those of his own adherents, and 'after acquiring much treasure in those regions . . . went back with great glory to London'. His conduct in 1152 was later described, however exaggeratedly, as holding 'the upper hand everywhere' and doing 'everything in the kingdom as he willed'.[112] But a sustained effort to restore royal control over the kingdom as a whole obviously had to wait until after the peace settlement. Stephen's Westminster charter of December 1153 had only two short sentences at the end which might be construed as a 'programme of reform', but, reading these alongside the various chronicle accounts, it seems reasonable to suggest that, at the very least, king and duke agreed that henceforth royal authority should be exercised throughout the kingdom with Henry's co-operation, that lands which had changed hands in the civil war should be restored to the pre-war holders (including royal demesne to revert to the Crown), and that castles built during

---

[108] W. Farrer, *Honors and Knights' Fees*, 3 vols. (London and Manchester, 1923–5), ii. 297.

[109] Stenton, *First Century*, 250–6, 286–8.

[110] D. Crouch, 'The Administration of the Norman Earldom', in *Earldom of Chester*, 82–3, 88–93.

[111] GS 150; *Rolls of the Justices in Eyre for Gloucs., Warwicks., [Salop], 1221, 1222*, ed. D. M. Stenton (Selden Soc. 59, 1940), no. 390; A. L. Poole, *From Domesday Book to Magna Carta*, 2nd edn. (Oxford, 1955), 151–3; Stenton, *First Century*, 247–8; Cronne, *Stephen*, 162–3. [112] HH 279; WN 57; GS 218, 226.

Stephen's reign should be demolished.[113] The key point, however, is that this was a conservative, backward-looking programme: king and duke were supposed to co-operate in reconstructing the England of 1135. Without seeking to apply the principle to every case regardless, both Stephen until his death in October 1154 and Henry II thereafter strove to give effect to this agreement. This is not to deny the significance of procedural innovation under Henry II, already beginning to be apparent before the 1150s were out,[114] but much of the basic work of restoring governmental and tenurial order was a matter of one king carrying on where another had left off.

Among government servants, there was a more obvious purge at the outset of Henry II's reign than there had been at the beginning of Stephen's. The only scribe whose handwriting has been identified in both kings' charters is Bishop's no. XIV, who never worked for Stephen after 1141.[115] Neither Stephen's chief steward, William Martel, nor his keeper of the seal, Baldric de Sigillo, retained their positions under Henry II, and, while it is clear from the cases of Richard de Lucy, Richard de Camville, and Henry of Essex[116] that the new king was willing to retain Stephen's adherents as advisers and administrators, these men were the exception not the rule. At the local level, although most comital titles were acknowledged and some baronial sheriffs left in post, there was also

[113] *RRAN* iii, no. 272; HH 289; RT 177; *GS* 240; SD ii. 331 (cf. GC i. 156); Howden, i. 212; *Radulphi de Diceto opera historica*, ed. W. Stubbs, 2 vols. (RS, 1876), i. 296; and comment in G. J. White, 'The End of Stephen's Reign', *History*, 75 (1990), esp. 11–12.

[114] e.g. by 1158 a royal ordinance offered protection, at least in church courts, against unsupported accusations: William fitz Stephen, *Vita Sancti Thomae*, in J. C. Robertson (ed.), *Materials for the History of Thomas Becket*, 7 vols. (RS, 1875–85), iii. 44. At Christmas 1159 Henry II, at Falaise, legislated on judicial procedure in Normandy: *Continuatio Beccensis*, in RT 327.

[115] Bishop, *Scriptores regis*, 24–5, pl. xvii(b); *RRAN* iii, p. xiv; iv, 11.

[116] E. M. Amt, 'Richard de Lucy, Henry II's Justiciar', *Medieval Prosopography*, 9 (1988), 61–87; Davis, *Stephen*, 67 and n. 8. Richard de Camville accompanied Henry II in his early reign in England, Normandy, Touraine, and on the Toulouse expedition of 1159: *Actes de Henri II*, i, nos. 6, 26, 53, 78, 85–6, 93, 95, 126, 128, 144, 166, 191, 204–5, etc. Henry of Essex was a frequent witness in England as constable for Henry II until July 1157, when he fled from the ambush in north Wales; in 1163 he was accused of cowardice and defeated in trial by battle: ibid., nos. 6–9, 26–8, 74; W. L. Warren, *Henry II* (London, 1973), 70; RT 218; *Chronicle of Jocelin of Brakelond*, ed. H. E. Butler (NMT, 1949), 68–71.

I. Castle Hedingham, Essex, interior of the great hall. The castle was a favourite residence of Stephen's queen Matilda, and was the place where she died in 1152.

II. Castle Rising, Norfolk: the east face of the keep seen from the gatehouse. The castle was built by earl William d'Aubigny after his marriage to Queen Adeliza, widow of Henry I.

III. New Buckenham, Norfolk. Castle mound of *c.*1150 and new town of the late 12th century. Earl William d'Aubigny moved here from Old Buckenham at the end of the civil war.

IV. Burwell, Cambs: view of the castle site from the south east. Built by Stephen on the edge of the fenland to control the activities of Geoffrey de Mandeville, who died here in 1144.

V. The coinage of the anarchy: substantive issues of Stephen and variants. All coins give details of the issuing authority, the moneyer, and the mint town. All illustrations are enlarged by 20%.

(a) Stephen, type 1, Stafford, moneyer Godric. Obv. +STIFNE REX:; rev. +GODRIC:ON:STAFO: (Lockett 1113).

(b) Stephen, type 2, Canterbury, moneyer Edward. Obv. +STIEFNE:; rev. +EDPARD:ON[:CANT] (Lockett 1123a).

(c) Stephen, type 6, Bedford, moneyer Tomas. Obv. [+ST]EFNE:; rev. +TOMAS:ON:BED: (Lockett 2961).

(d) Stephen, type 7, Sandwich, moneyer Wulfric. Obv. +STIEF[E]; rev. +P[VLF]RIC:ON:SAN (Lockett 2964).

(e) 'Pereric', type 1, London, moneyer Godric. Obv. +PERERIC:; rev. +GOD-RICVS·ON LV (Lockett 1169).

(f) Erased obverse die, Stephen, type 1, Thetford, moneyer Baldwine. Obv. [+STIE]FN[E:]; rev. +BALDEWI[:ON:TETE] (Lockett 1167).

VI. The coinage of the anarchy: non-substantive issues of Stephen and a coin of Roger II of Sicily.

(*a*) Erased obverse die, Stephen, type 1, Nottingham, moneyer Swein. Obv. +STIEFNE R; rev. {+S]PEIN:ON:S[NOT} (Lockett 2968).

(*b*) 'Stephen', type 3, mint uncertain. Obv. [   ]IFE; rev. +WH[   ]NI (Lockett 1132).

(*c*) 'Stephen', copy of Edward the Confessor's Sovereign/Eagles type reverse, Derby, moneyer Walchelin. Obv. +STEPHANUS REX; rev. +WAL-CHELINVS:DERBI (Fitzwilliam Museum).

(*d*) 'Stephen' Flag type, York. Obv. +STIEFNE R; rev. ornaments (Ashmolean Museum, *SCBI* 281).

(*e*) 'Stephen', Two-Figures type, York. Obv. +STIEFNE R; rev. ornaments (National Museum of Wales).

(*f*) Sicily, Roger II of Sicily and Roger, duke of Apulia, ducalis, 1140. Rev. R RX SLS (*Rogerius Rex Siciliae*) by the right-hand figure, R DX AP (*Rogerius Dux Apuliae*) by the left-hand figure, and AN R X (regnal year 10, i.e. 1140) between them (Fitzwilliam Museum).

VII. The coinage of the anarchy: coins of the empress and the baron-age.

(a) Robert of Stuteville, Horseman type, York. Obv. +ROBERTVS D[E STV]; rev. ornaments (National Museum of Wales).

(b) Eustace fitz John, Armoured Figure type, York, Obv. EVSTACIVS +; rev. +EBORACIEDTS, with ornaments (Ashmolean Museum, *SCBI* 285).

(c) Empress Matilda, type A (as Stephen type 1), Bristol, moneyer Turchil. Obv. :MATILD[I] IN:; rev. +[T]V[RChIL:]O[N]:BRI: (National Museum of Wales; ex Coed-y-Wenallt hoard, no. 26).

(d) Empress Matilda, type B. Cardiff, moneyer Joli de Brit. Obv. IM·HE·MA·; rev. +IOLI:DE:BRIT:C[AIE]R (National Museum of Wales; ex Coed-y-Wenallt hoard, no. 87).

(e) Henry de Neubourg, type B, Swansea, moneyer Henri. Obv. +hENR[ICI] dE NOVOB; rev. +HENRI:ON:S[W]EN (National Museum of Wales, ex Coed-y-Wenallt hoard, no. 98).

(f) 'Henry', rev. design as Henry I's type 15, Hereford, moneyer Witric? Obv. hENRICVS[ ]; rev. [ ]RIC:ON:hER (Lockett 1174).

VIII. The coinage of the anarchy: miscellaneous coins of Stephen, the baronage, a.. 1 Henry of Scotland.

(*a*) 'Henry', design as William I's type 5, Bristol, moneyer Arefin. Obv. +[HE]NRICV[S]; rev. [AR]EFIN:ON B[RI] (Lockett 2974).

(*b*) Brian fitz Count?, design as William I's type 5, mint uncertain. Obv. B·R:C·I·T·B·R·[ ]; rev. +BRIIT·P·ON·TO: (Lockett 1179).

(*c*) Patrick, earl of Salisbury?, Salisbury, moneyer Stanhung? Obv. [/COM]; rev. +S[   ]ON·S[A] (Lockett 1180).

(*d*) 'Stephen', Southampton, moneyer Sanson. Obv. +STEFNE·REX; rev. +SANSON:ON ANT (Lockett 1158).

(*e*) 'Stephen', Bamburgh?, moneyer Willem. Obv. +STIFENE RE; rev. +WI:LELM:ON:OBCI (Lockett 1159).

(*f*) Prince Henry of Scotland, Cross Fleury type, Carlisle, moneyer Willem. Obv. +N:ENCI:CON; rev. +WILLEN:ON:CARDI:C (Ashmolean Museum, *SCBI* 292).

an upheaval, with at least fourteen sheriffs replaced around Michaelmas 1155.[117]

But if the accession of a new king in 1154 brought a significant change in administrative personnel, it did not signal an immediate redirection in government policy, for the restoration of order had already begun. One of Henry II's first acts after his coronation was to order the destruction of castles built since 1135, apart from those he wanted for himself; with characteristic vigour he proceeded to enforce this upon the recalcitrant William of Aumale, Roger, earl of Hereford, and Hugh Mortimer.[118] But—despite Henry's complaints at Dunstable early in 1154 about the old king's lack of application to the task—Stephen had also attended to this matter; according to Roger of Howden, in summer 1154 Drax (Yorkshire) was only one of many castles captured and demolished in the months following the peace settlement.[119] Henry also made it a priority to recover royal demesne, issuing an edict ordering sworn recognitions into former crown lands and scrutinizing his predecessors' charters where royal grants were involved.[120] The 1155 pipe roll included *terrae datae* against the names of several barons in Dorset, Essex, Northamptonshire, Staffordshire, and Surrey—drawn from both sides in the civil war—which did not recur in subsequent years so were presumably recovered by the Crown,[121] although resumptions thereafter were largely a matter of opportunism.[122] All this was continuing Stephen's work, for among

---

[117] Comparison of those who apparently rendered account of shire farms at Michaelmas 1155 with those who did so in the following year: *Red Book*, ii. 648–58; *PR 2–4 Henry II*, 1–68.

[118] RT 183; GC i. 161–2; WN 102–5; Warren, *Henry II*, 59–61.

[119] HH 290; Howden, i. 213; WN 94.

[120] WN 103; *Gesta Abbatum Monasterii Sancti Albani*, ed. H. T. Riley, 3 vols. (RS, 1867–9), i. 123; *Chronicle of Battle*, 214–16.

[121] *Red Book*, ii. 651–7; names include Angevin supporters such as William Mauduit (in Northamptonshire) and Earl Patrick (in Dorset) as well as royalists like William of Aumale and Earl Simon (Northamptonshire), Hubert of St Clare (Essex) and Robert Marmion (Staffordshire).

[122] e.g. manors valued at over £400 p.a. in Lincolnshire, Nottinghamshire, Oxfordshire, and Suffolk were recovered from Thierry, count of Flanders, in 1160, probably on the marriage of his son Matthew to Stephen's daughter Mary: RT 207; *PR 6 Henry II*, 1, 8, 43, 45. Hamo Boterel in Hampshire, Jordan de Blosseville in Surrey, Walter Hose in Staffordshire were among those who apparently retained *terrae datae* until their deaths: last refs., *PR 11 Henry II*, 40; *PR 13 Henry II*, 203; *PR 18 Henry II*, 103–4.

the accounts rendered for a full twelve months at Michaelmas 1155 (and so dating back to the last weeks of Stephen's life) were the farms of Geddington, Kingsthorpe, and Silverstone (Northamptonshire), almost certainly taken back into crown hands following the death of Simon II de Senlis in August 1153.[123] The restoration of lands other than royal demesne to their pre-war holders also seems to have begun before Stephen's death. This, at least, is the interpretation that has been placed upon two episodes from the last year of the reign—Stephen's grants to William de Chesney in compensation for Mileham (Norfolk), which had been given to the rival fitz Alan family, and his siege of Drax so as to deprive Robert de Gant in the interests of Hugh and Fulk Paynel.[124] As Henry II was to find, the implementation of this policy was fraught with difficulties, as likely to exacerbate ill-feeling as to allay it, unless the parties could agree settlements among themselves; several tenants-in-chief unable to resolve their problems complained in the *cartae baronum* of 1166 that they had not yet recovered fiefs lost in the civil war.[125]

Stephen had acknowledged the problems caused by lack of royal justice by promising in his Westminster charter of December 1153 to exercise it throughout the kingdom. In the following summer he took a step in that direction by appointing Robert, bishop of Lincoln, as local justice of Lincoln and Lincolnshire, an office both previous bishops had held in their time.[126] The 1156 pipe roll records pleas imposed by him and also by Guy fitz Tyece in London which—since neither is known to have been a justice under Henry II—may well date to the last year of Stephen's reign.[127] Henry II also appointed local justices, although William of Newburgh was almost certainly exaggerating when he claimed that they were installed 'in all the districts of his kingdom . . . to coerce the boldness of the wicked and do justice to those seeking it, according to the merits of the cases'.[128] Early pipe rolls include pleas imposed by Henry de Pommeraye in Cambridgeshire and

---

[123] *Red Book*, ii. 655; comparisons with later pipe rolls (e.g. *PR 2–4 Henry II*, 104, 142) show the accounts to be for a full year. For Earl Simon's death, see HH 288; RT 172; *CP* vi. 643.

[124] *RRAN* iii, no. 177; C. T. Clay in *EYC* vi. 33; Davis, *Stephen*, 122.

[125] *Red Book*, i. 237, 251, 298, 401, 408–9.   [126] *RRAN* iii, no. 490.

[127] *PR 2–4 Henry II*, 5, 16, 115; White, 'End of Stephen's Reign', 19 n. 70.

[128] WN i. 102.

John of Kent in Somerset[129] but suggest that, otherwise, the king relied on *curiales* (such as Thomas Becket, Robert, earl of Leicester, and William fitz John), who heard pleas while visiting shires on special commissions to impose taxes or conduct inquests into the extent of royal demesne.[130] In the first decade of Henry II's reign there was considerable demand for the intervention of the king and his justices, and some new judicial processes were certainly devised.[131] Yet it could be frustrating and time-consuming to obtain a hearing *coram rege*,[132] and royal writs to prohibit impleading or order reseisin, couched in virtually identical phraseology to those of Stephen, might still fail to resolve disputes over tenure.[133]

Of the routine business of government in the mid-to-late 1150s, we know most about the handling of royal finances through the survival of the pipe rolls. Henry I's former treasurer Nigel, bishop of Ely, was brought in to oversee the restoration of the exchequer to working order; indeed, there are glimpses of his activity at the exchequer as early as 1155/6.[134] Henry II's early pipe rolls were clearly modelled from the outset on rolls such as that of 1130: the

[129] PR 2–4 Henry II, 15, 98; D. M. Stenton, 'England: Henry II', in *Cambridge Medieval History*, v (Cambridge, 1929), 584–5.

[130] Becket: PR 2–4 Henry II, 26, 65, 114, 164; Leicester: ibid. 26; fitz John: PR 6 Henry II, 28, 31, 51, 59; PR 7 Henry II, 36, 49. The years when most of these accounts fell due—1156, 1158, and 1160—were also years when the *donum comitatus* was levied; cf. D. M. Stenton, *English Justice between the Norman Conquest and the Great Charter, 1066–1215*, 69–70; G. J. White, 'The Restoration of Order in England, 1153–1165' (Univ. of Cambridge Ph.D. thesis, 1974), 225, 249, 340–3.

[131] Above, n. 114; also, *Letters of John of Salisbury*, i. *The Early Letters*, ed. W. J. Millor *et al.* (OMT, 1986), nos. 102, 115, and Van Caenegem, *Royal Writs*, no. 169, for legislation to protect seisin, all predating the Constitutions of Clarendon of 1163.

[132] Thus, P. M. Barnes, 'The Anstey Case', in P. M. Barnes and C. F. Slade (eds.), *A Medieval Miscellany for Doris Mary Stenton*, (PRS NS 36, 1960), 1–24; *Chronicle of Battle*, 212–14.

[133] *English Lawsuits*, ii, no. 361. For a long-running dispute over land at Cotes (Derbyshire), not settled in Burton Abbey's favour until *c.*1180 despite writs of Henry I, Stephen, and Henry II, see 'The Burton Chartulary', ed. G. Wrottesley, in *Collections for a History of Staffordshire*, v, pt. 1 (Wm. Salt Arch. Soc, 1884), 8–10; Van Caenegem, *Royal Writs*, nos. 139, 180; *RRAN* iii, no. 136; *English Lawsuits*, ii, no. 517. See also 'The Rydeware Chartulary', ed. G. Wrottesley, in *Staffordshire*, xvi (1895) 230–8, 274–80; *RRAN* iii, no. 715; 'The Staffordshire Chartulary', ed. R. W. Eyton, in *Staffordshire*, ii, pt. 1 (1881), 240–81; *English Lawsuits*, ii, no. 459, for the Ridware family's persistent insecurity of tenure in Edingale and Ridware despite writs of Stephen and Henry II ordering that they hold in peace.

[134] *Dialogus*, 50; PR 2–4 Henry II, 4, 65.

same concern to enter quittances down the right-hand side of the
membrane so that the eye could quickly read off accounts still due,
the same sequences in the itemizing of sheriffs' farms, the same distinction between old and new farms, following rules for the placing
of old farm accounts exactly as later described in *Dialogus de
Scaccario*.[135] Yet the frequent scribal errors in the rolls of 1156–8—
gaps left unfilled, entries begun and abandoned—and evident
uncertainty about the insertion of the *Nova placita et nove conventiones* heading betray a clerical staff by no means at ease with their
task. Alongside the entry in the 1156 pipe roll for 66s. 8d. spent on
the repair of exchequer buildings, these items clearly show that
there had been some decay in exchequer activity—certainly a
reduction in staff and in the scale of operation.[136] But there is
enough in these early Henrician pipe rolls to qualify Richard fitz
Nigel's assertion that the *scientia* of the exchequer had 'almost perished' under Stephen.[137] The 1156 pipe roll indicates that the old
Angevin loyalist Earl Patrick was already accounting to Stephen for
the shire farm of Wiltshire at Michaelmas 1154.[138] Stephen's charter of summer 1154 in favour of St Peter's Hospital, York, assigning
forty shillings yearly from the farm of the city, envisaged the customary Easter and Michaelmas sessions of the exchequer.[139] As the
Red Book copy of the 1155 pipe roll shows, the sheriffs of
Berkshire, Dorset, Essex, Northamptonshire, Staffordshire, Surrey,
and Wiltshire went on to render their farms for the full year
Michaelmas 1154 to Michaelmas 1155, and so had presumably
acknowledged their accountability to Stephen before his death.[140]
Although it took some years for the blanch or *numero* qualification
on sums accounted for to be entered with absolute consistency,[141]

---

[135] *Dialogus*, 92.

[136] *PR 2–4 Henry II*, 4: on this item, cf. Green, 'Financing Stephen's War',
110–11. The heading for *Nova placita et nove conventiones* was not used in the 1156
pipe roll and occurs in only nine shires in that of 1157, even though some new
accounts appear to merit the description: e.g. *PR 2–4 Henry II*, 76 (Ralf de Bealfo and
Edward of Yarmouth), 81 (William Patriz), 86 (citizens of York).

[137] *Dialogus*, 50.

[138] *PR 2–4 Henry II*, 56 (where he accounts for the farm of the 'third year' counting back from 1155/6); cf. Yoshitake, 'Exchequer', 956.

[139] *RRAN* iii, no. 993.

[140] *Red Book*, ii. 648–58; White, 'End of Stephen's Reign', 19 n. 66.

[141] In 1158, e.g., omission of the blanch or *numero* qualification on sums paid,
owing, or in surplus in accounts of shire farms occurred at *PR 2–4 Henry II*, 125, 139,

Stephen's government deserves credit for recovering revenues not only from the south-east but also from parts of the Midlands and south-west before the reign was over.

More remarkable, however, is the fact that many of the sheriffs' farms accounted for at Michaelmas 1155, whether for a full year or only for part, were calculated according to totals which would recur as standard in subsequent years. Allowing for minor deviations, this was the case for Berkshire, Dorset, Gloucestershire, Herefordshire, Staffordshire, Surrey, Sussex, Wiltshire, and Yorkshire. In the following year's pipe roll, that for 1155/6, of twenty-nine shire farms accounted for, eight matched the subsequent standard totals exactly and a further ten were only odd shillings or pence out, possibly as a result of scribal error. Of the remaining eleven, seven had achieved their standard totals by 1158/9, and all but one has done so by 1162/3.[142] All this would appear to refute Charles Johnson's suggestion, in his introduction to *Dialogus de Scaccario*, that early in Henry II's reign 'the sum of the farms remained uncertain because of the gradual restoration of estates devastated in the years of anarchy'.[143] The sums of the farms were not uncertain. Restoration of alienated royal demesne there certainly was, devastation there had been, failure to collect all that was due persisted as a problem; but the exchequer had entries to cover these difficulties, within the overall accounts of the farms.[144] At best, Johnson's comments can be valid only in a minority of cases,[145] for the farms' totals themselves—the sums to which the items paid in, allowed for, or left owing should add up—were known to the exchequer for some shires as early as

141, 156, 164, 179, 183. Not until 1163 did every relevant item carry the qualification.

[142] Full calculations are given in White, 'Restoration of Order', 237–46.

[143] *Dialogus*, p. xlviii.

[144] G. J. White, 'Were the Midlands "wasted" during Stephen's Reign?', *Midland History*, 10 (1985), 26–46, esp. 34–5. Entries in the accounts of the farms of Wiltshire from 1156/7 and Oxfordshire from 1157/8 show the exchequer handling the issue of whether or not to include parts of Marlborough and Benson as *terrae datae*. No payments were made for them by the sheriffs, but accumulating debts 'pro calumpnia' were recorded year after year pending final decisions, without affecting the totals accounted for: *PR 2–4 Henry II*, 79, 116, 150; *PR 5 Henry II*, 34, 39, etc.

[145] e.g. Norfolk and Suffolk, where totals accounted for from 1154/5 to 1156/7 (at most £341 10s. 6d. blanch) were less than half the sums in later years (standardized at £749 13s. 4d. blanch plus £50 *numero* in 1160/1).

1154/5 and for most by 1155/6. When were the totals worked out? They were not the farms of 1129/30, as comparison with Henry I's surviving pipe roll makes clear. But G. J. Turner believed that they had been fixed before Henry II's accession[146]—whether late in Henry I's reign or sometime in Stephen's—and, for those shires whose sheriffs accounted for standard totals for the whole year as from Michaelmas 1154 (Berkshire, Dorset, Staffordshire, Surrey, Wiltshire), this must surely be the case. This being so, Henry II's exchequer presumably had access to a 'roll of farms' recording totals to work to, bequeathed from the previous reign. To suggest that such a roll had been available to Stephen's exchequer is not to claim that shire farms had been regularly collected, except perhaps in a small part of the country, but it is to argue for a measure of administrative continuity.

It seems fair to suggest, in conclusion, that, while presenting his government as a return to the good old days of his grandfather Henry I—the theme of his coronation charter, reiterated in countless writs and charters which claimed to restore the situation in 1135—Henry II did in fact owe some debt to his predecessor. Under Stephen, chancery, household, and exchequer had all been depleted in personnel, and royal government had ceased to operate over much of the country, but in a limited area revenues had been raised, pleas had been heard before the king and his justices, royal writs had been sought to settle feudal disputes, all following procedures modelled on those of the previous reign. In the development of chancery formulae, and in the readiness to adjust financial arrangements to fit new realities, there may even have been some creative dynamism,[147] but the emphasis within Stephen's administration had been on the maintenance of established practice where possible. By the time he died in 1154, the king had already taken steps to recover crown lands, reinstate the disinherited, demolish castles, revive royal justice, and regain lost revenues, so setting in motion the restoration of the old order for which chroniclers heaped praise upon his successor. That Stephen's reign can be seen as significant in preserving governmental methods should occasion no surprise, for it was J. H. Round himself who drew attention to evidence of continuity, when analysing the charters of 1141: 'I

---

[146] G. J. Turner, 'The Sheriff's Farm', *TRHS* NS 12 (1898), 133.
[147] Above, nn. 79, 95.

have never been able to reconcile myself to the accepted view, as set forth by Dr Stubbs, of the "stoppage of the administrative machinery" under Stephen.'[148] A century later, we must agree that Round had the better of the argument.

[148] Round, *Geoffrey*, 99–100.

5

COINAGE AND CURRENCY

Mark Blackburn

THE coinage of Stephen's reign is one of the most complex and challenging in the English series, and potentially one of the most rewarding for the historian. The general outlines are clear enough—an orderly coinage at the beginning of the reign gives way, for the first time in English history, to a loss of royal control over minting in many parts of the country, followed towards the end of the reign by a restoration of the central mint administration. The evidence of civil war is manifest in the coinage, showing with surprising clarity the area and extent of baronial independence. Equally important, however, is the picture of continuity in royal control and administration that is evident from the coins issued from the eastern and south-eastern counties. The numismatic evidence corroborates, with particular precision, that of the chronicles, charters, writs, and later pipe rolls as to the breakdown of royal government in certain regions and its survival in others.

The foundations for the modern study of Stephen's coinage were laid in the mid-nineteenth century by two papers by Jonathan Rashleigh,[1] who was the first to identify some of the minor coin

I have benefited greatly from many people who have guided me or provided me with information, including Marion Archibald, Joe Bispham, Ian Blanchard, Michael Bonser, Marjorie Chibnall, Judith Green, William Lean, Derek Renn, David Roffe, Peter Seaby, Ian Short, and Tim Webb Ware. The text has been read in draft and commented upon by George Boon, William Conte, Paul Dalton, Edmund King, Jeffrey North, and Lord Stewartby. I am grateful to them all. Illustrations are courtesy of the Ashmolean Museum, Fitzwilliam Museum, National Museum of Wales, and British Numismatic Society (Lockett photographs).

[1] J. Rashleigh, 'Descriptive List of a Collection of Coins of Henry I and Stephen, Discovered in Hertfordshire, in 1818', *NC* 1:12 (1849), 138–69; 'An Account of Some Baronial and Other Coins of King Stephen's Reign', *NC* 1:13 (1850), 181–91.

types in the name of Stephen as baronial issues. This work was
built on by Evans, Longstaffe, Burns, Grueber, and others;[2] and
most notably by W. J. Andrew.[3] In 1916 G. C. Brooke published
his magisterial *British Museum Catalogue* of the coins of the
Norman kings.[4] Brooke's work was of such authority that for the
coinages of William I and II and Henry I it stultified further
research for many decades. But, in the case of Stephen, the com-
plexity of the coinage and the discovery of new material fuelled a
continuing flow of publications, mainly in the form of articles.
Some of these have recorded new hoards or individual finds,[5] while
others have considered particular topics—for example, questioning
the chronology of the issues, the attributions of some 'irregular'
types, and the significance of the erased or defaced dies. Because of
the variety of coin types and the poor legibility of most inscriptions, it is necessary to take account of almost every surviving specimen. Brooke realized this and consulted all the major public and
private collections of his day, describing and illustrating significant
coins not represented in the British Museum. Fifty years on, in
1966, R. P. Mack compiled a more comprehensive and well-illus-
trated catalogue, which listed for the commoner types significant
variants of reverse legend and for other types all the known specimens.[6] It is still the fundamental tool for anyone working on the
coinage of Stephen's reign, even though it is now somewhat out-
dated.[7]

---

[2] See particularly J. Evans, 'On Some Coins of the Empress Matilda, Queen of
England', *NC* 1:14 (1851), 66–71; [W. H. D. Longstaffe], 'Postscript by the Editor',
in D. H. Haigh, 'The Coins of the Danish Kings of Northumberland', *Archæologia
Æliana* 7 (1876), 21–77, at 72–7; E. Burns, *The Coinage of Scotland*, 3 vols.
(Edinburgh, 1887), i. 8–41; H. A. Grueber, 'A Find of Coins of Stephen and Henry II
at Awbridge, near Romsey', *NC* 4:5 (1905), 354–63.

[3] W. J. Andrew, 'A Numismatic History of the Reign of Stephen, A.D.
1135–1154: Parts 1–3', *BNJ* 6 (1909), 177–90; 8 (1911), 87–136; 10 (1913), 43–67;
ten further parts read to the British Numismatic Society were only summarized in *BNJ*
vols. 11–18, but his MS notes are preserved in the British Museum's Department of
Coins and Medals. Note also, 'A Remarkable Hoard of Silver Pennies and Halfpennies
of the Reign of Stephen, Found at Sheldon, Derbyshire, in 1867', *BNJ* 7 (1910),
27–89. While Andrew's detailed knowledge of the series was unsurpassed, his judgement was often unreliable.   [4] *BMC.*

[5] L. A. Lawrence, 'On a Hoard of Coins chiefly of King Stephen', *NC* 5:2 (1922),
49–83; Boon, *Welsh Hoards*, 37–82 (Coed-y-Wenallt hoard).

[6] Mack, 'Coinage of Stephen'.

[7] This has to some extent been rectified by E. J. Harris, 'The Moneyers of the

Apart from Mack, the principal post-war contributors to the study of Stephen's coinage have been F. Elmore Jones, Peter Seaby, George Boon, and Marion Archibald. Elmore Jones provided a detailed review of type 7, in the course of which he offered some penetrating observations on the coinage of the reign generally.[8] Seaby contributed a series of provocative articles on the unusual York issues, the erased dies, and the chronology of Stephen's types,[9] but many of his views have proved controversial. Boon has extended our knowledge of Matilda's coinage and of the Welsh mints in his exemplary publication of the Coed-y-Wenallt hoard.[10] Archibald has handled the two major English hoards—Prestwich and Wicklewood—and many single-finds that have been shown at the British Museum, and she has delivered a number of stimulating lectures, but in print her views are mainly to be found in the entries in the catalogue of the 1984 Romanesque exhibition and a paper on the chronology of type 1.[11] Stephen's coinage has not been assimilated into general historical research to the extent that it should have been. Cronne discussed it at some length, but based largely on references to mints and moneyers in charters rather than on the evidence of the coins themselves.[12] Most other historians have all but ignored it[13]—one notable exception being Edmund

---

Norman Kings and the Types they are Known to have Struck' (in twenty-seven parts), *Seaby Coin and Medal Bulletin* (1983–91), *passim*. A revised edition by Harris and Webb Ware is in preparation; I am grateful to Tim Webb Ware for lending me a draft.

[8] F. Elmore Jones, 'Stephen Type VII', *BNJ* 28 (1955–7), 537–54.

[9] These include P. J. Seaby, 'King Stephen and the Interdict of 1148', *BNJ* 50 (1980), 50–60; 'A New "Standard" Type for the Reign of King Stephen', *BNJ* 53 (1983), 14–18; 'Of Seals and Sceptres: King Stephen and the Advocate of St. Vaast's', in R. Margolis and H. Voegtli (eds.), *Numismatics—Witness to History* (Wetteren, 1986), 141–52. On his death in July 1992, Mr Seaby left a substantial unpublished manuscript of a paper read to the British Numismatic Society in 1980, 'The Pattern of Coinage in Stephen's Earldoms', copies of which are deposited at the British Museum and the Fitzwilliam Museum. He had kindly given me permission to draw upon this in the preparation of this chapter.

[10] Boon, *Welsh Hoards*, 37–82.

[11] M. M. Archibald, 'Coins', in G. Zarnecki *et al.* (eds.), *English Romanesque Art 1066–1200* (Arts Council exhibition, London, 1984), 320–41; 'Dating Stephen's First Type', *BNJ* 61 (1991), 9–21. This latter appeared in 1993, after this book had been delivered to the publisher, and only partial account of it could be taken here.

[12] Cronne, *Stephen*, 236–44.

[13] e.g. it is accorded only eleven lines in Davis, *Stephen*, 84–5; and not much more in Chibnall, *Matilda*, 121–2.

King, whose excellent concise survey of the Anarchy[14] has probably given the coin evidence a wider circulation than all the numismatic works together. The responsibility does not rest solely with the historians, however, for numismatists could have done more to make their arguments and conclusions accessible to the non-specialist.

The surviving coinage has grown considerably over the decades. Brooke knew of only nine hoards containing coins of Stephen, Mack cited seventeen, and we can now list thirty-seven, that is twenty-seven from Britain and a further ten from the Continent (see Appendix). The increase has come in part from archival work revealing evidence of older finds, but also from the discovery of new hoards, the most recent being one found in 1992 at West Meon in Hampshire. Since 1970 some 1,800 coins of the reign have been discovered in finds,[15] bringing the total recorded from the thirty-seven hoards listed in the Appendix to more than 3,600. Taking account of unrecorded hoards and the many single-finds, it is probable that more than 5,000 coins of Stephen's reign survive today.

Although the extant coinage is very substantial, one must be aware of its shortcomings as a representative sample of the original currency produced under Stephen. Most of the surviving coins come from a handful of large hoards that appear to have been deposited during the early or mid-1140s, which inflates the proportion of coins from earlier in the reign. Thus, of Stephen's first type (*BMC* 1) there must be well over 3,000 coins surviving, while for the last type (*BMC* 7) there are only some 300, and for the penultimate type (*BMC* 6) the figure is *c.*175. We do not as yet have any estimates of the comparative scales on which the various types were issued, but it is plain from the dates of deposit of the larger hoards that there must be some distortion in the surviving record, under-representing the later types. Single-finds, reflecting accidental losses from circulation, should give a truer representation of the relative sizes of the issues and the period of their currency. However, it is only in recent years that single-finds have been recorded systematically irrespective of their rarity or condition, and any comparative analysis should be restricted to them. The number

[14] King, 'Anarchy', 147–52. See also E. King, *Medieval England 1066–1485* (Oxford, 1988), 60–1.

[15] Regrettably, of these 1,800 coins only 107 (from the Wenallt hoard and a Finnish grave find) have as yet been fully published. For others one must rely on summary accounts and, where parts have been sold off, auctioneers' catalogues.

of single-finds of Stephen's four substantive types recorded during 1984–92 is compared with those from British hoards in Figs. 5.1 and 5.2. It can be seen that, while type 1 is still the most prolific, it does not dominate the single-finds to the same extent as in the hoards; type 1 makes up 78 per cent of the coins in the hoards, but 56 per cent of the single-finds. By contrast, Stephen's last issue, type 7, is the most poorly represented, comprising only 2 per cent of the hoard coins but 15 per cent of the single-finds. The hoards are indeed biased in favour of the earlier issues. What is perhaps surprising is that for types 2 and 6 and the 'baronial' issues (here taken as all other types) the proportions among hoards is only a little lower than among single-finds. The significance of this for the chronology of the issues will be discussed further below.

There is also a considerable bias in the geographical distribution of the finds, for the great majority of hoards come from south-western, western, and midland England. Indeed there are only two significant hoards from the south-eastern counties—Linton, Kent, and Wicklewood, Norfolk—and the latter was a very late hoard. The currency of south-east England during the earlier part of the reign is thus poorly represented in the hoards. The geographical bias can be seen in Figs 5.1 and 5.2, and in the underlying statistics, only 17 per cent of the coins from hoards having been found in the south-eastern counties, compared with 63 per cent among the single-finds. The single-finds give a truer picture of the currency, for throughout the Middle Ages there was more coinage in circulation in the south-east than elsewhere in the county. While it is hazardous to try to associate the deposit of hoards with particular events, the concentration of hoards in the south-west, west, and Midlands during the 1140s can be taken as an indication of a higher level of violence in these regions, just as the large number of hoards of the 860s and 870s reflects the activities of the Viking great army.

Since the eighth century foreign coins had been effectively excluded from circulation in England, and this continued throughout Stephen's reign; none occurs in hoards and they constitute only a small proportion of the single-finds. Money brought from Normandy or Boulogne to finance Stephen's or Matilda's campaigns, therefore, would have been reminted before it could be used in England.[16]

[16] On the ducal coinage of Normandy, see F. Dumas, 'Les Monnaies normandes

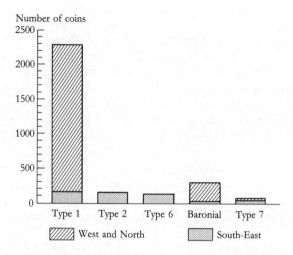

Fig. 5.1. Coins of Stephen's reign in British hoards

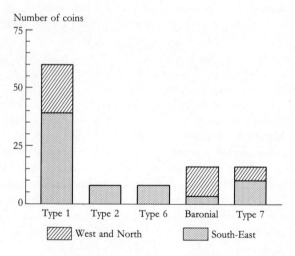

Fig. 5.2. Coins of Stephen's reign among single-finds, 1984–92
(108 finds)

STEPHEN'S OFFICIAL COINAGES

The late Anglo-Saxon and Anglo-Norman monetary system had been more sophisticated and more closely regulated than any other in Europe. Since Eadgar's monetary reform of c.973, the English coinage had settled into a regular pattern in which a single coin type was issued from all the mints, numbering as many as sixty-five at times, distributed throughout the country. (During Stephen's reign some seventy mints were active, although not all at once (Table 5.1).) Standards of weight and fineness were closely regulated, and each coin was inscribed with the name of the mint and the moneyer responsible for issuing it. But the coinage provided more than just a sound currency; it was a means of regular taxation in itself.

The type was changed periodically and a charge was levied by the moneyers for exchanging old coins for new. Domesday Book and the pipe rolls are our main sources of evidence for the financial arrangements for coin production, and from these it would seem that the moneyers did not account directly to the king for the proceeds of minting, but that the mints were farmed to the boroughs, with the moneyers paying certain additional fees. The principal charge for operating the mint had, since the time of William I, been laid on the borough in the form of an annual tax (*geld de moneta*) which varied from mint to mint according roughly to its size and likely output.[17] In addition, each moneyer had to purchase his dies in London from the royal *cuneator* or die-engraver, a hereditary office held in the later eleventh and twelfth centuries by the family of William fitz Otto.[18] In the twelfth century there are

(X^e–XIIe siècles) avec un répertoire des trouvailles', *Revue numismatique*, 6:21 (1979), 84–140; F. Dumas and J. Pilet-Lemière, 'La Monnaie normande—X^e–XIIe siècles: Le Point de la recherche en 1987', in H. Galinié (ed.), *Les Mondes normands (VIIe–XIIe siècles)* (Caen, 1989), 125–31.

[17] D. M. Metcalf, 'The Taxation of Moneyers under Edward the Confessor and in 1066', in J. C. Holt (ed.), *Domesday Studies* (Woodbridge, 1987), 279–93; P. Grierson, 'Domesday Book, the *geld de moneta* and *monetagium*: A Forgotten Minting Reform', *BNJ* 55 (1985), 84–94. Another coinage-related tax (*monetagium commune*) introduced by William I was apparently abolished by Henry I in his coronation charter: ibid. 90–4.

[18] D. F. Allen, *A Catalogue of English Coins in the British Museum: The Cross-and-Crosslet ('Tealby') Type of Henry II* (London, 1951), pp. cxii–cxiii.

also instances of moneyers making a payment on taking up or lay-
ing down office.[19] However, these may not have been the only
methods by which the Crown benefited from minting. The towns
for which Domesday Book or the pipe rolls refer to moneyers or
mint payments are only a minority of those with active mints, and
it has usually been assumed that in the other cases the payments
have been silently included in the general farm of the borough.[20]
But whether different arrangements applied at some mints, as
Pamela Nightingale has suggested,[21] with moneyers working for
the Crown and accounting for their receipts directly, not via the
sheriffs, we do not presently know.

Whatever systems operated, the coinage would have brought in
a moderate income to the king, and, if managed well, an additional
profit to the mint boroughs and moneyers. There is reason to think
that the periodic recoinages, which latterly had occurred on average
every 1.8 years, had been abandoned by Henry I in 1125 and that
his final type was the first of the immobilized coinages that were to
characterize the later Middle Ages.[22] At the same time, Henry I
also overhauled the mint administration, radically reducing the
number of mints. Such then was the closely controlled, efficient
monetary system that Stephen inherited; yet the most superficial
examination of the coinage will show that over much of England it
was not maintained.

It is now clear that there were essentially four official, substantive
coin types of Stephen which were, or were intended to be, general
issues struck from dies produced centrally, in London. These are
termed *BMC* types 1 (also known as the 'Watford' or 'Cross
Moline' type (Pl. V(*a*)), 2 (the 'Cross Voided and Mullets' type (Pl.
V(*b*)), 6 (the 'Cross and Piles' type (Pl. V(*c*)) and 7 (the 'Awbridge'
type (Pl. V(*d*)).[23] In addition to these four main issues, there are

---

[19] D. F. Allen, *A Catalogue of English Coins in the British Museum: The Cross-and-Crosslet ('Tealby') Type of Henry II* (London, 1951), p. lxxvi.

[20] Ibid., pp. lxxviii–lxxix.

[21] P. Nightingale, 'Some London Moneyers and Reflections on the Organization of
English Mints in the Eleventh and Twelfth Centuries', *NC* 142 (1982), 34–50 (at
44–5); '"The King's Profit": Trends in English Mint and Monetary Policy in the
Eleventh and Twelfth Centuries', in N. J. Mayhew and P. Spufford (eds.), *Later
Medieval Mints: Organization, Administration and Techniques* (BAR Internat. Ser. 389;
Oxford, 1988), 61–75.

[22] Blackburn, 'Coinage under Henry I', 64–75.

[23] *BMC* i, p. lxxiv; G. C. Brooke, *English Coins*, 3rd edn. (London, 1950), 91. The

many other types struck in Stephen's name that are generally termed irregular or regional issues, but which, as we shall see, appear to have been produced at the instigation of Stephen's earls. Before turning to this interesting if difficult category of material, there is a good deal to be learnt about the nature and extent of Stephen's authority from his regular issues alone.

In the overhaul of the mint organization carried out towards the end of Henry I's reign, probably in 1125, the number of mints was halved from the fifty-one operating in type 14 to only twenty-four in type 15.[24] This was evidently a process of rationalization, as the mints that were closed were generally the smaller ones with just one or two moneyers. Political as well as economic considerations must have weighed in the planning, for, while the small remote mints of Launceton, Pembroke, and Carlisle survived, a group of seven adjoining counties in the west Midlands were left without a mint between them. The boroughs, and the local earls where they held the third penny, must have been unhappy about the closure of their mints, since these were a source of revenue for them. It is significant, then, that, of the twenty-nine mints[25] suppressed by Henry I, nineteen reopened during Stephen's first issue and six more were back in business before the end of the reign (Table 5.1). In addition, at least six new mints (Rye, Dunwich, Richmond (Yorkshire),[26] Newcastle, Swansea, and an unidentified mint 'Delca') were established during the course of type 1, one in type 2 (Castle Rising), two in type 7 (Bramber and Hedon), and possibly several more whose identifications are less certain. Evidently Stephen yielded to pressure and restored minting rights to the boroughs that had lost them under Henry I and granted new rights to a number of others.

Can we gauge when in his reign he made these concessions? Fortunately the large type 1 coinage can be subdivided chronologically according to the form of the obverse inscription. The earliest dies have +STIFNE REX (or occasionally +STIEFNE REX), and this was superseded by +STIEFNE RE (or R), while the latest ones have just +STIEFNE. Such a sequence of contractions in the inscription is not

substantive status of types 1, 2, 6, and 7 was demonstrated in Elmore Jones, 'Stephen Type VII', 542–3, and has been reinforced by subsequent finds.

[24] Blackburn, 'Coinage under Henry I', 68.

[25] This figure includes one mint (Stafford) last recorded in Henry I's type 13.

[26] See below, n. 31.

TABLE 5.1. *Mints of Henry I's types 14 and 15, of Stephen's reign and of Henry II's cross-crosslet coinage*

	Henry I		Stephen					Henry II	
	Type 14	Type 15	Type 1	Type 2	Type 6	Baronial	Type 7	Class A	Class D–F
South-east (incl. East Anglia)									
London	x	x	x	x	x	—	x	x	x
Southwark	x	—	x	—	—	—	—	—	—
Canterbury	x	x	x	x	x	S	x	x	x
Sandwich	x	x	—	x	—	—	x	—	—
Dover	x	—	—	x	—	—	x	—	—
Romney	x	—	—	—	—	—	—	—	—
Rye	—	—	—	x	x	—	x	—	—
Hastings	x	—	x	x	x	—	x	—	—
Pevensey	x	—	x	x	—	S	x	—	—
Lewes	x	—	x	x	x	—	x	—	x
Bramber	—	—	x	—	—	—	x	—	—
Steyning?	—	—	—	—	—	—	x	—	—
Norwich	x	x	x	x	x	S	x	x	x
Castle Rising	—	—	x	x	x	—	x	—	—
Thetford	x	x	—	x	x	S	x	x	x
Bury St Edmunds	x	x	x	x	x	S	x	x	x
Dunwich	—	—	x	x	x	—	x	—	—
Ipswich	x	x	x	x	x	S	x	—	x

Place	1	2	3	4	5	6	7	8
Sudbury			×	S			×	×
Colchester	×	×	×		×	×	×	
EIE (Eye?)					×		×	
IERNEM (Yarmouth?)					×			
ME (Maldon?)							×	
RVCI					×			
WA (Walton?)					×			
Midlands								
Lincoln	×	×	×	S			×	×
Stamford			×		×		×	×
Nottingham			×	S			×	×
Derby				SO				×
Leicester		×		S			×	×
Northampton	×	×	×	S	×		×	×
Huntingdon			×	S				
Cambridge				S				
Bedford		?	×		×	×	×	
BVR (Peterborough?)			×					
North								
York	×	×	×	SO			×	×
Hedon			×					
Richmond							×	
Durham		×		S			×	×
Newcastle	×	×		SO			×	
Carlisle	×	×		SO				×

TABLE 5.1. (cont.) *Mints of Henry I's types 14 and 15, of Stephen's reign and of Henry II's cross-crosslet coinage*

| | Henry I | | Stephen | | | | | Henry II | |
	Type 14	Type 15	Type 1	Type 2	Type 6	Baronial	Type 7	Class A	Class D–F
North (cont.)									
Bamburgh	—	—	—	—	—	SO	—	—	—
Corbridge	—	—	—	—	—	O	—	—	—
West									
Chester	x	x	x	—	—	—	—	x	x
Tamworth	x	—	—	—	—	—	x	—	—
Stafford	—	—	x	—	—	—	—	x	—
Shrewsbury	x	—	x	—	—	—	—	x	—
Warwick	x	x	x	—	—	—	x	—	—
Hereford	x	x	x	—	—	O	x	x	—
Worcester	x	—	x	—	—	—	x	—	—
Gloucester	x	x	x	—	—	MO	x	x	—
Cardiff	x	—	x	—	—	MO	x	—	—
Swansea	—	—	x	—	—	O	—	x	—
Pembroke	x	x	x	—	—	—	—	x	—
South-west									
Chichester	x	—	x	—	—	—	—	—	—
Winchester	x	x	x	—	—	S	x	x	x
Southampton	—	—	—	—	—	—	—	—	—

Christchurch	×	—	—	—	—	—	—	—	—
Salisbury	×	—	×	—	—	O	×	×	—
Wilton	×	—	×	—	—	—	×	×	—
Wareham	×	—	×	—	—	MO?	—	—	—
Shaftesbury	×	—	×	—	—	—	—	—	—
Dorchester	×	×	—	—	—	O?	—	—	—
Exeter	×	×	×	—	—	—	×	×	×
Launceston	—	×	×	—	—	—	—	×	—
Barnstaple	×	—	—	—	—	—	—	—	—
Watchet	×	—	—	—	—	—	×	—	—
Taunton	×	—	—	—	—	—	×?	—	—
Ilchester	—	—	×	—	—	O	×?	×	×
Bath	×	—	—	—	—	—	—	—	—
Bristol	×	×	×	—	—	MO	—	×	×
Malmesbury	—	—	—	—	—	O	—	—	—
Cricklade	—	—	—	—	—	S	—	—	—
Oxford	×	×	×	×	—	SM	×	×	×
Wallingford	×	—	—	—	—	O?	—	×	—
DELCA	—	—	×	—	—	—	—	—	—
No. of mints	51	24	48+	17	19	34	40+	28+	19
No. of moneyers (min.)	139	97	162	50	47	?	80	100	54

Abbreviations: S = in the name of Stephen; M = Matilda; O = other.

uncommon in coin series, and in this type it is supported by various pieces of evidence, including hoards, moneyers' careers, stylistic developments, and spelling changes in the reverse inscriptions.[27] We cannot be sure that there was a strict progression in the abbreviation of the royal title from REX to RE to R to nothing. Indeed the development is likely to have been gradual and somewhat haphazard, as the use of larger, more spaced lettering resulted in greater abbreviation; but none the less, as a broad classification, the division holds good.[28] The obverse legends on coins from official (i.e centrally produced) dies thus provide some guide to the period of a mint's activity. Tables 5.2 and 5.3 record, for established mints and for ones opened or reopened during type 1, the forms of obverse inscription read from clear specimens from official dies. Most of the mints that had operated during Henry I's last type start with STIFNE REX dies and many use all the forms through to STIEFNE (Table 5.2). Of the nineteen mints that had been suppressed by Henry I, at least nine were reopened early in the type, since they use dies with the full reading STIFNE REX; at least five more were in operation by the middle of the type, using dies reading STIEFNE RE or STIEFNE R (Table 5.3). The number of mints known to have received the earliest dies might well increase as further legible coins are discovered, but the table even in its present form demonstrates that Stephen restored the minting rights to many of the boroughs very early in his reign—probably within the first two years or so— and it looks as if he may have done this as a general measure rather than on an *ad hoc* basis to individual boroughs as they asked or when interests dictated. Such a concession is consistent with other actions taken by Stephen in 1136/7 to secure his succession to the throne, notably the charter of liberties granted to the Church, yet

---

[27] The progression was first noted by Andrew, in 'A Numismatic History', *BNJ* 10 (1913), 57–8. The arguments were subsequently developed by others: Lawrence, 'On a Hoard of Coins', 56; R. J. Seaman, 'King Stephen's First Coinage, 1135–1141', *Seaby Coin and Medal Bulletin* (1968), 60–2; M. Dolley and K. A. Goddard, '. . . the Obverse Legends of English Coins of Stephen's First Substantive Type', *Proc. Royal Irish Academy*, 71.C (1971), 19–34; R. J. Seaman, 'A Re-examination of Some Hoards Containing Coins of Stephen', *BNJ* 48 (1978), 58–72; Archibald, 'Dating Stephen's First Type'. Archibald has further subdivided the +STIEFNE coins into three stylistic groups.

[28] The same chronology cannot safely be applied to locally cut dies of type 1 or to types that imitate type 1, as Seaby occasionally sought to do, e.g. in 'The Pattern of Coinage'.

TABLE 5.2. *Forms of obverse legends used at mints of type 1 continuing from Henry I's type 15*

	STIFNE REX	STIEFNE RE	STIEFNE R	STIEFNE
London	x	x	x	x
Canterbury	x	x	x	x
Norwich	x	x	x	x
Thetford	x		x	
Bury St Edmunds	x	x		x
Ipswich		x	x	x
Sudbury			x	
Lincoln	x	x	x	x
Stamford		x	x	x
Nottingham	x	x	x	
Northampton	x			x
York	x	x	x	x
Carlisle		[local dies]		
Chester		x	x	x
Hereford	x	x	?	x
Gloucester	x	x		
Pembroke		x		
Winchester	x	x	x	x
Exeter	x		x	x
Launceston	x			
Bristol	x		x	?[1]
Oxford	x	x	x	x

Note:

[1] Seaby ('King Stephen and the Interdict of 1148', *BNJ* 50 (1980), 54) notes that the defaced obverse die used at Bristol is of the STIEFNE variety, and Boon (*Welsh Hoards*, 68 n.53) cites another Bristol coin of this variety by the moneyer Gurdan, but the readings on both are very unclear.

it also constitutes an exception to the general principle that in his early years Stephen endeavoured to maintain the administrative system he inherited from Henry I.[29]

The new mints are too few to show a clear pattern, but it is likely that they were created on an *ad hoc* basis. For Castle Rising,

[29] See White, Ch. 4.

TABLE 5.3. *Forms of obverse legends used at mints opened or reopened in type 1*

	STIFNE REX	STIEFNE RE	STIEFNE R	STIEFNE
Southwark[a]			x	x
Rye[c]				
Hastings[a]		x	x	x
Pevensey?[a]				x
Lewes[a]	x	x	x	x
Dunwich[c]		x		x
Colchester[a]	x	x		x
ME (Maldon?)[c]				
EIE (Eye?)[c]	x			
IERNEM (Yarmouth?)[c]		x		
Leicester[a]	x		x	x
Bedford[a]				x
Richmond[c]		x	x	
Durham[a]		[local dies]		
Newcastle[c]				
Stafford[b]	x			
Shrewsbury[a]	x			
Warwick[a]		x	x	
Worcester[a]	x		x	x
Cardiff[a]	x			
Swansea[c]		[local dies]		
Chichester[a]	x	x	x	x
Salisbury[a]				
Wilton[a]	x	x	x	x
Wareham[a]		x		
Shaftesbury[a]		x		x
Taunton[a]	?			x
DELCA[c]	x			

Notes:
[a] Mints last recorded under Henry I's type 14.
[b] Mint last recorded under Henry I's type 13.
[c] Mints that had not operated under Henry I.

the historical context is reasonably clear. A new planned town and elaborate castle were built by William d'Aubigny II on his marriage to Adeliza of Louvain, the second wife and widow of King Henry I, in 1138.[30] The earliest coins of Castle Rising are of type 2, suggesting that a mint was established some seven years or more after the construction of the castle and town had begun.[31] The mint of Hedon offers a parallel later in the reign, for the town had been founded as a port with access to the Humber in the early twelfth century by Stephen, count of Aumale.[32] In the 1130s and 1140s it had been systematically developed as a seignoral borough by William of Aumale, earl of York, and subsequently he obtained a royal charter from Henry II sealing its burghal status. Before this charter, William evidently obtained a grant of minting rights for his borough from the king, for some coins of Stephen's last issue (type 7) were struck there c.1154–8. In neither of these cases do the charters granting new mints survive, and ironically in the two cases where they do—in favour of Lichfield, Staffordshire, c.1149–54 and Newark, Nottinghamshire, c.1153–4—no relevant coins attest the use of the minting rights.[33]

Broadly the same mints that were operating in type 1 were still active in Stephen's last issue, type 7. However, Henry II in his recoinage of 1158 implemented a radical reduction in the mint network along similar lines to that of Henry I. The number of mints was reduced from about forty to twenty-eight or twenty-nine in 1158, with a further reduction in c.1165 to some nineteen mints and in 1180 to thirteen mints. Stephen's restoration of minting rights had clearly been against the tide of change, though that is not to say that it may not have been expedient in 1135–6 to win or retain supporters. There is no evidence that he intended at that stage to reverse Henry I's other innovation, the abandonment of

[30] R. A. Brown, *Castles from the Air* (Cambridge, 1989), 80–2.

[31] The coins of type 1 by the moneyer Bertold and with the mint name RI formerly attributed to Castle Rising now appear to be from Richmond, Yorkshire. A striking of this in lead was found in 1987 below the walls of Richmond castle, which is strong evidence for the attribution, especially given that lead strikings would not usually travel far from their place of origin: M. M. Archibald, 'Anglo-Saxon and Norman Lead Objects with Official Coin Types', in A. Vince (ed.), *Aspects of Saxon and Norman London*, 2. *Finds and Environmental Evidence* (London and Middlesex Arch. Soc. Special Paper 12, 1991), 326–46, at 345.

[32] B. English, *The Lords of Holderness 1086–1260* (Oxford, 1979), 213–22.

[33] *RRAN* iii, nos. 457, 489.

periodic recoinages, since the first issue ran for at least six years, probably more, and it is likely that the following change of type was intended to remove from the currency the many low-weight coins of type 1 and its unofficial derivatives rather than to increase receipts from minting. The second recoinage, replacing type 2 by type 6, may have been planned as a means of raising revenue for the king, but equally it could have represented an attempt to impose Stephen's official coinage on a wider range of mints. The third and final recoinage, between types 6 and 7, had been agreed between Stephen and Duke Henry in 1153 and re-established a uniform coinage throughout England.

The two types from the middle of the reign, types 2 and 6, had both been rare until the discovery of the Wicklewood hoard in 1989, and it had not been clear what their relationship was or how extensively they were struck. Type 2 survived in a hundred or so specimens but these from only seventeen mints, while type 6 was known from only some thirty-five specimens struck at ten mints. The addition of 109 coins of type 2 and 134 of type 6 from Wicklewood was therefore of great significance, yet it added no new mints for type 2 and only eight for type 6. Single-finds have since added one further mint in type 6, and, even if a few more minor mints still remain to be discovered, we can now be reasonably confident that we know the broad geographical distribution of these two types. The contrast between the patterns of minting in types 1 and 7 and in types 2 and 6 is dramatic. The forty-eight mints of type 1 and the forty or so mints of type 7 are distributed throughout the country, while the seventeen mints of type 2 and the nineteen of type 6 are essentially limited to an area of south-eastern England bounded by a line from Lewes in the south through London to Northampton and Stamford in the north (Map 5.1)—coins of type 2 of Oxford being the only known exception.[34] Most of the mints that struck type 2 also struck type 6, and the small differences in the lists appear to have little significance, except for the addition in type 6 of the two east Midlands mints of Northampton and Stamford, which suggests that there was an extension of the minting area to include them during the currency of that type.

[34] *BMC* 409, no. 173A, and another in the collection of J. Bispham. The former weighs only 16.6 grains (1.08g) (see n. 47); the latter is too corroded for the weight to be of significance.

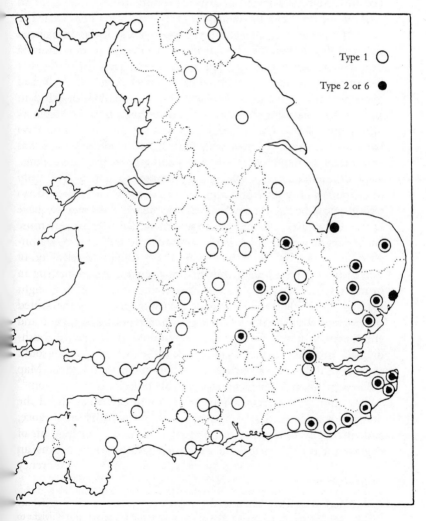

Map. 5.1   Mints active in types 1 and 2 or 6 during Stephen's reign

It would, however, be wrong to dismiss types 2 and 6 as merely regional issues. They have the attributes of full substantive types intended to replace the preceding issues. Significant for this is the fact that the dies, to judge from their style and uniformity, were metropolitan—that is, produced at the official workshop in London and distributed from there in the usual way. Moreover, London itself participated as a mint in both issues, with eight or nine moneyers striking coins in each type. Stephen evidently ordered a general recoinage, but the moneyers at less than half the country's mints responded by sending to London to purchase the new dies. In the rest of the country, as we shall see, the mints that remained in operation struck coins of novel design from locally made dies in the name of Stephen, Empress Matilda, or a baron, and most of the coins were distinctly lighter than those of Stephen's official substantive types. Oxford is the only mint in this area we know to have experimented with type 2, and it soon followed the example of so many other mints in issuing types that are deliberately differentiated from Stephen's substantive issues. The only direct copies of types 2 or 6 appear to be some from Leicester imitating type 2 but in the name of Earl Robert of Leicester. In parts of the south-east, notably East Anglia, there had been some irregular and light-weight coins issued towards the end of type 1, but after the introduction of type 2 only full-weight coins of these official types were minted, and the finds suggest that the currency of this region consisted almost exclusively of types 1, 2, or 6 (Figs. 5.1 and 5.2).[35] By contrast, outside the south-east the currency was dominated by the lighter local issues,[36] and types 2 and 6 are rarely encountered. For some eight or ten years, then, England was divided into two distinct regions with quite different currencies— the one of uniform type struck to the full-weight standard, and the other very mixed in character and variable in weight.

The moneyers at mints outside the south-east were effectively denying that Stephen's administration had authority over them, and, if they were refusing to purchase their dies from the official engraver, it is likely that these mints were also no longer rendering

[35] It is interesting to note that, among the recent single-finds from the south-eastern counties, the only 'irregular' or 'baronial' coins were three from the northern borders struck to the full weight standard.

[36] e.g. the Wenallt hoard contained coins only from the mints of Cardiff, Swansea, and Bristol.

to the king the annual *geld de moneta* and other dues. If payments from the mints were not reaching the king, was the same true of other revenues, such as those from the farms of the boroughs and from the shire courts? The fact that the geographical demarcation is so clear, and that so few of the mints outside the south-east appear even to have experimented with types 2 or 6, suggests that a firm pattern of administrative independence had developed throughout the region by the time that type 2 was introduced, which is also a factor to be considered in relation to the chronology of the issues.

The evidence provided by the coinage about the extent and effectiveness of the administration of the mints accords well with the interpretation of historians based on other aspects of royal government during the civil war. During the first five years of the reign Stephen's government appears to have functioned fairly effectively in all but the few western counties that supported the Empress Matilda after her arrival in England in 1139, but during the middle and later years of the reign the central administration failed in various respects. Stephen lost a number of his key officials without replacing them, and the size and output of the chancery scriptorium was diminished.[37] In a number of counties the sheriff, whose job it was to account for the king's revenue and expenditure, appears to have made only partial or no returns to the exchequer, which fell into such a bad state that subsequently Bishop Nigel of Ely, Henry I's former treasurer, had to be brought in to restore the exchequer to working order.[38] The authority and independence enjoyed by the sheriffs during Henry I's reign were undermined during Stephen's, in part because of political divisions during the civil war, but also as a result of Stephen's creation in 1137–8 of earls over many counties that had not previously had one. Judith Green has studied the political affiliations of Stephen's earls and sheriffs,[39] and has concluded that in the 1140s and early 1150s Stephen's strongest support was to be found in the counties of Norfolk, Suffolk, Essex, Kent, and Sussex and in the city of London—precisely those areas where his official coinage of types 2

[37] See White, Ch. 4; J. Green, 'Financing Stephen's War', *ANS* 14 (1992), 111–13.

[38] Cronne, *Stephen*, 221–36; K. Yoshitake, 'The Exchequer in the Reign of Stephen', *EHR* 103 (1988), 950–9.

[39] Green, 'Financing Stephen's War', 93–102.

and 6 were struck. Several western and south-western counties
(Cornwall, Devon, Gloucestershire, Herefordshire, and Worcestershire) were dominated by supporters of Matilda, and elsewhere
either there were conflicting interests or the earls acted with a measure of independence. Graeme White traces a broadly similar geographical division.[40] He finds evidence of continuing royal control,
as reflected in the provision of justice, taxation, the issue of charters, etc., most often in London, Kent, Essex, Suffolk, and Norfolk,
and occasionally in Surrey, Hertfordshire, Berkshire, Yorkshire, and
possibly Hampshire. Over much of England the king's control was
tenuous, and the earls, and some lesser barons, took substantial
power for themselves. White points out, for example that the boroughs of Derby, Hereford, Huntingdon, Lincoln, Northampton,
Nottingham, Stafford, Worcester, and York were all either
promised to earls or came under their effective control at some
stage in Stephen's reign. Earls issued private charters using the formulae of the royal chancery, and instances can be found of earls
levying taxation, hearing crown pleas, and attempting to control
castle-building—functions normally exercised by the Crown alone.

Apart from the coinage, the evidence for the extent of royal
authority is sporadic and often imprecisely dated, so that it is
difficult to chart in detail the chronological and geographical
changes. However, the event that seems to have prompted the
widespread assumption of power locally was not the dismissal of
the three bishops in June 1139 or the arrival of the empress three
months later, but the captivity of Stephen during 1141, when, as
White puts it, 'earls and other leading barons had both an opportunity and an obligation to carry on the business of government
without reference to the centre'.[41] Not until after the treaty of
Winchester (November 1153) was Stephen in a position to re-
establish central authority over the whole country, and indeed at
the very end of the reign improvements can be detected in various
branches of government, clearest of all in the coinage.

[40] See Ch. 4.
[41] Ibid. See also K. Yoshitake, 'The Arrest of the Bishops in 1139 and its consequences', *Journal of Medieval Hist.* 14 (1988), 97–114.

INDEPENDENT AND ANGEVIN ISSUES

The four substantive issues that we have considered account for about 90 per cent of the surviving coins of Stephen's reign. The remaining 10 per cent show enormous variety and they are particularly interesting historically. They comprise some thirty-five distinct types in the name of Stephen and a further twenty-five types with the names of Matilda, 'Henry', 'William', 'BR:CITBR . . .' (possibly Brian fitz Count), an uncertain earl (probably Patrick, earl of Salisbury), Henry of Neubourg at Swansea, an unidentified 'John' at Cardiff, 'Robert' (probably Earl Robert of Leicester at Leicester), in York Robert of Stuteville, Eustace fitz John, and a bishop Henry, and in the northern borders King David and Prince Henry of Scotland. Our knowledge of these issues must be very incomplete, for many of the types survive in just a few specimens with inscriptions that are only partially legible. Their mints of origin and their dating are often uncertain, so that their usefulness for historical interpretation is not as great as one might expect.

There are references in the chronicles to barons issuing their own coins. William of Malmesbury, writing in 1140–2 about events in 1140, complains that 'everything was deteriorating because of the lack of justice . . . and owing to the quantity of bad money; for there was such difficulty with the coinage that sometimes hardly twelve pennies could be accepted out of ten shillings or more'. 'It was said', he continued, 'that the king himself had ordered the weight of pennies to be reduced from what it had been in King Henry's time, because after exhausting his predecessor's huge treasure he could not meet the expense of so many knights.'[42] It is interesting, and perhaps significant, that William is complaining not of barons issuing their own coins, but of Stephen's mints reducing the weight of the penny from that ruling in Henry I's time. Complaints about the state of the coinage had been made in previous reigns and now often seem exaggerated,[43] but, as we shall see, William's comments—which we may take as applying particularly to the currency of south-west England, where he lived, in the period 1140–2—do seem to accord with the numismatic evidence.

[42] WM *HN* 42.
[43] e.g. *ASC, s.a.* 1125: 'the man who had a pound could not get a pennyworth at the market.'

Some mints, during the course of type 1, did reduce their weight standards dramatically, and this appears to have started in the south-west c.1140.

Two later writers are much more specific about baronial involvement. William of Newburgh, writing from Yorkshire at the end of the century, says that the tyrannical lords of castles each minted their own coinage.[44] Roger of Hoveden records that in 1149, when Henry of Anjou invaded England, he struck a new coin which obtained the name Duke's money (*moneta Ducis*), and that not only he but all the magnates, bishops, earls, and barons made their own money; but that, when Henry came (on which occasion it is not clear—1153 or even on his succession in 1154?), he put down the coins or the greater part of them.[45] The coins first referred to can only have acquired the name *moneta Ducis* after 1150 when Henry became duke of Normandy. The suppression of the magnates' coinage presumably refers to the recoinage which followed the treaty of Winchester in 1153. Despite certain difficulties with these accounts,[46] the general message is clear enough: that coins were struck by the barons on a significant scale.

There has been considerable uncertainty about the status of the non-substantive issues in Stephen's name. Some have been regarded as 'royalist' coinages and others issues of 'insurgents'. However, most of them should probably be regarded as independent issues of earls and other noblemen who, while owing their feudal allegiance to the king, were primarily acting in their own self-interest. If these issues are included with the overtly baronial ones, the coinages are as substantial as the chronicles imply. Indeed, as we have seen, they dominated the currency of western, midland, and northern England between the mid-1140s and 1154.

[44] 'Numerous castles had been raised in individual areas through the eager actions of factions, and in England there were in a sense as many kings, or rather tyrants, as there were lords of castles. Each minted his own coinage, and each like a king had the power to lay down the law for his subjects' (WN i. 69 (trans. from P. G. Walsh and M. J. Kennedy, *The History of English Affairs, Book 1* (Warminster, 1988), 99)).

[45] Howden, i. 211. Stubbs points out (Howden, i, p. l) that this is one of the few passages for the period 1148–69 that appears to be an original statement, not copied from the *Melrose Chronicle*.

[46] G. C. Brooke, 'Some Irregular Coinages of the Reign of Stephen', *NC* 4:15 (1915), 105–20, at 116; Boon, *Welsh Hoards*, 45.

Weights and fineness

The weight of the penny, having fluctuated somewhat during Henry I's reign, was raised and stabilized at *c.*22 grains (*c.*1.43g) on the introduction of his final issue (type 15) in 1125.[47] As Table 5.4 shows, Stephen's four substantive types maintain that standard remarkably well. The weight distributions of types 1, 2, and 6, with their mode or commonest weight falling at 21.5–22.0 grains, is very similar to that of Henry I's type 15. The slightly lower mode and average weight for type 7 may result from the sample being based on a complete corpus including more corroded or damaged coins; a sample of ten coins of type 7 from the Wicklewood hoard gave a higher mode and average weight than those for types 1, 2, and 6.[48] The continuity of weight standard among the substantive types is, however, broken towards the end of type 1, when some coins were issued at a much lower weight. The sample for type 1 in Table 5.4 is based only on coins from the Watford hoard, deposited midway through the period of the STIEFNE variety, but those hoards deposited at the very end of the type or later (such as South Kyme, Nottingham, or Sheldon) contain a large number of lighter coins and hence a significantly lower average weight.[49] Not all mints reduced their weights, and those that did so adopted various standards. This is neatly demonstrated by coins of a distinctive sub-group of type 1 dies that are among the latest products of the official London die-cutter. They have no inner circle on the obverse, large lettering, and a characteristic bust,[50] and are found at a range of mints including London, Southwark, Canterbury, Bedford, Bury, Norwich, Lincoln, and Warwick. We may assume that the coins of this variety are more or less contemporary. Based on the weights of some thirty-five specimens noted from published sources, coins of this sub-style from London and Southwark have an average weight of 21.0 grains (7 coins), while those from

[47] Blackburn, 'Coinage under Henry I', 52. Weights in this chapter are quoted in grains: 1g = 15.432 grains.

[48] Type 1 (average 19.9 grains), 2 (21.2 grains), 6 (21.2 grains), 7 (21.6 grains), based on the Wicklewood coins sold at Christies, 15 May 1990.

[49] R. J. Seaman, 'A Re-examination of Some Hoards Containing Coins of Stephen', *BNJ* 48 (1978), 58–72. Seaman also points out that, even within the Watford hoard, there is a small decline in weight, with each of the four categories of type 1 obverse, but the final decline is far more significant.

[50] e.g. *BMC,* pl. 50, no. 16; pl. 51, nos. 3, 11.

Table 5.4. *Weights of issues of Stephen's reign*

Weights (grains)	Stephen's substantive issues				East Anglia	Midlands	South-west	York	Northern borders
	Type 1 (%)	Type 2 (%)	Type 6 (%)	Type 7 (%)	(%)	(%)	(%)	(%)	(%)
23.0–23.4	3		6	2					9
22.5–22.9	12		17	10		2			9
22.0–22.4	17	23	13	12		**10**			4
21.5–21.9	**26**	**32**	**27**	12		2		2	**13**
21.0–21.4	18	13	6	**17**	4	4			9
20.5–20.9	9	11	2	12		6		2	4
20.0–20.4	5	4	10	9	4			4	9
19.5–19.9	8	7	2	6		2		4	**13**
19.0–19.4	2		2	6	8		1	13	9
18.5–18.9		7	2	3		2	1	11	9
18.0–18.4	2		4	6	4	2	1	**22**	4
17.5–17.9				2	13	2	1	7	4
17.0–17.4		2		1	**21**	6	7	7	4
16.5–16.9			4	1		10	**8**	4	
16.0–16.4			4	1	4	15	11	9	

Weight range									
15.5–15.9	2			1	**21**	**17**	**13**		
15.0–15.4						6	11	4	
14.5–14.9			2			12	8	7	
14.0–14.4						2	10		
13.5–13.9						2	6		
13.0–13.4							6	2	
12.5–12.9							3		
12.0–12.4							4		
11.5–11.9							2		
11.0–11.4							2		
Lower							4		
No. of coins	66	56	52	162	24	52	142	45	23
Average weight	21.4	21.1	21.0	20.6	17.0	16.1/21.6	14.8	17.8	20.4

Note:

Mode figures are shown in bold.

Sources: Type 1, 66 coins from Watford hoard listed in Seaman, 'A Re-examination of Some Hoards Containing Coins of Stephen', *BNJ* 48 (1978), 60–1; types 2 and 6, Mack and coins from Wicklewood hoard sold by Christies, 15 May 1990, lots 29–131; type 7, an unpublished corpus of type 7 by R. J. Seaman, *c.*1980, with additions from the Wicklewood hoard (Christie's sale, lots 132–42); East Anglia, variants of type 1—roundels, pelleted crown, and Thetford cross varieties, and coins from defaced dies based on Mack; Midlands, coins of type 1 from defaced or locally made dies and later independent types of the Midlands based on Mack (two weight standards, the higher representing Mack nos. 169–73, 175); south-west, coins of Stephen's type 1 from local dies, of Matilda, 'Henry', 'William', etc., and independent types in Stephen's name based on Mack and Boon, *Welsh Hoards*, 73–7; York, the ornamental group in the names of Stephen, Robert de Stuteville, Eustace fitz John, and independent types based on Mack; northern border, coins in the names of Stephen, David, or Henry of Scotland of type 1 from local dies and independent types based on Mack.

Lincoln average 18.2 grains (15 coins), from Norwich 18.7 grains (2 coins), and from Warwick only 13.1 grains (6 coins from one obverse die). Groups of light-weight coins struck from regular dies can also be identified at other mints, such as those of the Wilton moneyer Thomas averaging 18.8 grains (9 coins). It was probably weight reductions such as these that William of Malmesbury was complaining of in 1140–2. A detailed study of the metrology of the type 1 coinage, mint by mint, deserves to be made, as it appears to provide some of the earliest signs of breakdown in central control. It would be interesting to determine to what extent the reduction in weight preceded the anomalous variants of type 1, such as the use of altered, defaced, or locally made dies in East Anglia and the Midlands. These East Anglian variants of type 1 mostly have weights in the range 15–18 grains, as does the Lincoln–Stamford group from defaced dies, while the Nottingham defaced group has a particularly close distribution aimed at a standard of c.16.5 grains. These late type 1 variants can be seen as a prelude to the overtly independent issues that followed, when the pattern of disparate weight standards in different regions also continued.

Most of the independent or Angevin issues discussed below fall well below the official 22-grain standard. The lowest weights are to be found among the Angevin issues in the west and south-west in the names of Matilda, 'Henry', 'William', and others. Two successive standards of c.13 grains and c.14 grains can be identified at Cardiff, while at Bristol, Oxford, Hereford, and other mints of western England the standard followed was somewhat higher, around 16 or 17 grains.[51] The ornamental York issues followed a rather loose standard in the region of 18–19.5 grains, while the coinages of the Midlands mostly range between 15 and 19 grains, although two issues—at Lincoln (Mack nos. 169–73) and Derby (Mack no. 175)—evidently attempted to restore the official 22-grain standard. The only region outside the south-east that managed to retain the original 22-grain standard was the northern borders and Scotland under King David and Prince Henry, who had no shortage of silver thanks to the mines in Cumberland. The distributions in Table 5.4 show the general weight ranges to be found in each region, but

[51] Boon, *Welsh Hoards*, 58–9. The 'Pereric' coins of Bristol are struck to a standard of *c.* 19 grains.

they should not be taken as defining particular standards, since
these often differed from mint to mint and from type to type.

Little is known about the fineness of coinage of Stephen's reign.
During preparations for the publication of the Wenallt hoard,
some twenty analyses were made of coins from western mints,
which proved to be of surprisingly good silver, 89–97 per cent.[52]
The earlier coins of Matilda were of marginally weaker alloy than
the official coins of Stephen, but those of her later issue (type B)
were improved. Apart from these there are few useful analyses.[53]

There are three special categories of the type 1 coinage, which
should be discussed before a survey of the independent issues
region by region.

'Pereric' coins

One of the earliest and most problematic of the irregular groups is
a series of coins of type 1 struck from dies of good style, the work
of the official London die-cutter, and regular in every respect save
the obverse inscriptions, which read +PERERIC (Pl. V(e)) or occasionally +PERERICM. It is a large group, with more than seventy
specimens known, struck at seven different mints, namely Bristol,
Canterbury, Ipswich, Lincoln, London, Stamford, and
Winchester.[54] A variety of explanations for the legend have been
put forward, some of them fanciful and none entirely convincing.
The interpretation most generally followed is that it is a vernacular
form of 'Empress M(atilda)', citing in particular the suggestion of
H. W. C. Davis that it is derived from the standard medieval
French *empereriz*,[55] and this is rendered the more likely by Dolley's
and Goddard's demonstration that the same London die-cutter was

[52] Ibid. 63, 'silver' here taken to be the aggregate of silver, gold, and lead, which
would not have been distinguished.
[53] Five coins of type 1 with 74–90% silver, but inadequate identifications: J. S.
Forbes and D. B. Dalladay, 'Composition of English Silver Coins (870–1300)', *BNJ*
30 (1960–1), 82–7; E. J. Harris, 'Debasement of the Coinage', *Seaby Coin and Medal
Bulletin* (1961), 5–7. One coin of David I with 92% silver: Burns, *Coinage of Scotland,*
i. 40.
[54] Mack, 'Coinage of Stephen', 45–7, nos. 43–50. Ipswich is added by M. M.
Archibald, 'Medieval Series', in E. M. Besly (ed.), *Department of Coins and Medals:
New Acquisitions 1 (1976–77)* (British Museum Occ. Paper 25; London, 1981), 50–1,
no. 27.
[55] In correspondence reported in G. C. Brooke, 'PERERIC', *NC* 4:20 (1920), 273–6.

using vernacular rather than Latin forms of Stephen's name.[56]
Contemporary literary sources in Anglo-Norman have *empereïs*,[57]
or in Old English *emperic*,[58] and, while the precise form of ending
of the coin inscription is not a problem, the loss of the initial sylla-
ble *em-* does cause some difficulty, for no close parallels are to be
found.[59] Thus, while it is not impossible that PERERIC is a vernacular form of 'empress', it does require some special pleading.

   Whether one accepts this interpretation or, like Brooke, regards
the legend as a meaningless evasion,[60] there is still the problem of
explaining when and why these official dies should have been distributed from London to at least seven widely spread mints. The
most obvious period is during Stephen's captivity in 1141, but for
long it was thought that the 'Pereric' dies were produced relatively
early in type 1, based on the style of the portrait and certain features of the reverse inscriptions.[61] In consequence, Brooke attributed them to the first weeks after Henry I's death, before Stephen's
authority was fully established,[62] while Archibald and Boon suggested that they may have been produced in 1137 during Stephen's
absence in Normandy, when Bishop Roger of Salisbury was in
charge of England.[63] Neither attribution carried any conviction,

---

[56] Dolley and Goddard ('Obverse Legends'), regarded the forms on the coins as
Anglo-Norman, but Ian Short has commented (in correspondence) that, while they
could well be Anglo-Norman, they could just as well be English. In any event they are
vernacular, not Latin. I am grateful to Prof. Short for linguistic advice on the 'Pereric'
legend.

[57] Philippe de Thaon, *Livre de Sibile*, ed. H. Shields (Anglo-Norman Text Society,
37; London, 1979), l. 1211; the work is of 1139–48 and dedicated to the Empress.

[58] *Peterborough Chronicle*, ed. C. Clark, 2nd edn. (Oxford, 1970), *s.a.* 1140, 58, l.
20.

[59] Prof. Short (in correspondence) points out that aphetic forms appear frequently
in Anglo-Norman, particularly in the thirteenth and fourteenth centuries (cf. Eng. stable ≤ *estable*, staunch ≤ *estanchier*), and the parallel of *stefne*, if this form is indeed
Anglo-Norman, shows that it could happen in the twelfth century, at least in the case
of initial *es-*. However, he can find no early instances of the loss of the initial *em-*. He
concludes, 'as it stands, the most that I dare say of *pereric* is that it is not wildly
implausible that it means "Empress" '.

[60] Brooke, *English Coins*, 94–5.

[61] Lawrence, 'On a Hoard of Coins', 56–7; Brooke, *English Coins*, 94–5; Archibald,
'Coins', 335, no. 437. To confuse matters, one 'Pereric' obverse die was reused at
Lincoln towards the very end of type 1: Archibald, 'Dating Stephen's First Type', 12.

[62] Brooke, *English Coins*, 94–5.

[63] Archibald, 'Medieval Series', 50–1; 'Coins', 335, no. 437. Boon, *Coins of the
Anarchy 1135–54* (Cardiff, 1988), 6.

and the 'Pereric' group remained a real puzzle until Archibald, following further work on the Prestwich hoard, was able to argue that
the 'Pereric' dies do not belong as early in the series as had previously been thought.[64] She would now associate them stylistically
with dies reading STIEFNE, and specifically with the first of three
substyles identified among the dies with that inscription. This
allows an attribution to late spring 1141, when Matilda was briefly
in London and granted a charter to William fitz Otto, the official
in charge of die-cutting.[65] The existence of 'Pereric' coins from
mints such as Canterbury, Ipswich, Stamford, and Winchester does
not necessarily indicate explicit support from those towns for the
empress,[66] for, as Archibald points out, the moneyers would have
had little option but to accept whatever dies were sent out from
London, and indeed they may have been relatively unconcerned
about the legends on them. It is likely, then, that the 'Pereric' dies
date from the period of Stephen's captivity in 1141, and they may
well have been an official issue in the name of the empress produced and distributed from London during May or June 1141.

Coins of type 1 from locally cut dies

Not all the coins of type 1 are struck from metropolitan dies. In
other reigns one finds the occasional coin in an unusual or crude
style, suggesting that a local person had been asked to make a
replacement die, perhaps in an emergency when a die had broken,
but locally cut dies are significantly more plentiful in Stephen type
1. In wartime conditions one can imagine situations arising in
which dies had to be commissioned locally as travel to London
became hazardous. On the other hand, if a baron wished to usurp
the Crown's prerogative over the coinage, as the chronicles suggest
some did, one obvious way would be for him to issue coins of the
regular type without accounting for the *geld de moneta* or the payment for the dies.[67] Where the use of local dies is accompanied by
a reduction in the weight or silver content of the coins, it is a fair

---

[64] Archibald, 'Dating Stephen's First Type', 11–12.   [65] *RRAN* iii, no. 316.

[66] The pattern of minting was debated by Brooke and Andrew (*BMC* i, pp.
lxxxii–lxxxviii; Andrew, *BNJ* 15 (1919–20), 322–6; Brooke, 'PERERIC'), and, as Andrew
showed, a case can certainly be made for most of the 'Pereric' mints, including
Canterbury, being sympathetic to Matilda's cause in Spring 1141.

[67] The suggestion that usurping barons might have been responsible for some
copies of type 1 is not new: cf. Rashleigh, 'Some Baronial Coins'; *BMC* i, p. lxxiii.

assumption that the mint was defying the central administration. For example, all the known coins in the name of Stephen struck at Swansea are from non-metropolitan dies, and one could imagine that it may have been difficult to collect dies from London; although Pembroke had managed it. But, as the coins weigh only two-thirds of the proper weight and are followed by ones in the name of Henry of Neubourg, there can be little doubt that their issue was not sanctioned by the exchequer. Similarly, when, for example, Bristol, Hereford, and Shaftesbury start using non-metropolitan dies, the weight standard falls significantly. Locally cut dies of type 1 are also found at Carlisle, Durham, Ipswich, Lincoln, Newcastle, Norwich, Nottingham, Shrewsbury, and probably elsewhere. No systematic study of coins from local dies has yet been made, but it is a topic with considerable potential as a means of tracing the beginnings of the independent issues of the shires.

Erased or defaced dies

The third group of anomalous coins of type 1 are those struck from obverse dies that have been defaced by having marks or symbols punched into the dies (Mack nos. 136–57). In the nineteenth century they were seen as the work of supporters of Matilda.[68] Brooke thought they were dies that had been cancelled in times of trouble to make them useless if they fell into rival hands.[69] Seaby saw them as a political protest, related not to the war as such but to the Church's brief interdict of 1148.[70] Archibald, like Brooke, thinks they were cancelled, but at the time of a recoinage that was subsequently countermanded so that they were called back into use.[71] Coins struck from defaced dies are recorded from some fifteen mints: Lincoln, Stamford, Nottingham, Norwich, Thetford, Bury St Edmunds (or Eye?), Canterbury, Steyning?, Hastings, Chichester, Salisbury?, Bristol, York, and an unidentified southern mint, 'Whit'. Half of these mints lay within the south-eastern counties, where Stephen's authority was strongest. In practice they can be divided into three major groups—two from the east Midlands (Lincoln and Stamford, and Nottingham) and one from

---

[68] Canon Pownall, 'Defaced Coins of Stephen', *NC* 3:1 (1881), 42–7.

[69] *BMC* i, pp. lxxvi–lxxxi; Brooke, *English Coins*, 95.

[70] Seaby, 'King Stephen and the Interdict'; 'The Defaced Pennies of Stephen from Sussex Mints', *BNJ* 56 (1986), 102–7.

[71] Archibald, 'Coins', 336, no. 446; 'Dating Stephen's First Type', 19–20.

East Anglia (Norwich, Thetford, and Bury/Eye)—and miscellaneous other mints (Canterbury,[72] Steyning?, Hastings, Chichester, Salisbury?, Bristol, York, and 'Whit') each of which is known from only one or at most two defaced dies.

The cause of the defacement need not have been the same in each case. The one Bristol die has furious scratches over its surface, and this looks like an attempt to obliterate the king's image before the mint had begun striking Matilda's own coinage, to judge from the full 22-grain weight standard of the defaced coins. On the coins of Lincoln, Stamford, Chichester, and 'Whit' the dies have a small bar through the sceptre, which is similar to cancellation marks found on coins of Edward the Confessor and other rulers.[73] The York coin and another from an unidentified mint in the Prestwich hoard have two parallel strokes the full width of the die, and these could also be cancellation marks, as could the large round globule on two coins probably of Salisbury.[74] The large East Anglian group is distinctive and consistent in having two bold lines at right angles over the full width of the die (Pl. V(f)), but if these too are cancellation marks why should some dies also have one or two small crosses punched into the die? Why also should the bold lines be neatly finished with short cross-bars at the edge of the design, as is evident from some specimens (e.g. Mack no. 141), if they were intended merely to render the die useless? This East Anglian defaced group is struck to a lower weight standard than the regular type 1 coins, which suggests that they were being used at a time when the moneyers were defying the central authorities. Moreover, as will be seen below, there are other low-weight coins of similar date from East Anglian mints struck from reverse dies that have been altered by the addition of roundels or crosses, which are clearly not cancellation marks. The method used for defacing dies of the Nottingham group, a neatly serifed Latin cross (often with a pellet in one quarter) punched on to the king's face (Pl. VI(a)) or aligned over his sceptre, suggests that these altered dies were also intended to be used and seen, rather than returned to the workshop for destruction. Again this Nottingham group is struck to a

[72] J. Bispham, 'Coin Register 1987', *BNJ* 57 (1987), 144–5—the sceptre has been converted into a crozier.

[73] Boon, *Coins of the Anarchy*, 24; Archibald, 'Dating Stephen's First Type', 19–20.

[74] The Salisbury coins, from the Sheldon hoard (Andrew, no. 97) and the Prestwich hoard, are discussed in Seaby, 'The Pattern of Coinage'.

lighter standard than the type 1 coins that preceded it, and it should probably be regarded as the first of the distinctive independent baronial issues of the Midlands. However, the so-called 'hammering-out' of the legend on coins from Nottingham and elsewhere, that was often regarded as a form of defacement,[75] can be discounted, for this seems to be an accidental result of the method used for preparing the flans before striking,[76] a common practice at mints in western and southern Germany known as *Vorschlag* (pre-striking).

While some of the 'defaced' coins may be struck from dies that had been cancelled and later reused, others, including the major groups from Norfolk and Nottingham, seem to be from dies that were altered to make a political statement. However, they are probably to be dated several years earlier than the 1148 interdict with which Seaby wished to associate them.

Variants of type 1 from the south-eastern counties

Although the counties in the south-east display the strongest continuity of government, striking all four of Stephen's substantive types, their mints did produce some anomalous varieties of light weight among the later coins of type 1. These are in addition to the substantial series of defaced coins from Norfolk and some regular coins of reduced weight noted at certain south-eastern mints. From Norwich a local variant with pellets in place of fleurs in the crown has recently been recorded from three specimens in the Wicklewood hoard, from a fourth coin, and from a lead trial striking.[77] Its absence from the Nottingham, Sheldon, and Prestwich hoards, coupled with its light weight, suggests that it may have followed after the defaced coins of Norwich. At Thetford some rare coins were produced with a cross superimposed on the reverse design (Mack no. 174). From the Suffolk mints of Bury, Ipswich, and Sudbury there is a substantial group of type 1 coins that have one, two, or three large pellets punched into their reverse designs (Mack nos. 159–69—the 'roundels' group).[78] Some are struck

---

[75]　Mack, 'Coinage of Stephen', 45, 64; Seaby, 'Stephen and the Interdict', 53–4.

[76]　*BMC* i, p. lxxxi; Archibald, 'Dating Stephen's First Type', 19.

[77]　M. Blackburn, 'A Lead Striking of an East Anglian Variant of Stephen's Type 1', *NC* 163 (1993), 215–17.

[78]　Andrew, 'Sheldon Hoard', 74–6; N. C. Ballingal, 'An Unpublished Coin of Stephen from the Ipswich Mint', *BNJ* 32 (1963), 220–1; Mack, 'Coinage of Stephen'

from altered metropolitan dies with inscriptions reading STIEFNE R or STIEFNE, while others are from locally cut dies. Coins are known from dies before and after the addition of pellets, and in one case after the addition of two and then three pellets (Mack nos. 159 and 165). Andrew interpreted the 'roundels' as representing the bezants that occur on the badge of the house of Boulogne to which Stephen's wife, Queen Matilda, belonged, and he suggested that, during Stephen's captivity in 1141, the queen sought to raise money for her husband's cause. However, none of the mints lay actually within the honour of Boulogne, and the light weight and distinctive designs of all these East Anglian variants seem to signify a loss of royal control to some degree in East Anglia during the final phase of type 1. Did the influence of Hugh Bigod and his frequent revolts extend over a wider area than east Suffolk, where his castles were situated? What is clear is that the recoinage on the introduction of type 2 brought the mints of East Anglia once again under the central administration, imposing a common design, enforcing the centralized distribution of dies, and restoring the traditional weight standard of c.22 grains.

The other mints of the south-east show much less sign of irregularity, but there are some variants of type 1 in addition to the few defaced coins of Hastings, Steyning?, and Chichester mentioned above. From Canterbury there is a coin which has a mace in place of the usual sceptre (Mack no. 158), while from Pevensey there is one with a star at the end of the obverse legend.[79] In both cases the symbols are part of the original design, not later additions, yet they may be the work of the official die-cutter in the later style without an inner circle. From London there is a coin with a small crescent in front of the king's nose, part of a small group of coins in a distinctive, non-metropolitan style.[80] Although these variants are much rarer than the East Anglian ones—too rare for us to determine their weight distributions—they do suggest a degree of

65-7. The Thetford coin from the Prestwich hoard (*Coin Hoards* 1 (1976), 92, fig. 20.15) with four pellets on the arms of the cross is perhaps better regarded as belonging to the small group of Thetford coins with a heavy cross overlaying the normal reverse cross: Seaby, 'The Pattern of Coinage'.

[79] P. J. Seaby, 'A Stephen "Star" variant of Pevensey', *BNJ* 54 (1984), 291–2; the second coin discussed there (Mack no. 187y) has been shown by a subsequent find to be of Cambridge (see below, n. 85).

[80] Boon, *Coins of the Anarchy*, 33, no. 29; Archibald, 'Dating Stephen's First Type', 11.

political uncertainty in the extreme south-east at some stage during the currency of type 1, though whether during Matilda's brief occupation of London in June 1141 or later is not clear.

Independent issues of the Midlands

Most mints in the Midlands were active at least at some stage in the period following type 1, issuing various distinctive types and always, with one possible exception, in the name of Stephen. Rarely did two mints share the same design, and the very fact that they chose not to copy Stephen's substantive types 2 and 6 suggests that the earls were making a deliberate statement about their independence to manage the shires which they controlled. They follow on from the later coins of type 1 from Midlands mints struck to light-weight standards, and in some cases from locally made or defaced dies.

The Midlands was shared between four earldoms. Two mints, Lincoln and Stamford, fell within the territory of the earls of Lincoln—William of Aubigny (1139), William of Roumare (1140–9), and Gilbert of Gant (1149–53)—although during 1140–6 the city and royal castle at Lincoln was held by William of Roumare's half-brother, Earl Ranulf II of Chester, who was then the dominant power in the county, controlling the administration jointly with Earl William.[81] There are three distinct issues attributed to Lincoln (Mack nos. 169–73, 186–7, and 72–4 = *BMC* 4);[82] the latter type was also used at Nottingham (Mack no. 75). Mack nos. 169–73 represented an attempt to restore the weight standard to the full 22 grains, but the mint reverted to a lower standard with *BMC* type 4. It is interesting to note that, whichever chronology for the coinage is followed, the Lincoln mint continued to strike coins in Stephen's name during 1141–6, supporting Dalton's recent suggestion that Earl Ranulf, despite his dispute with Stephen, never formally terminated his homage and fealty with Stephen or performed homage to the empress.[83] The borough and castle of Stamford appears to have remained in the control of the king and his ally Gilbert of Gant, and this may explain why

---

[81] P. Dalton, in *Earldom of Chester*, 109–34.

[82] For the Lincoln attribution of Mack no. 186, formally given to Exeter, see Seaby, 'The Pattern of Coinage'.

[83] P. Dalton, '. . . Ranulf II Earl of Chester in King Stephen's Reign', *ANS* 14 (1992), 48–9.

no independent issues have as yet been attributed to the mint and why Stephen's substantive issue, type 6, should have been struck there.

After 1141 Northampton, Huntingdon, and Cambridge lay within the earldom of Simon II of Senlis. Northampton had one, possibly two, independent issues (Mack nos. 67–9 = *BMC* 3 (Pl. VI(*b*)) and 275?), and it also struck regular coins of Stephen's type 6. *BMC* 3 also seems to have been struck at Huntingdon,[84] and an independent issue of Cambridge, a variant of type 1, has recently come to light.[85] From Leicester, which was under the control of Simon of Senlis's father-in-law, Earl Robert of Leicester, there are two issues in the name of Stephen (Mack nos. 76 = *BMC* 5, and 177–8),[86] and a third, probably of Leicester, in the name of Robert himself (Mack 269).[87] Further west, the counties of Nottingham and Derby were held by Earl Robert of Ferrers, although Nottingham and its castle were largely controlled by William Peverel. Besides the distinctive group of 'defaced' coins of type 1 discussed above, two issues of Nottingham are known, one with a design loosely derived from the official type 2 (*SCBI Midlands Museums*, 723; not in Mack) and the other from *BMC* 4 (Mack no. 75), also struck at Lincoln although in a different style. The attribution of a third type (Mack no. 180) to Nottingham must be considered doubtful. From Derby there is an unusual type (Mack no. 175 (Pl. VI(*c*)) with a reverse copied from coins of Edward the Confessor's Sovereign issue, having four birds in the quarters of a cross,[88] and struck to the full 22-grain standard. Another type (Mack no. 179), undoubtedly the work of the same engraver

---

[84] One specimen of *BMC* 3 has a partially legible mint-signature, 'H . . .' (Mack no. 70), probably for Huntingdon.

[85] Sotheby sale, 26 Mar. 1987, lot 106. It is a die-duplicate of Mack no. 187y, which has an illegible reverse.

[86] Mack no. 177, sometimes attributed to Newark, Notts., appears to consist of blundered copies of no. 178.

[87] The design is a direct copy of Stephen's type 2, with 'ROBERTV . . .' on the obverse, and the mint name '. . . ERE', which has been interpreted as either HERE for Hereford (and Robert of Gloucester) or LERE for Leicester (and Robert of Leicester). But two coins from the Sheldon hoard (Andrew, nos. 35–6) also copying type 2 are clearly of the Leicester moneyer Simund; their obverse legends are illegible.

[88] For an interpretation of the design, see Archibald, 'Coins', 335, no. 438. At least ten specimens survive, from two pairs of dies, and most of them come from the 1788 Ashby-de-la-Zouch hoard.

although struck to the lower weight standard, has the mint name
STO or STV, which has been attributed to either Nottingham
(*Snotingeham*) or Tutbury (*Stutesberia*)[89]—the latter, although otherwise unknown as a mint, was a borough and the site of Earl
Robert's castle. At least three other types appear to have been
struck in the Midlands, although their mints cannot be determined,[90] and further types and mints may well await discovery.

York issues

Another major group was struck at York, and has been the subject
of considerable attention. It consists of ten elaborately decorated or
unusual pictorial types, five bearing the name of Stephen, others
with the names of local magnates and a bishop.[91] Two types are
atrributed to Robert III of Stuteville: one with an armed figure on
horseback and inscribed +RODBERTVS DE STV (Pl. VII(*a*)) and the
other in quite a different style copying type 1 but with
+RODBDS[T·HE?].[92] Two other types are attributed to Eustace fitz
John: one with a standing figure in armour holding a sword and
+EVSTACIVS (Pl. VII(*b*)); the second showing a prancing lion and
reading +EISTAOHIVS or, on one damaged specimen, +[   ]CII FII IOA-
NIS (for *Eustacius filius Iohannis*). The final type has the crowned
bust of Stephen's type 1, but with a crosier in place of the sceptre
and inscribed HENRICVS EPC (Bishop Henry).

The York moneyers had struck all four varieties of type 1 from
metropolitan dies and to the full weight standard, but they did not
so far as we are aware purchase dies of types 2 and 6 from London.
The ornamental series that followed was struck to a lower weight
standard, using elaborate locally made dies mostly without the
name of the moneyer or mint, although some coins of the Eustace

[89] Andrew, *BNJ* 5 (1908), 440; *BMC* i, p. xcvi.

[90] These are Mack no. 197, a specimen of which was found in excavations in
Leicester (*SCBI Midlands Museums*, 728); Mack no. 273, which has the same obverse
type as *BMC* 3 and a hammered flan typical of mints in the Midlands; and a coin from
the Sheldon hoard (*BNJ* 7 (1910), 46, pl. 2, no. 25), which has a type 1 obverse but a
reverse similar to the Nottingham issue (*SCBI Midlands Museums*, 723). The Sheldon
coin was attributed to David I, but given to the Midlands by Seaby, 'The Pattern of
Coinage'.

[91] The types are Mack nos. 215–18, 220–9, and a newly discovered type with the
king standing: Seaby, 'A New "Standard" Type'.

[92] Mack no. 227; illustrated in G. C. Boon, 'Robert de Stuteville, type I',
Numismatic Circular, 93 (1985), 41.

Figure type include the mint name EBORACI (York) or a moneyer's name. One type in the name of Stephen (known as the 'Flag' type) is based on type 1 but shows the king holding a banner or flag (Pl. VI(*d*)), which has been seen as representing the elaborate standard to which Stephen's troops rallied at the battle of the Standard in 1138; in consequence the issue has been dated to 1138/9.[93] Another type with two standing figures (Pl. VI(e)), usually identified as Stephen and his wife, Queen Matilda, has been attributed to the period of Stephen's captivity in 1141. The whole series is generally dated 1138–41, but Boon has suggested that it may have begun in 1141 with the Two-Figures type and continued for some years, with the Eustace fitz John coins belonging towards its close in 1146–50.[94] Indeed, if one sets aside the historical associations that have been proposed for this coinage, the numismatic evidence points to an even later date, with the series starting no earlier than *c.*1145 and continuing into the early 1150s.

These ornamental York issues have occurred in only three hoards, Winterslow deposited in the later 1140s, 'Kent' in the mid-1150s, and Catal, for which there is no independent dating evidence. Their complete absence from all the major hoards of the early and mid-1140s—namely, those from Watford, South Kyme, Dartford, Nottingham, Sheldon, Paris region ('Beauvais'), and most significantly Prestwich, the latter containing sixty-four coins of type 1 from York—shows that the series belongs after *c.*1145.[95] That the ornamental series survives in such large numbers—some ninety specimens are known—is due largely to the hoard found at Catal, Yorks, in 1684. Although contemporary reports indicate only that it included three of the York types (Two-Figures; Robert of Stuteville Horseman; and Eustace Lion), it is likely that most of the surviving specimens of these types and of the Eustace Figure and Bishop Henry types come from this hoard, since they have provenances that can be traced back to the eighteenth or first half

[93] Alternative interpretations of the banner are discussed in Seaby, 'A New "Standard" Type'. In a later, unpublished paper, Seaby drew attention to the fact that the seals of Earl William and of his father Stephen, count of Aumale, have him on horseback also holding a banner: English, *Lords of Holderness*, figs. 2 and 3.

[94] Boon, 'Robert de Stuteville, type I'; *Welsh Hoards*, 70–1 n. 83; *Coins of the Anarchy*, 33, 37–41.

[95] After *c.*1145 on the chronology suggested below, or after *c.*1142 on the traditional chronology of type 1.

of the nineteenth century.[96] The only type that has been found in
significant numbers among modern single-finds is the Flag type.
That some of the York types are in effect over-represented in the
surviving material by virtue of the Catal find is confirmed by a
recent die-study of the York mint made by Lean.[97] He has shown
that the twenty-two Eustace Lion coins are struck from two pairs
of dies, the eighteen Two-Figures coins from three pairs of dies,
and the fourteen Eustace Figure coins from six obverse and eight
reverse dies. By contrast, the twenty-one Flag coins are struck from
seventeen obverse and eighteen reverse dies—which implies that
there were even more dies of this type originally in use and that the
issue was far larger than any of the others. It is not surprising, then,
that more Flag pennies than other types have occurred as single-
finds, in Yorkshire and elsewhere, and it makes their absence from
the major hoards still more significant.

If the series began sometime after c.1145, the Flag type was
probably the principal issue during the second half of the 1140s.
The Two-Figures, Robert Horseman, and Eustace Figure and Lion
types—that were clearly the most recent issues when the Catal
hoard was assembled—should be dated c.1150 or even later. The
Lozenge–Sceptre and Bishop Henry coins (known from four and
two specimens respectively) appear to be related to the later types
through their reverse designs and the Latin inscriptions of the
Bishop Henry coins.

These York issues have often been regarded as a 'royalist coinage'
par excellence, overseen by the king's loyal supporter, William of
Aumale, earl of York.[98] There can be little doubt that they were
issued at the instigation of William, who was appointed earl in
1138 and apparently controlled the royal castle and exercised the
jurisdictional authority normally enjoyed by the sheriff in York, but
doubt has recently been cast on William's reputation as a strong
supporter of Stephen. Work by Dalton casts him in a rather different light, as one who by the 1140s was principally interested in
extending his own influence and wealth, and whose actions at
times conflicted with the interests of the king, prompting Stephen
to come to York in 1142 and 1149 to attempt to reassert royal
authority. To this extent he was typical of many barons, Earl

[96] Boon, *Welsh Hoards*, 71 n. 83.
[97] I am grateful to William Lean for allowing me to draw on his unpublished work.
[98] Mack, 'Coinage of Stephen', 77–85.

Ranulf of Chester included, who owed their allegiance to Stephen, but looked to their own interests first. The distinctive York coins in the name of Stephen can properly be regarded as the baronial issues of Earl William. William must also have authorized as a concession the issues in the names of Robert of Stuteville and Eustace fitz John, two local magnates with whom he had close associations. Indeed, the revised dating for their coinages is more compatible with the documentary evidence, for, although both were active in the early 1140s, it is in the late 1140s and early 1150s that Dalton has found evidence of their close association with Earl William.[99] Moreover, there is one moneyer whose name (+THOMAS FILIVS VLF) can be recognized on some coins of the Eustace Figure type, and who has been plausibly identified with the Thomas fitz Ulvieth, sometime alderman of the Merchants' Guild of York, to whom William of Aumale gave the vill of Bonwick in Holderness c.1150.[100]

The two coins inscribed +HENRICVS EPC on the obverse and +STEPHANUS REX on the reverse have consistently been attributed to the king's brother, Henry of Blois, bishop of Winchester, although not without difficulty. It is most unlikely that Henry of Winchester would personally have usurped the regalian right of coinage, less still at York where he had no formal standing, even though he was a strong supporter of Archbishop William fitz Herbert and the treasurer of York, Hugh of Puiset. King regarded the suggestion that Henry of Winchester himself issued the coins as 'preposterous', and wondered whether in a period of uncertainty his name might have been used as that of a safe figure of authority, just as Henry I's was in western England.[101] Even this suggestion carries little conviction, since the coins carry Stephen's name on the reverse, and the York coinages, unlike those from western mints, have obverse legends that are consistently literate and purposeful. There were only two bishops named Henry during Stephen's reign, Henry of Winchester (1129–71) and Henry Murdac, archbishop

---

[99] P. Dalton, 'William Earl of York and Royal Authority in Yorkshire in the Reign of Stephen', *Haskins Soc. Journal*, 2 (1990), 155–65; *Conquest, Anarchy and Lordship: Yorkshire 1066–1154* (Cambridge, forthcoming), ch. 4. I am grateful to Dr Dalton for lending me a copy of his typescript for this chapter.

[100] C. T. Clay, 'A Holderness Charter of William Count of Aumale', *Yorkshire Arch. Journal*, 39 (1956–8), 339–42.

[101] King, 'Anarchy', 151.

of York (1147/51–3). Although Henry Murdac was consecrated archbishop and received his pallium in 1147, he was disapproved of by Stephen and denied admission to York until January 1151.[102] For two years he exercised his office, which included the right to strike coins at York, although since the ninth century these had borne the name of the king rather than the archbishop. With the revised dating of this issue to *c*.1150, an attribution to Henry Murdac is clearly a possibility. An argument against this is the use of the title *episcopus* rather than *archiepiscopus*. Henry Murdac was, of course, a bishop as well, but in documents the full archiepiscopal title would be used. If these coins are to be attributed to Archbishop Henry, as they probably should be, the die-cutter must have used the shorter title EPC for reasons of space or to balance the REX on the other coin face.

Incidentally, a later dating for the series opens the possibility of a reidentification of the figures depicted on the Two-Figures type. It has long been thought to represent a man and woman—Stephen and Queen Matilda[103]—but both figures appear to be holding swords by their sides (Pl. VI(*e*)). Archibald has pointed to a likely model for the design,[104] the splendid ducalis of Roger II of Sicily issued in 1140 which depicts Roger and his son, another Roger, duke of Apulia, standing either side of a tall cross-on-steps (Pl. VI(*f*)).[105] It is possible—I would put it no higher—that the York issue represents Stephen, on the right in ceremonial costume with a pendant crown,[106] and his son Eustace to the left, in a helmet and armour similar to that on the coins of Robert of Stuteville and Eustace fitz John. By the late 1140s Eustace had been knighted, had led troops in battle, and was being promoted by Stephen as his rightful heir. Both were in York in 1149, and Eustace may have remained there looking after Stephen's interests and negotiating

---

[102] It seems that William of Aumale was sympathetic to Henry Murdac's cause before 1151: Dalton, *Conquest, Anarchy and Lordship*, ch. 4.

[103] For the most recent discussion, see Boon, *Coins of the Anarchy*, 41–2.

[104] Archibald, 'Coins', 335, no. 439.

[105] R. Spahr, *Le Monete Siciliane dai Bizantini a Carlo I d'Angio (582–1282)* (Zurich and Graz, 1976), 153, no. 72.

[106] The form of head-gear of the right-hand figure is problematic, and on two of the three known dies it does resemble loose hair or a veil. On the third (*BMC* 261) and most careful die, however, it might be interpreted as a pendant crown of the type worn by Roger II on the ducalis.

with Henry Murdac in 1150.[107] If this design does in fact depict Eustace with his father, it does not follow that the Eustace Figure type with the sample legend +EVSTACIVS was struck for the prince rather than Eustace fitz John, for he would not readily have usurped the royal prerogative over the coinage by omitting Stephen's name.

In a number of papers Seaby has argued fervently that this whole 'York' series of coins was in fact struck either in Flanders or for use in Flanders, and that the coins in the name of Eustace are of Prince Eustace of Boulogne and those of Robert are of Robert le Roux, lord of Bethune.[108] Elements of their design, particularly the use of various symbols breaking the inscriptions, have close parallels in the contemporary coinage of Saint-Omer. However, the denomination and weight standard is quite incompatible with that used in Flanders or Boulogne, none is known with certainty to have been found on the Continent, but there is a very clear find distribution in England which concentrates on Yorkshire. Moreover, as we have seen, several of the inscriptions give the series clear York connections. In short, Seaby's attributions cannot be accepted, and the Flemish influence on the coin designs probably stems from the use of a Flemish die-cutter and the presence of a significant Flemish community in York.

Issues of the west and south-west

Whereas the independent coinages of the Midlands were in Stephen's name, those of western England and south Wales were essentially in the names of Matilda, 'Henry', 'William', and some individual barons. In central southern England (Oxfordshire, Hampshire, and Wiltshire) some issues have the names of barons but others name 'Stephen'. At Bristol, Hereford, Wareham, and Cardiff the local 'Stephen' dies probably date to 1140 and 1141, following Matilda's arrival in England.[109]

Our knowledge of Matilda's coinage has been revolutionized by

---

[107] Dalton, *Conquest, Anarchy and Lordship*, ch. 4.

[108] P. J. Seaby, 'Some Coins of Stephen and Eustace and Related Issues of Western Flanders', in N. J. Mayhew (ed.), *Coinage in the Low Countries (880–1500)*, (BAR Int. Ser. 54; Oxford, 1979), 49–53; 'A New "Standard" Type'; 'Of Seals and Sceptres'.

[109] An alternative date of 1138–9 has also been suggested (Boon, *Welsh Hoards*, 55), but this would imply a still earlier end to the supply of metropolitan dies to these mints (see below, Chronology).

the discovery and swift publication of the Coed-y-Wenallt hoard in 1980, which trebled the number of extant coins of the empress. We now see that her coinage—other than the 'Pereric' issue discussed above—consisted of two types. The first copies that of Stephen's type 1, but with the title MATILLIS IMPER (MATILDIS IMP, etc.) or simply IMPERATR, and the dies are locally cut (Pl. VII (c)). It is known from the mints of Bristol, Cardiff, Oxford, and Wareham. The second type, only discovered in the 1980 Wenallt hoard, has a similar obverse but a cross over a saltire fleury on the reverse, and provides an additional inscription, IM·HE·MA·, which Boon interprets as IM[peratrix] HE[res] MA[thildis] (Pl. VII (d)). The new type is known for Matilda from the mints of Bristol and Cardiff, for a certain John (whom Boon tentatively identifies as a member of the St John family)[110] also from Cardiff, and for Henry of Neubourg (+hENRICI dE NOVOB) from Swansea (Pl. VII (e)).

Although about 100 coins of Matilda are now known from several hoards, they are heavily die-linked, and the coinage would have been a relatively small one. The Oxford coins must have been struck between Matilda's first arrival there in July 1141 and her dramatic escape in December 1142. The coins of Bristol, Cardiff, and Wareham could in theory have been struck at any time after the arrival in the south-west of the empress and Earl Robert in late September–October 1139, but a number of factors suggest that her coins were not produced until late 1140 or 1141.[111] It is quite likely, then, that Matilda's coinage started only after the battle of Lincoln (February 1141).

The two other substantial groups of coins from western mints are those in the name of a 'Henry' and a 'William' (Mack nos. 241–61, 262–8). These have usually been attributed to Henry of Anjou and Earl William of Gloucester (1147–83), son of Robert, but Archibald has suggested that some of these—perhaps all—

---

[110] Boon, *Welsh Hoards*, 52–3; 'A Second Penny in the Name of John from the Wenallt Find', *Numismatic Circular*, 95 (1987), 253.

[111] This is based on the existence of local 'Stephen' type 1 dies, on the hoard evidence, in particular the absence of Matilda coins from the Watford hoard (which included Cardiff coins from local dies in Stephen's name), and on the small size of the issues. However, Boon would date Matilda's first type late 1139–spring 1141, and her second type spring 1141–summer 1142, but this is influenced in part by his dating of the Nottingham hoard to September 1140: Boon, *Welsh Hoards*, 55.

invoke the name of Henry I or William I or II.[112] In both groups there are several designs, but they are all copied or adapted from three earlier issues: Stephen's type 1, Henry I's type 15, and William I's type 5. (Elsewhere in the country coin designs from previous reigns are rarely invoked.) Most of the 'Henry' coins read merely HENRICVS, which is the inscription on Henry I's type 15, but some read HENRICVS REX (as found on Henry I's type 14) and this is clearly inappropriate to Henry of Anjou. One coin (Mack no. 244, from the Nottingham hoard) reads merely REX AN, without a personal name, and this title was probably copied from William I's type 5.[113] The presence of three of the 'Henry' coins in the Prestwich hoard indicates that some of these belong to the currency of type 1, and belong to a period in the earlier 1140s when Henry of Anjou was a boy and not a serious contender for the throne. The 'Henry' and 'William' coins appear to fall into two broad groups. Ones of 'Henry' with designs based on Stephen's type 1 or Henry I's type 15 (Pl. VII (f)) were struck mainly at Gloucester and Hereford towards the end of type 1, while Bristol and Cardiff were striking coins of Matilda. A somewhat later group, from the more southerly mints of Bristol, Malmesbury, Dorchester, Wareham, Sherborne?, and Ilchester?, comprises the coins in the name of 'William' and those of 'Henry' with designs taken from William I's type 5 (Pl. VII(a)). This type was by then seventy years old and no longer in circulation, but evidently some coins had been found which inspired Angevin mint officials. Also associated with this group is a unique coin of the same type but with an obverse reading +BR:CITBR[   ] (Mack no. 270 (Pl. VIII(b)), which has doubtfully been attributed to Brian fitz Count, constable of Wallingford.[114] I am inclined to regard all the 'Henry' coins, and probably those of 'William', as invoking the name of earlier kings. As Edmund King has observed, the barons who placed their names on the coinage during Stephen's reign were, with few exceptions, men of the second rank.[115] The bishops and earls, although they

---

[112] Archibald, 'Coins', 337, no. 448; followed by King, 'Anarchy', 150. Boon (*Coins of the Anarchy*, 32–3) would prefer to attribute some of the 'Henry' coins to Henry of Anjou.

[113] Earlier types generally have a longer form of *Anglorum*, while subsequent types usually omit it altogether.

[114] See discussion in Boon, *Coins of the Anarchy*, 29–32, no. 24. The mint-signature 'TO' poses a real difficulty for the attribution.   [115] King, 'Anarchy', 151.

often controlled mints that issued independent types, shrank from signing these coins with their own name. It is evident that there was a strong respect for the tradition that the issuing of coins was a royal prerogative, and for those who had renounced their homage to Stephen it was good enough that they should use the name of a former king, William or Henry.

In the central counties of southern England there are two related types in the name of Stephen, each having a rosette inserted at the end of the obverse legend. One is based on the type 1 design (Mack nos. 184–5), and the only legible mint name is Cricklade (Wiltshire), at which a castle was built in 1144. The other has a reverse derived from type 2, and significantly it was struck by at least two moneyers at Oxford—the one mint outside the south-east that we know had received official dies of type 2. Rather than ordering further type 2 dies from London, the moneyers appear to have reverted to local dies with an adaptation of this type. From Salisbury there is an overtly baronial issue showing a figure in armour holding a sword, known from two specimens both found locally (Pl. VIII(c)).[116] Unfortunately, the obverse legend is only partly legible, [ ]COM, but, given that the mint attribution is secure, it has not unreasonably been completed as *Patricius comes*, for Patrick of Salisbury, whom Matilda created earl of Wiltshire between 1141 and 1147.

There are a number of mints that were active in type 1 but to which no coins of the following period, prior to type 7, can be attributed. These include Chester, Shrewsbury, Stafford, Warwick, Worcester, Exeter, Shaftesbury, and Winchester. Our knowledge of the coinage of this period is by no means complete, and for some of these mints coinages may yet be discovered, though even so they are likely to have been relatively small.[117] Winchester was one of the largest mints in the region, with eight moneyers striking type 1 from the full range of dies and maintaining a high weight standard,[118] but we know no coins from it until the end of the reign, when two moneyers struck type 7. In Survey II of the

[116] Mack no. 271; Archibald, 'Coins', 336, no. 443.
[117] There are a number of types with illegible or blundered reverses for which no attribution can presently be proposed, e.g. Mack 176 (from the Watford hoard) and 206.
[118] I am grateful to Yvonne Harvey for allowing me to consult her die-study of the mint.

Winton Domesday made in 1148, which falls during the period of inactivity according to the chronology preferred below, six of the eight type 1 moneyers can be identified, occupying properties mainly in the High Street that have previous connections with minting.[119] Another man, Sanson, is named in the Survey as a *monetarius*, occupying three properties in the same area of the High Street. He is not known from any coins of Winchester, but he did strike an independent type in Stephen's name at Southampton ('ANT' or 'ANTOI' for *Hanton* (Pl. VIII(*d*))),[120] which had been inactive as a mint for over a hundred years. A second moneyer named W[ ] striking this type at Southampton[121] may well be the Willem who minted at Winchester in Henry II's cross–crosslet coinage and in 1148 had premises adjacent to Sanson's in the High Street. It would seem as if for much of the civil war Henry of Blois, bishop of Winchester, may have placed a moratorium on minting in Winchester, or imposed conditions such as the maintenance of a 22-grain standard that made it uneconomic,[122] but that two moneyers, to avoid the restrictions, issued their coins in nearby Southampton. Whether these were actually struck there or in their premises in Winchester High Street we cannot know.

Issues of the northern borders

The coinage of northern England is intimately linked with the beginning of coinage in Scotland, since for much of the reign the area was under the control of King David and Prince Henry of Scotland. Within weeks of Stephen's accession the Scots invaded

[119] M. Biddle and D. J. Keen, 'Winchester in the Eleventh and Twelfth centuries', in M. Biddle (ed.), *Winchester in the Early Middle Ages* (Winchester Studies 1; Oxford, 1976), 241–448 (at 415–19). Only one of these men is described as a *monetarius*, but the same was true of the earlier survey and need not imply that the others were inactive. One of the moneyers had died by 1148.

[120] Mack nos. 207–13, as probably of the Canterbury mint, following Elmore Jones, 'Stephen Type VII', 541. The previous Southampton attribution has more recently been restored, relying on the form of the mint-name, on further local finds (e.g. *BNJ* 57 (1987), 144, no. 196), and on the Winton Domesday entry, which was known already to Andrew.

[121] Mack no. 213A, and a second specimen said to have been acquired in the Portsmouth–Havant district: Seaby, 'The Pattern of Coinage'.

[122] Andrew (*BNJ* 18 (1925–6), 261–2) suggested that minting ceased due to the destruction of the city in 1141, but the Winton Domesday shows that it had largely been rebuilt by 1148.

and secured Carlisle and much of Cumberland and Westmorland. In 1138 they moved into Northumberland, Durham, and north Yorkshire, and, although they were repulsed at Northallerton at the battle of the Standard, it is not clear to what extent they were deprived of their immediate gains. The following year, as part of a treaty, Stephen granted Prince Henry the earldom of Northumbria (i.e. Northumberland, Durham, Cumberland, Westmorland, and north Lancashire). These northern counties were only regained by Henry II in 1157. Cumberland was particularly prized in the 1130s and 1140s as it included the very rich silver mines below Nenthead, near Alston, which were succeeded in the 1150s and 1160s by even more productive mines near Blanchland over the Northumberland border and at Rookhope in County Durham.[123] This silver made the Carlisle mint particularly important, and it also fed indirectly the other northern English and Scottish mints.

The coinage of this region has been described with admirable clarity by Stewart,[124] and only the general outlines will be described here. Some rare coins of David I struck at Carlisle copying Henry I's last type were probably produced soon after his capture of the town in January 1136. These apart, the earliest coins of the borders and of Scotland bore the designs of Stephen's type 1. At Newcastle, Durham, and Carlisle they were in the name of Stephen, but only Newcastle obtained official dies from London, and it subsequently followed the other two mints in using locally made dies. At Corbridge the coins were in the name of Prince Henry (HENRIC ERL or HENRICUS) and at Edinburgh and Roxburgh in the name of David. These mints were closely related, sharing common moneyers—Erebald at Carlisle, Corbridge, and Edinburgh, and Willem (probably Erebald's son) at Carlisle, Newcastle, and later Bamburgh. There is a unique coin of Edinburgh in the name of Stephen, but it shares an obverse die with a Carlisle coin, and it is likely that the Edinburgh reverse die

[123] I. Blanchard, 'Lothian and Beyond: The Economy of the "English Empire" of David I'. I am grateful to Dr Blanchard for showing me this unpublished paper and for discussing it with me.

[124] I. Stewart, 'Scottish Mints', in R. A. G. Carson (ed.), Mints, Dies and Currency (London, 1971), 165–289 (at 191–202). However, this was written prior to the discovery in 1972 of the Prestwich hoard, which is of critical importance for the early Scottish and border coinage containing some sixty-five coins of the region, but which unfortunately remains essentially unpublished.

had been brought back to Carlisle by Erebald and used there by mistake. Newcastle and Durham soon abandoned type 1 in favour of local variants (Mack nos. 189–90, Newcastle; and 118, Durham), the same die-cutter apparently serving both mints.[125]

The next phase, beginning probably in the early 1140s, saw the adoption of a distinctive reverse design (a cross and four pelleted annulets) for David's coinage (Stewart[126] type IVc), which was struck at Carlisle and Newcastle as well as at some Scottish mints.[127] In the mid- or late 1140s a new mint, probably Bamburgh, operated for Prince Henry striking a bold cross–crosslet type, and rather surprisingly one of the obverse dies used there was in Stephen's name (Mack nos. 288–9 (Pl. VIII(e))). A further distinctive type with a cross fleury reverse was adopted for the, by now growing, Scottish coinage and this was struck at Carlisle for both David (d. 1153) and Henry (d. 1152) (Pl. VIII(f)).

All these northern issues, except for those of Durham, were struck to the full 22-grain standard. There was no shortage of silver, and it was in David's interests to produce a coinage that would be acceptable internationally. One of the questions that arises is what significance should be attached to the use of Stephen's name on several issues of the later 1130s and on the small group from Bamburgh of the mid- or late 1140s. Except for the earliest coins of Newcastle, all the 'Stephen' issues from the Borders are from local dies and many have their own distinctive designs, features that elsewhere in the country would suggest coinages of earls who managed their shires independently, while acknowledging Stephen's ultimate sovereignty over them. The same may well be true of these border issues, and, if so, it sheds interesting light on David's perception of his possession of Carlisle, and the change that came about in the early 1140s when he started putting his own and his son's names on the coins there.

[125] The attribution of Mack no. 193, which is related to the Durham coins but has the mint-signature EI, is uncertain.

[126] I. Stewart, *The Coinage of Scotland*, 2nd edn. (London, 1967), 132.

[127] Newcastle and Perth were added by the Prestwich hoard: *Coin Hoards*, 1 (1975), 92.

CHRONOLOGY

The chronology of the coinages is of critical importance to historians and numismatists alike, but it is problematic and controversial and for this reason has been left until the end. Firm dating evidence has proved surprisingly elusive. There are essentially two theories that are current, a high chronology and a low chronology (Table 5.5). The traditional or high chronology would have type 1 lasting until, but not much beyond, Stephen's release from captivity in November 1141, attributing types 2 and 6 to the following twelve years. There is more general agreement that the last issue, type 7, must belong to the settled period after the treaty of Winchester (November 1153, promulgated at Westminster in December), as part of which, according to Ralph de Diceto, Stephen and Henry of Anjou agreed to reform the coinage.[128] Type 7, then, would have been introduced in 1154, the last year of Stephen's reign, and it continued until Henry II's recoinage of 1158, a date established from several chronicles and the pipe rolls.[129]

TABLE 5.5. *Chronology of Stephen's substantive issues*

Type	Seaman–Seaby	Archibald	Blackburn preferred
Type 1	*c.*1135–49/50	1135/6–42	*c.*1136–45
STIFNE REX	1135–41		
STIEFNE RE	1141–5		
STIEFNE R	1145–7		
STIEFNE	1147–9/50		
Type 2	*c.*1150–2	1142–*c.*1148	*c.*1145–50
Type 6	*c.*1153	*c.*1148–53	*c.*1150–4
Type 7	*c.*1153–8	1153–8	*c.*1154–8
Matilda	1142 or poss. 1147	1141–	*c.*1141–5?

[128] 'Forma publica percussa eadem in regno celebris erit ubique moneta' (*Radulph de Diceto opera historica*, i. 296–7, *s.a.* 1153).
[129] Allen, *BMC Henry II*, pp. lxiv–lxv.

The low chronology, first mooted by Dolley,[130] and subsequently developed by Seaman and Seaby,[131] has type 1 lasting until the late 1140s, and gives types 2 and 6 to the early 1150s. Dolley based his argument on the relative proportions of the surviving coins and on there being more continuity of moneyers from type 2 into the later types than into type 1. Seaman took account of this, but was influenced mainly by his proposed dating for the coins attributed to Henry of Anjou to 1151–2 (or possibly 1149) and a similar dating for the Nottingham hoard which included one of these but was composed mainly of type 1 coins. Within type 1 he also assigns an absolute chronology to the four forms of obverse inscription (see Table 5.4). The shortest form he dates *c*.1147–49/50 because it is unknown, or at least extremely rare, for the mints of Bristol and Gloucester, which would not have struck coins for the king after 1146. The long period of issue for the STIFNE REX coins, *c*.1135–41, is probably intended to permit the PERERIC coins to be assigned to 1141, although he does not expressly say so. Seaby has associated the coins of type 1 struck from defaced or cancelled dies with the interdict of 1148. None of these arguments is conclusive. Doubt has been cast on the attribution of the coins reading HENRICVS to Henry of Anjou, the Bristol and Gloucester mints probably stopped receiving metropolitan dies long before 1146, and Seaby's explanation for the defaced dies is not convincing.

The high chronology has its origins in observations of Andrew and Brooke that type 1 must have lasted until *at least* the king's captivity in 1141,[132] and, although no very strong argument that he ordered a recoinage on his release was put forward, a date of 1135–*c*.1141/2 had been generally adopted.[133] This dating was supported by Andrew's belief, widely followed, that the Nottingham hoard was lost as a result of the destruction and burning of the city by Robert of Gloucester in September 1141.

[130] M. Dolley, 'The Anglo-Norman Coins in the Uppsala University Cabinet', *BNJ* 37 (1968), 29–34.

[131] Seaman, 'A Re-examination of Some Hoards'; Seaby, 'Stephen and the Interdict'.

[132] Andrew, 'Sheldon Hoard', 42–3; *BMC* i, pp. lxix, lxxv; Mack, 'Coinage of Stephen', 39, 48.

[133] Ibid. 40; J. J. North, *English Hammered Coinage*, i, 2nd edn. (London, 1980), 164; Archibald, 'Coins', 333.

Unfortunately, as Boon has pointed out, Robert's raid on Nottingham was in September 1140,[134] an impossibly early date for the deposit of the hoard since it contained a coin of Matilda minted at Oxford after June 1141! This is not the first time that numismatists have been misled by an excessive desire to associate hoards with recorded events, rather than allowing the contents to speak for themselves, and it takes away one of the few points in the chronology that had been regarded as reasonably secure.

Responding to the papers by Seaman and Seaby, Archibald and Boon have supported the earlier chronology. Boon has argued that the Bristol mint coins struck from official dies of Stephen, which include ones reading STIEFNE R but few if any reading STIEFNE, must have been struck before Matilda's arrival there in October 1139.[135] A similar case could be made for Gloucester, Matilda's principal residence from early 1140 until the battle of Lincoln (February 1141) and an Angevin stronghold thereafter, which appears only to have used metropolitan dies ending REX or RE. Equally Hereford could perhaps provide dating evidence, since it came under the control of Miles of Gloucester in December 1139, yet its moneyers used official dies of all four varieties, including several with STIEFNE, before one moneyer resorted to locally made ones. The evidence from these three mints is somewhat inconsistent, each implying a slightly different stage in the sequence of type 1 dies that had been reached by the end of 1139. The reason for the disparity is likely to be in part that the sequence of obverse legends was not as distinct as we are inclined to think—i.e. there was some overlap between the various forms—and in part that the moneyers may not have stopped acquiring official London dies immediately—it was in their and the Angevin party's interests that their coins should be readily accepted in currency. Indeed at Bristol and Hereford, as at Cardiff and Swansea, there had been a period when local dies in Stephen's name were employed before those of Matilda or 'Henry'. Even though these mints may not provide a precise chronology for the development of type 1, they all point in the same general direction, and we may reasonably conclude that the shortest STIEFNE form was in use at the latest by 1140 or 1141. Archibald has reached a similar conclusion, but by a quite different route.[136] She

[134] Boon, *Welsh Hoards*, 55 n. 85; the text is FW ii. 128.
[135] Boon, *Welsh Hoards*, 50, 68 n. 53; *Coins of the Anarchy*, 17.
[136] Archibald, 'Dating Stephen's First Type'. She had proposed a slightly different

argues that the Angevin mints continued to use metropolitan dies of Stephen until the second half of 1141, but bases her support for the high chronology essentially on her identification of the 'Pereric' coins as issues of Matilda in mid-1141 and her argument that these are associated stylistically with the STIEFNE series of dies.[137] On either approach, the Seaman–Seaby chronology, which has the STIEFNE form introduced c.1147, does appear to be wrong, but that does not mean that we must accept that type 1 ended in 1141/2. We should be particularly wary of the argument that this was an appropriate time for a recoinage. It may not have seemed so at the time, and governments often do not do things at the most appropriate moment. Boon has suggested that type 2 was not introduced until c.1145,[138] and there is much to favour such a date.

Between the earliest STIEFNE coins of type 1 and the introduction of type 2 one must allow for the substantial STIEFNE coinage as well as the use of some local dies, of defaced dies and of variants, accompanied by a weight reduction at some mints. It is difficult to provide a reliable estimate of the time this might have taken, but there are two factors already touched upon that have a bearing on this. At its height the STIEFNE coinage was being struck at most mints in the country, but by the beginning of type 2 a major political change had occurred which discouraged two-thirds of the mints from purchasing the new metropolitan dies. The event that is likely to have triggered that change is the nine months of Stephen's captivity (February–November 1141), which prompted some earls and lesser barons to join the Angevin party, and others, of necessity, to assume control of their own counties and manage them on their own account. The fact that types 2 and 6 show such a clear and stable geographical pattern suggests that there had been ample time for the independence of the counties outside the south-east to be well established, and for royal control of East Anglia to be restored.

The second factor is that raised by Dolley, namely the relative number of surviving coins of each type, though now we can base this on the more representative evidence of single-finds. In theory

chronology in 'Coins', 321, 333–4; 'English Medieval Coins as Dating Evidence', in J. Casey and R. Reece (eds.), *Coins and the Archaeologist*, 2nd edn. (1988), 280.

[137] Archibald places the 'Pereric' dies after the first of the three sub-varieties of STIEFNE dies, but on the published evidence they could come a little earlier in the STIEFNE series.

[138] Boon, *Coins of the Anarchy*, 43.

the number of single-finds should reflect the volume of coinage in circulation and the period for which the type was in use. Unfortunately, we cannot assume there will be a close correlation between the duration of a coin type and the number of finds, because there may well have been changes in mint output and the size of the currency during the reign. It is difficult to predict what effect the civil war would have had on the size of the currency, for, while it may have drawn into circulation silver from the treasury's reserve, from church and domestic plate, and from abroad, it will also have interrupted international trade, which normally brought silver into the country. None the less it is worth considering the single-find evidence in relation to the chronology. The analysis in Table 5.6 of 108 single-finds is based on the hypothesis that the number of finds is proportionate to the duration of the issue. This theoretical model implies a duration of some twelve years for type 1, about three years each for types 2 and 6, and three and a half years for type 7. The estimate for type 7 corresponds remarkably well with the established dates, c.1154–8, and the fact that the finds from the south-east give such similar results to those from the Midlands, north, and west encourages one to think that some weight should be given to the results. At least they suggest that the five or six years attributed to type 1 by the traditional chronology (c.1136–41/2) are too short.

TABLE 5.6. *Theoretical chronology implied by single-finds* (based on 108 finds of 1984–92, cf. Fig. 5.2)

Finds	Duration of issues (years)				
	Type 1	Type 2	Type 6	Baronial/ independent	Type 7
South-east	12.6	2.6	2.6	1.0	3.2
Midlands, north, and west	11.6			7.2	3.3
All	12.2		6.5		3.3

	Resultant theoretical chronology			
	Type 1	Type 2	Type 6	Type 7
	c.1136–48	c.1148–51	c.1151–4	c.1154–8

Taking all these points into account, it is likely that type 1 extended at least into the mid-1140s, while types 2 and 6 on present evidence appear to be of roughly similar length. Translating this into a chronology that does not appear unduly precise is difficult, but I would suggest the following: type 1, c.1136–45; type 2, c.1145–50; type 6, c.1150–4; type 7, c.1154–8. The Angevin issues in the name of Matilda and others seem to have begun in 1140 or more likely 1141, while most of the independent issues in the name of Stephen would belong to the period from c.1145 (or a little earlier) to 1154. In the Appendix the hoards are arranged in order of their deposition, and tentative dates have been assigned to them based on this chronology, but it must be stressed that the absolute dating of these hoards is not as precise as the table would seem to imply.

CONCLUSION

The coinage offers evidence on a range of topics of importance for the historian, a number of which have been touched upon here. Henry I's policy of restructuring and reducing the size of the mint network was reversed by Stephen early in his reign, by restoring minting rights to boroughs that had previously enjoyed them and by creating a number of new mints. For the first four years the mint administration worked more or less as normal, but the arrival of Matilda prompted a breakdown of control, initially over mints in the west, and the breakdown became more widespread after the king's capture in February 1141. Only the mints in the extreme south-east appear to have remained under effective royal control throughout the reign. Around the mid-1140s, it is suggested, authority was restored over the East Anglian mints, but in the remainder of the country the coinage was managed by the local earls or other barons, and coin circulation became highly regionalized. In general the major magnates—the earls and bishops—did not strike coins in their own names, and to this extent they respected the royal prerogative of coinage. More detailed work is required, but it would seem that those who owed homage to Stephen issued coins in his name, while those who had given their allegiance to Matilda issued their coins either in her name or apparently in that of a previous king, Henry or William. Only a handful of mostly lesser barons placed their own name on the coins.

Much work remains to be done on this intricate coinage, particularly in defining the points within type 1 at which the various mints broke free from central authority, determining the pattern and chronology of the independent issues region by region, and assessing the economic implications of changes in the output of the mints in different regions through the reign. As more single-finds and hoards come to light and are published, these issues should become clearer, but there is already ample material for real progress to be made.

NOTES: TO THE APPENDIX

These notes generally give the principal modern references for the numismatic content of each find, from which fuller details and references can be found, although some earlier major publications of the hoards are also cited. The dates of deposit suggested in the table are approximate; for the continental hoards, an indication of the *terminus post quem* (*t.p.q.*) of the non-English element of the find is also given below. The following abbreviations are used:

Inv.   J. D. A. Thompson, *Inventory of British Coin Hoards A.D. 600–1500* (London, 1956)

Kluge   B. Kluge, 'Das angelsächsische Element in den slawischen Münzfunden des 10. bis 12. Jahrunderts. Aspekte einer Analyse', in M. A. S. Blackburn and D. M. Metcalf (eds.), *Viking-Age Coinage in the Northern Lands* (BAR Internat. Ser. 122; Oxford, 1981), i. 257–327

Molvõgin   A. Molvõgin, 'Normannische Fundmünzen in Estland und anderen Ostseeländern', in K. Jonsson and B. Malmer (eds.), *Sigtuna Papers* (Stockholm, 1990), 241–9

Seaman   R. J. Seaman, 'A Re-examination of Some Hoards Containing Coins of Stephen', *BNJ* 48 (1978), 58–72

1. R. H. M. Dolley, 'A Small Find of Stephen Pennies from Berkshire', *BNJ* 31 (1962), 162–4; Mack, 107.
2. *Inv.* 372; J. Rashleigh, 'Descriptive List of a Collection of Coins of Henry I and Stephen, Discovered in Hertfordshire, in 1818', *NC* 1:12 (1849), 138–69; Mack, 103; I. Stewart, 'A London Penny of Matilda?', *BNJ* 46 (1986), 76–7 (but see Boon, *Welsh Hoards*, 71 n. 90); Seaman, 60–1. Another group of about 100 coins of Stephen is said to have been found in Watford in the same year (known as the 'Smaller Watford Hoard'), but it is not clear whether it is a parcel from the main deposit: *Inv.* 373; Mack, 103.
3. R. Seaman, 'A Find of Stephen Coins at Rayleigh Mount', *BNJ* 38 (1969), 186–8.
4. *Inv.* 230; Mack, 105; C. E. Blunt and F. Elmore Jones, 'Two Wiltshire Coin-Hoards of the Time of Stephen', *Wilts. Arch. Mag.* 64 (1969), 65–70; P. Robinson, 'The Latton Hoard: A Further Note', *Numismatic Circular*, 92 (1984), 252–3. One coin of Henry I, type xv, is published in *Sylloge of Coins of the British Isles, Bristol*, 64.
5. *Inv.* 337; L. A. Lawrence, 'On a Hoard of Coins chiefly of King Stephen', *NC* 5:2 (1922), 49–83; Mack, 106–7; Seaman, 61.
6. *Coin Hoards*, 1 (1975), no. 360. Part of hoard sold at auction: Sotheby, 6 Dec. 1974, lots 1–107; Glendining, 13 Nov. 1974, lots 1–228; Glendining, 10 Nov. 1976, lots 121–420; and privately by one of the finders who produced a list illustrating some 300 coins: Henry Tasker, 'A Sales Catalogue of the Prestwich Hoard of Silver Pennies' (Prestwich, n.d., *c.*1975).
7. *Inv.* 116; J. Rashleigh, 'An Account of Some Baronial and Other Coins of King Stephen's Reign', *NC* 1:13 (1850), 181–91; Mack, 103–4; C. E. Blunt, F. Elmore Jones, and P. H. Robinson, 'On Some Hoards of the Time of Stephen', *BNJ* 37 (1968), 35–42, at 39–40.
8. Boon, *Welsh Hoards*, 37–82; G. C. Boon, 'A Second Penny in the Name of John from the Wenallt Find', *Numismatic Circular*, 95 (1987), 253.

APPENDIX: *British and continental hoards containing coins from the reign of Stephen*

	Deposit date	Henry I	In Stephen's name					Independent	Matilda	Other	Uncertain	Tealby	Total
			Type 1	Erased	Type 2	Type 6	Type 7						
1. Henley-on-Thames, Berks., 1881	c.1138	—	5	—	—	—	—	—	—	—	—	—	5
2. Watford, Herts, 1818	1140/1	477	646	—	—	—	—	—	—	—	3	—	1,127+
3. Rayleigh, Essex, 1909–10/1961	c.1141	x	9	—	—	—	—	—	—	—	—	—	9
4. Latton, Wilts., 1860–82	?	—	2	—	—	—	—	—	—	—	47+	—	50+
5. South Kyme, Lincs., pre-1922	c.1143	11	315	1	—	—	—	4	1	1	—	—	334
6. Prestwich, Lancs., 1972	c.1144	66	873	32	—	—	—	45	5	44	—	—	1,065
7. Dartford/Gravesend, Kent 1817/25	c.1145	4	44+	1	—	—	—	6	5	2	—	—	c.70
8. Coed-y-Wenallt, Glam., 1980	c.1145	—	25	—	—	—	—	—	73	8	—	—	106
9. Nottingham, 1880	c.1145	14	89+	41	—	1?	—	27	5	1	—	—	178+
10. Sheldon, Derby, 1867	c.1147	3	77	14	2?	—	—	2	—	—	—	—	101
11. Linton, Kent, 1883	c.1148	7	42+	38+	—	—	—	6	—	—	—	—	c.150
12. Ashby-de-la-Zouch, Leics., 1788/9	c.1150?	x	4+	—	—	—	—	4+	—	—	400+	—	c.450
13. Winterslow, Wilts., c.1804	c.1150	—	1	—	5	—	—	3	—	9	—	—	20+
14. Catal, Yorks., 1684	c.1152	—	—	—	—	—	—	x	—	—	—	—	?
15. Kent?, 1986	c.1155	—	1	—	—	1	11	1	—	—	—	—	14
16. Bute, Isle of, 1863	c.1155	—	3	—	—	—	—	—	—	15	9	—	27
17. Crosthwaite, Cumb., 1841	?	—	—	—	—	—	—	—	—	—	x	—	?
18. Norfolk?, 1660	?	—	—	—	—	—	—	—	—	—	60	—	60?
19. Bamburgh castle?, Northumb., 1844	c.1160?	—	1	—	—	—	—	—	—	7	—	—	7
20. Awbridge, Hants, 1902	c.1165	—	—	—	—	—	31+	3	—	—	—	104+	c.180

	Deposit date	Henry I	Type 1	Erased	Type 2	Type 6	Type 7	Independent	Matilda	Other	Uncertain	Tealby	Total
			In Stephen's name										
21. Wicklewood, Norfolk, 1989	c.1170	17	44	2	109	134	29	5	1	1	—	140	482
22. West Meon, Hants, 1992	c.1170	—	—	—	2	1	—	1	—	—	—	31	34
23. London Bridge, c.1850	?	—	—	—	—	—	—	—	—	2	x	x	?
24. Outchester, Northumb., 1817	c.1170	—	—	—	—	—	—	—	—	11+	—	20+	c.1,000
25. Lark Hill, Worcs, 1853	c.1175	—	—	—	—	—	1?	—	—	2	—	208	229
26. Isle of Man, pre-1769	c.1180	—	—	—	—	—	1	—	—	4	—	2	7+?
27. Colchester, Essex, 1902	c.1260	2	—	—	—	—	1	—	—	—	—	—	10,926
28. Paris region ('Beauvais'), France, c.1987,c.1150		174	143	—	—	—	—	6	1	1	—	—	339
29. Taskula (grave 5), Maaria, Finland, 1938,c.1150		—	1	—	—	—	—	—	—	—	—	—	2
30. Kirkkomäki (grave F), Kaarina, Finland, 1984	c.1150	—	1	—	—	—	—	—	—	—	—	—	2
31. Lazyn, Poland, 1887	c.1150	1	—	—	—	—	—	—	—	—	2	—	c.1,725
32. Vaide, Estonia, 1896/7	c.1160	14	18	—	—	—	54	—	—	—	—	—	447
33. Estonia, 1936	c.1160	—	—	—	—	1	1	—	—	—	—	—	77
34. Padikila, Estonia, 1927	c.1160	12	1	—	1	—	—	—	—	—	—	4	110
35. Dæli, Hedmark, Norway, 1840	c.1200	—	—	—	—	—	1	—	—	—	—	—	c.5,000
36. Lower Normandy?, France, pre-1905	c.1210	—	1	—	—	—	—	—	—	—	—	4	54+
37. Galicia, Spain, pre-1988	?	—	—	—	—	—	—	—	—	—	—	—	?
Total recorded in hoards (minimum)		2,275		91	158	138	149	113	92	108	521		

9. *Inv.* 295; Mack, 105; E. W. Danson, 'The Nottingham Find of 1880: A Stephen Hoard Re-examined', *BNJ* 37 (1968), 43–64; Seaman, 62–3.

10. *Inv.* 329; W. J. Andrew, 'A Remarkable Hoard of Silver Pennies and Halfpennies of the Reign of Stephen, Found at Sheldon, Derbyshire, in 1867', *BNJ* 7 (1910), 27–89; Mack, 104–5; Seaman, 62.

11. *Inv.* 235; Mack, 105–6; Seaman, 63–4.

12. *Inv.*—; Mack, 102; Blunt, Elmore Jones, and Robinson, 'On Some Hoards', 35–8.

13. *Inv.* 378; Mack, 102; C. E. Blunt and F. Elmore Jones, 'Two Wiltshire Coin-Hoards of the Time of Stephen', *Wilts. Arch. Mag.* 64 (1969), 65–70.

14. *Inv.* 80; Mack, 102.

15. D. J. Rogers, 'Two Farthings', *Newsletter, Journal of the London Numismatic Club,* 7.13 (1988), 38–40.

16. *Inv.* 63; Mack, 104.

17. *Inv.* 108; Mack, 104.

18. Blunt, Elmore Jones, and Robinson, 'On Some Hoards', 41–2.

19. *Inv.* 31; D. M. Metcalf, 'The Evidence of Scottish Coin Hoards for Monetary History, 1100–1600', in D. M. Metcalf (ed.), *Coinage in Medieval Scotland (1100–1600)* (BAR Brit. Ser. 45; Oxford, 1977), 1–59, no. 4 (citing I. Stewart's view that this is merely a parcel from the Outchester hoard).

20. *Inv.* 16; H. A. Grueber, 'A Find of Coins of Stephen and Henry II at Awbridge, near Romsey', *NC* 4:5 (1905), 354–63; Mack, 106.

21. Unpublished; information M. M. Archibald. 324 coins sold by Christies, 15 May 1993, lots 1–159 (all Stephen illus.).

22. Unpublished; information M. M. Archibald.

23. *Inv.* 246; Mack, 104; Blunt, Elmore Jones, and Robinson, 'On Some Hoards', 41.

24. *Inv.* 299; Mack, 106; Metcalf, 'The Evidence of Scottish Coin Hoards', no. 5.

25. *Inv.* 381; Allen, *BMC Henry II*, pp. liv–lvi.

26. *Inv.*—; I. Stewart, 'An Eighteenth-Century Manx Find of Early Scottish sterlings', *BNJ* 33 (1964), 48–56.

27. *Inv.* 94; Mack, 107.

28. Glendining auction, London, 4 Nov. 1987, lots 1–161, with an introduction by Peter Mitchell; M. A. S. Blackburn, 'Les Monnaies de Beauvais dans un Trésor découvert aux environs de Paris vers 1987 (la soi-disant "trouvaille de Beauvais")', *Bulletin de la Société française de numismatique* (1991), 110–16. This hoard, now thought to have been found in the Paris region, was given the name 'Beauvais' only because those were the most plentiful of the continental coins in the parcel. A full photographic record of the hoard was made by A. H. Baldwin & Sons Ltd. *T.p.q.* (non-English) mid-12th cent.

29. P. Sarvas, 'Fynd av utländska mynt från brytningen mellan den förhistoriska perioden och medeltid i Finland', *Nordisk Numismatisk Årsskrift* (1968), 78–87, no. 1; *SCBI Finland,* 917. *T.p.q.* (non-English) 1056.

30. T. Talvio, 'The Coin from the Kirkkomäaki excavations in 1973 and 1984', *Fennoscandia archaeologica,* 9 (1992), 90–2. *T.p.q.* (non-English) 786.

31. *SCBI Berlin,* 35, no. 48. *T.p.q.* (non-English) *c.*1100.

32. Kluge E 52; Molvõgin, table 1, no. 16. F. Elmore Jones and C. E. Blunt, 'A Remarkable Parcel of Norman Pennies in Moscow', *BNJ* 36 (1967), 86–92; A Molvõgin, 'An Estonian Hoard of English Coins from the Twelfth Century' *Numismatic Circular,* 1980, 307; I. Leimus, *Der Münzfund von Kose aus dem zweite*

Viertel des 12. Jahrhunderts (Tallinn, 1986), 64; and information from Leimus and Molvõgin, who are preparing an article on the hoard. *T.p.q.* (non-English) 1111.

33. Kluge E 51; Molvõgin, table 1, no. 15. *T.p.q.* (non-English) 1134.

34. Molvõgin, table 1, no. 18. *T.p.q.* (non-English) 1157.

35. H. Holst, 'Funn av myntskatter i Norge inntil slutten av 19. århundre', *Nordisk Numismatisk Årsskrift* (1936), 5–26, at 14, B1; 'Mynter og myntlignede metallpreg fra de Britiske Öyer i norske funn, nedlagt etter år 1100', *Nordisk Numismatisk Årsskrift* (1939), 103–24, at 110–12; *BMC Henry II,* pp. liii–liv. *T.p.q.* (non-English) 1198.

36. J. Duplessy, *Les Trésors monétaires médiévaux et modernes découverts en France,* i. *751–1223* (Paris, 1985), no. 397; to the references cited there add J. Yvon, 'Esterlins à la croix courte dans les trésors français de la fin du XIIe et de la première moité du XIIIe siècle', *BNJ* 39 (1970), 24–60, at 49–50. Duplessy questions whether this group of fifty-four English and Irish coins spanning William I, type 8, to the Short Cross coinage could derive from a single hoard.

37. Unpublished. One coin of Stephen, type 1 (reading +ALFPINE ON CA[   ], was among a group of coins acquired by the Cabinet des Medailles, Paris, in 1988, selected from a larger parcel of twelfth-century coins reputedly from a hoard found in Galicia, Spain. Information Michel Dhénin. *T.p.q.* (non-English)?

6

THE CHURCH

Christopher Holdsworth

AT first sight, my title involves an impossible task, since, in one sense, everyone was part of the Church in the Middle Ages, except for those who were expelled from it as heretics, or who never belonged to it because they were Jews or Moslems. One chapter is not large enough to consider how everyone behaved as members of the Church. But I hope it will prove possible to consider some aspects of the Church as an institution and of those who belonged to its professional 'classes', the clergy and monks. Before going further it is interesting to remind ourselves that this whole area was one to which Round devoted scarcely any space at all in his great book: most of the problems which will concern us are not to be found there. The first aspect of the Church to appreciate is that it was part of a much wider body, dispersed from Spain to Scandinavia, or from the north-west of Donegal to the southernmost parts of Sicily, and which to some extent, varying a good deal over time and space, looked to the church in Rome and its leader for direction, and discipline. So our first question must be how did England seem from the angle of the popes and their Curiae?

During Stephen's reign no less that five popes occupied the see of Peter and Paul: Innocent II, Celestine II, Lucius II, Eugenius III, Anastasius IV. Neither Celestine nor Lucius survived in office for as long as a year, and Anastasius lasted scarcely fifteen months.[1] Of course, some of the cardinals served them longer, but they were a group which also changed through death. Probably the moment at which they felt a common 'policy' most was when they shared in

---

[1] J. N. D. Kelly, *The Oxford Dictionary of Popes* (Oxford, 1986), 167–73.

the election of a new pope, whose aims may have corresponded with theirs at that time. But it is difficult now to discern continuities of policy at the top, so to speak, or among the court which served succeeding popes. But the centre did face some abiding problems.

The fact that popes were often on the road whilst Stephen tried to rule England is the superficial sign of three interlocking difficulties. When Stephen seized the throne, Innocent II was in Pisa, because Rome was controlled by the supporters of Anacletus II, as it had been in fact since the outbreak of schism in February 1130, apart from a few months in the spring of 1133. Although we may think that the Schism was over by the summer of 1131, since the emperor and the king of France, as well as Henry I, had by then declared for Innocent, it did not in fact end until Anacletus's successor, Victor IV, submitted to Innocent on 29 May 1138. For contemporaries in 1135 there were no certain signs that the longest split yet experienced in the Western church (not to be surpassed until the Great Schism) was coming to an end.[2] Some of them, like us, were, on the other hand, aware that schism was sustained by two things, divisions among the nobility of Rome, and the support for Anacletus of one great ruler, Roger of Sicily.[3] These same two forces contributed to the difficulties of popes even after the Schism collapsed. Rome remained scarcely amenable to papal control as successively a commune, an independent senate, and Arnold of Brescia made the place extremely unruly. Relations with Roger, too, remained tense.[4] So, to refer to only the most striking events, Lucius II died leading his troops against his Roman enemies, whilst Innocent II suffered a shattering military defeat at Roger's hands, the very hands which in 1148 helped Eugenius to return (but briefly) to the eternal city. Papal concerns, then, were focused on three things whilst Stephen tried to rule England: the ending of the Schism, gaining control of Rome, and coming to some sort of settlement with the Sicilians. A fourth cause, that of the Holy War to defend the land where Christ had lived and died, was also close to any pope's heart, leading Eugenius to launch a second wave of warriors on Palestine, with almost uniformly disastrous results.

[2] M. Stroll, *The Jewish Pope: Ideology and Politics in the Papal Schism of 1130* (Leiden, 1987).

[3] RH 168; WM *HN* 6–10. *GS*, in contrast, says nothing of the Schism.

[4] D. Matthew, *The Norman Kingdom of Sicily* (Cambridge, 1992), 32–61.

Set against this background, the stance of 'Rome' towards Stephen seems entirely predictable. To Innocent, stuck in Pisa, the news that the former king's nephew had been crowned and anointed by the proper authority in England can hardly have seemed disturbing, especially when the news came with letters supporting what had happened from the king of France (Stephen's overlord for Normandy) and Theobald of Blois (who, as his elder brother, might have been thought to have had a stronger claim to inherit).[5] If Matilda approached Innocent at this point, early in 1136—and clear evidence is lacking—it is conceivable that Innocent's court would have recalled that she had been married to an excommunicated German ruler, and so had a somewhat chequered past. Admittedly, Henry V had come to terms with Rome in 1122, but that was not long enough away by 1136 for memories of papal tensions with the emperor to have been forgotten. Her present husband, Geoffrey, if he had already gained the reputation as an enemy of the Church which he was to have later in 1141, could have made her even less acceptable.[6] Again, from a Roman point of view, all Matilda's main supporters in 1136 could have sounded suspect: Robert of Gloucester, her half-brother, was a royal bastard, whilst her uncle the king of Scots, under the influence of his chief bishop, John of Glasgow, seems to have been deciding to throw in his lot with Anacletus at this very juncture.[7] All these considerations lead to the belief that, if Matilda's cause had been made at Pisa early in 1136, it would have seemed distinctly unattractive to Innocent.

On the other hand, application of the Gregorian principle of *idoneitas*—suitability—to the situation would have pointed towards Stephen.[8] Innocent's letter recognizing Stephen's claim, a

---

[5] RH 147–8; see Chibnall, *Matilda*, 69, and below, n. 9.

[6] Peter the Venerable, Ep. 101, in *The Letters of Peter the Venerable*, ed. G. Constable (Cambridge, Mass., 1967), i. 262; Bernard of Clairvaux, Ep. 348.2, in *Sancti Bernardi opera* ed. J. Leclercq and H. Rochais (Rome, 1977), viii. 292a: 'Comes Andegavensis, malleus bonorum, oppressor pacis et libertatis Ecclesiae.' These two letters were written in late 1141 on behalf of Arnulf, whom Geoffrey refused to recognize as bishop of Lisieux, because he had attacked Matilda's claim in 1139: see C. P. Schriber, *The Dilemma of Arnulf of Lisieux* (Bloomington, Ind., 1990), 17–19.

[7] RH 170, a passage referring to the situation in 1138. See Barrow, *Kingdom of Scots*, 176 and n.; A. A. M. Duncan, *Scotland: The Making of the Kingdom* (Edinburgh, 1975), 260–1. Stroll (*Jewish Pope*) has nothing on Scotland.

[8] I. S. Robinson, *The Papacy 1073–1198* (Cambridge, 1990), 316.

document preserved only by Richard of Hexham, and scarcely discussed by modern historians, says that the king was elected to avoid disorder, and mentions two other things about the new king which commended him: that he had promised obedience and reverence to St Peter on the day of his coronation, and that he was closely related to the dead king, with whose praise the letter begins.[9] One can, I suggest, read it as Innocent's reward to a relative of the great king who had recognized his own claim to be the rightful pope when some others had not made up their minds.

Three years later, in April 1139, Matilda did succeed in getting her case presented at the Second Lateran Council, but without obtaining any clear decision, or even a formal postponement of consideration to a later date.[10] One scrap of evidence, recorded only by William of Malmesbury, suggests that Innocent may have been in two minds about it. In 1138, when Robert of Gloucester came out as a supporter of his half-sister, he claimed to have received a letter from the pope telling him that he ought to observe the oath which he had taken to her in the presence of her father.[11] There is no means of knowing whether such a letter really existed, but clearly William thought that his readers would find the idea plausible. In any case, a year later the pope seems to have felt that the best way of avoiding disorder in England was for him to do as little as he could: the empress had, after all, not yet put her claim to the test of battle there. In any case, Innocent had far more pressing affairs on his hands in southern Italy. The lowest point in his whole career, capture by King Roger near Galluccio on the River Garigliano, occurred on 22 July 1139, just three months after his

---

[9] RH 147–8 (= Jaffé-Loewenfeld, *Regesta Pontificum Romanorum* (Leipzig, 1885–8), no. 7804 (5567), 873). The letter is not dated, but presumably arrived by the April Oxford meeting. Davis (*Stephen*, 18) has nothing; Cronne (*Stephen*, 30) little. Chibnall (*Matilda*, 69) mentions the letter, without details. *Councils and Synods* (i:2, 762) makes no reference. Round (*Geoffrey*, 257–8) quotes the letter in arguing that Matilda did make a case in 1136. Relationship to the Norman line, and hence to the Confessor, was mentioned in Stephen's letter of 1139 supporting Westminster Abbey's plea to have him recognized as a saint: *The Letters of Osbert of Clare*, ed. E. W. Williamson (Oxford, 1920), 84; for date, see F. Barlow, *Edward the Confessor* (London, 1970), 274–6.

[10] Chibnall, *Matilda*, 75–6. Sources fully discussed, in Constable, *Letters of Peter the Venerable*, ii. 252–6.

[11] WM *HN* 23. William added: 'I will take care to insert a page of this decree in a later book'; but did not.

great Council.[12] It was also, unfortunately for Matilda, less than a
month after Stephen arrested the three bishops, the one act which
might have led Innocent to conclude that Stephen had shown himself unsuitable for rule. Later, when some people saw in the king's
capture at the battle of Lincoln a clear sign from the world beyond
that right was not on his side, Innocent appears to have remained
firm.[13] William of Malmesbury, again, is the only one to record the
fact that, at the Council of Westminster, Henry of Winchester produced a letter in which the pope reprimanded him for having done
little to get his brother released and urged him 'to gird himself to
procure . . . [his release] by any means, ecclesiastical or secular'.[14]
By the Council, Stephen was, of course, at liberty, but one wonders
who, if not Henry himself, had told the pope of events. In any
case, the letter must have cheered Stephen and his party, whilst
depressing the empress. So, Innocent's recognition of 1136, and
disinclination to reopen the question in 1139, proved to be decisive.

Later, in 1143, when a cardinal who had argued against
Innocent's attitude in 1139 became pope as Celestine II, another
significant statement was made—that there should be no change in
the Crown of England.[15] At the time this hardly helped Matilda,
but later, in 1148 and 1151, it seems to have been behind
Eugenius' refusal to allow Stephen to have his son Eustace crowned
during his own lifetime, which could have blocked the succession
of the young Henry.[16] Presumably by then the papacy had come to
feel that *idoneitas* now pointed towards the young duke, since
Stephen had provided evidence of his own unsuitability largely
through his persistent refusal to come to heel over the York election. Three years after Eugenius had reiterated his refusal, Stephen's
hopes completely collapsed with the death of Eustace, not distantly
followed by his own. We may note here the words with which the
Gesta commented upon the deaths of the king's heir, Simon of St
Liz, Ranulf of Chester, and others in 1153: they were 'signs it

[12] Matthew, *Kingdom of Sicily*, 51–2. For the actual date, see J. J. Norwich, *The Kingdom in the Sun* (London, 1970), 67–8.

[13] e.g. *GS* 113; HH 271; WM *HN* 53: all, of course, writing some time afterwards.

[14] 'I heard that a letter from the Pope was read' (WM *HN* 62).

[15] JS *HP* 85–6.

[16] Chibnall, *Matilda*, 141; M. Chibnall, 'The Empress Matilda and Church Reform', *TRHS* 5:38 (1988), 121–3.

could readily be understood that God, who determines all we do, wished to summon the duke of sovereignty and thus put an end at last to the obstinate struggle'.[17]

So, throughout the reign the bishops in England had to work within the Roman view that Stephen was their rightful king. Now this leads us to a second area of enquiry: what sort of people were the bishops, and how likely were they to go along with Stephen?

There were seventeen dioceses in England during Stephen's reign, which were occupied by thirty-four bishops, an average of two per diocese (I have excluded from this total Anselm the Younger and Philip Harcourt neither of whom seems to have exercised episcopal functions in London or Salisbury).[18] Four sees— Bath, Carlisle, Ely, and Winchester—had one leader whose episcopate spanned the whole reign and more, but most sees had two or three bishops. They divide by their previous experience into three very unequally sized groups. The smallest group, of three, were canons regular, although the group included one archbishop (William of Corbeil), and one man who nearly achieved recognition as a saint (Robert of Béthune, bishop of Hereford). Then came a group of twelve who were monks, all, save one—Murdac— Benedictines. Among them, three belonged to the Cluniac tradition (Henry of Blois, Winchester; Robert of Lewes, Bath; Gilbert Foliot, Hereford). The other monks came from a variety of black monk houses: Bec; Christ Church, Canterbury; Glastonbury; Norwich; Reading.[19] But by far the largest number of bishops were secular clerks: nineteen in all. This group can readily be divided into two, depending on whether their career had involved service in the household of the king or queen. By far the majority of the secular clerks had not served there, but rather had made their way in the world of archdeaconries and major offices in cathedrals: only six had spent significant time in a royal household, though we may

[17] GS 239.

[18] *Handbook of British Chronology*, ed. E. B. Fryde *et al.*, 3rd edn. (London, 1986), for chronology, and F. Barlow, *The English Church 1066–1154*, (London, 1979), 76–103, for careers.

[19] *The Heads of Religious Houses England and Wales 940–1216* (ed. D. Knowles, C. N. L. Brooke, and V. C. M. London (Cambridge, 1972), 63) has Reading among independent Benedictine houses, but *Reading Abbey Cartularies* (ed. B. R. Kemp (CS 4:31, 1986), i. 14–15) notes it had 'all the benefits of the Cluniac observance but without the juridical ties to Cluny'.

note that at least one of the monks, Robert de Sigillo, had, as his name suggests, been so engaged before he entered Reading. Frank Barlow noticed in 1978 that the proportion of royal clerks to monks and canons, or episcopal clerks, in the episcopacy fell as the reign went on, and this may well reflect a less tight royal influence over elections.[20] But, taken as a whole, this bench was not undistinguished. Only one may have been saintly, but another, William fitz Herbert, because of the odd circumstances of his death, did make a mark, and finally achieved formal sanctity in 1227. At the other extreme, so to say, only two impressed contemporaries by their failings: Seffrid of Chichester and Everard of Norwich, both deposed by a papal legate in 1145. Four had attended the greatest school of their day in Laon, and one of those had also studied in Paris. With an archbishop who had been a monk at Bec, and two others who had spent time at Cluny, the group contained men well aware of some of the changes taking place south of the Channel. At least one, Hilary of Chichester, knew the papal court well, whilst others had visited it. How did such backgrounds prepare them to serve the Church under Stephen?

It seems to me highly likely that most of those already in post in December 1135, as well as those appointed subsequently, would accept the papal decision and work with the consecrated monarch, whether he had played a crucial role in their own appointment or not. All the teaching that they had absorbed would dispose them so to do, and at first, when Stephen's great Charter of Liberties appeared to promise what they had come to feel the Church wanted, they must have been reassured. Even when Stephen turned against Roger of Salisbury and his nephews, his actions did not lack episcopal support, though it appears only to have been voiced by the archbishop of Rouen.[21] Still more significant, surely, is the fact that on the whole they avoided Matilda, except during her palmy days in 1141.[22] Even then, two bishops, those of Norwich and Rochester, cannot be found among witnesses to her charters, and it is well known that Theobald of Canterbury, very correctly, refused to accept her as Lady until Stephen permitted him so to do.[23] The same basic attitude was revealed later in 1148, when Gilbert Foliot, having been consecrated by Theobald in Flanders

---

[20] Barlow, *English Church 1066–1154*, 318.

[21] WM *HN* 22–3.

[22] Chibnall, *Matilda*, 99; *RRAN* iii *passim*.

[23] Saltman, *Theobald*, 16.

on condition that he would do fealty to Duke Henry, and not to
Stephen, went precisely to the king when he crossed over to
England, even though the area in which his diocese lay was controlled, not by the king, but by the Angevins, with whose claims he
had expressed sympathy in his famous letter to Brian fitz Count
written three or four years before.[24] The failure of the Interdict
which Theobald laid on England in the autumn of the same year
(even Saltman calls it 'almost a complete fiasco') shows how, when
the pope wanted to put pressure upon the king, in this case for trying to prevent the bishops from attending the Council of Reims,
they were not willing to take a stand.[25]

Life cannot have been easy for any of them, especially when
sieges and their attendant devastation of the countryside occurred,
but, on the whole, as far as I am aware, no cathedrals were
destroyed. On the other hand, although it is notoriously hard to
date building programmes, they were definitely going forward at
Ely, Lincoln, and Norwich in the 1140s, and an enormous amount
of monastic building was also needed, for reasons to be explored
later.[26] Yet the bishops must have longed for peace, and tried to
bring it about by various means.[27] As early as December 1138 at
the Council of Westminster canons were passed with the aim of
protecting the clergy and their possessions, and these were added to
in 1143, but all the evidence suggests that they had little effect,
almost certainly because their only sanction was excommunica-
tion.[28] As the *Gesta* commented, it was 'the sword that the
Church's warfare uses', and it was 'adamantine', but unfortunately
its edge did not cut very deep.[29] Similarly, when in 1140 Henry of
Winchester excommunicated those who 'broke into graveyards and
outraged churches and laid hands on men of a holy or religious
order or their servants', the historian could only lament that the
bishop 'accomplished hardly anything by these efforts'.[30] Some of
the bishops, notably those of Ely and Lincoln, according to the

---

[24] Chibnall, *Matilda*, 146; whereas Saltman (*Theobald*, 30) has Theobald instruct
him to swear fealty to Stephen. For Gilbert's sympathies, see Chibnall, *Matilda*, 84–7.

[25] Saltman, *Theobald*, 29.

[26] T. S. R. Boase, *English Art 1100–1216* (Oxford, 1953), 114–16, 118–21.

[27] C. Holdsworth, 'War and Peace in the Twelfth Century: The Reign of Stephen
Reconsidered', in B. P. McGuire (ed.), *War and Peace in the Middle Ages*
(Copenhagen, 1987), 67–93.

[28] *Councils and Synods*, i:2, 776–7, 800–4.   [29] *GS* 169, 215.

[30] Ibid. 40.

same source, had large military retinues, which were felt to be most unsuitable for a bishop and hardly a good example for the lay nobility.[31] So it is scarcely surprising that at Peterborough the chronicler commented: 'The bishops and learned men were always excommunicating them [the disturbers of the peace], but they thought nothing of it because they were all utterly accursed and perjured and doomed to destruction.'[32]

It was not until the Council of March 1151 that the Church drew up new methods, forbidding those excommunicated for longer than a year from being heard at law *in testimoniis neque in causis*, which I take to mean in cases concerning wills, and other matters which might be pursued in Church courts.[33] Here the threat to inheritance may have cut deeper, but it is hard to link it with any changes in the next two years.

This lack of ecclesiastical enterprise in the field of peace-keeping may reflect the degree to which bishops in England had come to think that this was something which could be left to kings, unlike some of their contemporaries in mainland Europe. Monarchy had been effective, and so the Peace of God and Truce of God had not taken root.[34] It was, therefore, hard for bishops to adjust themselves to a situation in which a king proved himself less able than his predecessors. Nor, as negotiators between the two sides, did they score many successes before 1153, but this surely reflected an impasse not of their making. As sureties for baronial 'treaties' they had perhaps more success, but those very agreements reflected the collapse of royal control.[35] On the whole, the evidence suggests that the bishops were unable to contribute anything very positive to lessen disorder from 1139 onwards: they were weaponless peacewishers, working in a situation for which previous experience provided no guide.

But one aspect of the field in which the bishops laboured was changing under their eyes during this period, and in some cases

---

[31] Ibid. 155–6. Only Robert of Hereford is praised: ibid., 159–61.

[32] *ASC, s.a.* 1137.

[33] *Councils and Synods*, i:2, 825 (ch. v). Ch. i, 823: 'novas nos cogunt medicinas querere . . .'

[34] H. E. J. Cowdrey, 'The Peace and Truce of God in the Eleventh Century', *Past and Present*, 46 (1970), 42–67; P. Contamine, *War in the Middle Ages* (Oxford, 1984), 50–4.   [35] See Holdsworth, 'War and Peace', 84–6, on negotiation and sureties.

they helped this change forward very materially, and in some cases they did not. I refer here, of course, to the extraordinary efflorescence of monastic foundations. When I started to think about this chapter, I had no idea of the total number which I would find. According to my calculations something approaching 180 houses (175 precisely, of which 171 were in England, and four in the southern parts of Wales) were founded in the reign of Stephen, a huge number and probably greater than that made in any similar number of years in the Middle Ages. Many years ago David Knowles described the increase, calculating that between 1135 and 1175 the number of houses almost doubled, and that, of this increase, 80 per cent occurred under Stephen, when some 114 houses were established.[36] It is not easy to be sure just what he included, but my much larger figure encompasses preceptories of the Hospitallers and Templars (of which there were eighteen in all), which he certainly omitted. I also count a number of small priories and cells which he may well have rejected just because they were small and, therefore, according to him, could not have supported a regular liturgical life.[37] It may be on such grounds that, whereas he counted only seven new houses of black monks (including Cluniacs) in the reign, I found twenty-four. His viewpoint, however, does seem to me anachronistic, owing more, perhaps, to his own concern for the proper organization of Benedictine life in the twentieth century than to medieval standards. I am sure that, when, for example, Baldwin de Redvers established Cluniac monks at St James, outside Exeter, he believed that their prayers would be effective, even though he provided such slender resources that only four of them could live there.[38] In any case, even though our totals differ, it is absolutely clear that the number of houses existing at the death of Henry I (some of which had a long history back to the tenth century) increased by at least 50 per cent in his successor's

[36] D. Knowles, The *Monastic Order in England*, 2nd edn. (Cambridge, 1963), 297–8, 711. The fuller tables in D. Knowles and R. N. Hadcock, *Religious Houses, England and Wales* (2nd edn. (London, 1971), 488–95), include Stephen's reign in the longer period 1100–54.

[37] 'To count the numerous cells and "alien" priories would be as misleading as, at the present day, to equate small groups of regulars on parish work with organised *domus formatae*' (Knowles, *Monastic Order*, 711).

[38] G. Oliver (*Monasticon Dioecesis Exoniensis* (Exeter, 1846), 191–4), giving no authority for the number of monks; the house seems to have had an income of c.£16 in the early 15th century.

reign. And it is worth remembering that existing houses generally continued to flourish, and that most received new benefactions. That side of the situation I have excluded from consideration here, but it would create a much wider pattern of interest in monasticism than that reflected in new foundations. That pattern would widen still further if one were to include foundations made in Normandy.

Two main themes in the new monasteries of Stephen's reign have attracted my attention: their geographical distribution, and the kind of people who founded them; I have looked especially for any evidence which might suggest a connection between political allegiance and the type of monasticism favoured. Before going further a word must be said upon methodology.

I began by making cards for every house listed in Knowles and Hadcock which appeared to have been founded within the reign. I then consulted cartularies edited since Knowles and Hadcock was published, and some secondary works, most notably Sally Thompson's recent book on nunneries, and revised the dates given by Knowles and Hadcock where the reasons for doing so seemed convincing.[39] As is well known, only a minority of houses can be clearly assigned to a particular year; the others present a problem. Those with an approximate date, like c.1150, or pre-1153, I included if the date was between 1136 and 1154. Where houses had two dates, e.g. 1137–45, I included them when the earliest date fell within the reign, unless the median between the two was outside; for example, a house assigned to 1150–62 was not included, because the median, 1156, was after Stephen's death.

Knowles considered distribution by counties, but it seems to me that it may be more revealing to look at dioceses. This for two reasons: first, bishops had had a general responsibility for the oversight of monasteries going back to the Council of Chalcedon; and, secondly, some of the new orders, most notably the Cistercians, required the bishop to assent to a house being set up in their diocese.[40]

---

[39] S. Thompson, *Women Religious: The Founding of English Nunneries after the Norman Conquest* (Oxford, 1991). Space is lacking in this chapter to give evidence.

[40] Chalcedon, ch. 4 (*Conciliorum Oecumenicorum Decreta*, ed. J. Alberigo *et al.* (Basel, 1962), 65); *Carta caritatis posterior*, preface: 'no abbey should be founded in the diocese of any bishop before he approved and confirmed the decree enacted between the abbot of Citeaux and its filiations' (L. J. Lekai, *The Cistercians, Ideals and Reality* (Kent, Ohio, 1977), 461). This provision is adopted from *prior*, the earliest *Carta*.

The total of 171 foundations over the seventeen English dioceses gives an average of 10 per diocese—a very unreal figure, of course, since dioceses varied hugely in size. Even so, two groups diverge considerably from this norm: first those ten with half, or fewer, of the average, i.e. five houses or less (Bath, Canterbury, Carlisle, Chichester, Durham, Ely, Exeter, Hereford, Rochester, and Winchester), and a smaller group of three with very considerable numbers, twice or more than the average: Chester with twenty, York with thirty-four, and Lincoln with fifty-six. What may these considerable variations mean? Let us turn to the low-scoring group first.

Some of these dioceses may well have had a high proportion of their land devoted to monasteries already: I suspect this may be the case in Canterbury, Ely, and Rochester, none of which ever had many additional foundations.[41] The same may partly explain the poor harvest in Bath, Chichester, and Winchester. At Canterbury and Rochester the enormous estates of Christ Church, Canterbury, occupied much territory; whilst Ely was dominated by its own estate, and that of the monastery from which it had been carved. The centre of Bath diocese was taken up by the ancient estates of Glastonbury, whilst, more recently, Lewes Priory and Boxgrove had taken some of the best land in the diocese of Chichester. Winchester, the heartland of the tenth-century reformation, was the home of old rich houses, which included its own two monasteries, Romsey and Wherwell. Carlisle and Durham, on the other hand, had plenty of 'spare' land, but under Stephen were very much in dispute with the Scots, and so may have been too unsettled to encourage many lords to attempt to settle new monks. With Exeter and Hereford we see dioceses without a great deal of land already devoted to monks or nuns, but which in the former case certainly had a very extensive episcopal estate which had mopped up much of the best low-lying land.[42] Yet both Exeter and Hereford did see new foundations being made after 1154, as

[41] The two Ordnance Survey maps, *Monastic Britain*, help to make the points in this paragraph.
[42] C. Holdsworth, 'From 1050 to 1307', in *Unity and Variety: A History of the Church in Devon and Cornwall*, ed. N. Orme (Exeter, 1991), 24–5. W. J. Corbett's Domesday figures have Exeter £360, Hereford, £280: *Cambridge Medieval History*, v (Cambridge, 1926), 511. Barlow (*English Church 1066–1154*, 117) has both paying £200+ a year net to the exchequer under Henry II.

indeed did Bath and Chichester. This has lead me to wonder whether bishops of these four dioceses were less well disposed to religious than some of their colleagues, and/or whether lords in these areas may have been less concerned for them. Is it a mere coincidence that Bath, Exeter, and Hereford were largely under 'Angevin' control?

Bath occurs also with four other low-scoring dioceses (Canterbury, Chichester, Rochester, Winchester) which lacked any new Cistercian foundation. For two of them, Canterbury and Rochester, the argument about lack of space may be conclusive, but it is striking that the other three are all linked with one person, Henry of Blois. Robert of Lewes, bishop of Bath for the whole reign, was, like Henry, a Cluniac, and was widely recognized as his protégé, whilst Hilary, admittedly only bishop of Chichester from 1147, had been his clerk.[43] Now not every Cluniac was an enemy of the Cistercians; after all, Flaxley was founded under the Cluniac Gilbert Foliot, and there is clear evidence that he admired Bernard of Clairvaux.[44] But, just as the abbot of Clairvaux came to have a very low opinion of Henry, it is surely highly likely that the feeling was mutual, particularly once the dispute over the election at York had broken out.[45] There is some attraction, therefore, in the idea that the lack of new foundations in these three dioceses, especially the absence of the Cistercians, is connected with their being directed by Henry and his friends. I suspect that some may accuse me here of 'trailing my tail' in the sea to make a storm, rather as Eugenius III accused Henry of Blois himself of doing.[46]

The three dioceses with very large numbers of new foundations will not surprise. Broadly speaking they encompassed an area almost nude of houses in 1066, since it had been unaffected by the Wessex-centred reforms of the tenth century, but one where from the Conquest onwards landholders had begun to put resources into monasteries. The role of Alexander at Lincoln has long been recognized.[47] Henry of Huntingdon (to go back to the beginning) thought that he was far too generous with his own resources, and

---

[43] Barlow, *English Church 1066–1154*, 92–3, 98.   [44] GF, *Letters*, no. 108.
[45] Bernard of Clairvaux, Ep. 520 (*Opera*, viii. 480–1), discussed in C. Holdsworth, 'St Bernard and England', *ANS* 8 (1986), 149–51.
[46] JS *HP* 79.
[47] A. G. Dyson, 'The Monastic Patronage of Bishop Alexander of Lincoln', *Journal of Ecclesiastical History*, 26 (1975), 1–24.

recent work has revealed how much he encouraged those who wanted to found Cistercian houses, or houses of regular canons, and what a crucial role he played in the life of Gilbert of Sempringham.[48] Thurstan at York has also been seen as one who fostered monks and nuns, but he died in 1140, and yet the flood of foundations continued unabated.[49] Indeed, according to my calculations, only two houses were founded within the diocese of York between 1135 and 1140, and no less than thirty-two afterwards. This fact should perhaps make one pause before concluding that a necessary condition for the growth of monasticism in a diocese was a strong and sympathetic bishop, since neither William fitz Herbert nor Murdac was in effective control of the diocese for very long. Maybe we should deduce that a bishop could act as a helpful stimulus where others wished to create houses, yet this positive role was not so significant as its reverse: where a bishop was unsympathetic, little development would take place.

Now let me move on to a second area: just who founded monasteries? The quick answer here is a very wide variety of people, from the king (and to a much lesser degree the empress) at the top, to quite humble holders of land at the bottom. Let us look at Stephen's foundations first. In all he can be firmly connected with eight foundations (not counting the hermitage at Stoneleigh, which the empress turned into a monastery), which were established fairly evenly in time across his reign.[50] His queen made three others, whilst the empress and her son in a strict sense founded only two houses, but 'took over' Waleran of Meulan's Bordesley as well.[51] Marjorie Chibnall and David Crouch have both discussed this case, the former stressing how Matilda was unwilling to recog-

---

[48] *The Book of St Gilbert*, ed. R. Foreville and G. Keir (OMT; Oxford, 1987), pp. xix–xliii.

[49] D. Nicholl, *Thurstan, Archbishop of York (1114–1140)* (York, 1964), 151–212.

[50] In chronological order: Thornholme (Lincolnshire, Augustinian); Buckfast (Devon, Savigniac); Eagle (Lincolnshire, Templars); Temple Dinsley (Hertfordshire). *Religious Houses*, 295, has Bernard de Balliol as founder, but his grant was made in 1147, while Stephen's charters date 1142–3 onwards: *Monasticon*, vi:2, 819; *RRAN* iii, no. 858); Witham (Essex, Templars); Faversham (Kent, Benedictine); Higham (or Lillechurch, Kent, Benedictine nuns); Ivychurch (Wiltshire, Augustinian).

[51] The queen: Cressing (Essex, Templars), Temple Cowley (Oxfordshire), Coggeshall (Essex, Savigniac): the empress: Stoneleigh/Radmore (Warwickshire, Cistercian), Stanley (Wiltshire, Cistercian). For the monastic patronage of the empress, see Chibnall, *Matilda*, 127–37.

nize as effective any alienation of land which had been royal demesne which had not had her prior approval.[52] This seems a convincing argument, and I believe that what look like takeovers lower down society by barons or greater lords of their tenants' foundations may have had a similar motive: they objected to houses being placed without their assent on what had once been land from which they took knight service.[53]

Moving on to the level of great magnates, we find this group well represented. To mention only those earls with more than one house to their credit, we can note Ranulf, earl of Chester (with four: Chester for nuns, Kersal, Maltby, and Trentham), Robert, earl of Gloucester (two: Bristol St James, Margam), Robert, earl of Leicester (two: Leicester, Nuneaton), Simon, earl of Northampton (two: Delapré, Northampton; Sawtry), William le Gros, count of Aumâle, earl of Yorkshire (three: Thornton, Vaudey, Meaux). When one adds in earls with one house, like William of Warenne, who enjoyed various titles and was the founder of Thetford priory, twenty of the thirty-three earls existing in 1135 or created later in the reign appear as founders: exceptions include Patrick of Salisbury and Hervey Brito, earls of Wiltshire, lying in a diocese with few new houses.[54] Below the great and not always good, there were many much lesser men. Richard de Camville, for instance, founder of Combe, Warwickshire, a Cistercian house, was a tenant of Mowbray who held that land from the earl of Leicester. The land involved in Combe represented one knights' fee, but how many fees he held in all we do not, I think, know. A probable cousin held nine knights' fees in 1166.[55] How large a holding, we

[52] Ibid. 134–5; Crouch, *Beaumont Twins*, 39–40.

[53] e.g. Alcester (see below, n. 63) was claimed by Robert of Leicester as his ('fundavi ecclesiam de Insula'), although Robert the butler founded it: *Monasticon*, iv. 172. Exeter, St James, of which Baldwin de Redvers was reckoned as founder (see above, n. 38), appears from his son's confirmation, and a charter of Bishop Robert I of Exeter, to have been on land held by Walter son of Wulfward, which he had asked Baldwin to give for the priory: *Monasticon*, v. 106–7. At Combe, founded by Richard de Camville, the monks asked Robert, earl of Leicester, to become 'principalis fundator', according to Robert: BL, Cotton MS Vitel. A.1, fo. 37ᵛ.

[54] I worked from the list in Davis, *Stephen*, 133; it omits Roger, earl of Hereford, mentioned ibid. 131, and index 161.

[55] J. Burton, 'The Foundation of British Cistercian Houses', in C. Norton and D. Park (eds.), *Cistercian Art and Architecture in the British Isles* (Cambridge, 1986), 29; *Mowbray Charters*, pp. xlix–1, 58–68, 225.

may also wonder, did Akarius fitz Bardolf, founder of what became
Jervaulx, hold of the Richmond fee, or William de Batevileyn,
founder of Pipewell? One of the two founders of Roche appears to
have been a six knights' fee man in 1164/5.[56]

When I started compiling cards and plumbing into the
Monasticon and some, but not all, of the cartularies, I had hoped
that I would find that political allegiances would have at least some
reflection in patronage, that men on the same 'side' would support
the same kind of religious, and that the timing of foundations
might reflect wider events: that, for instance, the worsening crisis
after the outbreak of war in 1139 might result in a larger number
of houses being founded. But, I have found nothing very
significant about the rate of foundation, except that it seems fairly
even.

As a check on this overall result we can isolate one group of
houses for which accurate foundation dates are known: the
Cistercians. We know from the account of the foundation of
Jervaulx that every year at General Chapter lists were drawn up of
houses established in the previous year.[57] These lists were needed
because Cistercian abbots visiting other houses had to defer to each
other according to the seniority of their foundations, not their own
seniority in abbatial office.[58] Any abbot, one may suppose, would
have known when he had been elected, but might have been hazy
about the establishment of his monastery. These dates show that
no less than eight of the eighteen Cistercian houses founded under
Stephen by people closely associated with him date from the years
1146–8. Has this anything to do with the political situation?
Barbara English suggested some years ago that one of the eight,
Vaudey, might represent William of Aumâle's acceptance of
Murdac's claim to be the rightful archbishop of York.[59] I myself
thought that Rufford (1146), another of the group, might be connected with the influence which Ranulf of Chester had over

[56] *The Cartulary of Blyth Priory*, ed. R. T. Timson (Royal Commission on
Historical Manuscripts, Joint Publication, 17; London, 1973), p. xvii.

[57] *Monasticon*, v. 571.

[58] *Carta caritatis posterior*, ch. 10, where seniority is explained, 'seniors' also, ch. 5:
Lekai, *Cistercians*, 463. See the earlier *Summa cartae caritatis*, iii, for a similar provision: Lekai, *Cistercians*, 445.

[59] B. English, *The Lords of Holderness 1086–1260* (Oxford, 1979), 20, who also
connects Meaux, 1151.

Gilbert de Gant at that time.[60] But, in view of the number of
houses involved, and of the fact that three Cistercian houses
founded by supporters of the empress also date from the same
three years, I now wonder whether some more internal rhythm of
monastic life is not involved. The bunching of foundations
between 1146 and 1148 may reflect the speed with which a
mother-house could recruit and train novices, rather than some
external circumstance. One has, of course, to bear in mind, too,
that no house could come into existence overnight: perhaps two or
three years were needed for negotiations over a suitable site, and
putting up the basic buildings.[61] Was something significant happening in the 'political' area around 1143–5 which could have
resulted in this bulge in foundations three years later? So far I have
not been able to come up with any satisfactory general conclusion,
but I suspect purely local conditions may have most to do with it.

These considerations lead naturally on to the wider question
whether there are any significant differences between the foundations made by Stephen and those people who supported him fairly
consistently, and foundations of the empress and those who from
1139 were mainly on the Angevin side. I realize only too well how
hazardous such concepts are, particularly in view of other comments made in this volume, or in other recent work—for example,
Paul Dalton's on Ranulf of Chester.[62] And I can admit that I found
myself placing a lot of people in a third group of 'neutrals', including four bishops, Roger de Clinton (Chester), Alexander and
Robert de Chesney (Lincoln), Robert de Béthune (Hereford). I
drew a line between the others depending upon whom people
seemed to support most of the time, using as indicators the *Regesta*,
and the standard works by Cronne and Davis. I have to admit that
the division is open to severe question.

When I began, I can now admit, I had hoped to find that many
founders would, as it were, proclaim their allegiance by the names
of those they wanted 'their' monks to pray for, but so far I have

[60] *Rufford Charters*, ed. C. Holdsworth (Thoroton Soc., Rec. Ser. 29, 1972), pp.
xxii–iii.
[61] Brightley, later Forde, suggests three years: C. Holdsworth, 'The Cistercians in
Devon', in C. Harper-Bill *et al.* (eds.), *Studies in Medieval History Presented to R. Allen
Brown* (Woodbridge, 1989), 182.
[62] P. Dalton, '. . . Ranulf II Earl of Chester in King Stephen's Reign', *ANS* 14
(1992), 39–59.

come across only four cases among 175 where founders mentioned either king or empress. A nice example is provided by Ralph the butler to the count of Meulan, who established Alcester Abbey in 1140 so that his monks could pray for the souls of William the Conqueror, Matilda his queen, William the Younger, Henry and Matilda his queen, King Stephen and Matilda his queen, Roger of Beaumont and Atheline his wife, Robert, count of Meulan, and Isabel his countess, Robert, earl of Leicester, and Avice his wife, and their son, Waleran, count of Meulan, the donor's father and mother, himself and Avice his wife.[63] Would that more donors had been so explicit and wide-ranging.

Another avenue into the evidence, namely to look at the range of houses founded by a great lord and his dependants, proved not very decisive either. We may take here, as examples, the cases of Ranulf of Chester and William of Aumâle, and their associates. The first, as we have seen, founded four houses during the reign. These were of four different kinds: Chester, for Benedictine nuns; Kersal, for Cluniac monks; Trentham, for Augustinian canons; and Maltby, for the Knights Hospitallers. Earlier, in 1131, under Henry I, Ranulf had established Savigniacs at Basingwerk, and two years later helped one of his vassals, Hugh Maubank, found Combermere, also for Savigniacs.[64] Among those close to him we find a nephew, Richard Bacon, placing Augustinians at Rocester, his half-brother, William de Roumare, Cistercians at Revesby, and Robert his butler, Savigniacs at what became Dieulacres.[65] Just as Ranulf himself spread his patronage, so did his men. The same is

---

[63] *Monasticon*, v. 174; the rulers involved are William I, William II (Rufus), Henry I, and Stephen: on the house, see Crouch, *Beaumont Twins*, 135, 142–3. Cf.: Buckenham, by William d'Aubigny, 'pro salute Stephani regis Angliae, et Matildis reginae uxoris suae, et filiorum suorum, et pro salute mea, et pro anima Athelizae reginae, uxoris meae' (*Monasticon*, vi. 419); Littlemore, by Robert de Sandford, for the soul of the empress 'et pro domino nostro Henrici' (*Monasticon*, iv. 492; the latter phrase might suggest that Henry was king, but Robert was dead by 1156: Thompson, *Women Religious*, 224); Monks Horton, a grant by Robert de Vere, the constable, 'pro redemptione et salute animae Regis Henrici et Regis Stephani' (*Monasticon*, v. 34–5). Deeper search beyond 'foundation' charters would no doubt produce similar examples.

[64] Burton, 'Foundation', 31 n. 31. The range of his patronage included others' foundations, e.g. Robert of Leicester's Leicester (Augustinian) and Waleran of Meulan's Bordesley: *The Charters of the Anglo-Norman Earls of Chester*, ed. G. Barraclough (Rec. Soc. of Lancashire and Cheshire 126, 1988), nos. 83, 100.

[65] Ibid., nos. 43, 68 (Rocester); C. Holdsworth, *The Piper and the Tune: Medieval Patrons and Monks* (Stenton Lecture for 1990; Reading, 1991), 6–13 (Revesby).

true for William, the founder of one Augustinian house, Thornton, and two Cistercian, Vaudey and Meaux. His tenants founded one house of Benedictine nuns (Nunkeeling by Agnes de Arches), one for Cistercian nuns (Nun Cotham by Alan de Monceaux and his wife), and one for Gilbertines (North Ormsby by Gilbert fitz Robert of Ormsby).[66] There seems no sign of imitation here to keep in with their lord, with this second group, but, conceivably, a division of labour, since the lesser people founded houses for women.

Other aspects of the growth in houses emerges from examination of royal and Angevin charters confirming gifts or making grants to these new houses; first, something from their geographical distribution, and, secondly, their chronology. Nine houses received 'Angevin' charters, all, with one exception, in the southwest, the southern part of the Welsh March, or the Thames Valley (taken broadly).[67] The twenty-three monasteries with royal charters were scattered much more widely, from Yorkshire in the north, through the eastern Midlands (with an interesting gap, Lincolnshire), to East Anglia and the south-east.[68] Clearly this scatter reflects the areas controlled by Matilda or Stephen quite well. A small group, four in all, received charters from both 'sides'. Biddlesden, Lilleshall, and Meaux founded by royal supporters benefited from Angevin charters, whilst St Augustine's, Bristol, founded by Earl Robert, got a charter from Stephen. This process of recognizing benefactions by the other 'side' all seems to have taken place after the succession had been settled in 1153–4, except in the case of Lilleshall, where Stephen's charter dates from 1145, and the Angevin ones from 1148–51. This suggests that in most cases charters, which almost certainly had to be paid for, though at

[66] English, *Lords of Holderness*, 147, 150 (Nunkeeling), 157 (Nun Cotham).

[67] Biddlesden, Buckinghamshire; St Augustine's, Bristol; Dorchester, Oxfordshire; St James's, Exeter; Kingswood, Gloucestershire; Lilleshall, Shropshire; Llanthony II, Gloucestershire; Meaux, East Riding of Yorkshire; Ogbourne, Wiltshire.

[68] Alcester, Worcestershire; Biddlesden, Buckinghamshire; Bisham, Berkshire; Bordesley, Worcestershire; St Augustine's, Bristol; Combe, Warwickshire; Oxford, Norfolk; Delapré, Northamptonshire; St James's, Derbyshire; Hatfield Broad Oak, Essex; Leicester (Aug.); Lilleshall, Shropshire; Meaux, East Riding of Yorkshire; Newburgh, North Riding of Yorkshire; Norwich Carrow, Norfolk; Rufford, Nottinghamshire; Sawley, West Riding of Yorkshire; Sibton, Suffolk; Thoby, Essex; Throwley, Kent; Walden, Essex; Welbeck, Nottinghamshire; Wickham Skeyth, Suffolk. The charters of Stephen and the empress can be readily found in *RRAN* iii.

what rate we do not know, were only sought by a monastery from the person who controlled their area, and whose protection was worth having.

These conclusions can be confirmed, on the whole, if we turn to examine the very much larger number of charters of gift and confirmation issued for English houses founded before the reign.[69] Eighty-five houses are involved, some, like Reading or St John's, Colchester, receiving many charters: thirty-eight in the first case, and thirty-three in the second. In general these charters, like those just discussed, followed closely the areas which the opposing forces controlled. As for the time when they were issued, whilst Stephen's are spread across the whole reign, the Angevin charters do not, with one possible exception, predate 1141: most of the empress's come from then or 1142, whilst Henry's are concentrated in 1153–4. And if one next looks at the group of sixteen houses which received charters from both parties, Stephen's cluster at the beginning of the reign, whilst those of the empress or Henry cluster in 1141–2, or 1153–4. Places like Bath, Glastonbury, and Shrewsbury, in what became Angevin areas, got charters from the king early in the reign, but not later, whilst places normally under the king, like St John's, Colchester (Essex), and St Benet's Holme (Norfolk), were only favoured by the Angevins in 1141 or 1153–4, when Stephen was in prison, or Henry's star was rising.

Stephen himself, to return to the Cistercian houses, was not a patron of the white monks, although he and his wife did support the Savigniacs, founding Buckfast and Coggeshall, respectively, in 1136 and 1140.[70] Since he was such a generous founder of houses representing all the main types of monasticism, his disinterest in the white monks seems to be connected with the fact that the abbots of Rievaulx and Fountains, aided and abetted by Bernard at Clairvaux, deeply offended him over the York election. This impression receives some confirmation if one looks at charters of gift, or confirmation, which he gave to Cistercian houses. These concern eleven of the thirty-nine Cistercian houses established during his reign, for which he issued in all sixteen charters.[71] With two exceptions—Kirkstead, founded by Hugh Brito, and Thame, founded by Alexander, bishop of Lincoln—the founders were

---

[69] I forbear listing the names because of their number.   [70] See above, nn. 50, 51.

[71] Biddlesden, Bordesley, Buckfast, Kirkstead, Meaux, Rufford, Sawtry, Sibton, Stoneleigh, Thame, Warden.

people who fought on Stephen's side, and to whom he might have felt himself obligated; the four charters in favour of Gilbert de Gant's Rufford are particularly striking. But, equally, if one considers two already existing houses which opposed him over the York election, Fountains and Rievaulx, it is suggestive that the former's charter well precedes the fracas, dating from February 1136, whilst Fountains had to wait until much later, 1151–3. Is it not possible that the abbot realized that he would be unlikely to receive a welcome if he were to ask for a charter earlier? One cannot, in the nature of the case, be certain, but here are signs that, just as the foundation of a house might have political connections, so the gaining of a gift or a charter of confirmation might involve political loyalties.

The fundamental question behind all these houses is why were they so numerous? David Knowles attributed this largely to the 'renaissance of spiritual life and ecclesiastical discipline' taking place all over north-western Europe, besides relating it to the European outlook of people like Theobald, Thurstan, Murdac, and others, including Henry of Winchester.[72] To what extent can we endorse his broader judgement?

There may well be something in it, but, as we have already seen, Henry founded no house, whilst Theobald, Thurstan, and Murdac had no direct hand in developments in their dioceses during the reign. None the less, their general influence must have been significant. To understand more we may need to reconsider how those much nearer to the times viewed developments. William of Newburgh called monasteries 'the castles of God in which the knights fighting for Christ the King could fight against spiritual wickedness'.[73] This seems fair, but it still does not help us with the question: why so many new houses just then? A few—very few the evidence suggests—were founded by men who regretted their actions in the anarchy; another handful can be connected with the crusade.[74] But most houses, I would suggest, reflect the need felt by men high and lower in society to have their own castle of prayer,

---

[72] Knowles, *Monastic Order*, 296.   [73] WN i. 53.

[74] e.g. Thomas of Cuckney establishing Welbeck for a range of people 'et eorum omnium quibus ego sua injuste diripui' (*Monasticon*, vi:2, 873). Ranulf of Chester made reparations for damage to Bardney, Chester Cathedral priory, Lincoln Cathedral: *Charters of Earls of Chester*, nos. 96, 34, 106. Crusade connection: Thremhall (Essex, Augustinian), and Wroxall (Warwickshire, OSB nuns, the evidence is late).

like their own castle for protection; and in about thirty cases the two were placed quite close to one another.[75] A small house would do; the point was that a personal spiritual stronghold would concentrate upon prayer for the founder, his family, and friends.

A related point—that the lack of such a defence might in such disturbed times result in the loss of all a man had—emerges from words written at Rievaulx, not far away from William's Newburgh. A little over ten years after Stephen died, Walter Daniel, describing Ailred's skill in developing Revesby, wrote that he knew that for men to give to monks 'helped the possessors of goods to their salvation, and that, if they did not give, they might well lose both life and goods without any payment in return'.[76] The words are striking with their sense that the man in the world who gave to monks would have certain reward in the world to come, but, if he did not give, there was little surety here below. Walter Daniel was, of course, a monk, and there is no means of being sure that laymen would have put the case in quite the same way. But we do know that laymen responded in an unprecedented manner to the offer which monks represented in a time of great disturbance. Of course we know that benefactors often gave their monks very little, or gave them land to which they had a very dubious title, leaving many problems for the inhabitants of these citadels of prayer in the future, but give they did.[77]

This very limited survey of the Church has attempted to explain why, on the whole, the Church stuck with Stephen, in the hope that he might keep the peace, whilst his failure to do so stimulated some people to protect themselves both here and in the hereafter by founding monasteries. But life was not so disturbed that monks and female religious were threatened. Most houses existed without suffering enormous damage, and somehow or other a huge pro-

---

[75] M. W. Thompson, 'Associated Monasteries and Castles in the Middle Ages', *Arch. Journal,* 143 (1986), 305–21, has seventy-nine cases for the whole 12th century. I am grateful to Dr Robert Higham for drawing this article to my attention.

[76] *The Life of Ailred by Walter Daniel,* ed. F. M. Powicke (NMT, 1950), 28.

[77] Some examples in Holdsworth, *Piper and Tune,* 23–6. Foundations on a woman's land, either from her husband, or her own family, may have been a means of providing a bolt-hole; e.g. Baysdale (North Riding of Yorkshire, Cistercian nuns), Nunkeeling (East Riding of Yorkshire, OSB nuns); see Thompson, *Women Religious,* 175, 177.

gramme of putting up buildings at these new houses, as well as at older houses, went on: one may recall, for example, the completion of the huge church at Lewes, dedicated somewhere between 1142 and 1147.[78] The scale of resources in materials and labour required was vast, and apparently forthcoming, despite the ebbs and flows of high political manœuvring. So Stephen's reign is remarkable for the continuation of an old practice, but at a new level of intensity.

Other aspects of the life of the Church, most notably life at 'parish' level in town and countryside, must be left on one side, but I suspect they are worth new consideration. I conclude with two brief notes: each reflects the tensions of the times. In the very year of Stephen's death, an anchorite, Wulfric of Haselbury, also died.[79] He had foretold to Stephen and his brother Henry that Stephen would succeed his uncle; and, to the local lord, the king's capture.[80] He may stand for that group of men and women who found a powerful role on the margins of normal society, where they filled some of the functions of trouble-shooters and peace-makers. Their heyday is not confined to this reign, but it certainly included it.[81] In 1141 the first case in western Europe of responsibility for the murder of a young boy being attributed to the Jews occurred in Norwich, which lead to the quick development of a tragic cult after the election of William Turbe, prior to the cathedral priory, as bishop in 1146.[82] Here we see a portentous twist in the terrible history of anti-Semitism, providing us with a final glimpse of a troubled society. Sometimes it sought relief for its tensions by directing them on to the next world when it founded monasteries, or by turning to a holy man or woman for guidance, both with, on the whole, benign results. But its third escape, to project their disturbance on to the most obvious strangers in their midst, was an utter disaster.

[78] Boase, *English Art*, 53–6.

[79] *Wulfric of Haselbury by John, Abbot of Ford*, ed. M. Bell (Somerset Rec. Soc., 47; 1933), p. xxxiii.

[80] ibid. 117–18 (ch. 91); cf. 21, 108–9 (chs. 7, 81).

[81] C. Holdsworth, 'Hermits and the Powers of the Frontier', *Reading Medieval Studies*, 16 (1990), 55–76.

[82] R. I. Moore, *The Formation of a Persecuting Society* (Oxford, 1987), 36.

7

THE SCOTS AND
THE NORTH OF ENGLAND

G. W. S. Barrow

THE title of this chapter was given to me by the organizers of the conference at Battle; it was one I was happy to accept at the time, and one with which I still have no quarrel. My remit seemed to be clear, compact, and well defined. But the longer I have thought about it, the more I have come to feel that the title begs at least two questions. Who, in the days of King Stephen and Geoffrey de Mandeville, were the Scots? And what, in their time, was the north of England? I shall argue that, in the mid-twelfth-century situation, these were far from being merely semantic questions. Some mystery inevitably attaches to the beginnings of states and nations, much as it does to the sources of streams and rivers. When the Loire, for example, begins life as a dark evil-smelling pool looking almost like slurry and trickles away southward across the fields in the direction of the Mediterranean, is it bound to become the Loire of Orléans, Blois, Angers, or Saint-Nazaire? Obviously the answer is yes, as things stand now and have done for many thousands if not millions of years. But whether the infant Loire was always so bound is perhaps a harder question, the answer to which presumably lies in the realms of geomorphology. Historians have no geomorphology to fall back on. If they are in the habit of assuming that the older nation-states with which they are familiar had to begin and grow and acquire their distinctive characteristics in the way that they did, this is less likely to be due to a conscious and deliberate philosophy of determinism than to sheer intellectual laziness. After all, the habit of attributing a history to England, for example (as distinct from histories of the English people, or of the kings or bishops or church of England), has been around since the later fourteenth century,[1] and may be said to have hardened into standard usage by *c.*1400.[2] By that time the notion of a history of Scotland was probably gaining ground. Even though the neatly entitled 'Scotichronicon' doubtless indicated a chronicle of the Scots rather than of Scotland, nevertheless in Walter Bower's recension, dating from the 1440s, the combination of geography with ethnology points unmistakably to an entity, Scotland, which possessed a legitimate, valid history—a standpoint epigrammatically summed up in Bower's colophon:

> That man is no true Scot, O Christ,
> Who thinks this book too highly priced.[3]

Our habit, therefore, of thinking, writing, and publishing histories of England and Scotland has become ingrained over many centuries. Although it does not arise from a false judgement about the past, it may—and often does—encourage a false anachronism. This does not matter too much if the anachronism is merely a bit of mischievous fun, as when the late and most learned Kenneth Jackson entitled his translation of Aneurin's *Gododdin* 'The Oldest Scottish Poem';[4] or even, perhaps—to cite an analogy from further afield—if it is palpably preposterous, as in the case of Sir Mortimer Wheeler's *Five Thousand Years of Pakistan* (1950). It is convenient to think of William the Bastard achieving the conquest of England, and it would be pedantic in the extreme to qualify that concept every time by adding, 'What William actually did was to conquer the kingdom of Edward the Confessor, recently taken over by Harold, earl of Wessex.' Nevertheless, the Normans' devastation of Yorkshire, Cheshire, and parts of Derbyshire and Staffordshire in 1069 raises serious questions regarding King William's concept of the English kingdom.[5] Sir Clifford Darby wrote many years ago:

---

[1] One of Thomas Walsingham's productions is entitled *Chronicon Angliae* (i.e. not *Anglicanum* or *Anglorum*). It concludes in 1388, and Walsingham died *c.*1422.

[2] John Capgrave (d. 1464) wrote 'The chronicle of England', which ends in 1417: E. B. Graves, *A Bibliography of English History* (Oxford, 1975), no. 2808.

[3] *Scotichronicon by Walter Bower in Latin and English*, viii, ed. D. E. R. Watt (Aberdeen, 1987), 340: 'Non Scotus est, Christe | Cui liber non placet iste.' The translation used here is by David McRoberts, *Innes Review*, 19 (1968), 6.

[4] K. H. Jackson, *The Gododdin: The Oldest Scottish Poem* (Edinburgh, 1969).

[5] *The Domesday Geography of Northern England*, ed. H. C. Darby and I. S. Maxwell (Cambridge, 1962), shows clearly and conveniently the extent of post-Conquest waste in the first three of these counties; see esp. 66, 140, 219, 318, 365. For Staffordshire

'The Domesday Inquest did not cover the whole of northern England. Descriptions of Northumberland, Durham, Cumberland and Westmorland are wanting.'[6] As a statement of fact with reference to the England of modern times, this is unexceptionable. As a piece of historical analysis, it begs a large question. One might as well say, 'Descriptions of Teviotdale, Tweeddale and the Merse of Berwickshire are wanting,' or even, 'Just as Domesday incorporated Flint and much of Denbigh so also it included twenty-eight vills or manors in Westmorland and Cumberland (specifically Lonsdale, Kentdale, Furness and the southern extremity of Copeland).' Those four county descriptions which Darby found wanting were wanting only for those who thought they ought to have been there in the first place—in other words, persons thoroughly steeped in modern English geography. The fact that the Domesday Commissioners did not concern themselves with, broadly speaking, the territory north of the River Tees, the Howgill Fells, and lower Lonsdale must surely signify that the lands to the north of this approximate line were not seen in 1086 as forming part of the English realm—as distinct from what King William might claim lordship over—any more than the lands west of the fluctuating western edge of Herefordshire and Shropshire were seen as part of the English realm. That does not mean, of course, that the country north of Tees could not be Anglia, 'England': on the contrary, version E of the Old English Chronicle reports that in 1091 the king of Scots led his army 'out of Scotland into Lothian in England',[7] while the first settlement of monks at Selkirk in 1113 was described by a knowledgeable contemporary as the coming of the Tironensians to England.[8] That usage applied, as far as I can see, to Northumbria east of the Pennines and the corresponding watershed north of the Tyne Gap, in other words to Bernicia and Lothian. How early the words Anglia or England were ever applied to any part of Cumbria I have not discovered, but I would be extremely surprised if what we have now learnt to call 'Cumbria' was even thought of, let alone formally labelled, as England much before the closing decades of the twelfth century, the period when the later counties of Westmorland and Cumberland were taking

see *The Domesday Geography of Midland England*, ed. H. C. Darby and I. B. Terrett, 2nd edn. (Cambridge, 1971), 203.

[6] *Domesday Geography of Northern England*, 419.   [7] *ASC* E, *s.a.* 1091.

[8] SD ii. 247.

recognizable shape. At least I hope I have said enough to persuade you that, in the context of King Stephen's reign, the phrase 'the north of England' is one which should be handled with care.

Likewise with the phrase 'king of Scots' or even simply 'the Scots'. The kingdom ruled by Kenneth mac Alpin, his brother Donald, and Kenneth's sons Constantine and Aed, all of whom are styled 'kings of the Picts' by the Ulster Annals,[9] had settled down by AD 900 into a kingdom of Scotland, or Alba. This kingdom was ruled by a dynasty which, whatever biological ingredients had contributed to its make-up, thought of itself not only as the Cenél nGabráin, a principal ruling house among the Gaelic-speaking dynasties of Ireland and northern Britain, but also, because it had succeeded to the older Pictish kings of Fortriu, as the unchallenged rulers of Alba, the whole of Scotland north of Clyde and Forth together with its islands to the west and north (already since c.800 under threat from Scandinavian incursions). It is, I believe, to the tenth century that we may date the beginning of the process, more or less completed by the twelfth, by which the words Scotia and Scoti came to refer to Scotland and the Scots, rather than to Ireland or the Irish. And in the English-speaking parts of Britain, too, the words Scotland and Scots came to bear this sense of the northern part of the island and its inhabitants.[10]

It was also in the middle of the tenth century that the kings of Alba acquired, as part of their lordship but as yet hardly as part of their realm, the territory of Lothian and the Merse—that is to say from the River Avon to the River Tweed—on the east, indubitably part of Bernicia or northern Northumbria, and also, on the west, the still Brittonic kingdom of Cumbria or Strathclyde.[11] The circumstances under which these large and agriculturally rich and important territories came under Scottish governance have been much debated, and will probably never become clear. The weight of later, medieval, English opinion has, not surprisingly, favoured the view that the Scots benefited from conditional concessions gra-

[9] *The Annals of Ulster (to A.D. 1131)*, ed. S. MacAirt and G. MacNiocaill, i (Dublin, 1983), 316, 318, 330, 332.

[10] e.g. *ASC* C, *s.a.* 934. See also R. L. G. Ritchie, *The Normans in Scotland* (Edinburgh, 1954), p. xxviii.

[11] Barrow, *Kingdom of Scots*, 142–3; D. P. Kirby, 'Strathclyde and Cumbria: A Survey of Historical Development to 1092', *Trans. Cumberland and Westmorland Antiq. and Arch. Soc.*, NS 62 (1962), 77–94.

ciously bestowed by west Saxon rulers. Such Scottish tradition as
survives points, equally predictably, to conquest obtained by force
of arms. I do not propose to enter here into what can easily become
a somewhat arid controversy fraught with anachronism. What I
believe is much more firmly based on contemporary source material is that, within the ambit of Scottish rule, within, that is to say,
the sphere of control or lordship exercised by kings of Scots, the
distinction between Scotia/Alba on the one hand and Lothian,
Cumbria, and Galloway on the other remained clear-cut in people's
minds and firmly delineated in linguistic usage far into the thirteenth century. The justiciarships of Scotia and Lothian, for example, were clearly distinguished at least until the fourteenth century,
and in a manner of speaking the former retained its identity till
1836.[12] The Melrose Chronicle reports contemporaneously on the
activities of armies raised by the king in Scotland in the early
decades of the thirteenth century, some of which contained Scots
while others did not.[13] Matthew Paris, the St Albans historian, was
well informed when he wrote that in the 1240s the Scots built two
castles which alarmed Henry III, one in Lothian, the other in
Galloway.[14] Undoubtedly the reference is to Hermitage in
Roxburghshire and Caerlaverock in Dumfriesshire respectively, the
localities being perfectly compatible with mid-thirteenth-century
usage.[15] The large diocese of Glasgow, although included within
the *ecclesia Scoticana* in Pope Celestine III's famous letter *Cum uni-
versi Christi* of 1192,[16] was always treated separately and distinctly
from the dioceses north of the Forth. In many respects Glasgow
was seen as *the* southern Scottish diocese, even though the St

[12] Barrow, *Kingdom of the Scots*, 85, 104–6, 108–9, 128–9. The justiciarship of
Scotia, later the justiciarship on the north side of the water of Forth, became eventually
the office of Lord Justice General, virtually hereditary in the family of Campbell of
Argyll from 1514 to 1628, and held by the earl of Ilay, afterwards 3rd duke of Argyll,
from 1710 to 1761.

[13] *Scotland in the Reign of Alexander III, 1249–1286*, ed. N. H. Reid (Edinburgh,
1990), 136.

[14] *Matthaei Parisiensis chronica majora*, ed. H. R. Luard, 7 vols. (RS, 1872–84), iv.
380; *Scotichronicon by Walter Bower*, v, ed. S. Taylor *et al.* (Aberdeen, 1990), 185.

[15] For the wider sense of 'Lothian', see G. W. S. Barrow, 'Midlothian—or the Shire
of Edinburgh?', *Book of the Old Edinburgh Club*, xxxv (1985), 141–2; for the larger
'Galloway', see *RRS* i. 38.

[16] R. Somerville, *Scotia pontificia* (Oxford, 1982), no. 156; full text in A. C. Lawrie,
Annals of the Reigns of Malcolm and William, Kings of Scotland, A.D. 1153–1214
(Glasgow, 1910), 275–6 (wrongly attributed to Clement III).

Andrews diocese embraced the archdeaconry of Lothian, which reached from Stirling to Kelso and Berwick upon Tweed.[17]

Senior ecclesiastics in the Middle Ages were, it is true, much given to making preposterous claims and extravagant gestures. But, when the English bishop of Glasgow, John of Cheam, declared in the 1260s that his diocese ought by rights to reach as far south as the Rere (or Rey) Cross on Stainmore, above Brough, he was surely indulging in optimism rather than fantasy.[18] After all, the church of Glasgow was historically the church of Strathclyde or Cumbria; and had not the first of the three bishops appointed to the see by David I, the Briton—or just possibly Breton—named Michael, been buried at Morland near Appleby, almost as though he intended his grave to mark the southernmost boundary of his sprawling diocese?[19]

Outside the Scottish realm, these distinctions were much less faithfully observed as the twelfth century proceeded, if indeed they were observed at all. What was ruled over by the king of Scots was all Scotland, his lieges all Scots, as far as English or French or other outsiders were concerned.[20] So much so, in fact, that in the thirteenth century a Northumberland jury refused to meddle with business arising in the Liberty of Tynedale because this was in Scotland and beyond the reach of their jurisdiction.[21] But even outside Scotland it took some time for these attitudes to develop.

[17] e.g., when six guardians were elected to govern Scotland after the death of Alexander III, the bishop of Glasgow was chosen as one of the three representing the south, while the bishop of St Andrews was among three representing the north: *Scotichronicon by Walter Bower*, vi, ed. N. F. Shead *et al.* (Aberdeen, 1991), 2.

[18] *Chronicon de Lanercost, 1201–1346*, ed. J. Stevenson (Bannatyne Club, Edinburgh, 1839), 65.

[19] J. Dowden, *The Bishops of Scotland*, ed. J. M. Thomson (Glasgow, 1912), 294–5.

[20] A good early illustration of this is contained in a charter issued by Stephen for Ranulf II, earl of Chester *c.*1146 (*RRAN* iii, no. 178). The earl was put in possession of all the land (with some stated exceptions) once held by Roger of Poitou 'from Northampton as far as Scotia'. Clearly 'Scotia' did not mean the country north of Forth and Clyde, but must have indicated the land ruled by the king of the Scots, the Scottish kingdom. Another clear illustration of English usage appears in *GS* 54, where the writer says, 'There was a king in Scotland (*Scotia*), which borders on England, with a river fixing the boundary between the two kingdoms.' Obviously, this river was the Tweed, and for the author of the *Gesta Stephani* Scotia began immediately north of it.

[21] *Calendar of Documents relating to Scotland*, ed. J. Bain, ii (1884), 46: 'the jurors attest that the trespass alleged was done in Tynedale in the kingdom of Scotland out of the kingdom of England, and the truth cannot be enquired into here' (AD 1279).

In the first half of the twelfth century we may not confidently speak of Scotland, Alba, Scotia, Écosse as extending south of the Firth of Forth or south and east of the Firth of Clyde. Nor may we confidently speak of England, Anglia, Angleterre as extending on the west much if at all beyond Stainmore Common in the north-west corner of the North Riding of Yorkshire, although on the eastern side of the country, and in a cultural or linguistic sense, it stretched as far north as the Forth. Twelfth-century writers habitually employed the Bedan terminology in referring to the territory between Tweed and Tees as Northumbria; for the country between Tweed and Forth both English and Scottish writers used the name Lothian, which is never found in Bede—or, indeed, much before 1100.[22] In the south-west of what is now Scotland they recognized the separateness of Galloway (Galwidia, Galwithia, Gauveye) and were more inclined to people it with Gallovidians (Galwithienses) than with Scots.[23] The Hexham writers of Stephen's reign, perhaps misunderstanding Bede's famous story of how the Gallovidian Ninian converted the southern Picts, rather absurdly applied the term 'Picts' to the inhabitants of Galloway, thus adding their own special brand of confusion to the general muddle into which many historians right down to modern times have been apt to fall.[24]

We must try to look at 'northern England' from the standpoint of a king of Scots in the first half of the twelfth century. To the east, the province of Lothian, rich in agricultural resources and in defensible strong points such as Edinburgh, Linlithgow, and Dunbar, passed without any formidable physical barrier into the Merse or lower Tweed Valley, which in turn formed part of the north Northumberland plain; both districts were distinguished for their advanced agricultural technology in the earlier nineteenth century. Beyond lay the series of river valleys—Aln, Coquet, Wansbeck—all of which provided some shelter and fertility without generating any outstanding prosperity. The valley of the Tyne, formed, of course, by the confluence of the very substantial tributary valleys of south and north Tyne, the whole constituting the

[22] Barrow, 'Midlothian—or the Shire of Edinburgh?', 141–8.
[23] e.g. in the racial addresses of royal charters, for which see *RRS* i. 74; ii. 76–7.
[24] There is an unduly extensive literature on the 'Picts' of Galloway, for whose status see, *inter alia*, J. MacQueen, *St. Nynia: A Study of the Literary and Linguistic Evidence* (Edinburgh, 1961), 39–43 (new edn. (Edinburgh, 1990), 39–53).

major river system of northernmost England, provided in many respects a parallel to the Tweed river system, though with almost all its features save the hills on a larger scale. Beyond the Tyne lay Saint Cuthbert's land—of which, of course, there were sizeable outlying pockets between Tweed and Tyne, especially Norhamshire, Islandshire, and Bedlingtonshire—and beyond that again only the territory of Hart and Harterness and the wapentake of Sadberge before the River Tees was reached, the boundary of what I suspect Alexander I and David I would have recognized as 'true' England.

These kings and their predecessors were surely brought up on a clear understanding that the country between Forth and Tees formed the ancient province (kingdom or earldom) of Bernicia. That this was understood by Malcolm III is demonstrated by the fact that he not only acknowledged the refugee Northumbrian Earl Cospatric, son of Maldred, by that title but bestowed upon him a large cluster of estates based on Dunbar (as an earldom which significantly bore no name) and presumably arranged that his own eldest son Duncan should marry Uctreda, Cospatric's daughter and granddaughter of Uhtred, last earl of Bernicia of the old Bamburgh line.[25]

In other words, the kings of Scots looked upon Bernicia, of which they already held the northern part, fairly densely settled by people of Gaelic speech who formed more than a mere uppercrust of warrior aristocracy, at least as proprietorially as did their counterparts in the south, kings of Wessex and England. I have never been convinced by the arguments often used to justify David I's lengthy involvement in English Northumbria, namely that he had 'inherited' a claim to this territory through his wife Maud, daughter and only child of Earl Waltheof, son of Siward. On the contrary, it seems to me, that, where Northumberland was concerned, David I was a true son of his father Malcolm III, who had invaded the province no fewer than five times, ultimately meeting his death there in 1093 at the hands of the treacherous Archil Morel. Most of Malcolm's raids across the Tweed seem to have been assertions of lordship rather than belligerent hostility.[26]

Even where Saint Cuthbert and his land were concerned, the Scots kings maintained a proprietorial and beneficent role—as well

[25] *The Scots Peerage*, ed. J. B. Paul, iii (Edinburgh, 1906), 242–5. Uctreda is called Aethelreda at 245.

[26] Ritchie, *Normans in Scotland*, 15–16, 26, 49–51, 55–6, 60.

they might, for, if the *Gododdin* is the oldest 'Scottish' poem, Cuthbert may plausibly be claimed as one of the best loved and most widely venerated of 'Scottish' saints.[27] He was in fact the favourite saint of Queen Margaret;[28] her husband Malcolm III had laid one of the foundation stones for the new—that is to say the present—cathedral of Durham in 1093;[29] and their anniversaries were celebrated at Durham with as much solemnity as that of King Athelstan.[30] Of their sons, Duncan II had abortively granted Tynninghame to Cuthbert and his monks,[31] Edgar granted Coldingham,[32] while Alexander I was privileged to be the only layman present when the saint's tomb was opened in 1104.[33] David I's kindnesses to Durham were substantial, not least his establishment of Coldingham as a full daughter-house of the cathedral under its own prior.[34]

Scottish royal interest in, and proprietory attitudes towards, Northumberland can be seen throughout David I's reign and survived to constitute something of a *damnosa haereditas* in the time of William the Lion and even until the treaty of York of 1237. For example, Udard, hereditary sheriff—I take that to mean 'thane'—of Bamburghshire, and his father Liulf, son of Eadulf, had some proprietorial rights in Swinton in Berwickshire which were duly acknowledged by David I.[35] The same king granted to Hextilda, daughter of Uhtred, son of Waltheof, in marriage with Richard Cumin, a nephew of David's chancellor, the ambitious William Cumin, four estates in lower Tynedale, namely Walwick, Thornton, Stonecroft, and Henshaw—all on or round about the Roman Wall as it climbs westward from Chesters out of the valley

---

[27] *Two Lives of Saint Cuthbert*, ed. B. Colgrave (Cambridge, 1940), 91. The anonymous life locates Cuthbert's early upbringing in a small village called Hruringaham, unidentified but evidently aligned W–E because in a strong east wind it was threatened with destruction by a fire at the east end. Perhaps the village was Whittingham in East Lothian, which is so aligned. Hwitingaham in insular lettering could have been misread as Hruringaham. In any case, Cuthbert was evidently born in what is now Scotland.

[28] Ritchie, *Normans in Scotland*, 117–18.   [29] Ibid. 59.   [30] Ibid. 117.

[31] Lawrie, *Charters*, no. 12. For discussion as to the authenticity of this famous charter, see A. A. M. Duncan, 'The Earliest Scottish Charters', *Scottish Hist. Rev.* 37 (1958), 103–35, and J. Donnelly, 'The Earliest Scottish Charters?', ibid. 68 (1989), 1–22.

[32] Lawrie, *Charters*, nos. 18, 19.   [33] Ritchie, *Normans in Scotland*, 114.

[34] Barrow, *Kingdom of Scots*, 168–9.   [35] Lawrie, *Charters*, nos. 100, 101.

of the North Tyne.[36] About 1118 Uhtred, son of Waltheof, had
sworn an oath affirming certain named lands—none, as it happens,
in what is now England—to the church of Glasgow.[37] In 1131 or
1132, in the process of making an agreement with the prior of
Durham regarding Staindropshire, Dolfin, son of Uhtred, son of
Maldred, reserved his allegiance to David I.[38] The hereditary succession of men who were earls of Dunbar from the time of the
refugee Cospatric, son of Maldred, to whom Malcolm III had
granted (or perhaps merely confirmed) many lands in east Lothian
and Berwickshire, down to Waltheof, Earl Patrick I, and beyond,
also held Beanley, Hedgeley, and other properties in north
Northumberland, apparently by very ancient tenure.[39] In this context it is in no way surprising that it was Earl Henry of Scotland
who built the first castle of Warkworth or that he and his father
issued charters and brieves in favour of Hexham Priory,
Tynemouth Priory, Newminster Abbey, St Bartholomew's Priory in
Newcastle, and several Northumbrian lay men.[40]

It was not an altogether different prospect which greeted a king
of Scots in the early part of the twelfth century, if he looked due
south from Edinburgh to the west side of the Tyne–Eden watershed and the Pennine Hills. Before 1092 the whole territory of
Clydesdale, Annandale, Eskdale, and Liddesdale had been lumped
with what is now English Cumbria to form the principality—formerly the kingdom—of Cumbria or Strathclyde.[41] Carlisle had
obviously been one of the centres for governing this territory, but it
was not the only one; Renfrew, Rutherglen, Cadzow, and Lanark
must all have played their part. The chief church was at St Mungo's
shrine of Glasgow, far to the north; much of the province's wealth,

---

[36] *RRS* i, no. 103. A charter issued by Richard Cumin and his wife granting land at
Stonecroft to Rievaulx Abbey is in *Cartularium Abbathiae de Rievalle*, ed. J. C.
Atkinson (Surtees Soc. 83, 1889), no. 305, and this was confirmed by Hextilda after
she had married her second husband, Malcolm, earl of Atholl: no. 306.

[37] Lawrie, *Charters*, no. 50 (p. 46).

[38] *Durham Episcopal Charters, 1071–1152*, ed. H. S. Offler (Surtees Soc. 179,
1964), 76.

[39] *History of Northumberland*, xiv, ed. M. Hope Dodds (Newcastle, 1935), 399,
422. See also ibid. vii, ed. J. C. Hodgson (1904), 29–31.

[40] Lawrie, *Charters*, and *RRS* i *passim*.

[41] Kirby, 'Strathclyde and Cumbria', 92–4; P. A. Wilson, 'On the Use of the terms
"Strathclyde" and "Cumbria"', *Trans. Cumberland and Westmorland Antiq. and Arch.
Soc.*, NS 66 (1966), 57–92.

however, must have come from well to the south, the rich agricultural lands of Copeland, Allerdale, and the Eden Valley and the silver mines of Alston—theoretically in Northumberland but perhaps
already being exploited, for convenience, from Carlisle.[42]

Abruptly in 1092 William Rufus severed the southern from the
northern part of Cumbria and sent peasant colonists from the
south to settle and cultivate the district around Carlisle.[43] With
ample use of hindsight we may see this as a 'regularization' of the
Anglo-Scottish border, since the Solway–Cheviot–Tweed line constituted a much simpler and more clear-cut frontier than the uncertain boundaries involved in the use of the Rere Cross, Lonsdale,
and the Furness Fells. But here again David I was his father's son.
Although neither his predecessors nor he himself could prevent
Rufus and Henry I putting new men into what we may just begin
to see as the north-west of England—for example, Roger the
Poitevin, Ivo Taillebois, Nigel d'Aubigny, Ranulf le Meschin, and
the future King Stephen himself—and although David in particular could not prevent Henry I's erection of the see of Carlisle in
1133, nevertheless personalities and features of the old unitary
Cumbria remained in place through the 1110s and 1120s. A
double act, namely Oggu and Leising, *Cumbrenses judices*—the
Cumbrian dempsters or lawmen—make their appearance at the
court of Edgar (died 1107) and at the court of David I (*c.*1128),
and in between took the oath required to affirm the possessions of
Glasgow.[44] They did so not only with Uhtred of Tynedale but also
with that Gille (Gillise), son of Boed, from whom the large north-
eastern Cumbrian district of Gilsland evidently derives its name.[45]
David seems to have had no difficulty in taking over southern
Cumbria as soon as the news reached him of Henry I's death.
Carlisle became, and remained, one of his chief seats of government. There is no evidence of any general reshuffle of landowner-
ship in favour of the Scots, but King David's nephew William, son
of King Duncan II, received in marriage—with resultant enormous
accretion of landed wealth—Alice de Romilly, the heiress of

---

[42] They were certainly so exploited in Henry I's reign, as is clear from *PR 31 Henry I*, 142.

[43] *ASC* E, *s.a.* 1092.

[44] Lawrie, *Charters*, nos. 20, 50 (p. 46), 153 (p. 119).

[45] Ibid., nos. 50 (p. 46), 153 (p. 119, where Gillise probably denotes Gille son of Boed). For the connection with Gilsland, see *VCH Cumberland*, i. 305–6.

Egremont, daughter of Cecily de Romilly, lady of Craven.[46] Moreover, it looks as though one of the Scottish king's right-hand men, Hugh de Morville, was given the lordship of Appleby—that is, Westmorland north of the Howgill Fells—by David himself.[47] This would surely have taken place by 1141, or earlier, for, in the detailed account of William Cumin's attempt to take over the see of Durham in succession to Geoffrey Rufus which is to be found in the First Continuation of Simeon of Durham, Hugh de Morville is listed among the baronial adherents of David I who were ready to take Cumin's part.[48] Understandable as such tactics would have been for men such as Robert de Brus, Bernard de Balliol, and Eustace fitz John, who all figure on the continuator's list, they would make sense for de Morville, lord of Lauderdale and perhaps of Cunningham, only if he was a landowner much closer to the bishopric of Durham than his Scottish fiefs brought him.

The aristocratic network of southern Cumbria in David I's time undoubtedly included many incomers, men of recent Norman or at least continental origin. But what must chiefly impress us is the persistent presence of wealthy and powerful families of obviously native stock, whether of northern England or of southern Scotland. Individuals associated with such families included Adam, son of Swain, son of Alvric, who held property from west Cumberland across to Yorkshire;[49] Cospatric, son of Orm, son of Ketill, ancestor of the Curwens of Workington;[50] Ketill himself, son of Eldred, and his brother Gilbert, ancestor of the family which took its surname from Lancaster;[51] and Ethelreda, daughter of Waltheof of Allerdale, who brought a large dowry to her husband Ranulf de

[46] Ritchie, *Normans in Scotland*, 400–1.

[47] Barrow, *Anglo-Norman Era*, 73.   [48] SD i. 144.

[49] See *PR 31 Henry I*, 25, 142, for references to Svein, son of Alric, and Svein's deceased widow (under Carlisle, Yorkshire, and Northumberland). See also W. Farrer, *Lancashire Pipe Rolls and Early Charters* (Liverpool, 1902), 238, 294; *PR 2–4 Henry II*, 146, 177, 179; *Domesday Book* (general editor John Morris), xxx *Yorkshire*, ed. M. L. Faull and M. Stinson (Chichester, 1986), pt. 2, app. 3, Biographies of Tenants, English, s.v. ALRIC (i.e. Adam's grandfather).

[50] F. W. Ragg, 'De Culwen', *Trans. Cumberland and Westmorland Antiq. and Arch. Soc.*, NS 14 (1914), 343–8 and table between 432 and 433; F. W. Ragg, 'Charters to St Peter's (St Leonard's) Hospital, York, and to Byland Abbey', ibid., NS 9 (1909), 237–9.

[51] F. W. Ragg, 'De Lancaster', ibid., NS 10 (1910), 395–494 and table I facing 494; Farrer, *Lancashire Pipe Rolls*, 295–6.

Lindsay.[52] This situation closely parallels that which prevailed in Northumbria east of the Pennines. How far back this native aristocracy could trace its roots within the region we hardly possess evidence to judge. What is noticeable is that there does not seem to be any marked prevalence among the personal names favoured by this network of families of any one of the four vernaculars employed—Old English, Scandinavian (both west and east), Gaelic, and Cumbric or Brittonic. South of the Eden Valley and east of the Pennines we may perhaps detect a slight preponderance of Anglo-Saxon names, just as in the Cumbrian 'melting-pot' Scandinavian and Celtic names may slightly predominate. But, if we simply look at two indisputably Scottish families of this period, we should be hard put to it to say which linguistic register was preferred.[53] The first lord—or king—of Galloway we know of in the twelfth century was Fergus (Gaelic). His two sons were Gilbert— either 'Norman' or an assimilation into Anglo-Norman of a Gaelic Gillebhrigde—and Uhtred (Old English). Gilbert's eldest son and heir was Duncan; he in turn was succeeded by Neil (both Gaelic names). Uhtred's heir bore the Gaelic name of Lochlan = Lachlan,[54] which was rendered more manageable to incomers of Norman French speech by being transformed into Roland (Rothlandus), while Lachlan's son was called Alan, which, although a Celtic name, came to Scotland from the Continent. A similar mixture may be found in the family which held the lordship of Nithsdale. Its first known head was Dunegal, a name which, as recorded, was probably Gaelic, although it may disguise a Cumbric name.[55] His sons were called Radulf,[56] a name of continental type, Gillepatrick, and Domnall (Duuenaldus), names of Gaelic

[52] Lawrie, *Charters*, 356.

[53] The names used by the lords of Galloway may be found in *Scots Peerage*, iv (1907), 135–41. The names used by the family of Dunegal, lord of Strathnith or Nithsdale, may be found in Lawrie, *Charters*, and in the cartularies of Holyrood, Kelso, and Melrose abbeys published by the Bannatyne Club.

[54] *Liber cartarum Sancte Crucis* (Bannatyne Club, Edinburgh, 1840), no. 24; *Cal. Docs. Scotland*, ed. J. Bain, ii. 422 (Lohlan, son of Huddredy, i.e. Lachlan or Roland, son of Uhtred).

[55] Donngal was a common Irish personal name, but here may represent a Brittonic equivalent, originally Dunnagual (*Annales Cambriae*, ed. E. Phiilimore, *Y Cymmrodor*, ix, 1888), *s.a.* 760.

[56] Lawrie, *Charters*, nos. 109, 125, 189, 230.

character, though the latter may embody a Brittonic form;[57] while
Domnall's son and heir bore the name Eadgar (Old English),[58] and
Eadgar named his daughter Affrica and son Gillechonaill (both
Gaelic).[59] Further south we should undoubtedly encounter fewer
Gaelic names and more Scandinavian and Old English forms, but
there would nevertheless still be a mixture.

This thoroughgoing mingling of vernacular languages at the
turn of the eleventh and twelfth centuries, persisting as it seems to
have done well through the twelfth century, points surely to an
aristocracy possessed of fairly deep roots which had existed long
enough to allow for some merging or fusion of different linguistic
and ethnic elements.

It is against this social, cultural, and geographical background that
we must appraise the interaction between the Scots and the north
of England during the twenty years of Stephen's reign. At the outset of that deeply formative couple of decades the territory that we
know as the north of England had scarcely come to terms with the
Norman Conquest as that was known and understood from the
English Channel to the Tees. It is this consideration which under-
lies the profound dissatisfaction which I cannot help feeling whenever I read the account of David I's reign in A. L. Poole's volume of
the Oxford History of England.[60] Poole admittedly was not alone
among historians in judging David's conduct to have been discred-
itable and his policy merely opportunistic. Poole says that it suited
David's policy to abide by the oath he had taken to support his
niece the empress in 1127 (and, incidentally, again in 1131).[61]
Although almost all the contemporary chroniclers mention, and
some emphasize, the oath,[62] Poole merely says that 'it provided a

[57] The Brittonic equivalent of Domnall, Dumnagual (Dyfnwal), occurred several
times in the ruling family of Cumbria; see e.g. Kirby, 'Strathclyde and Cumbria', 78.
This is the personal name contained in the Lakeland pass name Dunmail Raise.

[58] *Liber S. Marie de Calchou* (Bannatyne Club, Edinburgh, 1846), nos. 340, 347.

[59] Ibid., no. 340; *Liber S. Marie de Melros* (Bannatyne Club, Edinburgh, 1837),
nos. 199, 200, 201.

[60] A. L. Poole, *From Domesday Book to Magna Carta*, 2nd edn. (Oxford, 1955),
269–73.

[61] Ibid. 270; Barrow, *David I*, 17.

[62] *ASC* E, *s.a.* 1127, describes how David I and the magnates took the oath, but
does not link David's conduct between 1135 and 1141 with the oath. But the continuator of Symeon of Durham (SD i. 142), John of Hexham (SD ii. 287), Ailred of

motive for invasions across the border, the ostensible object of which was support of the empress's cause, the real object to secure Northumberland which he claimed in right of his wife . . . It was a war of ambition and aggression . . . the empress was altogether forgotten.'[63] I do not believe that David I's claim to Northumberland was derived from his wife, but from his father Malcolm III and earlier Scottish kings. Just as in the eyes of West Saxon and Norman rulers of England Lothian must have seemed merely an extension of Northumbria, to which they laid prescriptive claim which it was unnecessary to justify, so Northumbria between Tweed and Tees must have seemed an extension of Lothian in the eyes of Scottish kings. Nevertheless, it appears that David I was prepared to hold this territory under the English Crown or negotiate for his son and heir Henry to hold it. Had the empress made good her own claim to the English throne, I have no doubt whatever that David I would have insisted on being given control of Northumberland, for which either he or Henry of Scotland would have done homage. The essential point was that David was determined to have Northumberland, no matter who was ruler of England. Admitting defeat as long as Henry I was alive, David bided his time and put forward his claim as soon as Stephen had made himself king. To that extent David was indeed an opportunist.

Cumbria was a different matter altogether. In Scottish eyes it was and remained an integral part of an ancient kingdom which had passed into the hands of the kings of Scots as long ago as the middle of the tenth century, and had been governed directly by the Scottish royal house since the death of its last Cumbric king Owain, c.1018.[64] It seems quite clear that David never seriously accepted Rufus's actions of 1092 as a *fait accompli*. The vital distinction between Northumberland and Cumbria is ignored by Poole.[65] The misconception by which his account is flawed is surely betrayed by two details of his narrative. He says that

Rievaulx (*Saints of Hexham*, in *The Priory of Hexham*, ed. J. Raine, i (Surtees Soc. 44, 1864), 183), Henry of Huntingdon (HH 259), the *Gesta Stephani* (*GS* 52–4), Orderic Vitalis (OV vi. 518) and William of Newburgh (WN i. 103) all refer specifically to the oath in accounting for David's invasion of Northumbria, although Henry of Huntingdon (HH 260) adds that the oath appeared to give Scottish atrocities the veil of sanctity.

[63] Poole, *Domesday Book to Magna Carta*, 270.
[64] Kirby, 'Strathclyde and Cumbria', 84–94.
[65] They are distinguished by Richard of Hexham, *De Gestis Regis Stephani*: RH 170.

'Stephen had not long been crowned before David was *over the Tweed*'.[66] The chroniclers state clearly that David seized five castles beginning with Carlisle,[67] and there seems no reason to doubt that that was the true order of his priorities. Poole also expresses surprise that, even after his heavy defeat on Cowton Moor by Northallerton in August 1138, David I 'made good his escape to Carlisle' and 'was not yet prepared to retire to his own kingdom'.[68] I would have no doubt whatever that King David felt himself safely in his own kingdom once he crossed the Pennines and reached the Eden Valley. When in the aftermath of the battle of the Standard the king of Scots held council with the papal legate, Alberic, cardinal bishop of Ostia, in the presence of the Scottish bishops, abbots, priors, and barons, he chose to do so at Carlisle, obviously treated as a chief place of Scottish government.[69]

It seems to me that the policy pursued by David I from 1136 to the 1140s—indeed, all the way through to 1153, the year of his death (at Carlisle be it remembered)—was remarkably consistent. He believed in the validity of the claim of the empress, who was his niece, to the English throne, but it would surely be completely unrealistic to expect David to refuse Stephen all recognition when he had effectively made himself king and had even won conditional recognition from Robert of Gloucester. But David I also believed with equal conviction in his own claim, as king of Scotland, to Cumbria and northern Northumbria. This was why he lost no time in seizing the castles of Carlisle, Wark on Tweed, Alnwick, Norham, and Newcastle upon Tyne.[70] This was why by the first treaty of Durham (February 1136) David retained Cumbria ('by grant of King Stephen' report two of the English chroniclers, surely saving face),[71] refused homage to Stephen, relinquished the Northumberland castles, and allowed his son to succeed to the honour of Huntingdon, along with Doncaster, to be held, of course, in homage to Stephen.[72] This was why at the end of November 1137, after a nine-month truce, David again demanded Northumberland from Stephen and was unwilling to renew the truce when the demand was refused.[73] This was why, when the Scots captured Norham castle in early summer 1138, David told Geoffrey Rufus, the bishop of Durham—i.e.

---

[66] Poole, *Domesday Book to Magna Carta*, 270.   [67] HH 258; RH 145.
[68] Poole, *Domesday Book to Magna Carta*, 272.   [69] RH 170.
[70] Ibid. 145.   [71] Ibid. 146; John of Hexham: SD ii. 287.
[72] RH 146.   [73] Ibid. 151.

bishop of northern Northumbria—that he could have Norham restored to him if he would renounce his fealty to Stephen and acknowledge the king of Scots as his secular superior.[74] And, of course, this was why David was at first very willing that his chancellor William Cumin, Geoffrey Rufus's former disciple, should strain every nerve and sinew to obtain the see of Durham in 1141, only pulling back in the following year when it seemed that Cumin's ambition o'erleapt itself and that his unscrupulous tactics would bring David himself into disrepute.[75]

The second treaty of Durham (9 April 1139) was largely inspired by the legate Alberic and by King David's other niece Matilda, who was, of course, Stephen's queen.[76] She, let us not forget, was said by a contemporary not particularly friendly towards the Scots to have loved her uncle and her cousin Henry greatly.[77] By this treaty Henry of Scotland was confirmed in his possession of the honour of Huntingdon and was granted the earldom of Northumberland—we are not told on what, if any, terms and conditions. Richard of Hexham says that the castles of Bamburgh and Newcastle were withheld by Stephen, and Earl Henry was to be allowed two equivalent places in southern England.[78] There is no evidence, as far as I am aware, that Henry ever received these additional or substitute places (whether castles, boroughs, or manors, there seems no way of knowing: Richard's word is *urbes*, perhaps meaning 'shires'). On the other hand, the surviving written acts of Earl Henry and his father show clearly that the Scots did hold both Bamburgh and Newcastle.[79] Either the treaty, as reported to Richard of Hexham, was subsequently modified, or the Scots used *force majeure*. Even though Warkworth castle, in its earliest phase, was probably built for Earl Henry in this period, it would not have been easy for the Scots to control the whole country from Tweed to Tees—and William of Newburgh noted the contrast during the 1140s between its peacefulness and the disturbed state of the Midlands and south of England[80]—unless they had had command of Bamburgh and Newcastle.

---

[74] Ibid. 157.
[75] A. Young, *William Cumin: Border Politics and the Bishopric of Durham 1141–1144* (Borthwick Paper, 54; York, 1978). 10–25.
[76] RH 176.   [77] Ibid.   [78] Ibid. 177.
[79] *RRS* i, nos. 23, 25, 27, 28, 30, 31, 32; Lawrie, *Charters*, no. 129.
[80] WN i. 70.

It is, I believe, significant that Richard of Hexham, in reporting
that by the second treaty of Durham Stephen commanded the
baronial tenants of the earldom of Northumberland to do homage
and be obedient to Henry of Scotland, adds, 'this *most of them*
did'.[81] Generally speaking, it was the incoming feudatories of continental origin—Normans, Picards, Flemings, and Bretons—who
held fast to the English Crown, whether worn by Henry I,
Stephen, or Henry II. It seems safe to guess that those who dis-
obeyed Stephen in 1139 and refused homage to Earl Henry
belonged to these incoming conquest families. Bearing in mind the
allegiance to the king of Scotland (as well as to the king of
England) reserved in 1131 by Dolfin, son of Uhtred, son of
Maldred; bearing in mind the prominent part taken in Scottish
military operations in Northumbria in 1138 by Edgar Unnithing, a
son of Earl Cospatric II of Dunbar and ancestor of the Caistrons of
that ilk,[82] and by Robert and Uhtred, sons of Maldred,[83] who were
perhaps nephews of Dolfin, Uhtred's son;[84] bearing in mind the
continued adherence to the Scots of Edgar Unnithing as late as
the 1170s[85] and the similar adherence of Cospatric, son of Orm
(the 'old white-headed Englishman' of Jordan Fantosme's poem),
landowner in Westmorland[86]—there may, after all, be something
in the unprovenanced statement of Orderic Vitalis, referring to the
situation after Henry I's death, when he says that certain evildoers

[81] RH 177.
[82] Ibid. 166–7; W. P. Hedley, *Northumberland Families*, i (Newcastle upon Tyne, 1968), 244–5.
[83] RH 166–7.
[84] The suggested family tree is:

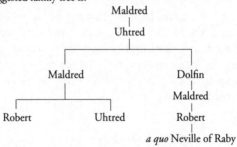

[85] *History of Northumberland*, vii (1904), 40–3.
[86] *Jordan Fantosme's Chronicle*, ed. R. C. Johnston (Oxford, 1981), 108 (laisse 151); *PR 22 Henry II*, 119.

plotted a conspiracy to massacre all Normans on a prearranged date and hand over the government of the English kingdom to the Scots.[87]

Of course there were exceptions to the general rule. If the elder Robert de Brus, though a friend of David of Scotland since youth, took Stephen's side in 1138, his younger son Robert took the Scottish side. Opponents of Stephen—such as the Somerset Lovels and other kinsmen of Robert of Bampton,[88] or the fitz Alans from Shropshire,[89] or Manasser Marmion probably uncle of the strongly pro-Stephen Robert Marmion I,[90] or the hugely ambitious Eustace fitz John, who supported Stephen till 1138 and again c.1146[91]—flocked to David I's standard from almost all quarters. Eustace's career, in particular, is almost a *locus classicus* in illustrating how the 'anarchy' of Stephen's reign could be exploited by an able man of knight's rank and training to build for himself a baronial power base, in his case centred upon Malton in Yorkshire and Alnwick in Northumberland, but also including the constableship of the earldom of Chester. Paul Dalton has drawn attention to the significant part played by Eustace fitz John in the process by which Earl Ranulf II of Chester consolidated his power in north Lincolnshire, especially after the battle of Lincoln in 1141.[92] It was evidently with Eustace's help that Earl Ranulf won the battle and captured King Stephen, with momentous consequences for the Angevin cause. The earl of Chester rewarded Eustace by compelling the young Roger de Mowbray to grant him a large beneficial enfeoffment—fourteen knights' fees for only eleven knights' service.[93] Dalton might have added that Eustace fitz John almost made a habit of accumulating beneficial enfeoffments, for in the period 1139–41 Henry of Scotland, earl of Northumberland and lord of the honour of Huntingdon, not only confirmed Eustace in his

[87] OV vi. 494.   [88] Barrow, *Anglo-Norman Era*, 100–2.

[89] Walter, younger brother of William fitz Alan and ancestor of the Stewarts, seems to have entered the service of David I as early as 1136: Barrow, *Kingdom of Scots*, 337. He and his brother William witnessed acts of the Empress Matilda at Oxford in 1141 and perhaps elsewhere: *RRAN* iii, nos. 377, 378, 821. See also OV vi. 520–2.

[90] Lawrie, *Charters*, nos. 100 (c.1136) and 119 (1138), were witnessed by Manasser Marmion, for whose place in the Marmion descent see *CP* viii. 507.

[91] R. H. C. Davis, *From Alfred the Great to Stephen* (London, 1991), 194; *RRAN* iii, no. 494; for Eustace's activity in the intervening period, see P. Dalton, in *Earldom of Chester*, 118–20.

[92] Ibid. 118–19.   [93] Ibid.

Northumbrian tenancies in chief but also put him in beneficial possession of five principal demesne manors of the honour of Huntingdon, Earls Barton, Potton, Great Paxton, Stukeley, and Tottenham, with the five-knight fee of Robert de Muntuit thrown in for good measure.[94] Eustace seems to have made himself indispensable to the king of Scots and to the earl of Chester, and it is of no little interest that, through his holdings in the East Riding, Eustace controlled one of the vitally important ferries across the Humber—surely used by the Scottish kings[95]—and, as constable of Chester, controlled another vital ferry across the Mersey at Runcorn.[96]

On the other hand, there were families and individuals in Scotland of Old English descent who do not seem to figure prominently or at all in the Scottish intervention in English politics of Stephen's reign or in the Scottish recovery of what we now think of as the northern English counties. The earls of Dunbar—Cospatric I, who owed his commanding position to the kindness of Malcolm III, Cospatric II, who fell at the battle of the Standard in 1138, and their close kin—seem to have been active on the Scottish king's side, perhaps not surprisingly. But we do not hear anything in northern England of the family which in several generations favoured the personal name Merleswain, borne by the prominent thegn, sometime sheriff of Lincoln, who fled from England into Scotland in 1067 and again in 1070,[97] or of the family supposed to be descended from the Yorkshire or Durham thegn Arkil, son of Ecgfrith, whose son and grandson may have served the Scottish kings as *rannaire*, 'distributors of food', *dapiferi*.[98] What the

[94] *RRS* i, nos. 11, 12.

[95] Ibid. ii, no. 551, records a grant of land in Fife (Knights Ward in Carnbee) by William the Lion to the Templars of North Ferriby, pointing to a royal link with Ferriby which is likely to have arisen through use of the Humber ferries.

[96] A. T. Thacker, in *Earldom of Chester*, 9–10, 12–13; Dalton, ibid., 120 and n. 64.

[97] For Merleswain in England, see *Domesday Book*, xx (ed. Faull and Stinson), pt. 2, app. 3, Biographies of Tenants, English, s.v. MERLESVEINN. In Scotland Ardross and Kennoway in Fife, including the farm of Kilmux, belonged to Merleswain, son of Colban, and his son Merleswain in the mid-twelfth century, almost certainly descendants of the Domesday pre-Conquest tenant; moreover, the Colban who held the earldom of Buchan *jure uxoris* in the 1170s evidently belonged to this family : *RRS* ii, no. 137; *Liber cartarum Prioratus S. Andree in Scotia* (Bannatyne Club, Edinburgh, 1841), 251–9.

[98] Arkil, son of Ecgfrith, is said to have been put to flight and made an exile at the Norman Conquest in the anonymous tract *De obsessione Dunelmi*: SD i. 220. He may

twelfth-century documents make us aware of is a remarkably stable middling nobility of mixed English, Celtic, and Scandinavian descent supporting a by no means completely overwhelming intrusion of Normans and other continentals for the most part slightly higher up the ladder of lordship and power. It was not at all a foregone conclusion that this dynamic mixture would end up as part of 'England' rather than 'Scotland'.

A. L. Poole seems to me to come perilously close to joining what one might not unfairly call the '1066 and All That' school of history when he says that David I had an easy task winning Cumbria and Northumbria from a weak king, Stephen, and it was not to be expected that his grandsons could hold these territories once a strong king, Henry II, came to the throne.[99] Contemporaries would surely not at once label the two Henrys as strong kings or Stephen a weak one. They had to take things as they found them, and could not know that both David I and Stephen would lose the sons, of whom they had such high expectations, almost within a single year.[100] Poole writes[101] as if he doubted the truth of the account transmitted by William of Newburgh and Roger of Howden of how the young Henry of Anjou, coming to Carlisle in 1149 to be knighted by King David, swore an oath that, if he became king of England, the Scots would be left in possession of Newcastle upon Tyne and all Northumbria—*a fortiori* Cumbria we may be sure—but this story, which neither Newburgh nor Howden could have had any incentive to invent or even gossip about, rings true: it is precisely in line with David I's singleness of mind about Northumbria and precisely what he would have wished to obtain from either the empress or her son.

Until the death of his only son Earl Henry, *rex designatus* of Scotland, in June 1152, David I may have felt confident that the balance of power in Cumbria and Northumbria had shifted substantially in favour of the Scots. Between his severe defeat at the Standard in August 1138 and the capture of Stephen at Lincoln David had had to make some concessions to the English king, none of them of fundamental importance. David and his son

have been ancestor of Alfwine, son of (or mac) Arkil, *rannaire* of David I and father of Gilleanndrais mac Alfwine, *rannaire* of Malcolm IV: *RRS* i. 32–3.

[99] Poole, *Domesday Book to Magna Carta*, 275.
[100] Henry of Scotland died 12 June 1152, Eustace of England 17 August 1153.
[101] Poole, *Domesday Book to Magna Carta*, 275. See WN i. 105, Howden, i. 211.

undertook to keep peace with Stephen and remain loyal to him,
and in token of this the Scots agreed to hand over five young
nobles of high rank.[102] Whether the choice of these hostages lay
with Stephen or the Scots, their identity seems to show that the
treaty of 1139 was between two kingdoms and not primarily concerned with what is now northern England or with feudal vassals
whose loyalty might oscillate between Anjou and Blois. The young
men chosen were the sons (presumably the heirs) of four Scottish
'earls'—Fergus, lord (or 'king') of Galloway, Cospatric III of
Dunbar, Malise of Strathearn[103] and Matad of Atholl.[104] The only
magnate of Anglo-Norman origin compelled to yield up a hostage
was King David's constable Hugh de Morville. This ties in with the
fact that the host which David led into Northumbria early in 1138
was drawn from Argyll, Moray, and the central territories of Scotia,
as well as from Galloway and Lothian and even from the Isles.[105]
And it also ties in with the fact that after Earl Henry's death David
I despatched Henry's eldest son Malcolm on a tour of Scotia to be
acknowledged as heir, while David himself installed Henry's second
son William in the earldom of Northumberland.[106] That installation, forced upon the Anglo-Norman barons of the earldom
against their will, as we are told,[107] and the closely contemporary
installation of Hugh du Puiset as bishop of Durham,[108] presaged a

---

[102] RH 178. The names of the Scots earls seem to have given the scribe of the MS
(Corpus Christi College, Cambridge, MS 139, fo. 47) some difficulty: he writes them
as Mel and Mac with marks of suspension. There can be little doubt that these names
stand for Malise and Madeth or Matad. Incidentally, Richard's use of Scottia here is
clearly in line with Scottish rather than English usage, meaning Scotland north of the
Forth.

[103] For Malise, earl of Strathearn, at the battle of the Standard, see Ailred of
Rievaulx, De Standardo, in Chronicles, iii. 190.

[104] Matad or Madeth, earl of Atholl, was the son of Maelmuire, who may have
been a younger brother of Malcolm III and Donald Ban. Matad married a daughter of
Paul II, earl of Orkney, and died perhaps soon after 1139, leaving a son and heir
Malcolm who was under age. See K. H. Jackson, The Gaelic Notes in the Book of Deer
(Cambridge, 1972), 81–3.

[105] Ailred of Rievaulx, De Standardo, 181, 190–1; RH 152.

[106] John of Hexham: SD ii. 327.

[107] John of Hexham (in SD ii. 327) says that King David took William to
Newcastle upon Tyne, presumably after Earl Henry's funeral at Kelso, and, in order to
enforce William's lordship over the Northumbrian magnates, took hostages from
them.

[108] Handbook of British Chronology, 241; Hugh du Puiset elected 22 January and consecrated 20 December 1153; he was installed at Durham on 2 May 1154 (SD i. 169).

new era, ushered in at the end of 1154 with the installation of Henry of Anjou as king of England. Even so, we must not allow ourselves to be carried away by concepts of weak kings and strong kings, old eras and new. Many of the old families survived, and with them many of the old ways. The palatine bishopric of Durham may have seemed an anomaly in 1300; it was certainly no anomaly in the twelfth century. And, along with the liberties of Redesdale and Hexhamshire, we should recall the liberty of Tynedale, which from David I's days till the 1290s gave the kings of Scotland a territory reaching from the Kielder Gap nearly all the way south to Cross Fell, overlooking Appleby, and also the honour of Penrith, which from 1237 to 1286 gave them a sizeable chunk of south-east Cumberland. The tidy, orderly Norman–Angevin pattern of shrievalties, sheriffs, deputy-sheriffs, coroners, escheators, and itinerant justices, so familiar to those of us put through the mill of English constitutional history as it used to be, had barely time to assert itself before the Anglo-Scottish war of 1296–1328 saw its supersession by other arrangements.

Before hindsight compels us to see that King David's vision was shattered in 1157 when Henry II resumed the possession of the 'northern counties' (as we must now learn to call them) enjoyed by his grandfather, we may be allowed a moment of surmise: what might have happened to Cumbria and Northumbria if William Cumin had become bishop of Durham in 1141—he lived, after all, till the late 1150s or 1160s[109]—and if David's son had succeeded as king of Scots? David was not the only opportunist. Henry of Anjou clearly took advantage of the youth of Malcolm IV and his brother when he seized Cumbria from the former and Northumberland (except Tynedale) from the latter. Had he been dealing with his older cousin and a bishop of Durham not only well established but also well affected to the Angevin house, it is just conceivable, I suppose, that he might have stayed his hand. As it was, David's vision, shattered or not, was bequeathed to William the Lion and his son and was to colour the relations of Scottish kings not only with their English counterparts but also with the land between Cheviot and Tees far into the thirteenth century.

[109] Young, *William Cumin*, 26–7.

8

THE MARCH AND
THE WELSH KINGS

David Crouch

A THIRTEENTH-CENTURY story tells of a baron on his death-bed. He was worried about how to divide his lands between his sons. Instead of falling back on tried and tested methods, he asked the boys what sort of bird each would have liked to be. The elder son might well have been puzzled by the question, but eventually he admitted that he would rather have liked to have been a hawk. In his turn, the younger said he would prefer to have been a starling. The father turned to the elder and addressed him thus: 'You, my son, as I see, wish to make your living out of preying on others, so I give you my lands in England, because it is a land of peace and justice, and you won't be able to thieve there and get away with it!' Then, turning to the younger, he said: 'Now you, my boy, who loves to live in neighbourliness—you shall have my lands in Wales, which is a land of strife and warfare. By your courtliness you will civilize the ill-nature of the natives.'[1] Here is the stock view of England and Wales neatly expressed—England the land of law, Wales the land of disorder, danger, and restless natives. We find it much earlier; indeed it is first strongly expressed in Henry I's reign. It is summed up by the prelate who set about writing the *Gesta Stephani* in the mid-1140s. He recalls the Anglo-Norman conquest of Wales and its aftermath:

they perseveringly civilized it after they had vigorously subdued its inhabitants; to encourage peace they imposed law and statutes on them; and they made the land so productive and abounding in all kinds of resources

The author thanks Professor R. R. Davies for his comments on an earlier draft of this chapter.

[1] *A Selection of Latin Stories*, ed. T. Wright (Percy Soc. 8, 1842), 36.

that you would have reckoned it in no wise inferior to the most fertile part of Britain.[2]

The irony is that the new reign, for which the writer is composing an apology, had reversed the relationship. It was Wales which eventually found a sort of stability and England which became a land of pillage, faction, and disorder.

The author of the *Gesta* had a simple explanation for Wales's fall from what he saw as grace. King Henry's death had taken away the great lion-tamer and his firm hand; the Welsh had reverted—in his words—to their 'animal type'.[3] The *Gesta* are not alone in linking the colonial disaster in Wales with Henry's death, but they make the most forceful case. So forceful is it that nobody seems to have gone to the trouble of questioning it. Yet a closer look at the sources does not support the link. The eventual explosion in Wales did not happen until six months or so after Henry died; it cannot be that the Welsh leaders were that slow on the uptake.

What happened in the immediate aftermath of Henry's death was a localized problem in the south of Wales. The Welsh of the area of Cantref Bychan and western Glamorgan descended on Gower and there inflicted a major defeat on the English in a pitched battle dated by one source as 1 January 1136. Almost all of the chronicles associated with the Severn Valley echo the shock of the event. In due course the author of the *Gesta Stephani* (who was probably Bishop Robert of Bath) used the disaster in Gower as his marker for the upset of English dominance in Wales. However, the Welsh chronicles fail to mention anything about this disaster for the English; for the Welsh the battle in Gower seems to have had only local significance. An argument against even linking the problem in Gower to Henry's death is the fact that both Orderic Vitalis and Gerald of Wales imply that troubles in Wales (and Gerald particularly refers to the troubles in the Gower area) had begun *just before* Henry died.[4] For the Welsh, the key event of 1136 happened

---

[2] *GS* 14. For the colonial mentality of the English in the early 12th century, see J. Gillingham, 'The Context and Purposes of Geoffrey of Monmouth's *History of the Kings of Britain*', *ANS* 13 (1991), 99–118, esp. 105–9.

[3] *GS* 14–16.

[4] The Gower fighting is dated by FW ii. 97, and mentioned in related or derivative texts: JW 40; *Annales Dorenses*, ed. F. Liebermann and R. Paul, in *Monumenta Germaniae Historicae: Scriptores*, xxvii (Hanover, 1885), 523; 'Winchcombe Annals' ed. R. R. Darlington, in P. M. Barnes and C. F. Slade (eds.), *A Medieval Miscellany for*

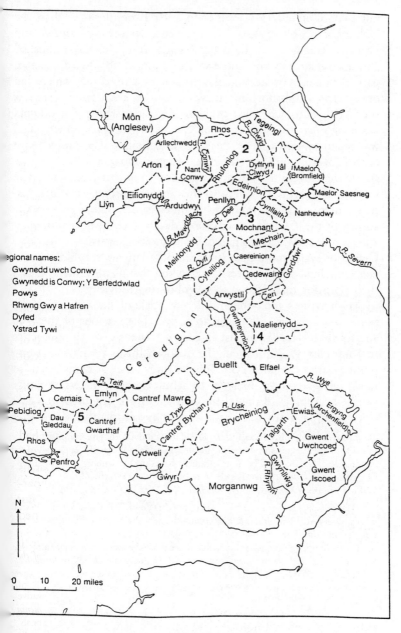

MAP 8.1. The Welsh regions

not in Gower but in Gwent, and several months later than the
January battle, on 15 April 1136. On that day the royal *curialis* and
lord of Ceredigion, Richard fitz Gilbert de Clare, was ambushed
and assassinated by the household of Morgan ab Owain, ruler of
part of upland Gwent, and descendant of a royal line which had
once ruled in Glamorgan.[5] It was after this event (*wedy hynny* as
the Welsh chronicle says, probably thus translating the original
Latin *post hoc*) that the army of Gwynedd and its southern allies
was set in motion against the English colonists. The problems of
early 1136 pale into insignificance when compared with the widespread violence of the summer and autumn of that year. The battle
in Gower owes its notoriety to the English chronicles, which fas-
tened upon it as an event with much shock value, and to the
author of the *Gesta* (writing over a decade later) who endowed it
with more retrospective significance than was perceived at the time.
Gerald of Wales more than hints that the January troubles were in
fact contained and even retrieved, when the Welsh leaders turned
their attention from Gower to neighbouring Kidwelly.[6]

Welsh writers took the murder of Richard fitz Gilbert as the
point when native rule began to revive. The versions of the *Brut*
and its abbreviated Latin sisters do not relate the Welsh resurgence
to King Henry's death at all. To establish this is to make a telling
point against Stephen. Sir John Lloyd—the protohistorian of
medieval Wales—was inclined to acquit Stephen of responsibility
for the beginnings of the rebellion at least.[7] His argument was that
since Henry's death was the spark for revolt, Stephen's character

Doris Mary Stenton (PRS NS 36, 1960), 127. These, and *GS* 16, give a similar number
of English casualties in Gower. For the involvement of the Welsh of Glamorgan in the
fighting, see D. Crouch, 'The Slow Death of Kingship in Glamorgan, 1067–1158',
Morgannwg, 29 (1985), 33–4. For the antedating of the 1136 troubles, see Gerald of
Wales, *Itinerarium Kambriae*, in *Opera*, vi, ed. J. F. Dimock (RS, 1868), 78.

[5] The principal account is in *GS* 16–18, but Gerald of Wales adds some colourful
details: *Opera*, vi. 47–8. *Brut* (*s.a.* 1136) notes the events in brief and says that Morgan
was the directing force; Gerald says that the deed was done by Iorwerth, Morgan's
brother (with other relations). It is possible to reconcile the accounts by suggesting that
Iorwerth was acting here as *penteulu* (or chief of the military household) for Morgan.

[6] *Opera*, vi. 78. Gerald, in the same passage, appears to date the campaign in Gower
to the last years of King Henry's reign, but other evidence (see above, n. 4) is against
him.

[7] Lloyd, *Wales*, ii. 462. Davies (*Wales*, 46), on the other hand, sees 'the personality
and power' of Stephen as important to the English failure in Wales at this time, despite
his seeing King Henry's death as the spark of rebellion.

MAP 8.2.   The Marcher lords in 1130

and capacities were irrelevant to it. However, if the rising did not begin until six months or so after Henry's death, then Stephen's first actions as king were relevant to its outbreak. The Welsh knew of King Henry's greatness and they understood the manipulation by which he had mastered them. But they also saw that his agents in Wales were their chief burden and constraint. The king's death had not removed these men. The old king would have retaliated smartly and in person to the fall of Richard fitz Gilbert—as he did in 1121 in the troubles following the death of Earl Richard of Chester. It was the real threat of Henry's intervention which had given his Welsh agents and allies shape and size. By mid-1136 the Welsh rulers knew Stephen to be indifferent to them, and month by month their conviction must have strengthened that the main player had quit the game of power in Wales. Welsh chronicles call Henry 'the Great' and describe his deeds at great length; they would do the same in due course for Henry II also. They noticed Stephen's accession and death, no more.

Stephen's apparent indifference to Wales matches his curious neglect of his own position in Normandy; it was attended by consequences quite as dire. Stephen's behaviour barely recognized the need to defend the authority and resources Henry had amassed in Wales and the March. His reaction to the emergency in Wales in 1136 was the same as his response to the crisis on the southern border of Normandy. He sent personal envoys to take charge, equipped with money and troops, but he himself appeared in neither theatre. In the case of Normandy, his selected lieutenant, Waleran of Meulan, was a man sufficient to deal with the problem.[8] In Wales, the king was not so lucky. He sent two known trouble-shooters to different parts of the March. In 1136, following Richard fitz Gilbert's death, he sent Richard's younger brother Baldwin into Ceredigion. The other agent was the Marcher lord, Robert fitz Harold of Ewyas. We are never told to where Robert was sent, but a process of elimination strongly indicates that he based himself at the royal fortress of Carmarthen in west Wales. Baldwin failed in his mission and got no further than Brecon, where 'he gave himself over entirely to gluttony and sloth'.[9] Robert

[8] Crouch, *Beaumont Twins*, 31–3.
[9] *GS* (16) notes that, when he first heard of the rising, Stephen sent hired knights and archers to Wales; this seems to refer to the *Gesta's* notice of Baldwin's mission elsewhere: ibid. 18–20.

MAP 8.3.   The Welsh magnates in 1130

had more success at the beginning of his mission and converted an unnamed castle (which must have been Carmarthen) into a forward base. However, force of circumstances, or the king himself, eventually obliged him to withdraw (probably in 1137).[10]

Stephen failed to follow up the efforts of his lieutenants in Wales by a personal appearance, and King Henry's system (and the accumulated prestige of five reigns) collapsed in Wales. Henry had peopled the March with many of his closest *curiales* (see Map 8.2). He had taken possession of large areas of the March himself, notably Pembrokeshire (after the fall of the Montgomery family) and Dyfed (after the murder of his client king, Hywel ap Gronw). King Henry had taken particular care to establish leading agents to inform him about Welsh affairs and to control them. To begin with he used Richard de Beaumeis, bishop of London, but later he employed Miles of Gloucester and Payn fitz John. These two men controlled for the king the middle and southern March, and the shires of Gloucester, Hereford, and Shropshire. As usual, Henry was both bestowing patronage and looking to his own security in an area that might be dangerous to him.[11] Stephen did not attempt to operate this system as such. The most important of the Marcher *curiales* (that is, Brian fitz Count, Miles of Gloucester, Payn fitz John, and Earl Robert of Gloucester) appeared at Stephen's Easter courts at Westminster and Oxford, indicating their support for his regime.[12] But neither Miles, Payn, nor Earl Robert was given overall responsibility for the March. Stephen chose in 1136 to turn to Robert of Ewyas, a man of lineage and enterprise, but no great weight. It is symptomatic of the new regime that Stephen chose to use Miles not against the Welsh but as a counterweight to the power and influence of Earl Robert, the late king's favourite bastard.

---

[10] *GS* (20) has Robert sent into Wales 'in another direction' to Baldwin; this would indicate a littoral direction to Robert's mission. The main reason for linking Robert with Carmarthen lies in the record of its successful defence, but eventual fall (probably late) in 1137; this would fit what the *Gesta* says about Robert's unnamed base: *Brut, s.a.* 1137; *AC, s.a.* 1137.

[11] For studies of King Henry's men and methods in Wales, see I. W. Rowlands, 'The Making of the March: Aspects of the Norman Settlement in Dyfed', *ANS* 3 (1980), 142–57; R. R. Davies, 'Henry I and Wales', in H. Mayr-Harting and R. I. Moore (eds.), *Studies in Medieval History Presented to R. H. C. Davis* (London, 1985), 132–47.

[12] For the personnel concerned at Westminster and Oxford, see Round, *Geoffrey*, 262–6.

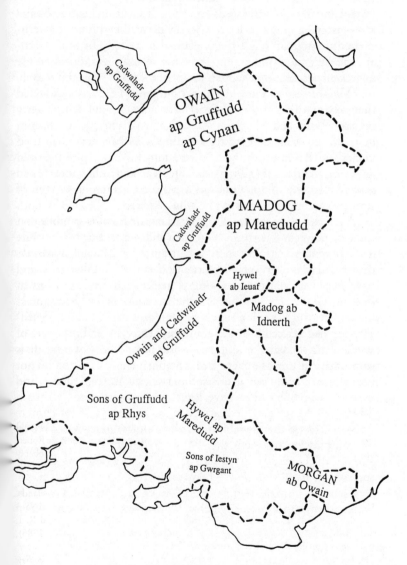

MAP 8.4.   The Welsh magnates in 1137

We may well ask what Stephen was up to in 1136, although any conclusive answer is unlikely. The author of the *Gesta Stephani* volunteers some ideas. In commenting upon the failure of Stephen's envoys to Wales in 1136, he portrays Stephen as unwilling to waste further money on Wales and—on the advice of unknown counsellors—as being ready to let the Welsh do as they please, expecting them to fall out amongst themselves soon enough. In time, famine and plague would follow on from their warfare—'and indeed', he says, 'we have seen this happen in a short while'.[13] But this was not so. Warfare lessened in 1137, not because the Welsh exhausted themselves with fighting—or at least no more than usual—but because Welsh and Marchers reached mutual agreements independent of the king. According to the *Gesta*, Stephen abandoned Henry's interventionism and bowed out of Wales. Its author may have been correct in saying that Stephen had other uses for his money (certainly Normandy was a drain on his resources), but his strategy can only be assessed as a wild gamble.

If we have to speculate about the reasons for this gamble, then the very power of Henry I's Marcher *curiales* might be one explanation. It may be that Stephen saw the greater Marcher lords as a threat and was wary of encouraging them. A number of writers have suggested that the new king was deeply suspicious of Robert, earl of Gloucester. Moreover, the *Gesta* describe Richard fitz Gilbert leaving the king's court in April 1136 upset because Stephen had refused him the grants for which he had petitioned.[14] It may be also that the king saw a turbulent Wales as a means of preoccupying the Marchers and keeping them out of his hair: it depends how ready one is to see Stephen as a Machiavellian. If this were true, Stephen must have been rather disconcerted when the Welsh and Marchers allied against him. Yet others of his contemporaries *did* see this possibility. Orderic notes under 1137 reports of conspiracies between the Welsh and the king's enemies.[15] Perhaps the closest we may ever get to Stephen's views on Wales are the comments of the *Gesta* when considering his refusal of Ranulf of Chester's humble request in 1146 for aid against Gwynedd. Stephen was easily persuaded that Ranulf was attempting to dupe

[13] *GS* 20.
[14] Ibid. 16. For Stephen and Robert of Gloucester, see the literature cited above Ch. 1 n. 65.
[15] OV vi. 494.

him; to lead him into the depths of Wales and do away with him. I find this the most revealing contemporary comment on the king. There was neither trust nor vision in Stephen, in Wales as elsewhere. He was a king unable to rise above his fears for his own dignity and throne.[16]

Stephen let Wales and the March run riot in 1136. His abdication of responsibility had its consequences, not least for the Welsh. As the *Gesta Stephani* put it, the Welsh were 'the stern masters of those before whom a little earlier they had bent compliant necks'.[17] The chagrin and surprise evident in this remark are either comical or tragic, and illustrate just how far the English had gone in the previous reign in writing off the Welsh.[18] Rees Davies has pointed out the extent of English influence in Wales at the time—no king of England until Edward I was to have so much influence there as Henry I.[19] But, although true enough, this comparison can mislead. What it sidesteps is the fragility of the English position in the March that the English had created. Henry's talent to manipulate cannot be denied, but much of his success was built on shifting circumstances. His predecessor and the Montgomery family had eliminated two of the established larger kingdoms of eleventh-century Wales: Glamorgan and Deheubarth. Henry had little to fear at the beginning of his reign from the other two: Gwynedd and Powys, or the lesser kingdoms clustered south of Powys. Gwynedd's king, Gruffudd ap Cynan, had forced himself upon north Wales, and it was all he could do to maintain himself there. It was in his interest to take on the part of client king.[20] The other major kingdom, Powys, was Henry's greatest asset in Wales. Although its dynasty and its allies had much of native-ruled Wales under its control, from Rhuddlan in the north to Cardigan in the south, it was a dynasty riven by murderous quarrels and rivalries. Thirteen sons and grandsons of the once-dominant king, Bleddyn ap Cynfyn (died 1075), were active in Henry's reign. Of these thirteen, six were murdered or mutilated by one or other of his relations before 1132. Henry assisted in this dynastic hecatomb by

[16] *GS* 192–6.   [17] Ibid. 18.   [18] JW 40.
[19] Davies, 'Henry I and Wales', 147.
[20] For Gruffudd's claim to Gwynedd, see Davies, *Wales*, 33; D. S. Evans, *A Medieval Prince of Wales: The Life of Gruffudd ap Cynan* (Llanerch, 1990), 11–15; K. L. Maund, *Ireland, Wales and England in the Eleventh Century* (Woodbridge, 1991), 82–90.

playing one kinglet off against the other, and remorselessly lessen-
ing the patrimony over which the competitors fought. It is of this
dynasty that the Welsh chronicler comments coolly that 'they were
all for killing one another'. The occasion was when, in 1111,
Bishop Richard of London was solicited at Shrewsbury by a
nephew asking red-handed for the lands of the uncle he had just
slaughtered.[21]

Such incidents may well have enhanced the feeling of moral and
cultural superiority which the English harboured against the
Welsh. But it was to betray them. The circumstances which Henry
I had exploited so ably had been more fortuitous than they realized. It was Stephen's hard luck that English fortunes were already
changing before 1135. In Gwynedd in the 1120s the aging
Gruffudd ap Cynan reaped the reward for his longevity and ceased
to be challenged by his nominal subjects. This change was advertised in 1121 when Gruffudd's two eldest sons made a damaging
raid along the northern March and into Cheshire on the news of
the death of Earl Richard of Chester.[22] Although checked on this
occasion, Gwynedd had signalled new ambitions in the north, but
until 1136 it satisfied itself in acquiring Welsh-ruled territory to its
east. In Powys, the kinstrife abated as the number of potential vic-
tims shrank. One king, Maredudd ap Bleddyn, established
supremacy over the remains of the kingdom, to be succeeded by his
son Madog. Maredudd died in 1132, commemorated by the Welsh
chronicles as 'the splendour and security of all Powys and its
defence'.[23] Between 1121 and 1135 the growing stability of the
surviving Welsh realms seems to have gone unnoticed, or at least
unheeded, by the English. Since Gwynedd satisfied its expansion-
ism during that time by chipping away at the former Powisian
domination of the north, this is not surprising, but it was ominous,
for the prospects for division and rule were fading fast. In this context, the Welsh challenge against English ascendancy had long been
threatening before 1135.[24]

---

[21] *Brut, s.a.* 1111.

[22] SD ii. 203–4. For the security and growth of Gruffudd's last years, see Evans,
Gruffudd ap Cynan, 81–2.

[23] *Brut, s.a.* 1132. The Welsh Latin chronicles call Maredudd, *dux Powisorum*: *AC,
s.a.* 1132.

[24] For Gwynedd's new ambitions, see Lloyd, *Wales*, ii. 465–7; J. B. Smith, 'Owain
Gwynedd', *Trans. Caernarvonshire Hist. Soc.* 32 (1971), 8–9, 10.

When the Welsh tide broke upon the March in 1136, its current was strong and dangerous. The Welsh had learnt that necessity was the mother of co-operation. Examples of fraternal goodwill occur in Stephen's reign in marked contrast to the bloody pruning of the branches of the Powisian family tree in the previous reign. It was the dispossessed dynasties which showed the most unity. The brothers Morgan and Iorwerth ab Owain worked happily together to restore their family's control over the Welsh of south-east Wales—they issued joint charters and, apparently, possessed a joint seal.[25] In Deheubarth, the sons of Gruffudd ap Rhys (Anarawd, Cadell, Maredudd, and Rhys) each assumed in turn the leadership of their reviving *regnum*, with the co-operation of his surviving siblings.[26] Even in Powys there is some evidence of the dominant king, Madog, attempting to accommodate his younger brother, Iorwerth, into a framework of co-operation: he offered him the position of *penteulu*—chief of the military household—and status in the kingdom equal to his own.[27] Welsh customary law offered possibilities by which family tension might be relaxed. Designation of an heir, an *edling*, by a ruling king—if it were accepted by other members of the family—would end the sort of arguments which ravaged Powys. This seems to have been what defused a potentially explosive situation in Deheubarth, where Gruffudd ap Rhys left at least five sons. It is also what seems to have happened in Glamorgan. Morgan ab Owain issued a charter there 'with the common assent and will' of his brother Iorwerth.[28] After Morgan's death, the succession went to Iorwerth despite the existence of at least one son, Morgan ap Morgan ab Owain.[29] The existence of the position of *penteulu* allowed a younger brother some of the reality of power while awaiting his succession. Since the *teulu* (plural: *teuloedd*; translated in Latin by *familia*) was the central element in Welsh lordship, its captain was of necessity the first

[25] D. Crouch, 'The Earliest Original Charter of a Welsh King', *Bull. of Board of Celtic Studies*, 36 (1989), 130. For the brothers' joint charters: PRO C53/76, m. 10; Berkeley Castle Muniments, Cartulary of St Augustine's, Bristol, fo. 27ᵛ.

[26] J. B. Smith, 'Dynastic Succession in Medieval Wales', *Bull. of Board of Celtic Studies*, 33 (1986), 212 and n.

[27] G. Jones and T. Jones, *The Mabinogion* (London, 1949), 137.

[28] PRO C53/76, m. 10.

[29] For the succession to Glamorgan, see *Brut, s.a.* 1158. For Morgan ap Morgan ab Owain, see Evreux, AD de l'Eure, H 9; *Historia et cartularium monasterii sancti Petri de Gloucestria*, ed. W. H. Hart, 3 vols. (RS, 1863–7), ii. 50.

minister of the king. Later redactions of the Welsh laws reserve the post for the sons and nephews of kings.[30]

As well as disappointing English expectations by failing to butcher one another, the leaders of the Welsh royal dynasties drew strength from another new source. The Welsh aristocracy had begun to Anglicize itself by 1135, in the matter of military technology at least. Welsh armies were accustomed by Stephen's reign to build and beseige castles, while their leaders and their *teuloedd* rode to war on horseback and (at least in part) in armour. The existence of the *teulu*, as has already been said, was an important aid to the Welsh. It was a permanent military force, devoted to its lord and subject to an élite ethos. Trained troops in some numbers were always at the disposal of Welsh kings.[31] Ultimately this was to have an effect on England too. It made possible the Welsh mercenary, with his king as contractor. Welsh contingents in English armies were a feature of Stephen's reign, the first reign in which English leaders resorted to this military option.[32]

So there were reasons why 1136 should be a year of euphoria for the Welsh and of shock for the English. Such was the extent of Welsh success that we can excuse those literary men who compiled the Welsh chronicles from reviving ideas of the *holl deyrnas y Brytanyeit*, the *regnum Britannorum*, or *tota Cambria*. They apparently saw as imminent the restoration of Wales—and perhaps all Britain—to its natural rulers. Some English writers feared the same too. It was an event which had been prophesied in Wales since the tenth century.[33] But such anticipation was more rhetorical than serious, and hardly deserves the attention given it by Sir John Lloyd, who once famously described the year 1136 under the heading 'the national revival'. This was his description of the consequences of Henry's death: 'Everywhere the foreign yoke was cast off, the power of the new settlers was dauntlessly challenged, and a

[30] *The Latin Texts of the Welsh Laws*, ed. H. E. Emmanuel (Cardiff, 1967), 109; *The Law of Hywel Dda*, trans. D. Jenkins (Llandysul, 1986), 8–9; Smith, 'Dynastic Succession', 210–16; Davies, *Wales*, 66–7.

[31] For the *teulu* and Welsh military technology at this time, see Davies, *Wales*, 66–7; D. Crouch, *The Image of Aristocracy in Britain, 1000–1300* (London, 1992), 156–61, 276–7.

[32] Welsh royalty was frequently to be found at the court of Henry I, but there is no evidence of Welsh troops being raised to assist his campaigns.

[33] W. Davies, *Wales in the Early Middle Ages* (Leicester, 1982), 114; for the phrase quoted, see *Brut, s.a.* 1136; *AC, s.a.* 1136.

new spirit of daring and independence seemed to have seized the whole Welsh race.[34] Things were, in fact, rather more prosaic. Once the Welsh had upset the work of the reigns of Rufus and Henry I, they were loath to take the good fight on into 1137, and that year saw the beginning of a new balance of power in Wales. Nor, in any case, did all the Welsh join in the struggle. We hear nothing about what the king of Powys contributed to the campaigns of 1136–7.

Since Gwynedd provided the leadership for the risings, and Gwynedd's ambitions had already led to fighting with—and conquest of territory from—Powys, it is unlikely that expulsion of the English colonists would have been the sole ambition of the leaders of the uprising in 1136. The strategy of Owain and Cadwaladr, sons of the aged and blind Gruffudd ap Cynan, was to establish a wide hegemony. They directed their efforts against Powys too in pursuit of the strategy. Owain and Cadwaladr worked to secure the former Marcher lordship of Ceredigion in 1136 and 1137, but alongside this they also snatched from Powys the provinces of Meirionydd and Penllyn.[35] No wonder then that no Powisian leaders are listed by the chroniclers as contributing to the expulsion of the English; they too were struggling to stem the tide. The brothers from Gwynedd were artful in allying with Powys's southern neighbours. The dynasties of Maelienydd, Brycheiniog, and Deheubarth all appeared allied to Gwynedd in the campaigns in Ceredigion. The exclusion of Powys, surrounded and victimized, negates any idea of a rising of the 'whole Welsh race' in 1136.

The watershed of the war in the March (and indeed the whole course of Anglo-Welsh relations in the twelfth century) can be located in October 1136, when the second campaign of Owain and Cadwaladr in Ceredigion rolled up to the gates of Cardigan. On the way it had finally eliminated much of the infrastructure of English lordship in Ceredigion. The English and Flemings of Pembrokeshire and Cemaes, further to the south-west, combined at this point to stem the flood and make sure that the line of the Teifi Valley was held. Either through desperation or hubris the Anglo-Flemish force risked a pitched battle near Cardigan. It was a catastrophe. Although the Marcher barons in the army escaped by

[34] Lloyd, *Wales*, ii. 462.
[35] *Brut, s.a.* 1136; *AC, s.a.* 1136, 1137; Lloyd, *Wales*, ii. 466–7.

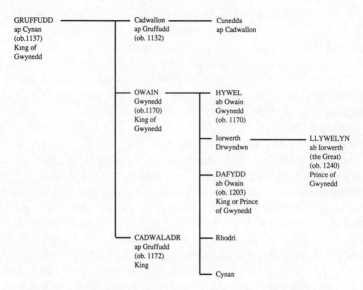

FIG. 8.1.   The royal house of Gwynedd in the twelfth century

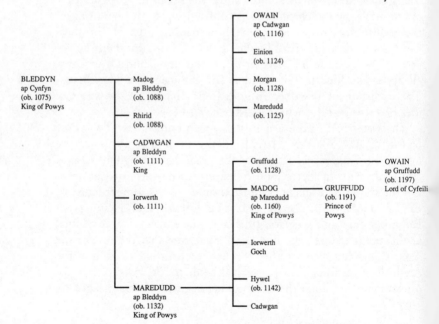

FIG. 8.2.   The royal house of Powys in the twelfth century

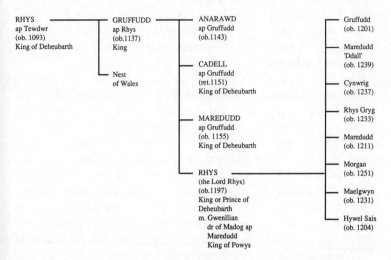

FIG. 8.3. The royal house of Deheubarth in the twelfth century

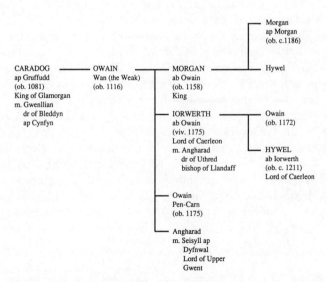

FIG. 8.4. The royal house of Glamorgan in the twelfth century

flight, much of the rest of it was overwhelmed. Cardigan castle did
not fall, and indeed it was relieved around the end of the year by a
freelance *coup* of Miles of Gloucester, but the battle of Cardigan
marked the end of unquestioned Anglo-Norman moral domination over the Welsh.[36] It would be several generations before the
English were again in as good a position as they had been in Wales
before the battle of Cardigan.

Another consequence of the battle was the abrupt re-emergence
of the royal house of Deheubarth as a force in west Wales. Its
leader, Gruffudd ap Rhys, who had been harried into the hills in
Henry's time, fought along with Owain and Cadwaladr of
Gwynedd at Cardigan. When they left after the battle, Gruffudd
was able to make good use of the English discomfiture for his own
purposes. A version of the Latin annals of Wales records significant
gains by Gruffudd and his eldest son Anarawd. The region of Rhos
was regained and a leading Fleming killed, after which, it appears,
the episcopal community of St Davids submitted to Anarawd's protection. But Gruffudd did not live long to enjoy the renaissance of
his family's fortunes. He was apparently betrayed by his wife and
killed during the course of 1137. But his sons Anarawd and Cadell
continued the fight, and before the end of the year they delivered a
major blow to English hopes by capturing the royal stronghold of
Carmarthen. It may have been in this campaign that Payn fitz
John, Henry's former sheriff of Hereford and Shropshire, met his
end in battle against the Welsh by means of a lance through
the head. This was as great a blow as the fall of Richard fitz Gilbert
the previous year; it removed one of the most experienced of the
Marcher lords remaining, one of Henry I's most trusted agents.[37]

A more surprising renaissance of 1136–7 was that of the royal
dynasty of Glamorgan. It had not been since 1081 that a
Welshman had exercised royal authority between the rivers Tawe
and Wye. He had been Caradog ap Gruffudd, a client of William
the Conqueror. Caradog's ambitions to extend his authority into
Deheubarth had brought him to death in battle. His grandsons,
Morgan and Iorwerth, appear to have controlled no more than that
part of upland Gwent known as Gwynllŵg. They burst on the

[36] *Brut, s.a.* 1136; *AC, s.a.* 1136; 'Winchcombe Annals', ed. Darlington, 128; FW
ii. 97.

[37] *AC, s.a.* 1137; JW 43. For a suggestion that Stephen was involved in an attempt
to salvage control of Carmarthen, see above, n. 10.

wider world with their killing of Richard fitz Gilbert near
Abergavenny in April 1136. We have no direct account of their
later campaigns, but charter evidence and the odd mention in
chronicles allow us to reconstruct in part their rise to power in
Gwent. By 1138 we know that Morgan was lord of the castle of
Usk—which tells us that he then dominated the lower Usk Valley
below Abergavenny.[38] Somewhere around this time he acquired the
lordships of Llefnydd and Edlogan and the castle of Caerleon. This
had probably happened by the end of 1136. We can say this
because by the end of 1136 Morgan and his brother had accepted
Earl Robert of Gloucester as their lord, receiving land in the earl's
honour of Newport, adjacent to their conquests. It is unlikely that
the earl would have treated the brothers so generously had they not
represented a power worth treating with.[39]

The successes of Gruffudd ap Rhys and his sons, and those of
Morgan ab Owain and his brother, were what came of King
Stephen's failure to take the initiative in the March. Unsupported
and unco-ordinated from England, the Marcher barons saw their
weakness made manifest.[40] The dynasties of Deheubarth and
Glamorgan advertised Stephen's failure and their own ambitions by
a conscious resumption of the language of kingship. Morgan is *rex*
twice—significantly, both times in English and not Welsh
sources.[41] If the English were acknowledging Morgan's kingship in
Stephen's reign, we may be sure that the Welsh were too. Gruffudd
ap Rhys of Deheubarth was referred to once as *rex* in a charter
issued by his son Cadell, of which the original survives. The title
was perhaps in recognition as much of his lineage as of his successes in 1136–7. Cadell himself appears described in a charter to
Haughmond Abbey as *rex Sudwallie* (i.e. Deheubarth) and his
younger brother Maredudd was regretted as *brenhin Keredigyawn
ac Ystrat Tywi a Dyvet* in an encomium inserted into the *Brut* on
the occasion of his death in 1155.[42]

---

[38] OV vi. 518.   [39] Crouch, 'Kingship in Glamorgan', 32–4.

[40] A point made in Davies, *Wales*, 46.

[41] The first occasion is an account of the battle of Lincoln, in which he took part:
Liber Eliensis, ed. E. O. Blake (CS 3:92, 1962), 321. The second occasion is in the witness list of a charter of his neighbour, Earl Roger of Hereford: 'Charters of the Earldom
of Hereford', ed. D. Walker, *Camden Miscellany XXII* (CS 4:1, 1964), no. 36.

[42] Crouch, 'Earliest Original Charter', 131; *The Cartulary of Haughmond Abbey*, ed.
U. Rees (Cardiff, 1985), 222–3; *Brut, s.a.* 1155.

Renewed kingship, self-confidence, and great territorial gains—
these were the effects of the indifference of King Stephen to Welsh
events. We will come back to the Welsh later, but for now we need
to turn to the effect of these reverses on the Marcher community. It
suffered losses, so much is clear. But it may be that the most serious
inroads were made in its sense of self-confidence rather than its territory. Ceredigion, Caerleon, and Llandovery—three seemingly
well-established Marcher lordships—were extinguished in the first
Welsh onsets. There were other losses. Carmarthen was lost to the
king for most of the reign. Later there would be land lost to Powys
and Gwynedd in the northern March. Yet, despite this catalogue of
failure, the territorial situation was not entirely one of gloom.
Although at first lost to the Welsh in 1136, Gower was reclaimed
by the mysterious (but obviously capable) baron, Henry du
Neubourg, before the end of the decade.[43] Cardigan, though
embattled in 1136 and under continuous threat thereafter, never
fell to the Welsh and remained an isolated outpost of Marcher
influence. Pembrokeshire and Glamorgan were crushed close to the
coast by Welsh pressure from inland, but they survived as units of
lordship. As Rees Davies points out, the individual Marcher lords
still left after the crisis of 1136 were tenacious and resourceful men.
They could still assert themselves on their own account, even if
they no longer had support from England. In the central March
the Briouze, Mortemer, and Say families were well able to expand
their lordships at Welsh expense in the 1140s.[44]

In 1145 we get a glimpse of what might have happened had
Stephen been other than he was. In that year, Gilbert fitz Gilbert,
earl of Pembroke and lord of Chepstow, entered the March and
took seisin of the earldom which Stephen had granted him in
1138. Earl Gilbert was one of Stephen's favourites. He had grown
wealthy on the king's favour. He had been given custody of the
earldom of Buckingham and the honour of Pevensey in Sussex,
lands of men who had retired to Normandy during the troubles of
the reign. The honour of Montfichet had come to him through the
wardship of his kinsman, Gilbert. Earl Gilbert was one of the few

[43] For Henry and Gower, see D. Crouch, 'Oddities in the Early History of the
Marcher Lordship of Gower', Bull. of Board of Celtic Studies, 31 (1984), 135–7; G. C.
Boon, 'Treasure Trove from Angevin Wales', Seaby Coin and Medal Bulletin, 775
(1981), 194–6.

[44] Brut, s.a. 1144, 1146; Davies, Wales, 51.

earls whose attendance on the king was constant and spanned the trauma of 1141. This great man left the court in 1145 and began a deliberate campaign of reconquest in west Wales; the fact that he was such a great man makes it likely that the king was involved in his decision in some degree. The Welsh dispersed before Gilbert like so much Celtic mist. He reclaimed Carmarthen and he recovered a good deal of Cantref Mawr from the Welsh, as appears from his building of a castle at 'Dinweilir' in the district of Mabudryd.[45] Was Gilbert acting in his own interest, or for the king, or both? When he returned to court, his reconquests swiftly fell once more to the Welsh; but, if he had stayed in the March with the king's support, one wonders what he might not have achieved. Gilbert's disgrace in 1147 led to the extinction of any Marcher interest at Stephen's court, and closed that avenue of intervention. Gilbert's subsequent death may well have enticed the brothers of Deheubarth into renewed assaults on Pembrokeshire. The fortresses of Wiston and Llanstephan fell to the Welsh. The disgrace at court of Ranulf of Chester in 1146 was to provoke a similar train of events.[46]

However, the story of Wales and the March after 1137 is by no means one of unrelieved hostility between Welsh and colonists. Quite the opposite, if anything. Working arrangements, even

[45] *Brut, s.a.* 1145.

[46] For the campaigns following Earl Gilbert's fall in Wales, see *Brut, s.a.* 1147; *AC, s.a.* 1147. For Gilbert's career, see in general *CP* x. 348–52. For his control of the honours of Pevensey and Montfichet, see College of Arms, Vincent MS 46, p. 120 (reference courtesy of Dr Nicholas Vincent); *Llandaff Episcopal Acta, 1140–1287,* ed. D. Crouch (South Wales Rec. Soc. 5, 1988), no. 15; *GS* 202. For Gilbert's control of manors of his cousin Earl Walter Giffard (and by extension of the honour of Giffard itself), see *The Norfolk Portion of the Chartulary of the Priory of St Pancras of Lewes,* ed. J. H. Bullock (Norfolk Rec. Soc. 12; 1939), 17 (Shouldham); *Reading Abbey Cartularies* (ed. B. R. Kemp (CS 4:31, 1986), i. 209–10 (Chelsfield). *The Cartulary of Worcester Cathedral Priory* (ed. R. R. Darlington (PRS NS 38, 1963) 134–6) preserves letters and writs of Earl Gilbert relating to Pembrokeshire. The earl resolved the tenure of the church of Daugleddau on his return from Wales by the way of Worcester, addressing writs to Walter fitz Wizo, lord of Wiston, William fitz Gerald, lord of Carew, and the archdeacon of St Davids. William fitz Gerald was one of the sons of Gerald of Windsor, and both he and Walter were the acknowledged leaders of the colonists of Pembrokeshire in battles against the Welsh in 1136 and 1146: *Brut, s.a.* 1136, 1146. By 1147 they had allied with the Welsh: *Brut, s.a.* 1147, 1153; *AC, s.a.* 1148. Earl Gilbert was with the king at Stamford early in 1146: *RRAN* iii, no. 494. For the earl's disgrace in 1147 and possible subsequent reconciliation with the king: *GS* 200–4; *RRAN* iii, nos. 845–7.

mutual dependence, flourished in many times and places in the March. This interdependence was closest in Deheubarth, where the royal dynasty and the principal Marcher families were related through the marriages of Nest, sister of Gruffudd ap Rhys (not to mention her illicit relationship with King Henry himself).[47] So we see on several occasions when they were not at each other's throats Welsh and Marchers in west Wales surprisingly cosy and co-operative.[48] John of Hexham was of the opinion that Wales quickly subsided into a state of peace after 1137, although he ascribes this—somehow—to the influence of King Stephen.[49] If Stephen did have anything to do with the relative peace in Wales, it was by impelling the Marcher lords into alliance with the Welsh, for their own survival and to protect their backs while they engaged the king to the east of Offa's Dyke.

The opposition to Stephen was focused by early 1138 on the southern March, with, as its captain, Earl Robert of Gloucester. Both Orderic Vitalis and Robert de Torigny favour us with lists of the disaffected. Of the combined list of twelve names, seven were barons of the southern or middle March, while a further three were barons of Somerset, within the area dominated by Robert of Gloucester.[50] Of the names from the March, that of Morgan ab Owain is the most significant. Orderic records him as the holder of the castle of Usk in the earl's interest. By 1138 Earl Robert was making a virtue of the necessity of coming to terms with the Welsh. His preparedness to use Welsh mercenaries against the royalist side was disdainfully noted by Orderic:

more than 10,000 *barbari* (as they are called) were let loose over England, and they spared neither hallowed places nor men of religion, but gave themselves up to pillage and burning and massacre. I cannot relate in

---

[47] For these relationships, see Rowlands, 'Making of the March', 157; Gerald of Wales, *Expugnatio Hibernica*, ed. A. B. Scott and F. X. Martin (Royal Irish Academy, 1978), 266.

[48] *Brut, s.a.* 1115, 1147.

[49] SD ii. 287.

[50] Robert de Torigny lists Earl Robert, Ralph Lovel (Somerset), Gervase Paynel (Ludlow and Dudley), William de Mohun (Somerset), Robert of Lincoln (Wareham), Eustace fitz John (brother of Payn, Yorkshire), William fitz Alan (Shrewsbury), Walchelin Maminot (nephew of William Peverel, Kent), Geoffrey Talbot (Hereford): RT 134–5. OV (vi. 518–20) gives in addition Morgan ab Owain (Usk), William Peverel (northern March, Kent), William fitz John (Somerset).

detail what sufferings the Church of God endured in her sons, who were daily slaughtered like cattle by the swords of the Welsh.[51]

The earl's own friends were embarrassed by this association. William of Malmesbury fastidiously failed to mention his earl's reliance on Welsh soldiery.

The culmination of the partnership between Welsh and Marchers came in 1141. Welsh soldiers formed a large proportion of the force which the earls of Gloucester and Chester brought to Lincoln against King Stephen. The various sources for the battle tell us the names of the Welsh kings the earls had recruited. From the independent account given by the *Liber Eliensis* we learn of the presence of Morgan (*Morgarus*) 'king of Wales', alias Morgan ab Owain of Glamorgan, whom we have already met allied to Earl Robert before 1138.[52] Orderic mentions 'two brothers', Cadwaladr and Maredudd, who fought for the earls. One must be Cadwaladr, younger brother of Owain ap Gruffudd ap Cynan. Since Cadwaladr had no known brother called Maredudd, this person has been understood to have been *Madog ap* Maredudd, king of Powys, who was in fact brother-in-law of Cadwaladr, even if he was not his brother germane.[53] Orderic regarded the participation of the Welsh at Lincoln as crucial to the earls' victory.[54] John of Hexham believed that the Welsh had made up about half the earls' army.[55] Both Orderic and Henry of Huntingdon stress the indiscipline and the recklessness of the Welsh, but this may be no more than racial stereotyping.[56] In fact the presence of the three Welsh kings at the battle would indicate that they had brought with them their *teuloedd*. It is possible that the presence of these quality Welsh troops swung the balance of the battle in the earls' favour, even if only by engaging the attention of royalist troops needed elsewhere.

[51] OV vi. 536.

[52] *Liber Eliensis*, 321.

[53] OV vi. 536. For Cadwaladr as *rex Nortwalie*, or *rex Waliarum*, see *The Charters of the Anglo-Norman Earls of Chester* ed. G. Barraclough (Rec. Soc. of Lancashire and Cheshire 126, 1988), nos. 28, 64, 84–5. On the identity of 'Maredudd', note that Cadwaladr's eldest son was called Maredudd: *Cartulary of Haughmond*, no. 794; it is possible, although less likely, that the son, rather than the brother-in-law, is intended by Orderic.

[54] OV vi. 542. The efficacy of the Welsh at Lincoln is a matter of disagreement amongst the sources. Orderic believed they helped make the victory for the earls, but HH (273) records that William of Aumale and William of Ypres drove the Welsh contingent from the field.

[55] SD ii. 307.

[56] OV vi. 542; HH 268.

In this way Stephen's indifference to Wales came home to him on the battlefield of Lincoln. He had made successful rebellion possible.

Of course, the intimacy of Welsh and Marchers was not always to the advantage of the Marchers. This was particularly the case in the north. Gwynedd had begun to show expansionist ambitions even in Henry's reign. In the 1130s the leaders of Gwynedd satisfied themselves by pushing into Powys and Ceredigion in the south. It was perhaps only a matter of time before the sons of Gruffudd ap Cynan began to move along the coast of north Wales towards Chester. In 1136 or 1137 John of Hexham reports that Ranulf of Chester had suffered a military disaster while opposing the new Welsh menace.[57] In 1141 he and the Welsh were co-operating, and it seems that he had profitable dealings with both Powys and Gwynedd at this time. But in 1146 he and Owain of Gwynedd had fallen out. In that year Owain raided over the River Clwyd and deep into the region of Tegeingl, and indeed beyond it. He captured the castle of Mold, seat of Ranulf's seneschal.[58] It would seem to have been this disaster which sent Ranulf to the king late in August 1146, begging aid and fearing that the Welsh would soon seize his entire earldom.[59] The reception that the earl got is well known, and his arrest was blamed by the Chester annals for the subsequent invasion of Cheshire by the Welsh. They penetrated as far eastward as either Nantwich or Northwich, where the seneschal of Chester is said to have gained his revenge by defeating and expelling the invaders on 3 September. The fact that the invasion took place a mere five days after the earl had been arrested at Stamford shows how deadly the intimacy between the Welsh and the Marcher community could be, if sensitive information could be so rapidly telegraphed across frontiers.[60]

The Welsh problem after 1146 may explain, at least in part, why Earl Ranulf became so amenable to agreements with his neighbours in the north of England later in the reign, just as alliance with Gwynedd may have assisted his earlier expansion into

[57] SD ii. 287. It is a suggestion worth pursuing that it was Ranulf's activity in the northern March which made the brothers' campaigns in Ceredigion so episodic.

[58] Brut, s.a. 1146. Smith ('Owain Gwynedd', 10 n.) disputes the identification of the castle of Wydgruc with Mold.

[59] GS 194.

[60] AC 20, s.a. 1146. There is a parallel to the raid on Cheshire in 1121.

Lincolnshire and Yorkshire.[61] That the earl regarded himself as at war with Gwynedd after 1146 is witnessed by the shelter offered at his court to his erstwhile mercenary and Owain's brother, Cadwaladr ap Gruffudd, who was fêted as 'king of Gwynedd', and 'king of the Welsh' in exile, in Ranulf's charters.[62] Earl Ranulf also enlisted Gwynedd's enemy, King Madog ap Maredudd of Powys, in his defence. In 1149 Owain moved his army into the region of Iâl and built a castle there.[63] Ranulf and King Madog retaliated the next year by a joint campaign in Tegeingl. It led only to failure and losses.[64] It is possible that Welsh distractions were behind the complaints of the Scots that Earl Ranulf had failed to provide the support he had promised to assist the campaign of Duke Henry and King David.[65]

Anglo-Welsh relations were less fraught in the south of Wales. The protracted struggles by which Cadell ap Gruffudd and his brothers obtained Ceredigion from Gwynedd, and, in the other direction, consolidated their rule in Dyfed, rarely touched on the southern March (although it did affect the English of Pembrokeshire). The alliance between Earl Robert of Gloucester and King Morgan ab Owain lasted until the earl's death in 1147 and indeed after it. Morgan and his brother made a pious grant to Bristol Abbey for the earl's soul. This alliance allowed Earl Robert the tranquillity to pursue his ambitions in England, supported by Welsh troops, as at Tetbury in 1144.[66] Anglo-Welsh peace in the south was matched by a more curious truce. The southern March contained lordships of barons committed to different sides in the conflict in England. There were more Angevin supporters than royalists, of course, but there were some significant royalists none the less. There is evidence that the civil war was not allowed to spill over into this area of the March. It was a trial bed for Ralph Davis's 'magnates' peace'.

The earliest examples of this phenomenon might perhaps have been the Marcher solidarity of 1138–9 in favour of the empress and Earl Robert of Gloucester, once the earl had declared for her cause in Normandy. There is an argument that twelfth-century

[61] For Earl Ranulf's agreements, see Davis, *Stephen*, 109–10.
[62] See above, n. 53.   [63] *Brut, s.a.* 1149.   [64] Ibid. *s.a.* 1150.
[65] SD ii. 323.
[66] For the grant to Bristol Abbey, see n. 25 above. For the attack on Tetbury, see *GS* 172.

lordship had a regional focus which was not based on (and indeed transcended) links of tenure. Earl Robert's dominance in the southern March drew to him lesser magnates anxious for his protection; these would have been included in the supporters who declared for him in 1138. In 1139, when the earl was campaigning in the area in person, magnates who had no previous links to him would have had to choose whether to join his affinity or fight against him. They would have had to weigh up their local interests and put them in the balance against their principles, if any. As a result there were several public defections to the earl away from the king. The most notable secession was that of Miles of Gloucester, who had received the king at Gloucester with honour only the previous year. Along with Miles came Robert of Ewyas, whom the king had earlier commissioned to attempt to retrieve his position in west Wales. Robert's brother, John, lord of Sudeley, followed him into the Angevin cause, quitting the affinity of Waleran, count of Meulan and Worcester. John clearly saw more danger in the offing from Earl Robert. Here we find the mechanisms of lordship pushing Marcher lords together inevitably, for protection against the king as much as against the Welsh. The fact that the king had proved so inept in the region of their interests may have made the decision to take part against him all the easier.[67]

However, the solidarity of the March even embraced those who still publicly espoused the cause of King Stephen after 1139. Throughout the 1140s Chepstow and the Clare lordships in the lower Wye Valley remained in the peaceful possession of Earl Gilbert fitz Gilbert of Pembroke, who was the king's good friend. This is striking, because on every side in Gwent and Gloucestershire his lands were hemmed in by Angevin supporters. Earl Gilbert remained a loyalist, except briefly in 1141, and again in 1147. Moreover, on a November day in a year sometime between 1139 and 1147, Earl Gilbert's sister Rohese married an Angevin supporter, Baderon, lord of Monmouth, the earl's neighbour to the north, and a steady ally of the earls, Miles and Roger of

---

[67] For Miles's defection, see *GS* 91; JW 117; *RRAN* iii, no. 391; D. Walker, 'Miles of Gloucester, earl of Hereford', *Trans. of Bristol and Gloucester Arch. Soc.* 76 (1958), 72–3; Chibnall, *Matilda*, 82–3. For the defection of John fitz Harold of Sudeley, see Crouch, *Beaumont Twins*, 47. Robert fitz Harold appears as constable of Earl Roger of Hereford after 1143, hinting that he might already have been attached to the Hereford affinity in 1139: 'Charters of Hereford', ed. Walker, nos. 11, 16, 40, 57.

Hereford.[68] The fact that the earl was not at Chepstow priory for the wedding and that he was represented by his brother Walter may indicate a way that troublesome loyalties might be circumvented. Walter might have been his brother's nominated governor for his honour in Gwent, a sort of trustee. We find the same arrangement in Gower, which had been the possession of the royalist Earl Roger of Warwick, but which was administered after 1138 by his younger brother, Henry du Neubourg.[69] Such arrangements would explain how the royalist Earl Gilbert might campaign successfully in west Wales, seemingly far behind 'enemy lines'. Whatever was happening in England, the barons of the March had their own overriding problems to worry about first.

In the period after the death of Robert of Gloucester in 1147 the situation in the southern March became ever more urbane. Two Marcher earls of the south, William of Gloucester and Roger of Hereford, were implicated in reaching treaties—not just mutually, but with the still royalist earl of Leicester, in or soon after 1148.[70] In 1149, notwithstanding, both these earls turned out to support Henry fitz Empress in his unsuccessful campaign against Stephen. Plainly the two earls saw no difficulty in temporizing to this extent. One of them, Earl Roger, was willing to go much further. It was Roger of Hereford who emerged in the last few years of Stephen's reign as the effective leader of the Angevin cause of England. The treaty he reached with William, earl of Gloucester, in either 1147 or 1148 shows how Roger had attained the ascendancy over the younger earl. The *obsides* of Earl William in the treaty are all his tenants, but those of Earl Roger include several lesser magnates who had committed themselves to his affinity: Baderon of Monmouth, Elias Giffard, Robert de Candos, and Walter of Clifford.[71] These lords occur in numbers of other acts of Earl Roger, confirming their relationship. These other acts also contain the attestations of other magnates who attended upon the earl:

---

[68] PRO E327/400, printed in T. Madox, *Formulare Anglicanum* (London, 1702), 241. The marriage is unlikely to have been carried out in 1141 or 1147, when Earl Gilbert was briefly an Angevin supporter (or at least, in the latter year, a rebel against Stephen). By November 1141 Gilbert was back in Stephen's camp. The rebellion in 1147 was too brief for a political marriage to be arranged.

[69] Crouch, 'Early History of Gower', 136–8.

[70] Crouch, *Beaumont Twins*, 84–5; R. H. C. Davis, 'Treaty between William Earl of Gloucester and Roger Earl of Hereford', in *Miscellany for D. M. Stenton*, 139–46.

[71] Ibid. 144–5.

Osbert fitz Hugh of Richard's Castle and our friend Robert fitz
Harold of Ewyas, who undertook the office of the earl's constable.
But one other attestor hints further at the nature of the earl's
power. On two occasions King Morgan ab Owain attests in the
earl's presence, on one occasion with his brother-in-law Seisyll ap
Dyfnwal, lord of the Welsh of Upper Gwent. It may be that Earl
Roger was now exploiting the Welsh connection previously used to
such good effect by Robert of Gloucester. It was by such support
that Earl Roger was able to extend his affinity deeper into England
to the east, beyond Herefordshire, where his power was well established. Earl Roger was able to draw into his affinity William de
Beauchamp, sheriff and castellan of Worcester, a dominating force
in the middle Severn Valley.[72]

Earl Roger's career has not yet received a great deal of attention,
despite the edition of his acts by David Walker. Yet he was the
magnate who represented the extreme of wilful power in England
in Stephen's reign. His control of the southern March was uncon-
tested in Stephen's last years. It seems likely that his cousin and
rival in Herefordshire, Gilbert de Lacy, had given up the struggle to
control the honour of Weobley at this time.[73] By 1150 Earl Roger's
ascendancy in the southern March had progressed to the point
where he was careless of offending his nominal party in the contest
for the throne. He went so far as to flirt with Stephen and his party
throughout the late 1140s and into the 1150s. Roger had come to
an understanding (the terms of which are unknown) with the royalist earl of Leicester around 1148, and this was not the only example of his dealing with the 'enemy'. At much the same time Roger
was to be found in company with Stephen's castellan of Oxford,
William de Chesney. Most significant were events in Worcester, in
or about 1151. Earl Roger had allied with the sheriff of Worcester,
William de Beauchamp of Elmley, a man of his own party. When

---

[72] 'Charters of Hereford', ed. Walker, *passim*.

[73] The progress of the Lacy–Hereford dispute during the 1140s in obscure. As the
treaty between Earl William and Earl Roger is specifically directed against Gilbert de
Lacy, we can conclude that that conflict was still continuing in 1148. W. E. Wightman
(*The Lacy Family in England and Normandy, 1066–1194* (Oxford, 1966), 188) suggests that Gilbert gained his inheritance in 1148 if not before; but this relies on a passage in the 1166 Lacy *carta* which cannot be trusted to prove that assertion. Earl
Roger's confident moves into Worcestershire, and the inability of any outside authority
to give judgement in favour of Gilbert's claim, suggest that Gilbert had been expelled
from Herefordshire in the early 1150s.

William got into severe local difficulties, Earl Roger invited King Stephen himself to campaign with him in order to seize Worcester. The bonds of affinity here may well have triumphed over those of party. We are free to believe or not the assurances of the *Gesta Stephani* that the earl's purpose was to distract the king from the assault on Wallingford, and that Roger was only pretending to assist the king.[74] The evidence of Roger's own charters tells us that William de Beauchamp and his brother Walter were frequently in company in the late 1140s. When William ended up imprisoned in his own castle by the knights of the earl of Worcester, no one else but the king would have been available for Roger to call on to get William out.

When Duke Henry returned to England on his final campaign in 1153, he did so according to the *Gesta*, at Earl Roger's urging.[75] But there are hints, indeed more than hints, that the duke returned aware of the problem represented by the earl. Earl Roger joined the duke not long after his arrival. He certainly received the duke at Gloucester in April 1153. Thereafter he accompanied the duke on his tour about England until at least January 1154.[76] At that time it is unlikely that the duke would have done other than flatter and conciliate his key supporters. The charters to the earl of Leicester and his son, and the outrageously extravagant charter to Earl Ranulf of Chester, show that largesse was there to be sprinkled. But, so far as we know, curiously little in the way of it came to the Marcher earls of the south. William of Gloucester, indeed, was the first known recipient of a writ, datable to December 1153, commanding the restoration of an estate to its owner as he had held it in the time of King Henry I.[77] Earl Roger is not known to have received such a writ, but nor does he seem to have picked up any grants or charters from the duke either, and there is reason to believe that no such grants were bestowed on him. What is significant is that Earl Roger had to watch the duke take his rival in Herefordshire, Gilbert de Lacy, into his court in the course of 1153, certainly by June.[78] It is possible that the Lacy claims on his lands inhibited any agreement with the duke. Earl Roger would

[74] *GS* 228.   [75] Ibid. 228–30.

[76] *RRAN* iii, nos. 180, 193, 339, 840, for appearances at Gloucester.

[77] D. Crouch, 'Earl William of Gloucester and the End of the Anarchy', *EHR* 103 (1988), 71–2.

[78] *RRAN* iii, no. 104.

have wanted his tenure sanctioned, but Gilbert would have wanted what he regarded as his inheritance back.

Once king, Henry II demonstrated a prompt appreciation of the problem of Wales and the March, an appreciation which Stephen had failed to display in all the years of his reign. Some of the new king's problems smoothed themselves away. Earl Ranulf had been conveniently removed during the course of 1153 by the grim reaper, who seems to have been working hard in Henry's interest in that year. But there still remained three earls of the Welsh March and several barons whose independence and ambition had been given free rein over the past decade and a half. Behind these loomed like their mountains the even less amenable kings of Wales, the baronial allies. It is hardly surprising therefore that the southern and middle March were among the first areas to discover the new king's temper. Henry had once had the inestimable advantage of the tutorship of his uncle, Earl Robert of Gloucester, for he had been under his care at Bristol as a boy. Henry had had plenty of opportunity to observe the mechanisms of power in the March. Earl William of Gloucester had already proved himself a minor character, and, apart from the withdrawal of the honour of Eudo dapifer which had been dangled before the earl at Dunstable in January 1154, William did not suffer too much from the new regime. The young Earl Richard fitz Gilbert of Pembroke, on the other hand, found that his father's acquisitions from the royal demesne were called in. Richard was unable to retain the region from which he continued to take his comital style, and was confined to his paternal estates in the Wye Valley, Essex, and Kent.[79]

The 'fall' of Earl Roger came about some four months after the new king's coronation. Since it represented the fall of the Anglo-Welsh order which had appeared late in the 1130s, it was an event of some importance. A pity then that the event itself is as obscure as it is. There are two main sources for it. The first is a charter from King Henry II to the earl confirming all that which his father had held in the time of Henry I. Roger also had confirmed to him all the royal demesne he had acquired between the Severn and the Wye in Gloucestershire, except the castle of St Briavels. In

---

[79] Crouch, 'Earl William of Gloucester', 74–5; M. T. Flanagan, 'Strongbow, Henry II and Anglo-Norman Intervention in Ireland', in J. Gillingham and J. C. Holt (eds), *War and Government in the Middle Ages* (Woodbridge, 1984), 64–5.

Herefordshire, Earl Roger retained his comital rights and his status in heredity, and also obtained the castle and shrievalty of Gloucester, as his father had held it in Henry's time. This charter allowed Earl Roger all he had gained in Stephen's reign, with the significant exception of the honour of Weobley, on which the charter is silent. We must assume from this silence that the honour had been awarded to Gilbert de Lacy (he appears holding it in 1157).[80] If we could narrow the charter's date, we would have some interesting evidence of the king's intentions towards Roger. Unfortunately there is no place-date in the surviving text which would have pinned a more precise date to its issue.

The second major piece of evidence which we have is Gervase of Canterbury's account of Roger's fall. This is by far the fullest account of the incident, but was written rather a long time after the event, whatever older sources it might have used. Still, according to Gervase, in March 1155 Earl Roger heard of a decree resuming the royal demesne. Quitting the royal court, Roger headed for Gloucester, determined to defend his possession of Hereford and Gloucester castles. Roger raised numbers of Welsh troops and allied with both Welsh and English magnates. Fortunately for the king (as Lewis Warren has said), Bishop Gilbert Foliot persuaded the earl to back off from confrontation. The next best account (that of Robert de Torigny) also reports the eruption of the row between earl and king. Unlike Gervase, he dates it to the Wallingford court of April 1155 and says it was over the possession of Gloucester castle, but gives no other details.[81]

Now, if we juggle the narrative accounts and the charter evidence, we could postulate a very sinister series of events. If the charter to Earl Roger belonged to King Henry's first months in England as king (and we know that Roger was at court in those months), then it might be suggested that the king had deliberately deceived the earl. It is possible that the charter had compensated the earl for his loss of the Lacy estates. Yet in March (or April) 1155 his tenure of Gloucester castle had been questioned. By this version of events the earl's outbreak into anger and militancy would be understandable. The young king had played him for a fool and was cheating him. But this is only one explanation which

---

[80] For the charter, see *Rotuli chartarum*, ed. T. D. Hardy (Rec. Com., 1837), 61; for Gilbert, see Wightman, *Lacy Family*, 188–9.

[81] GC i. 161–2; RT 184.

fits the facts as we have them. It is as likely that the dispute *pre-ceded* the issue of the charter. The charter would not then have been a deceit to lull Earl Roger into temporary quiescence, but a peace settlement between the two after the violent outbreak of March–April, as Eyton suggested.[82] Since the earl appears at court with the king after April, as late as September 1155 at Winchester, this interpretation is the more likely. We can therefore see the charter as one of the last of those *conventiones* between sovereign (and would-be sovereign) and subjects so characteristic of the period after 1138, and even into the first year of Henry II. Henry cannot, however, be acquitted of deceit even in this alternative scenario. Earl Roger fell ill towards the end of 1155, entered St Peter's Abbey at Gloucester, and died in a monastery which he had compelled to accept him as *advocatus* during Stephen's reign.[83] The earl's heir, Walter of Hereford, was not allowed to succeed either to the earldom or to his father's and brother's gains over the previous reign. Gloucester castle and a number of Herefordshire manors returned to the royal demesne.

Whatever the case, the events of 1155—particularly King Henry's dealings with Hugh de Mortemer over Bridgnorth—served notice that the king would no longer tolerate the free-for-all in the March that had been one of the characteristics of Stephen's reign. This was the easier of the king's two tasks in Wales to resolve. Half the danger from the Marcher barons had evaporated when there were no longer two factions competing for the throne; the rest of the job just required determination. But the second problem was that of the Welsh kings. In the end, as we know, it was not a problem he ever resolved in his own favour. Henry's intentions in 1155 seem to have been to put the question on ice, but there are at least signs that he was aware of its intricacies. He came to an agreement of some sort with the ever-amenable King Morgan ab Owain. It seems to have been much to the advantage of

[82] R. W. Eyton, *Court, Household and Itinerary of King Henry II* (London, 1878), 9. Eyton does not take account of the more contemporary evidence of Robert de Torigny.

[83] For Earl Roger's appearances at court after the dispute of March–April, see ibid. 11–12. For Roger's retirement in his last illness to Gloucester Abbey, see *Historia et cartularium de Gloucestria*, i. 88–9. There does not seem to be any warrant for the suggestion in *CP* (vi. 54–5) that Earl Roger retired to the abbey as a consequence of his disgrace at the royal court.

the Welshman. A charter was involved in the process. A grant by Morgan and his brother to Goldcliff Priory in Gwent refers to Henry II having formally conferred on the brothers their reconquests in Gwent (referred to as 'the honor of Caerleon'); this despite the fact that the former holders, the Candos family, were still active in Herefordshire. The same grant has the brothers referring to Henry II as *dominus noster*, implying some form of formal submission.[84] A significant help to the dating of this settlement is that the pipe rolls from 1155 up to Morgan's death in 1158 refer to an annual payment out of the revenues of Gloucestershire to Morgan at Caerleon of the sum of forty shillings.[85] Taken all together, the evidence suggests a meeting sometime in 1155 between King Henry and King Morgan, in which a charter was given, the *status quo* in Gwent accepted, a rent charge conferred, and homage given by the Welshman to the English king. It may well be that this was contemporary with the agreement with Earl Roger of Hereford, part of Henry's settlement of the southern March. By it the king had secured at least one Welsh king in a sensitive area to his own interests, for he had become Morgan's paymaster. Morgan remained in the king of England's pay until he was killed, along with his *teulu* and his court poet, somewhere north of Caerphilly in 1158, defeated by one of his Welsh neighbours who disputed his right to levy royal dues upon him.[86]

Henry II does not seem to have been able to deal with the other Welsh kings in the way he had dealt with Morgan ab Owain; either that, or he was not inclined to do so. We may suspect that Henry had already come to understand that Gwynedd under Owain ap Gruffudd was the main threat in 1155. Some confirmation of this is to be found in the pipe rolls. That of 1155 contains a generous payment out of the revenues of Shropshire of seven pounds to one Cadwaladr.[87] This was Cadwaladr ap Gruffudd, Owain's brother, in his English exile, being kept ready for future use by King Henry. Indeed it was in supposed support of Cadwaladr that Henry was to invade Gwynedd in concert with Powys in 1157.

So we see Henry in the first year of his reign dusting off the old tricks by which Henry I had managed the Welsh. He had secured

[84] PRO C53/76, m. 10.

[85] *PR 2–4 Henry II*, 49, 100, 167. After 1158 the payment was transferred to Morgan ap Morgan ab Owain.

[86] *Brut, s.a.* 1158.   [87] *PR 2–4 Henry II*, 43.

the March, negotiated client status with one king, and was preparing to exploit internal divisions within the principal Welsh royal dynasty. But, however he tried after 1155, the old gambits seemed not to work. Henry's armies failed him, and internal Welsh rivalries failed to ignite to any purpose. Indeed, the Welsh dynasties began to show an alarming tendency to unite against him, as they did in 1165. This is the point at which to weigh up Stephen's contribution to this state of affairs in Wales. Nobody now believes that a 'national revival' took place among the Welsh in 1136. Yet the aftermath of that year did change the Welsh. John Gillingham has recently pointed to the effect that the Arthurian legend had in Wales and England in Stephen's reign. One English writer even stated that he thought that the Welsh were deliberately trying (by means of Arthur) to regain lost Britain. We find this spirit of British recovery in south Wales, where Morgan ab Owain's re-establishment of his kingdom at Caerleon was held up to Geoffrey of Monmouth's literary mirror, and King Morgan saw himself dressed up as Arthur renewing the British kingdom against the Saxons. We find it late in the reign of Stephen in north Wales, where the author of the biography of Gruffudd ap Cynan compared his hero in adversity to Arthur 'king of the kings of the isle of Britain'. It may be significant that Gruffudd's dynasty was in the thirteenth century to cherish amongst its regalia an item described as 'Arthur's jewel'.[88]

Ideas such as these were potent ones, and were something new in Anglo-Welsh relations. They were champagne bubbles of the spirit, heady and elevating. The English had been catastrophically and irrevocably defeated in Stephen's first years. There are indications that the English position was becoming fragile before 1135, but Stephen's particular contribution to the problem was that the defeat was as catastrophic as it was; not only that, but his indolence allowed the appearance of a Wales where the Welsh were free not just to organize their own affairs, but to profit in coin, plunder, and opportunities by English events. The Welsh had believed of Henry I that only God could avail against him. But a clear generation had since grown up which knew nothing of such an ogre; it had learnt of new heroes, real and legendary, against whom the

[88] Gillingham, 'Geoffrey of Monmouth', 112–18; Evans, *Gruffudd ap Cynan*, 27, 33; Davies, *Wales*, 355.

English had availed not at all. What was Stephen to them? Why should they fear Henry Plantagenet? Angevin England had to begin all over again with Wales, not much better off than the Conqueror had been. Perhaps the English of 1154 were better informed of Wales and its rulers than had been the Normans of 1067, but they faced an enemy now as instructed as they were in military technology, with a hard-won record of success, and an uncomfortable knowledge of the wider problems of England and France, from which they had been allowed to profit. Owain ap Gruffudd ap Cynan of Gwynedd was to become a regular correspondent of Louis VII and Becket. This was the context of Henry II's ultimate failure to do much more in Wales than Stephen had done. It is to Stephen's indecision and indifference that we have to look for the alarming extent of the successes of the dynasties of Owain Gwynedd and Rhys of Deheubarth which made Wales such an uncomfortable place for the English for well over a century.

9

1153: THE TREATY OF WINCHESTER

J. C. Holt

THE settlement of 1153 was not part of J. H. Round's study of Geoffrey de Mandeville. He left us with what is still the best general account of King Stephen's younger son, William, count of Boulogne, and of the lands which came to him under the terms of the settlement.[1] But of the settlement itself he said very little;[2] and for this it was to Stubbs that Round's first readers would have had to turn and to the exact information and good sense of the *Constitutional History*.[3]

Round's reticence is a pity, for it detracted from his treatment of King Henry II's early charters.[4] Quite apart from that, he might have helped us with insights gained from his study of the charters of King Stephen's reign. At least he would have given us some hard grist. In the event, the settlement has become something of a muddle; or rather we have got into a muddle about it. For example, my title is not a slip. The settlement is very occasionally described as of Wallingford, sometimes of Winchester, more usually, now, of Westminster. Some have used more than one location, for good reason, or for no apparent reason at all.[5] I will justify my own use

I should like to thank Dr John Hudson for presenting this paper on my behalf to the conference. I am also grateful to him and to Professor Edmund King for summarizing the subsequent discussion and for commenting themselves. I have made some minor changes to the original text following their suggestions.

[1] J. H. Round, *Studies in Peerage and Family History* (London, 1907), 147–80.
[2] Round, *Geoffrey*, 176–7 n.
[3] Stubbs, *Constitutional History*, i. 359–63.
[4] Round, *Geoffrey*, 234–42.
[5] Stubbs refers to the Peace of Wallingford and Westminster, drawn up at Wallingford, adopted at Winchester, and published at Westminster. Le Patourel

of Winchester in what follows. Then, again, the document we know as the treaty of Westminster is not quite the same as the settlements described in the chronicle narratives. These promise the restoration of the disinherited, and this has no place in the Westminster document. Our responses to this have varied. No one has been prepared to reject the narrative sources, or even argue that promises made at Winchester were jettisoned at Westminster. On the contrary, Professor Palmer has treated the chronicle stories and the Westminster document as complementary arrangements of equal weight. Yet there are differences revealed in curious ways. At one pole, Professor Palmer has given us 'the Compromise', decked out with a capital; at the other, John Le Patourel cannily placed the 'Treaty of Winchester' in inverted commas.[6] Presumption has affected presentation.

Alongside this we have given the settlement of 1153 diverse roles in the development of the common law. For Davis it established heritability, of the Crown, of the great baronies, and hence, in time, for all the free landowning classes; it was an opinion he modified, but still held firmly in his final work.[7] Professor Warren looked to the settlement for the origins of *nemo tenetur*, the rule that no free man need answer for his free tenement except to the king's writ.[8] Professor Milsom suggested that the agreement under-

mentions Winchester, as does Dr Chibnall: Le Patourel, *Norman Empire*, 112; M. Chibnall, *Anglo-Norman England, 1066–1166* (Oxford, 1986), 99. Professor Warren refers to both Winchester and Westminster, as does Professor Hyams in different studies: W. L. Warren, *Henry II* (London, 1973), 62, 333; P. R. Hyams, review in *EHR* 93 (1978), 858; 'Warranty and Good Lordship in Twelfth-Century England', *Law and History Review*, 5 (1987), 497. R. H. C. Davis refers to Winchester in *GS* 240 n. 1, but uses both locations and elides the contents of the agreement in Davis, *Stephen*, 119, 122. Professor Biancalana uses Westminster, and is perfectly clear about the relationship of the Westminster document to the treaty: J. Biancalana, 'For Want of Justice: Legal Reforms of Henry II', *Columbia Law Review*, 88 (1988), 434, 467 n. Professor Palmer also favours Westminster, but with complications (on which see below, p. 295): R. C. Palmer, 'The Origins of Property in England', *Law and History Review*, 3 (1985), 8–9. I followed their usage in J. C. Holt, 'Magna Carta 1215–1217: The Legal and Social Context', in E. B. King and S. J. Ridyard (eds.), *Law in Mediaeval Life and Thought* (Sewanee Mediaeval Studies 5, 1990), 11–12, where I expressed an initial doubt about the accepted treatment of the settlement.

   [6] Palmer, 'Origins of Property', 8–13; Le Patourel, *Norman Empire*, 112.
   [7] R. H. C. Davis, 'What Happened in Stephen's Reign 1135–54', *History*, 49 (1964), 1–12, esp. 10–12; Davis, *Stephen*, 150–3.
   [8] Warren, *Henry II*, 334.

lay the emergence of the writ of right.[9] He also hinted very tentatively that it may have led to a distinction between right and seisin,
and this was developed into a full-blown theory by Professor
Palmer, who argued that the arrangement made in 1153 for the
descent of the Crown, whereby Stephen remained in seisin but
Henry was recognized as rightful heir, was used as a model for the
general territorial settlement and thereby differentiated seisin and
right both in real and procedural terms.[10] All this is hypothetical
and much of it has proved contentious.[11]

This is to select just a few of the many variant approaches. That
there is such a choice leaves a number of impressions. One is that
we have come to distance ourselves from the evidence, to give
structures pride of place over documents. Another arises from the
kind of structures we have built. If we turn to the documents seeking support for this or that model of the origins of the common
law, we shall assuredly find it. The trouble is that we shall all find
different things. The subject deserves better. We ought at least to
know what the evidence allows us to say and what it does not. It is
in this spirit that I turn first to the document we know as the treaty
of Westminster.[12]

The first thing to be said is that it is not a treaty. We have come
to think of it as such perhaps because it marked the end of the nineteen long winters of the anarchy; but it is not a treaty in the strict
diplomatic sense. It is not a bipartite document; it is in the name of
King Stephen, not King Stephen and Henry fitz Empress jointly. It
records no exchange of sureties. There are no named guarantors;
instead it is attested by great men drawn from both the opposing
parties, a point of some importance to which I shall return.

If not a treaty, what then is it? It states that it is a charter.[13] That

[9] S. F. C. Milsom, *The Legal Framework of English Feudalism* (Cambridge, 1976),
178–9.

[10] Palmer, 'Origins of Property', 8–13; foreshadowed in Palmer, 'The Feudal
Framework of English Law', *Michigan Law Review*, 79 (1981), 1142–9.

[11] For an alternative hypothesis to Davis, see J. C. Holt, 'Politics and Property in
Early Medieval England', *Past and Present*, 57 (1972), 3–52. For an alternative to
Warren, advocating the more gradual development of *nemo tenetur*, see Van
Caenegem, *Royal Writs*, 212–25, esp. 223–5. For considered criticisms of Palmer, see
Biancalana, 'For Want of Justice', 467–70, and Hyams, 'Warranty', 497–503.

[12] *RRAN* iii, no. 272. For further comment on the text and on earlier editions, see
EYC viii. 15–16.

[13] 'per conventiones inter nos prolocutas, que in hac carta continentur'.

was perhaps the best that could be said, but it does not fit the description at all exactly. Presumably (for it survives only in a copy) it bore the seal of King Stephen, but it does not grant anything specifically and it names no beneficiaries. It is *sui generis*, designed for a special occasion and a particular purpose, and it has no exact parallel in any other surviving document of the twelfth century. The settlement between Henry II and his sons which we know as the Treaty of Falaise of October 1174 is perhaps the nearest analogue, but that was a *conventio*, secured by hand of the Young King and his brothers.[14] If we cast the net more widely, the Westminster document is quite unlike the various treaties and agreements concluded between the great nobles of the anarchy or between them and King Stephen, the empress, or her son Henry. There is no *affidatio in manu*, no provision of guarantors, no *obsides fiducie*.[15] It certainly breathes of the atmosphere of the anarchy; its insistence on the adjudication and arbitration of the great churchmen is not unlike Matilda's call on the 'Christianity of England' to back her second concession to Geoffrey de Mandeville;[16] and here, as in other agreements of the anarchy, homage is the starting-point.[17] But in its construction and purpose it stands alone.

[14] *Actes de Henri II*, ii, no. 468. 'Notum sit . . . quod pax . . . in hunc modum Deo volente reformata est'. 'Hanc conventionem firmiter tenendam ex parte sua assecuravit Henricus rex filius regis in manu domini regis patris sui.' In the particular cases of the documents of 1153 and 1174 I am taking a somewhat stronger view of the distinction between *carta* and *conventio* than that in P. R. Hyams, 'The Charter as a Source for the Early Common Law', *Journal of Legal Hist.* 12 (1991), 173–89, esp. 174.

[15] For *affidatio in manu*, compare the charters of Matilda and Henry for Aubrey de Vere, earl of Oxford (*RRAN* iii, nos. 634–5), and for both this and the *obides fiducie*, see Matilda's second charter for Geoffrey de Mandeville, earl of Essex (*RRAN* iii, no. 275). The whole question is illuminated by Round in *Geoffrey*, 176–7, 384–7. Similar, if somewhat milder, language reappears in Duke Henry's grant of Bitton to Robert fitz Harding of 1153 (*RRAN* iii, no. 309) and, much more understandably, in his agreement with Jocelin, bishop of Salisbury, concerning the custody of Devizes castle, April 1153 (*RRAN* iii, no. 796). It is exceptional at this late date; it does not figure, for example, in Henry's charter for Ranulf, earl of Chester, of 1153 (*RRAN* iii, no. 180). It should be noted also that this section of the Bitton charter does not lie at all easily alongside Henry's grant of Berkeley (*RRAN* iii, no. 310) of roughly the same date, for which Robert fitz Harding paid 500 marks *in recognicione*. These inconsistencies increase the probability that the Bitton charter is spurious. See below, n. 58, for further discussion and references.

[16] *RRAN* iii, no. 275.

[17] E. King, 'Dispute Settlement in Anglo-Norman England', *ANS* 14 (1992),

The best description of it is Sir Charles Clay's: 'the King's notification of the treaty.'[18] That is not quite exact: *conventiones* in the Latin have become 'the treaty' in the English; and perhaps 'notification' is too weak a word for a document with such a potent list of witnesses. But it contains the root of the matter. The Westminster charter is a formal promulgation of terms previously agreed. Its purpose was to bring peace to the land through the publication of agreements necessary to that end. It is an administrative document pursuant to the treaty agreed at Winchester. As for the 'Treaty of Westminster', there was no such thing.

This may look like splitting hairs. Yet the consequences are important. First, there is no difficulty in accepting that certain matters agreed at Winchester might not be included in the Westminster charter. The one does not invalidate or call in question the other, so long as there is sufficient explanation of the differences. Secondly, there is no ground at all for treating Westminster and Winchester as 'two components' in which 'the Treaty of Westminster was the model for the restoration of the disinherited', as agreed at Winchester.[19] The two are not on a par; the one, Winchester, was a treaty, the other, Westminster, its administrative consequence; quite apart from that, Winchester came first.

The Westminster charter, therefore, states matters which are past and settled, *conventiones . . . prolocutas.* Stephen has recognized Henry as his heir. Henry has performed homage; Stephen has given security on oath to maintain him as a son and heir. William of Blois has performed homage to Henry, and Henry has conceded the enormous territorial endowment which William received in England and Normandy. Homage has been performed by the earls and barons of the two parties, Henry's to Stephen and Stephen's to Henry; archbishops, bishops, and abbots have performed fealty to Henry. Arrangements have been made and securities taken for the custody of the critical castles: Wallingford, the Tower, Windsor,

115–30. I am grateful to Professor King for letting me see a copy of his paper prior to publication. I do not, however, follow him in regarding the Westminster document as an exemplary *conventio.*

[18] *EYC* viii. 26. On occasion Davis used similar words: 'the terms agreed at Winchester on 6 November 1153, and subsequently promulgated in the form of a charter at Westminster' (*GS* 240 n. 1)—as did Biancalana: 'On Christmas at Westminster Stephen issued a charter containing the terms of the treaty' ('For Want of Justice', 467 n. 162). Neither, however, is consistent in his usage.

[19] Palmer, 'Origins of Property', 8–9.

Oxford, and Winchester. The charter is attested by the great men
of both parties; it is subject in some of its provisions to the advice
and arbitration of the archbishop and bishops, and *ecclesiastica jus-
ticia* is invoked against any contravention. In all this the
Westminster charter almost certainly gives us terms which were
first agreed at Winchester.

That, at least, is our best guess. There may well have been other
meetings; the assemblage of provisions may have been more miscellaneous in origin than a straightforward derivation from Winchester. Here and there, too, the Westminster charter speaks in the
language of an evidentiary rather than a historic past; how else
could it assert that the citizens and garrisons within the king's lordship had done homage and given security to the duke? At one point
it seems to reveal the gap in time between agreement and promulgation. It was arranged that Reginald de Warenne, uncle to the wife of
William of Blois, was to have custody of the castles of Bellencombre
and Mortemer, if he so wished. Yet Reginald was one of the witnesses to the Westminster charter. Why should he not have come to
a conclusion? The incongruity is perhaps best explained by the sup-
position that the Westminster charter states terms which had been
agreed at an earlier stage, when Reginald was still left with an
option or perhaps was not even present. But these are minor matters beside the most striking feature of the Westminster charter: it
scarcely ventures at all into the future. Apart from contingencies
which will require ecclesiastical intervention or arbitration, it
restricts itself to three general statements: the duke's family will support the settlement; the king will deal with the affairs of the realm
with the counsel of the duke; and the king will exercise his royal
justice throughout the realm, in the duke's part as in his own. The
last two were long-term promises. No one could know that Stephen
would be dead within a year. Before that Henry had departed for
France. Neither had the time or opportunity to feel encumbered.

So the Westminster charter contained some extended commit-
ments. It is all the more significant, therefore, that certain matters
agreed at Winchester on 6 November were not included. For these
we are entirely dependent on narrative sources. Henry of
Huntingdon gives the place. Robert of Torigny supplies the date,
and he and the *Gesta Stephani* provide detail of the content.[20]

---

[20] HH 289; RT 177; *GS* 240.

These are contemporary or nearly contemporary accounts which are mutually independent.[21] Torigny and the *Gesta* tell of two decisions which do not figure elsewhere: first, that adulterine castles were to be destroyed, and, secondly, that lands were to be restored to their rightful owners. It is reasonably easy to guess why these matters were omitted from the Westminster charter. That was designed to bring peace to the land. At this stage, a formal denunciation of adulterine castles would have been provocative, impossible to enforce. Likewise, a promulgation that lands were to be restored might well have launched many a demandant on the path of self-help. In any case, who was to judge a rightful claim? Both provisions were full of dangers; quite apart from that, who could gauge the extent of either? It was better to omit them from any promulgation of peace. Promises for the future were best kept general and preferably obscure.

On the restoration of land, the two chroniclers come closer than is normally allowed. According to Torigny, it was sworn that possessions which had been seized by intruders should be restored to the ancient and lawful possessors who had them in the time of good King Henry.[22] The *Gesta* simply state that the disinherited were to be restored *ad propria*.[23] Now *propria* means something more precise than 'their own'. It must be read as 'inheritances', as contrasted with 'acquisitions'. Quite apart from that being one of the prime senses of the word, this is what it clearly means in the particular context, for the agreement did not seek to give the stamp of approval to the 'acquisitions', the intrusions and enforced claims, of the anarchy. If we read the chronicles so, they coincide; the only difference is Torigny's reference to Henry I, to which I shall return. Moreover, what they are getting at is quite clear: inheritances were to be restored; acquisitions were at risk; unlawful acquisitions would be revoked.

It was a precise guide-line. Nevertheless, it brought its own particular difficulties. What, for example, was to be done when land, rights, and title acquired during and through exploitation of the anarchy had already been inherited, or at least subject to a

---

[21] Davis, *Stephen*, 144–6.

[22] 'Juratum est etiam, quod possessiones, quae direptae erant ab invasoribus, ad antiquos et legitimos possessores revocarentur, quorum fuerant tempore Henrici optim[i] regis.'

[23] 'exheredati ad propria revocarentur'.

succession, before 1153? This leads at once to the most famous case of all and the subject of Round's book, Geoffrey de Mandeville, who died in 1144. Now Round's account of the succession to Geoffrey is vitiated by his unquestioned assumption that the eldest surviving son, Arnulf, was legitimate—legitimate but disinherited. This was not so. There is overwhelming evidence that Arnulf was a bastard.[24] He cannot, therefore, have affected the straightforward succession of his legitimate half-brothers, Geoffrey and, subsequently, William, to the honour of Mandeville and the earldom of Essex. Hence, Arnulf's existence has nothing to do with the manner of Geoffrey's succession, and, regretfully, the gloomy sentence with which Round concluded his study truly belongs to the Gothic fiction which it sought to emulate.[25] We cannot piece together the complete story of the succession, because the charter which Matilda issued between 1144 and 1147 survives only in summary form. But, to take it at its face value, it was for Geoffrey, son of Geoffrey, earl of Essex—in short, the younger Geoffrey was not recognized as earl; and it distinguished between his 'whole inheritance' and 'all tenures which she had conceded to his father'.[26] The distinction on which the settlement of 1153 was to rely seems to have been made clearly enough. Now Geoffrey the

[24] Round, *Geoffrey*, 227–33, 238. *CP* (v. 116) suggests that Arnulf and Geoffrey may have been half-brothers, but includes them as brothers in the pedigree chart. Sidney Painter seems to be alone in stating that Arnulf was 'probably illegitimate', but he provides no evidence (*Feudalism and Liberty* (Baltimore, 1961), 216, 217 n.). The evidence of Arnulf's illegitimacy is:

(a) He attests charters of his father but never as son *and heir*, and he never occupies prime place in the lists of witnesses. The foundation charter of Walden priory is particularly significant (*Monasticon*, iv. 148–9).

(b) He accepted enfeoffment in Kingham from both his half-brothers, thereby recognizing their title—crucial evidence which Round used, but failed to appreciate.

(c) He also attests charters of his half-brother Geoffrey.

(d) Neither he nor his descendants ever laid claim to the Mandeville inheritance.

Taken together these arguments are overwhelming. Much of the charter evidence on which they are based is collected in A. Charlton, 'A Study of the Mandeville Family and its Estates, 1066–1236' (Univ. of Reading Ph.D. thesis, 1977).

[25] 'And as if by the very irony of fate, Ernulf, his disinherited son, alone continued the race, that there might not be wanting in his hapless heirs an everstanding monument to the greatness at once of the guilt and of the fall of the man whose story I have told' (Round, *Geoffrey*, 244).

[26] *RRAN* iii, no. 277. This is a summary in BL Lansdowne MS 229 of a copy in the lost volume of the Great Coucher of the Duchy of Lancaster.

younger certainly attested one of Matilda's subsequent charters as
earl of Essex, but that is not clinching evidence by itself.[27]
Moreover, beyond the general phrases of the summary of Matilda's
charter, there is nothing to show whether the younger Geoffrey
obtained all that his father had gained in 1140–1. What is certain
is that the whole matter was reviewed after the settlement of 1153.
Henry II, as king, now made Geoffrey earl of Essex, giving him the
title and the third penny of the pleas of the county, all to be held
hereditarie.[28] His charter uses the language of an initial creation,
not, as Round thought, because of the exclusion of Arnulf, but
because the terms of the settlement of 1153 put all acquisitions of
the time of war in question. It was as though they had never been.
Hence Geoffrey's earldom is presented as a new one.[29] For the rest,
Henry confirmed to Geoffrey and his heirs all the lands of his great
grandfather, grandfather, and father of whomsoever held. The
father, the first earl, is not mentioned without the others, either in
general or with regard to the family's privileges in London, which
gained special mention. It seems clear, in short, that only his inherited lands were now being confirmed to his son. The king also
quitclaimed for ever the lien which Henry I had held on the
manors of Walden, Sawbridgeworth, and Waltham, thereby releas-
ing the new earl from a long-standing hold which the Crown had
hitherto retained.[30] That apart, the title and third penny of pleas of
the county of Essex were all that the new earl retained of the massive gains which his father had made in 1140–1. It is worth noting
that Geoffrey de Mandeville had not been among those who
attested the Westminster promulgation of the terms of 1153.
Nevertheless, there is little sign that he or his descendants were dis-
gruntled with its consequences. They clearly nursed a claim to the
custody of the Tower of London which Geoffrey, the fifth earl,
revived in 1215, but that probably went back beyond the days of

[27] *RRAN* iii, no. 43, a charter of 1144 for Geoffrey Ridel, son of Richard Basset. It
survives as a transcript in the Basset roll, not as an original. This detracts somewhat
from its specification of Geoffrey's title. For an original charter of John, count of
Mortain, attested by Geoffrey fitz Peter as earl of Essex 1191–3, see *CDF*, no. 61. In
fact Geoffrey aquired the title in 1199.

[28] Round, *Geoffrey*, 235–6.   [29] It is so understood in *CP* v. 116–17.

[30] For the origin and later history of the lien, see C. W. Hollister, 'The Misfortunes
of the Mandevilles', in *Anglo-Norman World*, 117–27.

the first earl to his father, William, and perhaps earlier.[31] The rest of the settlement they seem to have accepted.

The Mandevilles provide a model of the application of the terms agreed at Winchester. But it was not the only model; or, rather, the logic which it followed could be made to yield quite different results. The Mandevilles had been no great friends of the Angevin party. Miles of Gloucester, earl of Hereford, and his son Roger, on the other hand, were. No charter survives to record the succession of Roger to Miles when Miles died in 1143, but it seems clear that Roger succeeded to the title and all the lands which Miles had acquired. It is certain that this was confirmed by Henry II in 1154–5; Henry, indeed, added further grants.[32] Now Henry's charter is of great interest, for a simple confirmation in fee and inheritance of the fee of his father and the fee of Bernard de Neufmarché, which Miles had acquired by marriage, was not seen to be enough. After confirming the lands which Roger inherited from his father and mother, the charter shifts from the language of confirmation, *reddidisse et concessise*, to the language of a fresh grant, *insuper etiam dedi et concessi*, and embraces not only Henry's own grant but also all the concessions which Miles had won from Matilda, along with the earldom, in 1141. These, granted *in feodo et hereditate*, are enumerated one by one, and, despite the language of a new grant, it is plain that Matilda's charter of 1141 was the model for Henry's of 1154–5.[33] Yet he did not mention it; no one reading his charter could suspect that there had been Matilda's. Acquisitions had to be conveyed afresh. In this case it did the Crown little harm. Roger took the habit in 1155, the title lapsed, and all the acquisitions were lost. Robert of Torigny noted that Roger's brother, Walter, succeeded *in paternam hereditatem tantum*.[34] It was not until 1200 that the title was revived for Henry de Bohun, Roger's nephew. In return he had to surrender the charter of 1154–5 and all the claims which might arise therefrom.

Where the original beneficiary of the anarchy still survived under the new king, the logic of Henry's charters was not so clear cut. In 1153 Hugh Bigod's position as earl was ambiguous, though

---

[31] J. C. Holt, *Magna Carta*, 2nd edn. (Cambridge, 1992), 208, 263–5. For the early associations of the Mandevilles with the Tower, see Round, *Geoffrey*, 38, 439.

[32] *CP*, vi. 454; D. Walker, 'The "Honours" of the Earls of Hereford in the Twelfth Century', *Trans. Bristol and Gloucestershire Arch. Soc.* 79:2 (1960), 180–2.

[33] *Rotuli chartarum*, 53. Cf. *RRAN* iii, no. 393.   [34] RT 185.

he appears as earl of Norfolk in the charters of Matilda as far back as 1141.[35] The original grant of the title does not survive, however, and there is even doubt as to who granted it, Stephen or Matilda. At all events, Henry II's charter of 1155, which made Hugh earl of Norfolk anew, is quite consistent with other charters which followed up the settlement of 1153. But it differs from them in one respect: Henry conceded to him 'all tenements of whomsoever's fee which he had reasonably acquired', and these, like the rest of the grant, were to be held by Hugh and his heirs.[36] We know nothing of the circumstances which lay behind this charter, which is unusual, if not unique, in leaving the acquisitions of the anarchy unenumerated and controlled by the single word *rationabiliter*.

In another case, such circumstances are very clear. By the accession of Henry II, Eustace fitz John had built up a vast accumulation of estates in which the main element came from his wife, Beatrice de Vescy.[37] With Walter Espec, he had been the greatest of Henry I's 'new men' in northern England. He was alienated by Stephen's seizure of castles in 1138 and fought on the Scottish side at Northallerton. A second marriage to the heiress of the constable of Chester then led him into the orbit of the earl of Chester. By the end of the reign of Stephen he had accumulated vast estates, including many undertenancies, the most important of which was a beneficial enfeoffment of fourteen fees which he obtained from Roger de Mowbray after the latter's capture at Lincoln in 1141.[38] He now set about securing the succession of his son William. First, he tried substitution. Some time in 1153–4, whether before or after the Winchester settlement is unclear, Duke Henry issued a charter to William, already called de Vescy, in which he confirmed the gift which his father Eustace had made to him, along with all the tenements he held on the day he had performed homage, and all his rights in England and Normandy.[39] We cannot know how much that embraced. Even so, the charter is a good illustration of the tactics to which an old hand like Eustace might resort. The rest was entirely accidental. Eustace fought with the king against the

---

[35] Davis, *Stephen*, 138–9.

[36] *Cartae antiquae Rolls 11–20*, ed. J. Conway Davies (PRS NS 33, 1957), no. 553.

[37] For an account of Eustace, see *CP* xii:2, 272–4, and app. B, 7–11. There is a useful summary in Green, *Henry I*, 250–2. For a disentanglement of the Tison–Vescy lands, see *EYC* xii. 1–4.

[38] *Mowbray Charters*, xxvii, no. 397.   [39] *RRAN* iii, no. 912.

Welsh in 1157 and was killed in an ambush. His ill fate was his son's good fortune, for within days, perhaps within hours, someone secured from the king at Rhuddlan a charter in favour of William de Vescy. The king was in a giving mood. The charter confirmed to William all the acquisitions which his father had made by marriage, by royal grant, and by other means. It embraced Alnwick and the honour of Yvo de Vescy, which came to Eustace by marriage with Beatrice; it specified all that Henry I had given him and included all he held of King David of Scotland and his son Henry; it recounted all the undertenancies he had obtained from the archbishops of York and the bishops of Durham, from Richmond, Mowbray, Paynel, Aumale, Clere, Mortain, and Gant; it included fees listed simply by place and tenant; and finally, to round matters off, it concluded with all other lands and tenures of the aforesaid Eustace fitz John. It is an unparalleled record of acquisitive achievement. And all was now confirmed to William de Vescy, not only *in feodo et hereditate*, but under the words of conveyance normally reserved for the confirmation of an inheritance—*Sciatis me reddidisse et concessisse.*[40] The charter was witnessed by the great men and household officers present in the army: William, the king's brother, Roger, earl of Clare, Geoffrey, earl of Essex, Richard du Hommet, constable [of Normandy], Henry of Essex, constable [of England], William de Briouze, Manasser Biset, steward, Warin fitz Gerold, chamberlain, Richard de Lucy, and others. For his family, nothing quite so became Eustace fitz John as the manner of his death.

Now it may be that Henry's generosity in this case is also to be explained by the probability that most of Eustace's acquisitions were made in the reign of Henry I, for Torigny tells us that in 1153 ancient and lawful ownership was referred to the time of good King Henry. Whether this is Torigny's gloss or the true wording of the settlement it is impossible to say. None of the documents I have discussed so far uses Henry I as point of reference, although they refer not infrequently to gifts made by him.[41] The fact was that reference to the time of King Henry or to the day on which King Henry was alive and dead could only complicate the settlement. Stephen, Matilda, and the young duke Henry had all used

---

[40] *The Percy Chartulary*, ed. M. T. Martin (Surtees Soc. 117, 1911), 291–4, summarized in Green, *Henry I*, 251–2.

[41] e.g. the charter to Roger, earl of Hereford: *Rotuli chartarum*, 53.

these or similar words as occasion demanded.[42] They were not, therefore, a very useful tool for separating sheep from goats. Moreover, they were potentially inconsistent with the main intention of restoring the disinherited, for some had been disinherited by Henry I: the Stutevilles, for example, after Tinchebrai, the Lacys of Pontefract in 1114–18. By 1153 both had eased or thrust their way back into the reckoning, Ilbert de Lacy reputedly through complicity in murder. His brother, Henry de Lacy, was now pardoned and restored, and Robert de Stuteville obtained fees from his Mowbray rivals.[43] In such cases, *tempus regis Henrici* was not merely useless: it was a positive impediment.[44] But this was perhaps no more than an eddy in the main stream. In all probability, tenure confirmed by Henry II would have been inherited. In all probability, the ancestor of the tenant would have held under Henry I. Wherever this common situation occurred, *tempus regis Henrici* would very likely be called in to reinforce his grandson's confirmations. Hence it appears very frequently in Henry II's early charters. Moreover, that much neglected document, the coronation charter of Henry II, confirmed to Church and laity all the concessions, gifts, liberties, and free customs which Henry I had granted. Witnessed by Richard de Lucy sole, it indicated that Henry I was to be the model for the government of Henry II.[45] More gradually the main principle of the settlement of 1153—that acquisitions made in the reign of Stephen were all subject to review—developed into the rule that no case would be accepted in the royal courts based on tenure *temporis gwerrae*. That was firmly in place in the first surviving *curia regis* rolls.[46] By then, 1194, rejection of

[42] For Stephen, see *RRAN* iii, nos. 10, 187, 255, 286, 386, 472, 678; for Matilda, see *RRAN* iii, nos. 274, 316, 343, 821, 897; for Henry, who mainly uses the formula *tempore regis Henrici avi mei*, see *RRAN* iii, nos. 130, 239 f., 462, 575, 653, 704, 710, 795, 902, 997.

[43] For Stuteville, see *EYC* ix. 1–6, 116–17, 200–1; *Mowbray Charters*, xxviii, 247. For Lacy, see W. E. Wightman, *The Lacy Family in England and Normandy, 1066–1194* (Oxford, 1966), 66–8, 87–8; *RRAN* iii, nos. 428, 429; *EYC* iii. 143–4.

[44] For further comment on the disherisons of Henry I, see Davis, *Stephen*, 151; R. W. Southern, 'King Henry I', in *Medieval Humanism and Other Studies* (Oxford, 1970), 211–25; Cronne, *Stephen*, 156–60.

[45] W. Stubbs, *Select Charters*, 9th edn. (Oxford, 1913), 157–8, where it is pointed out that the charter antedates the appointment of Becket as chancellor in January 1155.

[46] Milsom, *Legal Framework*, 178–9.

acquisitions under Stephen and reliance on the day on which King Henry was alive and dead had finally come together. But earlier there were cross currents. Very soon after 1154, certainly before 1162, a statute was promulgated, one effect of which was that English claimants could not recover land without proof of tenure on the day on which King Henry I was alive and dead *or later*. Here the deadline was used, not to underwrite tenure, but to prevent the English from attempting to reverse the expropriations of the Norman Conquest. It could be used as a *terminus post* as well as *ante quem*.[47]

How many cases were there, how were they settled, and how soon? I have already discussed Mandeville, Hereford, Bigod, and Vescy, and mentioned Lacy of Pontefract and Stuteville. To these we have to add charters for the earls of Arundel,[48] Gloucester,[49] Leicester,[50] and Oxford,[51] and for Richard de la Haye,[52] Fulk de Lisoures,[53] Payn de Montdubleaux,[54] and Warin fitz Gerold,[55] to name only the more certain items. It is very likely that most of these belong to 1154 and 1155;[56] the latest seem to be Aubrey de

[47] See Van Caenegem, *Royal Writs*, no. 169, for the prior and monks of Winchester. *Vel postea* cannot be dismissed as an error, for, although the phrase does not appear in a similar writ for the priory of Dover (ibid., no. 172) it does appear in the form of *vel post* in a writ for the prior and monks of Worcester (ibid., 217 n.). I am proposing above a simple, straightforward explanation of these writs. Cf. Professor Hyams's comment: '[the English] alone had to plead on facts from the reign of the despised Stephen!' ('Warranty', 500); and, for earlier views, see Van Caenegem, *Royal Writs*, 216–17; D. M. Stenton, *English Justice between the Norman Conquest and the Great Charter 1066–1215* (London, 1965), 31–2; P. R. Hyams, *Kings, Lords, and Peasants in Medieval England* (Oxford, 1980), 251–2; Biancalana, 'For Want of Justice', 502.

[48] For confirmation of the castle and honour of Arundel and the third penny of Sussex, see *Calendar Charter Rolls*, 4, 257.

[49] For general confirmation, including the privileges of Burford, see *Actes de Henry II*, i, no. 17.

[50] For general confirmation, see L. W. Vernon Harcourt, *His Grace the Steward and Trial of Peers* (London, 1907), 60.

[51] For allocation of title, see *Sir Christopher Hatton's Book of Seals*, ed. L. C. Loyd and D. M. Stenton (Oxford, 1950), no. 40.

[52] *Ancient Charters, Royal and Private, Prior to A.D. 1200*, ed. J. H. Round (PRS 10, 1888), no. 36.

[53] HMC, *Middleton Manuscripts*, 2–3.   [59] *Ancient Charters*, no. 34.

[55] H. G. Richardson and G. O. Sayles, *The Governance of Medieval England* (Edinburgh, 1963), 437.

[56] The Bigod, Lisoures, and Montdubleaux charters were all issued at Northampton in January 1155; the earl of Hereford's at Nottingham in February.

Vere's, issued at Dover prior to the king's crossing to the Continent in January 1156, and William of Gloucester's, issued at the siege of Chinon in 1156.

We simply do not know how large a tip of how large an iceberg these charters represent. Documentary survival was hazardous. Quite apart from that, some successions and confirmations may well have taken place without any written record. When that stalwart Angevin, Baldwin de Redvers, died in 1155, he was succeeded by his son Richard. Richard later made endowments for the souls of his father and mother and for that of the noble King Henry, 'who gave the land to my ancestors', but he made no reference to any confirmation by Henry II.[57] Others, like Reginald, earl of Cornwall, simply survived (in his case until 1177), secure in the support which they had given to the Angevin cause, requiring documentary confirmation of their position only if challenged. But not all Angevin supporters felt secure. Robert fitz Harding, for example, buttressed his advance into the baronial ranks with charter after charter, some of questionable authenticity, from Henry both as duke and king.[58] Disputed claims are the least documented of all. To all appearances some of the quarrels of the anarchy simply petered out, leaving none of the charters of confirmation characteristic of the years immediately following Henry II's accession. William de Roumare continued as earl of Lincoln to die as a monk of Revesby c.1161. His rival, Gilbert de Gant, one of Stephen's supporters, died in 1156 with his title denied or ignored, only for it to be reclaimed by his nephew in 1216.[59] The dispute over the associated earldoms of Huntingdon and Northampton followed a similar pattern. In 1153 these were held by Henry, son of King David of Scotland, and Simon de Senlis respectively. Both died in that year. Simon was succeeded by his son, also Simon, but the family lost the earldom on or shortly after the accession of Henry II. In 1157 it was incorporated in the earldom of Huntingdon,

[57] *CP* iv. 312–13.

[58] R. B. Patterson ('The Ducal and Royal *Acta* of Henry Fitz Empress in Berkeley Castle', *Trans. Bristol and Gloucestershire Arch. Soc.* 109 (1991), 117–37) mounts a powerful case for the authenticity of the charters. For my suspicion of one of them, see above, n. 15. A further difficulty is that doubt about one charter affects the rest, especially those written by the same scribe. For Robert fitz Harding more generally, much the best account is now Patterson, 'Robert Fitz Harding of Bristol', *Haskins Soc. Journal,* 1 (1989), 109–22.

[59] Davis, *Stephen,* 122, 134–5; *CP* vii. 669, 672–4.

when that was revived for the royal house of Scotland. It was separated once more and returned to Simon de Senlis after the Scottish
war of 1173–4.[60] No charters survive for any of these successions
or transfers. Not all disputes were a consequence of the anarchy.
The contention over the earldoms of Huntingdon–Northampton
lay in the half-blood, originating in the two marriages of Maud,
daughter of Earl Waltheof. Such issues were likely to occur in any
family; they fed on the anarchy, certainly, but would probably have
occurred, civil war or no. The quarrel between the Paynels and
Robert de Gant is yet another example.[61] The descent of the lands
of Lacy of Weobley was equally contentious.[62] Finally, within the
first year of the reign, the new king had to use force or the threat of
force to ensure the surrender of castles from supporters of both
sides: William, count of Aumale, Roger, earl of Hereford, Hugh
Mortimer, William Peverel, and Henry of Blois, bishop of
Winchester.[63] In all these ways the settlement was very untidy, and
this has to be kept in mind in considering how it was done.

How it was done is the most difficult question of all. Some of
the difficulties are of our making. First, the treaty of Winchester
was agreed on 6 November 1153. Nobody knew that Stephen
would be dead within the year. Arrangements which seem to us to
be very short term were conceived and planned with no term at all
in mind. So, when Stephen's men, for example, performed homage
to the duke and perhaps sought some kind of confirmation of their
position, they entered upon arrangements which could conceivably
last for years. Secondly, territorial settlements cannot have been

[60] K. J. Stringer, 'A Cistercian Archive: The Earliest Charters of Sawtry Abbey',
Journal of Soc. of Archivists, 6 (1980), 325–34; *CP* vi. 644; W. Farrer, *Honors and
Knights' Fees*, 3 vols. (London and Manchester, 1923–5), ii. 298.

[61] Cf. Davis, *Stephen*, 122. Henry's charter to Hugh Paynel of 1151–3, granting
Les Moutiers Hubert and all the barony of his father in Normandy and England (*EYC*
vi. 96–7) is sufficient evidence of Hugh's affiliation to the Angevin cause. The main
reason for thinking that Robert de Gant was of the other party seems to be that he was
brother of Gilbert, earl of Lincoln. However, the opposing claims were in the half-
blood, arising from the two marriages of William Paynel (d. 1145–7), and this was
complicated by the marriage portion of Alice, daughter of the second marriage and
wife to Robert de Gant. These were common sources of dispute. It is noteworthy that
Henry II, having recognized Hugh before his accession, not only conferred part of the
barony on Robert de Gant, but also divided the English holdings between Hugh and
his brother Fulk: *EYC* vi. 18, 32–4, 96–7, 160–1.

[62] Cronne, *Stephen*, 160–3.

[63] Davis, *Stephen*, 152; Warren, *Henry II*, 59–61.

imposed on the great men of the land at Winchester or as an immediate consequence of the agreement, partly because neither the king nor the duke, nor both together, can have known the extent and detail of all the disputes, and partly because there was no governmental machinery capable of doing so. Only one such settlement was included in the terms of Winchester, that in favour of William of Blois, which was carefully specified, with distinctions drawn between his patrimony derived from Stephen, the lands of his wife, Isabel de Warenne, the acquisitions, the *incrementum*, which had come to him from Stephen, and the further gifts now made for the first time by Henry, the whole secured by the testimony of the great men of both parties and the overriding arbitration of the Church. For the rest, compulsion derived solely from the homage which the duke's men now performed to the king, and the king's men to the duke. Within that it was up to each man to get the best deal he could.

Now the authorities of king and duke were not on a par. True, Stephen was king and recognized as such by Henry, now become his vassal, but the Westminster charter, and probably the treaty too, accepted that the realm fell into two parts, the king's and the duke's. Moreover, Stephen was on the way out and had been for some time.[64] It was the younger man and heir to whom men would look for security. Stephen had promised to govern *consilio ducis*, and apparently did so; there were at least six courts, which they both attended, between Winchester on 6 November and Henry's departure for Normandy in early March 1154, so that there were opportunities for co-operation. Homages were taken at Oxford on 13 January, and a later meeting at Dunstable was taken up with the suppression of adulterine castles, in which Henry had found Stephen dilatory.[65] But the concerted action which Davis saw in these meetings was limited, and on Henry's side strictly so. For example, no charter of King Stephen has yet been found attested by Duke Henry, yet after Winchester Henry was Stephen's man and indeed his heir. The simultaneous confirmations to which Davis attached importance are not quite what they seem.[66]

[64] J. Leedom, 'The English Settlement of 1153', *History*, 65 (1980), 347–64.
[65] HH 289–90.
[66] For Davis's opinions, see *Stephen*, 121, 122: 'The only way in which individuals could make certain of their lands which they claimed as their own, was by making treaties or marriage alliances with their rivals . . . or by getting their lands confirmed by

Practically all of them are consistent with two separate operations, even perhaps on two different occasions; none of them shares the same witness-list; even to share a witness is unusual. Typically, a charter of the king was copied for, or by, the duke. On two occasions this was reversed, and then the king, in confirming, referred to the duke's charter.[67] But Henry rarely repaid the compliment. He or his clerks were ready enough to copy the terms of confirmations by King Stephen for ecclesiastical beneficiaries, even verbatim.[68] But where so, there would be no reference to King Stephen. Indeed, Henry made specific reference to Stephen only where it concerned the royal demesne or other regalian rights: a confirmation of the grant of Stanton Harcourt to Milicent, wife of Richard de Camville, made originally by Queen Adeliza and now confirmed *petitione et precepto* of King Stephen; a confirmation of the grant by Stephen of the manor of Letcombe Regis to the monks of Cluny, which replaced a pension of 100 marks originally granted by Henry I; and a confirmation of Stephen's grant of a die and mint to the cathedral church of Lichfield.[69] That is all. None of Henry's charters confirming the lands, title, or rights of tenants-in-chief, either before or after his accession, acknowledges Stephen in any way.[70] Except for William of Blois, Henry was simply not prepared to warrant the concessions of his predecessor. He was ready enough

Stephen and Duke Henry simultaneously.' 'Now that the king and duke were acting in concert . . .'. He relied on *RRAN* iii, nos. 94–7 (all of which are brief summaries), 126–7, 215 and 239 f., 457–8, 583–4, 874–5.

[67] *RRAN* iii, nos. 126, 127, 130, 131.

[68] Ibid., nos. 94–5, 96–7, 874–5, and, for a verbatim copy for Meaux Abbey, nos. 583–4.

[69] Ibid., nos. 140, 204–6, 457–8. In the case of the charters for Cluny, Stephen's charter is dated 1136, seventeen years before Henry's confirmation.

[70] A possible exception to this was adduced by Hugh de Gournay in the *curia regis* in 1212: *Curia regis rolls*, vi. 272–3. This purported to be a grant of the manors of Wendover and Houghton Regis by Henry II to Milicent, widow of Hugh de Gournay [the elder], which included 'all the new land which King Stephen gave to Hugh de Gournay *ad sue hereditatis augmentum*, namely Wendover and Houghton'. Henry also conceded 'whatever her husband bought or acquired in any way, as his charter testifies and confirms to her'. The open-ended nature of this second concession, the unusual and somewhat irregular wording of the charter, and the fact that Hugh's opponent in the action produced a perfectly standard charter of Henry II and a confirmation of King Richard, conveying Wendover to the ancestor of the opposing party, Faramus de Boulogne, suggest that the charter produced by Hugh de Gournay was spurious. Even if genuine, however, it should be noted that the reference to Stephen occurs yet again in a charter concerning the royal demesne, for both manors were *terrae regis*.

now and then to provide warranty for others, even spelling it out to include compensation, *escambium*, for the bishop of Lincoln, Joscelin of Louvain, and William Mauduit.[71] But to Stephen's men he would not give an inch beyond the agreements of Winchester unless or until they made their particular peace with him. He had already acquired an arrogant majesty like that which had occasioned opposition to his mother in 1141. He spoke of land pertaining to the crown of the king: he did not mean Stephen.[72] Indeed, in his confirmation of the foundation charter of Biddlesden Abbey, 1153–April 1154, he granted quittance of suit of shire and hundred and other privileges, along with 'all customs pertaining to my crown'.[73] Henry knew that Henry was boss.

There is very little evidence, therefore, of joint action of the two protagonists in their meetings following the Winchester agreement. The Westminster charter stands out with its long list of witnesses of leading figures from each side. It was unique in this, and almost alone in revealing cross-witnessing of any kind. Some of Henry's men attested Stephen's confirmation to the fitz Harding house of St Augustine, Bristol,[74] and Richard de Lucy figures among the witnesses to Henry's confirmation of Stephen's grant to Cluny,[75] but Henry's confirmation for Meaux, which was a verbatim copy of Stephen's, had its own witnesses, Henry's men and none of Stephen's.[76]

We are led, therefore, in the end to a very simple model of resettlement. Take as an example Robert de Beaumont, earl of Leicester. Robert joined the Angevin cause in the spring of 1153 and quickly became a major figure in the duke's counsels. He attested the Westminster promulgation of the general settlement in December.[77] His new allegiance is reflected in three charters. First, from Henry as duke he obtained a confirmation of his hereditary lands in England and Normandy and of his wife's inheritance from William fitz Osbern; Henry also conceded the recent exchanges of land which Robert had made with Roger, earl of Warwick. Then,

[71] *RRAN* iii, nos. 306, 491, 568, 582.
[72] Ibid., no. 90. Cf. the empress's reference to pleas pertaining to her crown in 1141: ibid., no. 274.
[73] Ibid., no. 104.
[74] Ibid., no. 127. William de Chesney; Richard de Camville.
[75] Ibid., no. 206.   [76] Ibid., nos. 583, 584.
[77] Crouch, *Beaumont Twins*, 86–9.

like Eustace fitz John, the earl took steps to ensure the succession to his lands by obtaining an identical charter in favour of his son. Finally, Henry confirmed the arrangements, apparently in the very same terms, after his accession.[78] That, or something closely akin to it, was probably the common pattern. It is repeated fulsomely in the fitz Harding charters, an example which is all the more telling if they are less than authentic. It reappears, with variations, in the cases of Geoffrey de Mandeville, Roger, earl of Hereford, and Eustace fitz John.

What then happened when claims were disputed? It is well known that some were settled by marriage alliances, some by division or subenfeoffment of one of the parties by the other, some by the creation of life-tenures for the weaker party.[79] The solutions were miscellaneous and seem entirely *ad hoc*. In some cases the parties and their descendants wrangled on into the next century, leaving scattered traces of their quarrels in the plea rolls. Amongst these there are perhaps a dozen or so references to decisions or judgments by Henry II. It is a hopelessly inadequate number. Very few of these references can be dated, they cannot even be arranged sequentially, and they include much hearsay. Consider the dispute between Ruald, constable of Richmond, and Richard de Rollos which was recorded much later in an action in the *curia regis* in 1208.[80] The facts are well known and the case has been much used by legal and other historians. In 1135 the Constable's fee of the honour of Richmond was divided equally between Richard de Rollos and Ruald the Constable, possibly as a result of a division between co-heiresses late in the reign of Henry I.[81] De Rollos gave service to the empress (he had considerable Norman lands) and was deprived by King Stephen, who gave his portion to Ruald. Some time after 1154, so de Rollos's descendant claimed, King Henry

[78] For the two ducal charters, see *RRAN* iii, nos. 438, 439. The editors date the son's charter, which survives in the original, earlier than the father's, on the ground that the second gives Henry the title of duke of Aquitaine, which he adopted in June 1153. But the father's charter survives only in a copy and it may be that the title is misleading. On the other hand, as Professor King has kindly pointed out to me, the grant to the son may have come first as a particular favour during the negotiations between Henry and Robert of Leicester in 1153. Henry's charter as king survives only in summary form, but it is full enough to establish that it followed the ducal charters very closely. See Harcourt, *His Grace the Steward*, 60.

[79] Davis, *Stephen*, 120–2; Warren, *Henry II*, 333.

[80] *Curia regis Rolls*, v. 147–8.   [81] *EYC* v. 85–8, 95–9.

brought the parties to an agreement which divided the fee once again. It looks like a copy-book example of a compromise agreed in the royal court. But in 1208 Ruald's descendant would have none of it. He mentioned no agreement, he claimed the whole fee as his right, he argued that Henry II had disseised his grandfather unjustly and without judgment, and he paid £100 for an inquisition of lawful men of the neighbourhood. The inquisition took his view—Henry II had indeed disseised Ruald the grandfather unlawfully and without judgment. So who was right? What had happened? Can we even accept the verdict of the inquisition? And how would the case look if we had the argument of only one party or the other? For none of the pleadings of 1208 fits the facts. De Rollos's descendant argued that Henry II had left Ruald with nothing more than a life-interest in his half of the Constable's fee. Yet his son, Alan, was confirmed in his constabulary and in all the lands of his father by Conan, duke of Brittany and earl of Richmond, in 1158,[82] and it is plain that Alan and his son in turn retained his half of the fee until the whole was reunited after 1204.

Procedure is equally in doubt. The Rollos's claimant argued that there had been a concord in King Henry's court (*et postea venit rex Henricus et eos concordavit*). It is certain, on the other hand, that Alan, son of Ruald, was confirmed in his father's land by Duke Conan at Fougères. If his son's argument in 1208 was right, that Henry II had acted without judgment, the matter may never have come to the *curia regis*. Procedure often seems hazy. It is sometimes at its clearest outside royal jurisdiction. Robert de Stuteville and Roger de Mowbray settled their differences in a *conventio*, probably before 1157, but it was a private agreement which never came to the king's court.[83] An action between Suspirus de Bayeux and Osbert fitz Nigel, which revealed that an intruder had been given a life-tenancy, derived from a settlement concluded in the court of the honour of Richmond at Boston.[84] Now and then an intrusion was corrected in the court of King Henry,[85] but he could equally well act by simple gift, rightly or wrongly,[86] or even totally infor-

---

[82] Ibid. iv. 48–9.

[83] Howden, iv. 118; *Mowbray Charters*, no. 386; *EYC* ix. 5, 100, 116–17.

[84] *Curia regis Rolls*, v. 181–2; vi. 17–18.

[85] Ibid. viii. 18–20 (*Badele v. Tattershall*); even then the parties were not reconciled until the conclusion of a subsequent marriage-alliance.

[86] *Rotuli curiae regis*, i. 93 (*Raimes v. Welles*).

mally. Hugh de Gournay, according to a jury of 1212, was allowed
to keep Wendover *sine dono* and was then deprived on Henry's
return from Toulouse in 1159.[87] Descendants of these disputants
might produce Henry's charters in court: none produced a writ,
and writs are not mentioned by those who recalled these actions a
generation or more later.

We can now bring matters to a head. First, there was no principle at work in the treaty of Winchester and its consequences which
depended on the distinction between right and seisin, no '1153
issue', as it has been termed.[88] It is not sustained by the evidence.[89]
That difficulty apart, the agreement between King Stephen and
Duke Henry was no model for it. The treaty did not award seisin
to the one and title to the other. Stephen recognized Henry as his
heir *jure hereditario*, promising to sustain him as son and heir in all
things and against all men. How could he do that, what was the
point of doing so, unless he himself had title? How could Henry's
title possibly be based on Stephen's mere tenure? You cannot make
a man your lawful heir without appearing as his lawful ancestor.[90]

Secondly, inheritance in 1153 meant something very precise. To
assert that the treaty of Winchester established an irreversible
'hereditary principle'[91] is to miss the point. By asserting inheritance the treaty questioned acquisitions, including acquisitions to
which the intruder had a hereditary claim or the tenant a lawful
title. If there was a principle, it was that of Ockham's razor,
Ockham's *necessitas*, in this case a compound of the rules of succession, the procedures for conveyancing, and more than a dash of
political convenience. At one and the same time it confirmed and
restricted title.

Here perhaps there were links with the legal developments of
Henry II. The treaty was not confined to lay fee. When Stephen
succeeded to the throne, the great wave of Cistercian expansion
was getting under way, accompanied by the foundations of the

---

[87] *Curia regis Rolls*, vi. 272–3.   [88] Palmer, 'Origins of Property', 11 n.

[89] See the comments of Professor Biancalana and Professor Hyams mentioned
above, n. 11. It should be noted that Davis largely accepted Professor Palmer's case
(Davis *Stephen*, 153), but without considering the arguments of Biancalana and
Hyams.

[90] I leave on one side here the more general issues surrounding the concept of the
lawful *antecessor*. These are among the matters to be discussed in a forthcoming work
by Dr G. S. Garnett.

[91] Davis, *Stephen*, 121.

Augustinian and Premonstratensian canons. Nearly 120 monastic
houses were founded during the reign. All their endowments were
acquisitions. All benefactions to the older monastic foundations or
to the secular Church subsequent to 1135 were likewise acquisitions. The same applied to the actions of churchmen as lords. All
enfeoffments or leases made since 1135 were acquisitions. All
intrusions into church property were acquisitions. All these varied
rights of property and tenure, all actions, whether lawful or bla-
tantly invasive, might be subject to review. The Church was up to
its neck in the settlement and its execution, and this in two distinct
ways. First, it had suffered great loss during the anarchy: castles,
land, services, goods, *tenserie*. Secondly, it had made enormous
gains: grants in free alms, endowments of new foundations, to salve
the conscience of the robber baron and ensure salvation amidst
uncertain fortunes. Perhaps, on balance, the Church was the chief
beneficiary of the anarchy of Stephen. But it could not recover its
losses without risking its gains. It chose to risk its gains. But it was
no choice: it had to do so.

The Church's losses have been discussed by others.[92] That its
gains could be subject to review is demonstrated by the treaty of
Winchester, for Duke Henry confirmed King Stephen's foundation
of Faversham, which had been well endowed with lands of the
royal demesne in Faversham and elsewhere, along with Stephen's
benefactions to other churches. This was done *consilio sancte
ecclesie*. More than thirty years later, in a notification of 1186 or
1188, the whole question was reviewed with reference to acquisitions of the monks of Stanley in Faversham. In the time of the war
of the usurper King Stephen, so the notification runs, much was
lost and alienated from the demesnes of the realm, both knights'
fees and church alms (both, note, now viewed equally as purpres-
tures); in particular, the abbey of Thame had come to hold Worth
in Faringdon by gift of King Henry's enemies. On his accession
they had surrendered the land to the king. But it had been conferred upon a religious house; the Empress Matilda, Gilbert, abbot
of Cîteaux, and other abbots of the order pressed their petitions,
and Henry gave the land to the abbey of Stanley, the empress's own

---

[92] Stenton, *First Century*, 244–5; King, 'Anarchy', 133–42; Biancalana, 'For Want
of Justice', 471–3; M. Cheney, 'Inalienability in Mid-Twelfth Century England:
Enforcement and Conseqeunces', *Monumenta Iuris Canonici*, ser. C: *Subsidia* 7
(1985), 467–78, esp. 469–71.

foundation.[93] Unease and uncertainty is again manifest at Kirkstall, originally founded by Henry de Lacy at Barnoldswick in 1147 and transferred to its present site at Kirkstall in 1152. The tradition of the house was that Barnoldswick was a tenancy which Lacy held of Hugh Bigod, earl of Norfolk, and that the rent due from the land was in dispute. This is very likely.[94] In 1153–4 Abbot Alexander had to put matters in order. As a result Henry de Lacy issued a charter confirming Barnoldswick and Kirkstall along with other acquisitions in the neighbourhood of Kirkstall.[95] Hugh Bigod, earl of Norfolk, at the request of Henry, wrote to Roger, archbishop of York, notifying him that he had granted Barnoldswick to the monks at the request of Henry de Lacy.[96] Henry in turn wrote to Henry II informing him that Hugh's grant had been made at his request and humbly imploring the king to issue his own confirmation.[97] This King Henry duly did.[98] There are four surviving documents in all, with some probably missing— quite a deal of fuss.[99] The king's charter is of special importance. In

[93] *Actes de Henri II*, ii, no. 682; *Ancient Charters*, ed. Round, no. 52. As Round pointed out, the notification refers to earlier transactions which cannot have occurred later than 1167. In all likelihood they followed soon on Henry's accession. For comment on the document, see E. King, 'King Stephen and the Anglo-Norman Aristocracy', *History*, 59 (1974), 181; Chibnall, *Matilda*, 135.

[94] *The Coucher Book of the Cistercian Abbey of Kirkstall*, ed. W. T. Lancaster and W. P. Baildon (Thoresby Soc. 8, 1896–1904), pp. ix–x. For the text of the *Fundacio Abbatiae de Kyrkstall*, ed. E. K. Clark, see *Miscellanea* (Thoresby Soc., 4; 1895), 169–208. This refers simply to the failure of de Lacy to pay the annual rent of five marks and a hawk (at 174). However, this probably reflects a more serious dispute. In 1086 it was recorded that Berengar de Tosny had held twelve carucates of land in Barnoldswick which were now in castlery of Roger of Poitou (i.e. Clitheroe): DB i. 332a. The Tosny interest descended to Bigod: *EYC* i. 466–7, 507–8. Clitheroe was held by the Lacys from the time of William Rufus. Hence, the non-payment of rent by Henry de Lacy was probably intended as a denial of any Bigod title. According to the *Fundacio*, Hugh Bigod successfully claimed Barnoldswick in demesne in the king's court. He then reinstated the monks at the ancient rent. All this occurred sometime after 1152 and possibly still in Stephen's time. Henry II subsequently persuaded the earl to relax the rent and confirmed the earl's grant in free alms (at 180). This last stage is confirmed by the documents, but, even so, the *Fundacio* makes no mention of the intervention of Henry de Lacy, and the surviving charters and letters make no reference to the rent.

[95] *Croucher Book of Kirkstall*, 50–1.   [96] *EYC* i. 507–8.

[97] Ibid. i. 508.   [98] Ibid. iii. 152–3.

[99] There is no surviving charter for the original establishment at Barnoldswick, although a perambulation of the bounds issued by Henry de Lacy may have served the purpose: *EYC* i. 506–7.

addition to confirming the grants of Bigod and de Lacy, he ordered that the monks 'were not to be disseised by any writ of land for which they had charter and chirographs; nor were they to be impleaded therein except *coram me*'. That emphasizes the protection which documentary confirmations gave. It envisages that writs of seisin might be used to challenge tenure. It shows that, in the king's view, royal charters brought issues into the royal court. Henry's confirmation cannot be later than 1162[100] and should probably be dated to 1155. Some of the elements of his later system of justice were already in place.

Now it is true that the status of free alms gave the Church a protection to title beyond anything which the laity enjoyed. But at Winchester the status of free alms was not immediately in question. What was, was title derived from endowments of the past nineteen years, whether free alms or not. It has long been recognized that a very large number of the *acta* of Henry II come from the years before 1162.[101] A very high proportion of these were for ecclesiastical beneficiaries. By 1162 there was no cathedral church and few monasteries, ancient or new, which had not acquired King Henry's confirmation. The king's confirmation implied and involved the king's jurisdiction. It was from this massive output that legal innovation emerged: the protection of seisin, and, in the reinforcement of the action of tolt, the supervision of lower by higher jurisdiction, especially that of the king. In this royal authority mingled with canonical views of the churchman's duty to preserve, and if necessary recover, the church's rights and property. It was an explosive mixture which contributed directly to the king's quarrel with Becket.[102]

At Winchester in 1153 all that had yet to happen. Whether the participants in the negotiations foresaw that the terms of the treaty would lead to such a demand for royal confirmations may be

---

[100] It is attested by Thomas Becket as chancellor.

[101] T. A. M. Bishop (*Scriptores regis* (Oxford, 1961), 30–1) suggests 40%, which Hyams ('Warranty', 476–7 n.) regards as on the low side for the English *acta*. Becket's attestation as chancellor determines the date 1162. For further comment, see below, n. 103.

[102] Cheney, 'Inalienability'; 'The Litigation between John Marshal and Archbishop Thomas Becket in 1164', in J. A. Guy and H. G. Beale (eds.), *Law and Social Change in British History* (London, 1984), 9–26; 'A Decree of King Henry II on Defect of Justice', in D. Greenway *et al.* (eds.), *Tradition and Change: Essays in Honour of Marjorie Chibnall* (Cambridge, 1985), 183–93.

doubted. They certainly cannot have foreseen that it would begin within the year. And nothing in the past could have prepared them for its unprecedented scale.[103] They designed the settlement in other, older terms, of homage and its consequences, of a lord's capacity to nominate an heir, above all of the difference between inheritance and acquisition. These were securely embedded in the legal thought which they inherited themselves from the reign of Henry I.[104] It was to that security that they turned in 1153. The invention necessary to cope with the problems they created for themselves was for the future.

---

[103] Professor Hyams notes quite correctly that it was 'normal for kings to make a disproportionate number of grants at the start of the reign' ('Warranty', 477 n.). This is true in general, but it is important in any calculation to distinguish grants from confirmations. The extensive endowments of Stephen's reign, coupled with the terms of the treaty, meant that the situation in 1154 was very different from that in 1100 and 1135. A large number of confirmations were also issued in 1189–90 and again in 1199–1200, but in each case for reasons which did not apply in 1154. I suspect that for 1154 the estimate of the percentage of the early grants against the total *acta* is less significant than the comparison of English and continental *acta*. A high proportion of the early acts concern England alone, as indeed did the treaty of Winchester.

[104] For the nomination of an heir, admittedly in circumstances where the ancestor is deserted by his own son or other relative, see *Leges Henrici Primi*, ch. 88, 15 (ed. L. J. Downer (Oxford, 1972), 274–6). For a possible example from Stephen's reign, involving Waleran of Meulan and William de Beauchamp, see Davis, *Stephen*, 110 n. For inheritance and acquisition, see *Leges Henrici Primi*, ch. 70, 21 (ed. Downer, 224), and for background, see Holt, 'Politics and Property', 12–19.

INDEX

Henry, ct of Eu 43
Henry of Huntingdon 3–4, 5, 8, 10,
    13–14, 18, 21 n., 22, 36, 50, 72,
    219, 245 n., 277
Henry de Lacy 303, 314–15
Henry Murdac, abp of York 185–6,
    212, 220, 222, 227
Henry of Neubourg 167, 176, 188,
    274, 281
Henry of Oxford, sheriff of Berks. 131
Henry de Pommeraye 138
Henry (d. 1152), son of David kg of
    Scots 11, 12, 15, 167, 172, 191–3,
    240, 245, 246, 247, 248, 249, 251,
    252, 302, 305
Hereford 10, 134, 196; bp of, *see*
    Robert of Béthune, Gilbert Foliot;
    castle 18, 85, 127, 285; diocese
    212, 218–19; mint 156, 159, 172,
    176, 181 n., 187, 189, 196
Herefordshire 120, 127, 141, 166,
    233, 262, 282–3, 287; sheriff of 122
Hertford 126
Hertfordshire 131; shrievalty of 129
Hervey Brito (d. 1168), earl of
    Wiltshire 125, 221
Hexham (Northumb.), priory 240
Hexhamshire 253
Hextilda, daughter of Uhtred 239
Hilary, bp of Chichester 213, 219
Hospitallers 216
Hugh of Amiens, abp of Rouen 74,
    103, 213
Hugh Bigod (d. 1177), earl of Norfolk
    46, 48, 101, 119, 126, 179, 300,
    301, 314–15
Hugh of Buckland 56
Hugh le Poer, earl of Bedford 126
Hugh (d. 1101), earl of Chester 39,
    40, 43, 53
Hugh de Gournay I 308 n.
Hugh de Gournay II 308 n., 312
Hugh of Ing 105
Hugh of Leicester 56, 57
Hugh Maubank 224
Hugh de Montfort 40, 42, 62
Hugh Mortimer 137, 286
Hugh de Morville 242, 252

Hugh Paynel 138, 306 n.
Hugh du Puiset, bp of Durham 252
Hugh de Scalers 124
Humber, river ferries 250
Humphrey de Bohun 119 n., 122
Huntingdon 52, 134; honour of 11,
    246, 247, 250, 305–6; mint 155,
    181; priory 125
Huntingdonshire 55 n., 56, 120, 125
Hywel ap Gronw 262

Ilbert de Lacy 53, 120 n., 303
Ilchester (Som.), mint 157, 189
Innocent II, pope 1–11, 17, 22,
    207–11
Ipswich (Suff.), mint 154, 159, 173,
    175, 176, 178
Ireland 87, 234
Isabel de Warenne 307
Islandshire 238
Ivo Taillebois 241
Ivo de Vescy 302

Jocelin de Bussy 34 n.
Jocelin of Louvain 309
Jocelin, bp of Salisbury 294 n.
John, kg of England 76, 90, 94
John, baron at Cardiff 167, 188
John of Cheam, bp of Glasgow 209,
    236
John fitz Gilbert 119 n., 122
John of Kent 139
John of Hexham 15, 50, 244 n.,
    252 n., 276, 278
John the Marshall 21
John of Salisbury 30, 109 n.
John fitz Harold, of Sudeley 280
John, bp of Sées 103
John of Worcester 2, 14, 18, 20, 50
Juhel de Mayenne 97

Kelso (Borders) 236
Kenilworth (Warwicks.) castle 80, 81
Kent 131, 165
Ketill son of Aldred 242
Kidwelly (Dyfed) 258
Kirkstall (Yorks WR), abbey 314;
    Alexander, abbot of 314

Shropshire 50, 129, 233, 262
Simon de Beauchamp 119
Simon, ct of Evreux 104
Simon II of Senlis (d. 1153), earl of
Northampton 56, 58, 126, 133,
135, 137 n., 138, 181, 305;
religious foundations 211
Simon III of Senlis (d. 1184), earl of
Northampton 128 n., 305–6
Sleaford (Lincs.), castle 74, 80, 83, 91
Somerset 139, 277 n.
South Mimms (Middx.), castle 78, 81
Southampton (Hants.) 34 n.; mint
156, 191
Southwark (Surrey), mint 154, 160,
169
Southwell (Notts.), minster 128
Stafford 134; mint 153 n., 156, 160,
190
Staffordshire 120, 140, 141, 142, 232
Staindropshire 240
Stainmore (Yorks. NR) 237
Stamford (Lincs.) 275 n., 278; mint
155, 159, 162, 173, 175, 176–7,
180
Standard, battle of (1138) 14, 126,
128, 246, 250, 251, 301
Stanley (Wilts.), abbey 220 n.,
313–14
Stanton Harcourt (Oxon.) 308
Stephen, kg of England 42–3, 46, 47,
49–51, 53, 54–5, 65–6, 67–8, 80,
81, 83, 85 n., 92, 112, 208–12,
224–9, 236 n., 241, 282–3, 291,
301, 302, 303–4, 306–9, 312–13;
outline of reign 7–36; Charter of
Liberties (1136) 10, 12, 118–19,
158, 162; arrest of the bishops in
1139 16, 26, 61, 74, 104, 122,
211; capture and imprisonment in
1141 21–3, 26–7, 62, 81, 102,
122, 130, 277–8; peace settlement
of 1153, see Treaty of Winchester;
administration of England 57–64;
117–43; administration and loss of
Normandy 13, 60, 62–3, 96–7,
101–4, 114; castle policy 69–72,
74–5, 87–9; coinage of 25–6,

145–205; restoration of minting
rights 158–9, 161; his religious
foundations 220, 223, 226, 313;
and Scotland 11, 14–15, 244–53;
and Wales 258–65, 274–6, 289; his
sons, see Eustace, William; his wife,
see Matilda
Stephen, ct of Aumâle 161
Stephen of Mandeville 100
Stephen of Richmond (d. c.1136), ct
of Brittany 46
Stephen de Scalers 124
Stephen, son of Theobald IV of Blois
33, 110
Steyning (Sussex), mint(?) 154,
176–7, 179
Stirling (Central) 236
Stoneleigh (Warwicks.), abbey 220
Strathclyde 234, 236
Sudbury (Suff.), mint 155, 159, 178
Suffolk 120, 132, 165
Suger, abbot of Saint-Denis 75,
109–10
Sulpicius of Amboise 110, 113
Surrey 55 n., 56, 131, 140, 141, 142;
earldom of 128
Suspirus de Bayeux 311
Sussex 141, 165
Swansea (West Glam.), mint 153,
156, 160, 176, 188, 196
Swinton (Berwicks.) 239

Tamworth (Staffs.), mint 156
Tancarville, family 42; see also Rabel
Taunton (Som.), castle 80, 91; mint
157, 160
taxation 151–2, 164–5
Tees, river 14, 233, 237, 238
Tegeingl, Englefield, lordship of
278–9
Templars 35 n., 216
tenserie 30, 76
Tetbury (Glos.) 279
Tewkesbury (Glos.) 20
Thame (Oxon.), abbey 313
Theobald IV, ct of Blois and
Champagne 8, 13, 20, 23, 62, 95,
96, 98, 102, 103, 110, 111, 124, 209

INDEX